POISONED IVY

POISONED IVY

How Egos, Ideology, and Power Politics Almost Ruined
HARVARD LAW SCHOOL

ELEANOR KERLOW

St. Martin's Press　　New York

Design by Judith Stagnitto

Library of Congress Cataloging-in-Publication Data

Kerlow, Eleanor.
   Poisoned Ivy / Eleanor Kerlow.
     p. cm.
   "A Thomas Dunne Book."
   ISBN 0-312-11367-6
1. Harvard Law School.   2. Law schools—Massachusetts—Cambridge.
   I. Title.
   KF292.H34K47   1994
   340'.071'17444—dc20   94-17890
                                              CIP

First Edition: November 1994

10 9 8 7 6 5 4 3 2 1

To my grandmother, Ida Cohen, in loving memory

ACKNOWLEDGMENTS

When I started working on this book in 1991, Harvard Law School professors had recently fought the meanest tenure-appointment battles in the school's history. After almost five years of turmoil, the school was still divided among far-left, far-right, and centrist factions. Each camp wanted to determine the direction of the school, believing that whoever won could shape the future of law in America.

For the liberals, it was bad enough that leadership of the school had been placed in the hands of the factional leader of the right. To the right, things finally seemed to be under control, but there was no telling how long that would last.

At the heart of the debate was a school of thought advocated by the faculty on the left known as Critical Legal Studies. CLS is complex, and most people only understand it as a view that the law is not neutral but designed to preserve the power elite.

I wanted to learn more about CLS, its proponents and opponents. At the start of my work I wrote a letter to each member of the faculty, including emeritus professors, to give everyone a chance to participate. But no one was in a mood to talk to a reporter from Washington.

Those who did agree to see me, after receiving follow-up phone calls and sometimes surprise visits, inevitably wanted to

viii *A c k n o w l e d g m e n t s*

know if I was a lawyer. When I answered yes, they would ask, "Did you go to Harvard?" At first, I figured the question was intended to see if I had a vendetta, perhaps as a rejected applicant or student. Then, since I was neither of those, the question began to annoy me. I felt the professors were being arrogant and condescending, checking to see if I measured up before they would confide in me.

Then one time a professor asked the question in such a way that I realized he didn't know if I had been in any of his classes or not. I was flattered he thought I might have been one of his pupils. But I also realized most of these professors barely knew their own students. It was my first insight into the workings of Harvard Law.

Like all good stories, this one took on a life of its own. The school's most senior black professor declared a leave of absence to protest the school's lack of women and minority professors. A group of students had also sued Harvard for discrimination on the Law School faculty, and the case was moving forward. Tenure appointments were bottlenecked.

The school was also unsettled by the brutal murder of a professor's wife in the spring of 1991. She was a law professor at New England School of Law in Boston, and, like her husband, was prominent in Critical Legal Studies. On the one-year anniversary of her death, editors of the esteemed *Harvard Law Review* released a savage parody of her last work.

Calls came for their expulsion and an investigation into the *Law Review*. Many people blamed Harvard Law School for breeding malice and misogyny in its students. Something was clearly wrong at Harvard Law, and it went beyond the argument over Critical Legal Studies.

To understand the forces at work, I conducted nearly two hundred interviews of Harvard professors, administrators, staff members, former students, other academics, and leading practitioners. The two editors responsible for writing the most harmful part of the parody, however, declined to be interviewed. I read hundreds of pages of manuscript material at the Harvard Law Library and the Library of Congress.

Many people helped me during the two and a half years I

researched and wrote this book, and I want to thank them. At Harvard, Derek Bok, Robert Clark, Alan Dershowitz, Christopher Edley, Jr., Roger Fisher, Charles Fried, Morton Horowitz, David Kennedy, Duncan Kennedy, Louis Loss, Daniel Meltzer, Frank Michelman, Martha Minow, Charles Ogletree, Jr., David Shapiro, Donald Trautman, Laurence Tribe, James Vorenberg, and Paul Weiler were among those who were generous with their time. I would also like to thank Erwin Griswold for his help. My gratitude also goes to Derrick Bell, Jr., for sharing his Harvard trials and tribulations.

Without the coaching and advice from James Doyle and Jamin Raskin, this book would not have been written. Lynne Bernabei was also a great source of knowledge about Harvard Law School.

I am greatly appreciative of *American Lawyer*'s Steven Brill, Jill Abramson, and James Lyons for setting the standard in writing about law and lawyers and for teaching me the basics. Through their encouragement and experiences with their own books, Kim Eisler and Judy Sarasohn made the process much easier. For their help in the early stages of research and preparation of the proposal I thank Kelly McMurry, Alex Friend, and Larry Trask.

At *Legal Times*, the weekly Washington, D.C., newspaper that covers law and lobbying, where I worked for seven years, I thank Eric Effron and Ann Pelham for allowing me the time to write and Terence Moran, Jonathan Groner, Linda Himelstein, and Daniel Klaidman for being great colleagues. At *Of Counsel*, where I am managing editor, I thank Steve Nelson for giving me the time to put the finishing touches on the book.

My agent, Jane Dystel, helped secure the extra time I needed to complete the book, and St. Martin's editor Tom Dunne and his assistant Alyssa Vitrano were always enthusiastic about it. I also wish to thank Paul Sleven for his patient legal review of the manuscript.

In addition, I must thank Reva Kleppel and Jerry Plum for their Boston hospitality, and Pat Goodheart for making me feel at home in Cambridge. Ronna Pritikin and Jeff Berk, Ellyn and John Bank, Kathy Doyle and Tom Coffin, Victoria Gewirz,

Thomas Mounteer, Judy Lettes and Sandra Sue, Louise Zanar, and the Rodich family have been the most wonderful support system.

I want to express my deepest gratitude to my mother and father, Joan and Aaron Kerlow, and my brother, Eric, for their unwavering confidence and support. Most of all, I thank Isabel Blanco for creating a beautiful space in which to live and work and for never letting me give up.

CONTENTS

PROLOGUE

For generations, Harvard Law School was the gatekeeper of American legal education.

In the 1990s, it has become a mockery of itself. This is the story of what changed and why. A hulking institution, Harvard Law is the oldest and largest law school in the United States. Founded in 1817, it spawned the Socratic method of teaching used today in virtually every law school in the country. Its 28,000 living alumni occupy the highest strata of American life. Like other graduates of Harvard University, those who have completed the three-year law school curriculum reside everywhere from the Supreme Court to the White House to the corporate boardrooms of the largest companies to Sesame Street and the other most creative departments of our leading advertising, news, and entertainment industries.

During its early years, Harvard Law was a clubby, chummy, and decidedly male place. Christopher Columbus Langdell, the school's first dean, who is credited with inventing the case method, presided over a group of loyal students known as "Kit's freshmen." The Ames Moot Court competition was the intellectual equivalent of a law school football team, and groups like the Pow Wow Club and Lincoln's Inn were important social organizations.

Although the British influence was heavy, there was a mo-
nastic air about the place. Langdell himself, with his long white
beard and wrinkled face, looked like a friar. He would wear a
dark eyeshade with a green lining to cut the glare of the reading
lamps in the library, where he pored over the books of legal
opinions that formed the basis of his texts. Professors such as
future Supreme Court justices Oliver Wendell Holmes, Jr., and
Louis Brandeis, knew they were developing a science of legal
doctrine and that they were teaching law for the ages. Students
were subjected to rigorous questioning designed to teach them
to "think like a lawyer." Above all, each person, whether student or professor, knew he would be contributing to improving
the condition of humankind.

America was undergoing an industrial revolution, and the
law, as taught at Harvard, reflected a legal climate inclined to
help railroad, steamship, and manufacturing companies prosper
and to encourage merchants to enter into agreements more
freely. Throughout this golden era, Harvard Law School was a
beacon of reason, instilling in its students a sense of endless
promise, fair play, and public service.

Of course, there were glitches along the way, and times at
Harvard Law School were not always easy. At the height of the
Red Scare in the early and mid-1920s, then-professor Felix
Frankfurter supported a petition for clemency in the case of
two avowed Italian anarchists, Nicola Sacco and Bartolomeo
Vanzetti, who stood convicted of murder. In this legendary
case, Frankfurter believed the two men were denied a fair trial
and true justice. His opinion and outspokenness regarding the
case put him at odds with Harvard University's president, Abbott Lawrence Lowell. Lowell was one of three men picked to
review Vanzetti's clemency petition, and in a decision known
as the Lowell Report, the panel concluded that the two had
been tried fairly and convicted properly. Pressure mounted
against Frankfurter, and Law School faculty members and Harvard University leaders pressed unsuccessfully for his removal.

Following that episode, a feud between Frankfurter and
Harvard Law School's dean, Roscoe Pound, raged for nearly a
decade, from the late 1920s to the late 1930s. The progressive

Frankfurter resented Pound's timidity and unwillingness to stand up to an anti-Semitic Lowell. He also disapproved of Pound's support for Hitler. Pound believed Hitler could free Central Europe from Communist movements and accepted an honorary degree from the University of Berlin in 1935. Pound, in turn, opposed Frankfurter's involvement in Roosevelt's New Deal, of which Frankfurter was a leading advocate. He tried to limit Frankfurter's trips to Washington to work on New Deal reforms. Moreover, he accused Frankfurter of attempting to dominate the faculty. The school divided into two cliques: Frankfurter's versus Pound's.

They clashed over the appointment of three Jewish candidates, including Frankfurter's protégé James Landis, and Frankfurter lambasted Pound for not supporting the candidates because they were Jewish. Pound refused to acquiesce. But as Pound became more irrational and his temper more fiery, the Frankfurter faction grew stronger. When James Bryant Conant replaced President Lowell in 1934, Pound was left without an ally at the top. He resigned his deanship in 1936. Adding insult to injury, Frankfurter's disciple James Landis was named Pound's successor.

Although the Pound-Frankfurter imbroglio was bitter and ugly, it was not based on divergent views of the law. In that area they both agreed. Both resisted innovations in legal education, such as the theory known as "legal realism," then being expounded at Yale. To them, wrote the legal historian Laura Kalman, "intelligence made theory irrelevant." Indeed, they "prided themselves on their tolerance of all bright people." For his part, Pound's intelligence was vast; he was a pioneer in an area called "sociological jurisprudence," and Frankfurter was renowned for his writings on public law and the history of the Supreme Court.

The McCarthy years of the early 1950s were another turbulent period at Harvard Law School. This was a time when the values of the Law School were clearly in question: Would it defend academic and political freedom, or cave in to the inflammatory rhetoric of McCarthyism? Professors like civil libertarian Zechariah Chafee, Jr., advised the university that faculty members called to testify before the House Un-American Activities Committee or the Senate Subcommittee on Internal Security should not invoke the Fifth Amendment against self-incrimination. Numerous professors were called by Senator Joseph McCarthy, as he and members of the investigating committees deliberately targeted Harvard University "because of its prestige and importance as a symbol of the Eastern Establishment."

The Law School was not immune. The Senate Subcommittee on Internal Security called two twin brothers at the school to testify. Dean Erwin Griswold counseled against their taking the Fifth Amendment. Their doing so, he said, would provide a basis to infer guilt, in this case that the two brothers had been involved in radical organizations while they were undergraduates at Cornell. A faction of the faculty wanted the brothers expelled. After the brothers took the Fifth, the *Harvard Law Review* voted to deny one twin membership on the journal because of his alleged political beliefs. Their fellow students deprived them of positions they had won on the Law School newspaper and in the Legal Aid Society as well.

In the end, however, Griswold publicly opposed McCarthy. Reversing his earlier position on the Fifth Amendment, he became a champion of the right against self-incrimination. His writing on the subject was widely circulated and laid the groundwork for protecting the rights of criminal defendants.

Griswold's strong sense of what was right was more than personal. It reflected the ideals of the school he would dominate as dean for twenty-one years. A majority of professors, such as Henry Hart, Lon Fuller, constitutional expert Paul Freund, and Archibald Cox, who later became the Watergate special prosecutor, were a moral force. Many of them had served in Washington during the New Deal, writing the laws that became the basis of our welfare, labor, banking, and securities systems. They were united by a belief in Harvard as the epitome of merit and the paragon of legal education. They instilled in their students a sense of logic, reasoning, and fairness, to carry forth after they graduated. Many of those students went on to become lieutenants in the post–World War II government of

Dwight Eisenhower, in John F. Kennedy's New Frontier, and in Lyndon Johnson's Great Society. All were steeped in the tradition of Harvard Law.

Then came the civil rights and anti–Vietnam War movements, and the campus of Harvard Law School, mirroring colleges and universities throughout the country, erupted with student boycotts and demonstrations. Still, the school remained a surprisingly cohesive place. In a now-famous incident, Law School dean Derek Bok, then only forty-one years old, brought coffee and doughnuts into Langdell Library to quell an all-night sit-in and to listen to students' complaints. During this time, a record number of students felt compelled to practice public-interest law, and the Law School gladly helped accommodate them. Harvard Law was also becoming more open to the representation of women and minorities on the faculty and in the student body, though it remained entrenched in its dominant position in the legal profession, politics, and business.

In the late 1970s and early 1980s, however, life at the school began to take on a different tone. Books such as *The Paper Chase* and *One L* glorified the rigor of the legal training and the power of the professors, and students themselves became self-conscious, even giddy, about the spoils that would come to them from positions as associates and partners at Wall Street law firms. And professors such as Arthur Miller, Alan Dershowitz, and Laurence Tribe, with their television shows, appearances on "Nightline," and testimony before congressional committees, became media stars overnight.

But something deeper was shifting in direct response to the symbol of power that Harvard Law had become. The change came with the arrival of three young, brilliant, iconoclastic professors: Morton Horowitz, Roberto Unger, and Duncan Kennedy. At first they were welcomed for their innovative ideas, such as their suggestions for broadening the curriculum to include courses on legal history and to create clinical programs to give students hands-on experience. As they saw it, Harvard Law School was out of touch with the world. Moreover, it was teaching the wrong kind of law—law that pertained only to the elite and catered to the interests of the wealthy and the

powerful. Most professors assumed law was neutral and unbiased, when in fact it was not, they said.

They were reviled. By attacking the Langdellian formalism that was the centerpiece of Harvard Law School, they were accused of having gone too far. With their experimental sections and abandonment of the Socratic method, they had destroyed the peace of the first year, which emphasizes the traditional courses of contracts, torts, civil procedure, and property. They were also seen as trying to colonize the school and promote their philosophy of law, which they branded Critical Legal Studies, for its critique of the old system of law teaching. In the past, when professors had feuded with one another, no one had questioned any of the parties' loyalty to the institution. Now the essence of the institution was at issue. Every decision, even one as small as deciding how many paper clips to order, had meaning.

Members of the old guard of the faculty and some young New Right faculty members fought to save the school. Their strategy was twofold: first to thwart the appointment of assistant professors whom they saw as the progeny of the radicals, then to mount a widespread campaign against the cabal itself. Between 1987 and 1988, three visiting professors and one assistant professor were denied tenure. The case of the assistant professor, a woman named Clare Dalton, whose husband is Secretary of Labor Robert Reich, became a public debacle. Eventually, Dalton successfully sued the school for discrimination against women.

The campaign to attack the rebel professors began at a debate at the Harvard Club in New York City in 1985, when a little-known professor named Robert Clark publicly denounced the new breed for engaging in a "ritual slaying of the elders." His speech touched off the second phase of the attack, which resulted in a letter-writing drive to pressure the school to move against the "radical" professors. Dean James Vorenberg, to little avail, sent his own letter to the 28,000 living alumni to try to settle the dispute.

Vorenberg's inability to quell the tension led Harvard University's president, Derek Bok, to select Clark in 1989 as the

tenth dean of Harvard Law School. Bok believed Clark could restore order, though many professors felt Clark would only exacerbate tension. The controversy had marred Harvard Law School, but hadn't shaken it from its foundations. Calling himself a "traditionalist," Clark quickly moved to reinforce the fundamental, if perhaps outmoded, curriculum of Harvard Law School. He limited the influence of the vanguard professors by restacking administrative positions and choice committees, and placed himself at the head of the powerful appointments committee. In one of his first acts as dean, he created more controversy by eliminating the office of public-interest counseling, which he later reinstated after an uproar over his action. Most significant, he launched a $150-million capital campaign, the largest fund drive ever to have been conducted at any law school in the country. The purpose was not only to ensure Harvard Law School's future, but to protect its long-established reputation as the gatekeeper of the legal establishment.

This was the state of affairs in February 1991, when a group of students who were 1L's (first-year students) in Clark's initial year as dean were elected the leaders of the school's prestigious journal, the *Harvard Law Review*. Their terms would end just before they graduated in the spring of 1992. Harvard was not an especially happy place, though the factions had reached an uneasy truce. In April 1990, Derrick Bell, Jr., the school's first tenured black professor, went on a leave of absence in protest against the school's failure to have a single tenured woman of color. There were four tenured black males, including Bell, and only five tenured women, on a tenured faculty of fifty-seven. In addition, the university was fighting a suit, brought in November 1990 by a group of law students supporting Bell, alleging that the Law School's faculty hiring was discriminatory.

For the most part, though, the new leaders of the *Harvard Law Review* were impervious to these events. As third-year students, most of their time was occupied with applying for appellate clerkships, some of which would lead to stints as clerks on the Supreme Court; securing high-paying jobs at major firms; and in some cases obtaining plum teaching posts—all

promising careers that awaited them because of their status as
the stars of Harvard Law School.

That is, until January 1992, when they began considering
whether to publish a controversial article written by a Harvard
Law professor's wife who had been brutally murdered in the
spring of 1991, less than three hundred yards from her home.
Her death shattered the tranquillity of one of Cambridge's most
exclusive neighborhoods. It also unnerved the campuses of the
New England School of Law, where she taught contracts, and
Harvard Law School, where she had many friends. Because she
had been a pioneer in feminist legal jurisprudence, many people
feared her death was not random, that someone had stalked and
killed her because of who she was. No arrests were made, the
case stayed open, and her husband remained a popular teacher,
aligned with the wing of rebel professors.

It was her husband who wanted the *Law Review* to publish
the writing she was working on at the time of her death. The
article, a loose-knit piece with an almost free-association style,
examined the ways in which the law subjugated women. It
would have been published without hesitation if it hadn't contained profanity. In a nasty debate that seemed to wake these
students from their job-searching stupor, they fought over
whether to delete the words, run a disclaimer saying the piece
contained offensive language, or leave it unaltered. Finally the
Law Review editors voted to run the article in its original form
as a tribute to its author.

That didn't end the matter, however. A group of disgruntled
editors decided to parody the article in the *Law Review*'s annual April Fool's spoof issue. When the public learned about
this mockery—published exactly on the first anniversary of the
woman's death—many felt that Harvard Law School was training vicious, sexist students to be the future leaders of the legal
profession. Against the backdrop of Derrick Bell's leave of protest, a suit against the school for discrimination, and a string of
appointments of only white males, the parody prompted an
instant outcry against Harvard for cultivating anti-woman,
anti-minority, and conservative values.

School officials swiftly condemned the piece, but in the name of academic freedom and free speech they refused to punish the authors. Yet an administrative panel reprimanded a group of students who held an overnight sit-in to protest the lack of faculty diversity. This double standard only made things worse. Professors jumped into the fray, with premier constitutional law expert Laurence Tribe railing against the *Law Review*, and civil libertarian Alan Dershowitz defending the creators of the parody. Others blasted Dean Clark for not taking a harder line.

When the turmoil at Harvard Law School began to make national headlines, it was too late to turn back. All the forces that had been in play for years started to come to a head and, in the process, began tearing at the fiber of this great American institution. Grandstanding, name-calling, and score-settling were now at the heart of this once-enviable school. Egos ran amok, and ideology was a weapon. Lost was the backbone of the school—the sense of justice and mission to produce morally bound leaders of American society who could judge between right and wrong and foster a more humane world.

Instead, Harvard Law became a social metaphor for all of the themes confronting America in the 1990s: the tensions between excellence and diversity, feminism, free speech and political correctness, and the excesses of money, power, and greed. In many ways it was symbolic of debates—both academic and barroom—raging throughout America in the 1990s. This is the story of how it all happened.

CHAPTER 1

A MATTER OF TRADITION

It was 6:00 P.M. on Sunday, February 3, 1991, and David Ellen, a Philadelphia doctor's son, then in his second year at Harvard Law School, was three hours away from being elected president of the 105th volume of the *Harvard Law Review*. He would survive nearly thirteen hours of a grueling election that began at eight o'clock in the morning. Compared to some elections that have gone on past midnight, this would be considered swift. It was a day filled with tradition. As always, the election was held on the first Sunday in February. According to custom, the candidates remained in a kitchen somewhere, cooking dinner for the rest of the *Review* members. At the end of the election, the winner would emerge and serve everyone the meal. Ellen and five other candidates were confined in a large steel kitchen adjacent to the large Ropes & Gray meeting room on the second floor of Pound Hall, one of Harvard Law School's main classroom and faculty office buildings, where these election-night feasts had been prepared for the past few years. They were cooking gumbo, the meal the outgoing leaders of the *Review* had requested. Since they had to cook for all eighty-five members of the review, Ellen and the other finalists had plenty to keep themselves busy.

He advanced through several rounds of voting until he faced

one other candidate, and then won a majority in the final ballot. His predecessor, Baruch Obama, had been the first African-American to serve as the *Review*'s president in 103 years. Obama was friendly and outgoing, but the class succeeding him wanted a tougher editor to lead them. Ellen, quiet and fair-haired, had graduated *summa cum laude* in history and science from Harvard College in 1987. He had worked at *The New Republic* in 1989, the summer before starting law school, and was seen as someone who would be a more rigorous blue-penciler. But he understood that the job was much larger than simply line-editing legal text.

The tradition of electing a new president to assume control of the *Review* is one of those important transfers of power that occur so quietly that few people know about it. All the presidents, dating back to when the *Review* was founded in 1887, have selected and supervised the editing of articles written by the leading academics, practitioners, and jurists of their time. Those pieces have shaped the law and guided those who apply it. It is remarkable that students publish the leading journals of the legal profession. The *Harvard Law Review* has been the pinnacle of legal scholarship. It is the oldest, most prestigious, and most widely imitated academic journal of its kind in the United States. Its competitor, the *Yale Law Journal*, cites Harvard articles and notes more often than it cites its own. State and federal courts refer to the *Harvard Law Review* far more often than to any of its rivals. And professors, especially those wanting tenure or tenure-track appointments, scramble to publish in it.

The *Harvard Law Review* is one of the greatest strengths of Harvard Law School. Among others, all of the following served as editors of the *Review:* Supreme Court Justices Felix Frankfurter ('06), Ruth Bader Ginsburg ('58), and Antonin Scalia ('60); federal appeals court judges Henry Friendly ('27), Learned Hand ('96), and Richard Posner ('62); former Yale Law School dean Thomas Swan ('03); Nuremberg trial counsel Telford Taylor ('32); former U.S. cabinet members Dean Acheson ('18), Joseph Califano, Jr. ('55), Elliott Richardson ('44), and William Coleman ('43); Senators Thomas Eagleton ('53) and Robert Taft ('42); former president of the American Civil Liberties Union Norman Dorsen ('53); poet Archibald MacLeish ('19); former dean of Harvard Law School and past president of Harvard University Derek Bok ('54); former Yale president Kingman Brewster ('47); former *Washington Post* publisher Philip Graham ('39); and accused spy Alger Hiss ('29).

Of course, many in this illustrious bunch could have reached their positions through their own ambition, social connections, and intelligence. But those who served on the *Harvard Law Review* held a golden passport. Winning a position on the *Review* has been the law school equivalent of receiving a Phi Beta Kappa key. It rewards the students deemed to be the highest achievers academically, and presumably develops the sharpest legal minds in the country, training members to be disciplined and judicious. At a banquet for the *Review*'s ninety-second anniversary, former Secretary of Health, Education and Welfare Joseph Califano, Jr., told the editors, "You are the kind of people society depends upon to shape its institutions and to solve its problems."

This wasn't just faint praise. Indeed, those who have attained a position on the *Harvard Law Review* have entered a stratum of power that affects nearly every facet of American life, from the classroom to the courtroom to the boardroom to the White House. They have made and will continue to make the most important judgments about our lives. This is part of the glorious tradition of Harvard Law School.

Located five miles west of Boston, not far from the banks of the Charles River, Harvard Law School, with its eighteen buildings, sprawls like a prep school around a shady, oak-studded quadrangle known as Holmes Field, at the north end of Harvard Yard. All of the buildings are connected by underground tunnels, making passage easier in the harsh New England winters. One can still sense the ghosts of faculty giants such as Zechariah Chafee and Edward H. "Bull" Warren, the prototype for *The Paper Chase*'s Professor Kingsfield, roaming the halls of Austin Hall and Langdell Hall, two of the school's oldest buildings, or floating between the oil portraits of distinguished English barristers and famous American jurists that hang everywhere.

It is a curious place, self-conscious of its power. Harvard Law School has its own Cambridge address. Faculty members have their own library, their own dining room, and they used to have their own bathrooms. They are among the highest-paid law professors in the country and enjoy the most job security. Any of the professors can call one of the television networks or major newspapers to comment on a Supreme Court opinion or on the legal angle of a news story, and be virtually assured of getting airtime or ink. They are instant experts. Professors like Alan Dershowitz, Laurence Tribe, and Arthur Miller— with their best-sellers, movies, consulting arrangements and television shows—are media stars in their own right.

Other professors admire the members of the Harvard Law faculty for their academic writings and envy them their advisory roles on cases, appeals, and congressional inquiries. Much of the Harvard Law faculty's clout comes from the professors' having a foot in both worlds, the academic one and the real one.

"Undoubtedly the most prestigious and notorious branch of the university, the Harvard Law School has had an incalculable influence in the legal, political and economic affairs of this nation," wrote Enrique Hank Lopez in his 1979 book, *The Harvard Mystique.* The school, both faculty and students, provided the brain power for the New Deal, functioned through the 1950s and 1960s as the West Point of legal education, and sent eager second lieutenants into the New Frontier and the Great Society. With close to six hundred students graduating every year, and another thirty thousand living alumni, Harvard Law School continues to pump an army of lawyers into the highest levels of American society, where they in turn wield enormous power.

Of the 111 justices who had served on the Supreme Court by 1993, Harvard Law School had produced twenty-one of them, including Oliver Wendell Holmes, Jr., Louis Brandeis, and Felix Frankfurter. Four out of the nine justices sitting on the Supreme Court in 1993 were Harvard Law graduates: Harry Blackmun, Jr., Antonin Scalia, Anthony Kennedy, and David Souter. Justice Ruth Bader Ginsburg left Harvard after her first year to join her husband in New York. Harvard sent more graduates to clerk on the Supreme Court than any other school, thirteen in the 1992–93 term alone. In the United States House and Senate, twenty-three graduates were sworn into the 104th Congress in 1992, including Representatives Barney Frank ('77) and Patricia Schroeder ('64) and Alaska Senator Ted Stevens ('50). Three solicitors general in three decades came from Harvard: Archibald Cox, 1961–65; Erwin Griswold, 1967–72; and Charles Fried, 1985–89. Attorney General Janet Reno graduated from Harvard in 1963.

The *Harvard Law Review* was a microcosm of the Harvard Law School, representing the best of its great training. But it also mirrored the failings of this great institution: its arrogance, its corporate culture, and its fractiousness. In his one-year term as president, David Ellen would contend with all those issues. He would have to motivate prima donna members who refused assignments, watch as the offices emptied out while editors flew around the country interviewing for jobs at law firms and clerkships with judges, and referee personality disputes. In one of the most painful episodes of the Law School's history, he would find that like the school, the *Review* maintained something more dangerous, an atmosphere of intolerance. His own lack of leadership, a lesson that would come to him painfully, would reflect the serious deficiency of this hallowed institution.

But first he would have to manage the sheer work of the *Review*. Having to turn out a highly refined law journal required students to throw themselves completely into the job, while still maintaining a full class load. It was so tense and so absorbing that it added a new dimension to their legal education. Their abilities as legal thinkers and scholars were lifted to a higher level than they were in the first year of law school. Some students logged almost as many hours as a full-time job would have required.

They practically lived at the *Review* offices in Gannett House, a plain, three-story white frame mansion built in the Greek Revival style. Located on the southeastern edge of the Law School campus, it was named for Caleb Gannett, an eighteenth-century tutor and steward of Harvard College, who had lived there. The building was later used to house students, and then was converted into offices. Gannett House was "a second home for most of us," said one former *Law Review* editor. "There are always lights on at night."

While Gannett House was a home away from home for some students, the intense deadlines and fiercely competitive nature of the editors also turned the *Review* into a pressure cooker. As it was, the members of the *Review* squeezed into cramped, cluttered offices on the second floor. The *Review*'s business office was also located on the second floor, and the Harvard Legal Aid and Defender Bureau worked out of rooms on the first floor. Gannett House "was crowded when I knew it, with thirty-five members on the *Law Review* board," observed Erwin Griswold, a former president of the *Review*, who later served as dean of the law school for twenty-one years until he was appointed U.S. Solicitor General. "How the present administration operates, with a board of more than eighty members, has long been beyond my comprehension."

From spring 1991 to spring 1992, *Review* president Ellen would have to make do with small space and long hours. The day after he was elected, he met over lunch with his predecessor Obama, and the day after that he was in the office, supervising the *Review*'s operations and finances. He was responsible for the entire April, May, and June issues of volume 104, and the November, December, January, February, and March issues of volume 105, in the 1991–92 school year—eight issues in all, about two thousand pages total. And it was the president's job to read every line and every word of every proof sheet before it was sent to the printer. Six months after beginning his work as a member of the *Review*, Ellen was in charge of running it.

His first major project was the May "Developments" issue, devoted to discussing recent developments in the law. He would have the summer to plan the rest of the issues and to brace himself for the large "Supreme Court" number distributed every November, which deals exclusively with the upcoming term of the high court. Each of these issues contained a major student-written article, a "Note on Developments" in the law, and the "Supreme Court Note" respectively. The last evolved from articles published in the *Review* by Felix

Frankfurter when he was a professor at the law school, and James Landis, his protégé, who later became dean. The foreword to the Supreme Court issue is the only piece that the *Review* ever commissions, making it the most coveted assignment in legal scholarship.

To help produce these eight issues, including the two massive ones, nine officers worked directly beneath Ellen: a treasurer, a managing editor, four executive editors, and three supervising editors. These were masthead positions. Under *Review* rules, a president may appoint the treasurer, though in recent years the job has been offered to the runner-up for president. Elections for the masthead positions take place three days after the election for president, and operate according to their own set of procedures. Also reporting to Ellen were the chairpersons or co-chairpersons of four separate departments: one office to handle the principal articles, one for the Supreme Court issue, one for the Developments issue, and one for book reviews and commentaries.

This was basically the same structure and format originally conceived for the *Review* more than one hundred years ago. It was founded in 1887, at the height of the deanship of Christopher Columbus Langdell. Although the school had been founded sixty years earlier, Langdell was its first dean. A "bookworm" and something of a "brilliant neurotic," he has been credited with inventing the case method of law teaching that is the cornerstone of modern legal education. The case method was built on the premise that every published court opinion contained a legal principle, and that the growth of the law could be traced by studying the principles in a series of cases. By discerning these immutable general principles, one learned logical reasoning, or how to "think like a lawyer." His idea was that law was a kind of natural science and that a library was its laboratory, since all that one needed to know was contained in books.

Langdell's innovations had a profound effect on the study of law in America, and at Harvard he injected new life and energy into the Law School. Law journals had begun to appear at other schools, such as Albany Law School and Columbia Law School.

It was only fitting that Harvard have one too. Stated in the 1887 prospectus for the *Review* was the desire that Harvard's journal might "show something of the progressive and scientific spirit which now characterizes the study of law."

As outlined back then, the *Review* would contain "articles on subjects relating to the law contributed *chiefly* by those who are connected to the school, either as alumni, professors or students, . . . editorials . . . reports of moot court trials . . . statements of doctrine and theory enunciated from time to time by the professors in their lectures . . . a record of current decisions of the courts of the United States . . . book reviews, correspondence from friends of the school at home and abroad, and items of news interesting to both past and present members of the school."

More than a century later, each issue still contained several articles by leading practitioners and professors, student-written case notes and comments, and book reviews. Ellen would supervise it all. Student-written articles, notes, and case comments received the toughest treatment. Drafts were written with extensive footnote citations. They were rewritten and edited many times, in what was known as the "S-1" phase. Once a student author and a supervising editor produced a publishable manuscript, it was given to a member of the law review "pool" for the footnotes and the draft to be "sub-cited," to make sure that the proper references had been used. After that, further drafts were written and then edited by the supervising editor in what was known as the "S-2" phase. Finally the piece went to the president for a "P-read" when it was considered about ready to be published.

Following any further revisions, a pool member "tech-cited" the piece, making sure every citation and quotation was accurate, that articles started on the pages the author said they did, and that cases said what they purported to say. And as if that weren't enough attention, the piece went to an executive editor who might suggest other stylistic changes, and who made sure the citations were in the proper form. The work was then typed in "galleys," after which it was proofread and then sent to the printer. It was amazing that the magazine got published at all.

But through this arduous routine, every member of the *Review* shared in helping achieve the highest standards of scholarship. Still, the president bore the greatest responsibility. No piece was published until he or she completed the "P-read" and declared it suitable for publication. Thus, no person had a greater impact on the quality of the work published in the *Review* than did the president.

The president and the members of the *Review* also had the luxury of being able to work freely and autonomously. At forty dollars per issue and selling more than eighty thousand copies annually, the *Harvard Law Review* was the only completely self-supporting law review in the country. Although the *Review* operated under the aegis of the Law School, it was managed independently by a five-person, nonprofit governing board known as the Harvard Law Review Association. This was an idea of Louis Brandeis. As the first secretary of the school's alumni association, Brandeis solicited alumni contributions to publish and distribute the first issue of the *Review*. He then helped establish the Harvard Law Review Fund to allow the magazine to operate continuously. Later the trustees of the fund were made part of the Law Review Association.

The association's main function was to manage the magazine's finances, and they were considerable. Not only did the *Review* generate revenue by selling subscriptions, but it published and sold *The Uniform System of Citation*, a style book known for short as "the Blue Book." This is the bible of legal citation, now used in almost every law firm and by almost every law student and lawyer in the country. The copyright for the Blue Book is held jointly by the law schools of Harvard, Yale, Columbia, and the University of Pennsylvania, and royalties are divided among them. The revenues, however, are significant. In 1984, Blue Book sales reached $288,402, just shy of the $303,836 generated by subscriptions. In that year, with interest paid on stocks and bonds held in trust and subscription sales, the *Review* generated $665,456. After paying expenses of $636,532, the *Review* still had $50,146 to spend. By 1993, Blue Book sales were running in the $700,000–$800,000 range, and *Law Review* subscriptions were generating close to $300,000.

The *Review* was still making more than enough to cover its expenses.

Still, nothing would get done if the president didn't delegate the task of checking the references cited in specific articles to the remaining "pool" of second- and third-year members of the *Review.* When Ellen took over the *Review,* there were eighty-five members, half second-year and half third-year students. They came from a range of backgrounds, from wealthy to middle class to poor. About half the members were women, and there were Asians, Hispanics, and African-Americans as well, though that's not to say their presence was abundant.

Like the rest of legal education, in its early years the *Review* comprised mainly the sons of the wealthy. And for many years, despite what some observers might say, the *Harvard Law Review* rejected Jews, women, and blacks. Adolf Augustus Berle, Jr., a child prodigy who graduated from Harvard College at age sixteen and maintained an "A" average in law school, was blackballed from the *Review* in 1914 because he was Jewish. Thirty-five years later, the leaders of the *Review* drew the line of people with the highest grades who would automatically be invited to join just above an African-American student named Clarence Clyde Ferguson. In its first eighty-five years, the *Review* had three black members: Charles Hamilton Houston, later a civil rights attorney and then president of Howard University; William Henry Hastie, who became a U.S. appeals court judge, and former cabinet secretary William Coleman.

It took the *Review* 103 years to elect its first black president. The law school began admitting women in 1950, and a few women, such as Ruth Bader Ginsburg, won positions on the *Review.* But the *Review* did not elect its first woman president until 1976, and only two women had served in the top post prior to the 1991 election. No woman had yet been named a managing editor by David Ellen's time. The first was chosen during his term.

Still, all of the members had one thing in common: they had distinguished themselves by winning a competition that had also varied only slightly since its inception. They were selected on the basis of their academic success. Instead of being picked solely for having the highest grades after the first year of law school, students also engaged in a writing competition. Some students could be selected on the basis of their writing alone, or by grades alone, if they thought their grades would be more outstanding than their writing, or they could combine their grades and their writing, with 70 percent of the weight given to their grades and 30 percent to their writing.

From the *Review*'s beginning, grades were considered the great equalizer. Felix Frankfurter, known for his "quasi-religious devotion" to the Harvard Law School, called winning a slot on the *Review* "one of the most complete practices in democracy" he had ever known. "This system, the objectivity of the marking, and the other considerations . . . creates an atmosphere and habits of objectivity and disinterestedness, respect for professional excellence, and a zest for being very good at this business which is the law," Frankfurter told the historian Harlan Phillips in 1960. "A fellow who gets an A gets it for something. He might be a grind. Well, that's important in the practice of law."

Leaders of the *Review* once held a meeting with lawyers at the Boston law firm Ropes & Gray to find out "what renders a *Review* man more valuable to an office?" Four answers were already identified on the agenda: He has wider acquaintance with the law and legal sophistication. He is already broken in. He has superior techniques of law work, and his review status is evidence of superior work. Firm Chairman John (Jack) Richardson, a distant relative of former U.S. Attorney General Elliot Richardson, explained what partners at most law firms would accept today. "People know that the *Review* man is bright and quick, and of course they would rather have such a man, in addition to his techniques; they have greater confidence in him. . . . At least grades good enough for *Review* are something you can put your finger on." The *Review* yielded "certified brainpower," Richardson (HLS '35) told the four other attorneys of his firm and three *Review* officers gathered that day at his firm. Ironically, Richardson had not been a member of the *Review*.

That meeting took place in 1949, and nearly forty years later, former dean Griswold, fondly regarded as "the conscience of the *Review*" because of the "Grizzer-grams" he sent to the editorial board monthly, usually complaining that articles were too long, still agreed that high grades were "reasonably accurate in measuring certain types of legal ability." Six out of the eighty-five people on the *Review* were still automatically picked on grades alone: the three people with the highest second-year grades, and the three people with the highest first- and second-year grades combined.

If high grades proved talent and merit, they also yielded elitism. Even at the meeting at Ropes & Gray, partners and editors wondered if they shouldn't make other *Review*-type training available to more students "to help dispel the feeling that *Review* editors have a monopoly on all the most advantageous aspects of law school." That same year, Warren Abner Seavey, one of the Law School's senior and more cantankerous professors, complained that "the *Review* men are just a bunch of lucky stiffs who have a facility of phrase." As he saw it, "from the standpoint of the school it would be better if every other man on the *Review* was a low C man—if more poor men could do the kind of work that is done by the *Review*. The *Review* men need the training least of all. The *Review* might go to hell, but from the standpoint of education it would be better if half your men were selected from those who got seventy or below, or by lot." Of course, this was a theoretical proposal. Seavey himself didn't want to recommend it to the faculty.

From 1902 to 1968, members were selected entirely on the basis of grades. Finally, in 1969, the ranks began to open. Editors instituted the writing competition to fill about half of the positions. The purpose was to open the ranks to women and minorities who had been denied membership because of years of exclusion. It was a controversial and hotly debated decision. Many former members of the *Review* criticized the change as "diluting" the valuable "cachet" of membership and "undermining" the organization's meritocratic foundation, and "[t]he small acknowledgment that writing ability might merit a place

next to legal scholarship produced a menacing rumble from
Harvard Law Review alumni," reported the legal columnist
David Margolick.

As it was, the writing competition yielded only some of the
desired effects. In 1979, eleven years after the writing component was added, 10 percent of the law school student body was
black, yet only three of the *Review*'s members were black. Two
years later, in 1981, the writing competition led to nineteen new
members being admitted, only one of whom was a woman, and
none of whom was from a minority group. Out of a total of
eighty-nine members, eleven were women and one was a member of a minority, in this case an Asian-American. Student
editors felt that an affirmative-action plan was needed.

In the winter of 1981 a plan emerged after a series of long,
bitter meetings in which a quota system was suggested, accepted, and then rejected. Two editors resigned. Finally the *Review* agreed to take forty students from the second-year class,
selecting sixteen people on the basis of grades alone, and sixteen on the basis of the writing competition. If a "non-
representative" number of women and minorities was selected
through that process, another eight students would be picked
through a combination of grades, writing, and the racial, sexual,
or other "societal" obstacles they had overcome. Applicants
who wanted those additional factors considered could indicate
that desire in a separate statement to the *Review*. The revised
plan was still controversial. A *New York Times* editorial denounced it as a radical departure from "absolute merit."

Dozens of alumni wrote letters to the *Review*, Dean Albert
Sacks formed a faculty committee to study other recommendations, and students tinkered with alternative ideas for two
more years. To the school's credit, the administration and the
faculty gave the *Law Review* the ultimate authority for deciding how it would manage its own affairs. Even that decision
was rooted in history. For example, during the 1950s, at the
height of the McCarthy era, the *Review* voted to deny Jonathan
Lubell membership, because he and his brother, David, also a
second-year student, had invoked the Fifth Amendment privilege against self-incrimination before Senator William Jenner's

roving Senate Subcommittee on Internal Security. Jenner had targeted them because they had been organizers for radical groups while in college at Cornell University.

A faction of the faculty, led by Professor W. Barton Leach, wanted the Lubells expelled, and Dean Erwin Griswold believed taking the Fifth was an admission of guilt. But Griswold, reversing his position on the Fifth Amendment privilege, recommended that the faculty table a vote on whether to expel the Lubells, and he told Andrew Kaufman, who was then president of the *Review* and is now a professor at Harvard, that the decision whether to elect Jonathan Lubell a member "belonged to the students" on the *Review*. Nearly twenty-five years later, in 1978, the editors of the *Review* voted to reinstate Jonathan Lubell as a member.

In the early 1990s, the *Review*'s affirmative-action plan remained essentially intact, with eight slots each year held for minorities if an insufficient number made it through the grade-writing competition. As with most affirmative-action plans, however, this one gave some people the impression that the *Review*'s standards had been lowered and that the beneficiaries might be of inferior caliber.

Still, it was hard to see where "merit" disappeared. Regardless of their sex, race, or national origin, each of the forty new members of the *Review* was among those 540 students in a class who got straight A's all their lives, near perfect LSAT scores, and were selected from more than 8,500 applicants to attend Harvard Law School. They were still among the best and the brightest.

The selection process and the cachet of being a member of the *Harvard Law Review* endured precisely because the payoffs were so great. Once students made it to the *Review*, they became part of a social and professional aristocracy that endowed them with privileges and pampering for the rest of their lives. They were Harvard Law School's crown jewels. Even as students, they received certain perks unavailable to the student body at large. Each morning they found muffins and bagels delivered at Gannett House. At 10:00 P.M. each weeknight, an "evening provider" brought snack food, for which he or she was reimbursed up to twelve dollars. Each year there were cocktail parties, a Christmas party, several faculty luncheons, and an annual banquet attended by the leading practitioners, judges, and politicians in the country. While anyone at the Harvard Law School could use LEXIS, a national legal database, the LEXIS machines at the *Law Review* were Cadillacs compared with the older models at the library in Langdell Hall.

The greatest advantage *Review* members had over their classmates was the built-in opportunity to develop personal relationships with faculty members. This would come through the many social events or by editing the articles submitted by professors. To secure a clerkship to an appellate judge, nothing was more valuable than having a Harvard Law professor write an editor a letter of recommendation. It was a luxury that most of the five hundred other students in a class never had.

Derek Bok, dean of the law school for three years before becoming president of Harvard University in 1971, recognized that Harvard Law School, where, he said, "lots of attention is lavished on people on the *Law Review* and the rest of the people are just kind of left there," needed to be less "hierarchical" than it had been.

He tried to remedy that imbalance by conceiving additional *Law Review*–type publications: "Instead of just having the very top students involved in these activities, which taught them a lot about law and got them a lot of faculty attention and so forth, we thought we'd try to get as many students as possible involved in activities like legal service or research-type work which would improve their education and get them faculty supervision and support." In addition to the *Review,* in the 1990s Harvard had nine other student-run law journals, including the *Harvard Journal on Legislation,* the *Harvard Journal of International Law,* and the *Harvard Civil Rights–Civil Liberties Law Review.*

But the biggest spoils kept coming to the *Review,* primarily from the outside, where the legal bar wooed members with annual salaries of $75,000 or more (plus moving expenses, bar review class stipends, and sign-on bonuses.) That all members of the *Harvard Law Review* were called "editors" provided a résumé enhancer that law firms and businesses gladly accepted. Satisfying the appetite of America's corporate law firms was a relationship Harvard also willingly accommodated. Sending its graduates off to lucrative jobs not only provided the firms with a steady stream of labor, but as those lawyers and firms prospered, so did Harvard in the generous support of alumni and firm contributions.

Each fall the courting ritual began, with various firms hosting a series of lavish receptions at several elegant Cambridge hotels. Firms opened the interviewing season for all second-year students seeking jobs as summer associates and for any interested third-year students. *Law Review* members were the most coveted. The firms would then "fly out" candidates to their home offices, putting students up in luxury hotels and dining them in fine restaurants while they interviewed with a firm's hiring partners. Corporations and government agencies pursued *Review* members almost as vigorously.

The plum for most editors was being able to parlay membership on the *Review* into a judicial clerkship. The members of the *Review* had their pick of positions as law clerks, a kind of special personal assistant, to the highest judges in the country. Those lucky enough to receive a one-year clerkship to a federal appellate judge, especially at the Second Circuit or D.C. Circuit, often went on to clerk for justices of the Supreme Court. Each year, about a dozen former members of the *Review* wound up as Supreme Court clerks. Justices Oliver Wendell Holmes and Louis Brandeis started the trend by automatically selecting two *Harvard Law Review* editors, usually the president and the treasurer, to spend a year as their clerks. Members now had to apply for all the clerkships, but many judges still automatically vied for an officer or member of the *Review*. An array of faculty members, present and past clerks, provided an intricate network for information, leads, and personal recommendations.

Those prize clerkships often led back to promising academic careers or to even larger bonuses and salaries from private firms. As it was, many people were on the *Law Review* because they wanted to join a law faculty, and there was no one an elite law school wanted more than a member of the *Harvard Law Review*. That included Harvard. At Harvard, for example, 74 percent of the sixty-one full-time professors on the faculty in 1989 had been members of the *Law Review*, and 61 percent had clerked for judges.

Joel Seligman, in *The High Citadel*, his 1979 book on Harvard Law School, criticized this rewards system of the *Law Review*, calling it "demeaning, distorting of values," and "arbitrary." Compared to medical schools, "where incentives are designed to insure that each student will be a competent practitioner, law review exaggerates the worth of a tiny minority of students, lessens respect for all non–law review related activities, and encourages students to value self-aggrandizement more than service to others," he wrote.

Indeed, this seemed to be the *Harvard Law Review* in the 1980s, when law firms and investment banks engaged in a virtual bidding war for Harvard's highest achievers. With the sense of entitlement that people used to so much special treatment possess, many officers and members of the *Review* took advantage of the perks. Some members used "fly-outs" to see who could earn the most frequent-flier miles. Others compared how many "extras" they could wrest from a firm, like tickets to Broadway shows or sporting events, while away on an interview. Some even arranged party weekends around interviews.

"I remember one time a group of editors planned a weekend in New York," recalls Jamin Raskin, class of '87. "They all arranged to interview either on a Friday or a Monday, and had the firms put them up at the same hotel. They spent the entire weekend partying, at the firms' expense, of course. It was reportedly wild. When they got back, one woman even bragged she had taken a bath in champagne. There was real license given to extraordinary self-indulgence. And a sense of entitlement to it all, that by getting to Harvard Law School and doing well at Harvard Law School you were entitled to all that." All of the corrupting influences of the 1980s seem to have corrupted the *Harvard Law Review*.

But David Ellen wasn't concerned with flying around the country or feasting on fancy meals. He had already tasted the life of big firm practice, spending the summer after his first year at the Washington, D.C., office of the large Chicago firm Jenner & Block, and he was planning to spend the summer after his second year at another major one, New York's Paul, Weiss, Rifkind, Wharton & Garrison. He was an intellectual, preferring to delve into his work with the various articles' authors and sifting through the arguments in each piece.

By the end of the 1990–91 school year, Ellen was proud of the first three issues he'd overseen, and was eager to begin working on the Supreme Court issue, due out the following November. It was to be an issue dedicated to Justice Thurgood Marshall, who would retire a year later. Harvard Law professor Charles Ogletree, Jr., an African-American and former public defender who represented Anita Hill in her charges of sexual harassment against then Supreme Court nominee Clarence Thomas, was submitting an article analyzing a recent court decision on criminal law. In addition to overseeing that article and others, Ellen would be primarily responsible for editing the foreword, to be written by then–Yale Law School dean Guido Calabresi.

During the summer, as he was organizing the articles appearing in that issue, he received a call from Gerald "Jerry" Frug, one of the professors at the Law School. Frug, a well-liked contracts and local government law teacher, wanted to know if the *Review* would be interested in publishing a manuscript his wife, Mary Joe, had been writing. "It was her best work," he told Ellen, who responded that he looked forward to reading it.

Ellen understood why the piece was so important to Frug. On April 4, 1991, nearly two months after Ellen became president, Mary Joe Frug had been murdered in a brutal stabbing less than three hundred yards from her home in the exclusive Brattle Street neighborhood in Cambridge. Her death had sent chills throughout the Harvard community. It had occurred in the center of the quietest section of Cambridge, where many Harvard Law professors, including Alan Dershowitz and Laurence Tribe, lived. The case was still unsolved.

He knew that Mary Joe had been a respected professor at the

New England School of Law and a pioneer in developing feminist legal theory. She and her husband were also prominent members of the Critical Legal Studies movement, a group comprising mainly law professors who challenged the conventional ways of teaching law and the larger role of law in society. In the early to mid-1980s, Harvard professors involved with CLS had tried to block appointments of professors they disliked, and to win promotions for other professors aligned with them. A faction of professors fought back and blocked CLS appointments. Tenure battles were so acrimonious that Harvard became known as "the Beirut of legal education."

In 1984, one professor told *The New Yorker*'s Calvin Trillin that the faculty was engaged in "a struggle for the soul of this institution." The conflicts centered around some of the same issues confronted at the *Review:* balancing the idea of meritocracy and elitism against openness and inclusion. As it was, Harvard Law School and membership in the *Law Review* stood as the symbol of the ultimate meritocracy, playing "a vital role in the American dream of meritocratic success and power," Dr. Alan Stone, a psychiatrist on the law faculty, told Trillin. Challenging the notion of who was qualified to be a Harvard Law professor or a member of the law review undercut this ingrained idea of merit.

The CLS professors had lost the political engagement. Robert Clark, who led the conservative faction's attack on CLS, had been placed at the helm of the Law School. This was not surprising, given the ideological shift in the country. Conservatives reigned in the Supreme Court and dominated the presidency in the administrations of Ronald Reagan and George Bush, then in power. It was more prestigious and valuable to a law student's career to be a member of the Federalist Society than of the National Lawyers Guild. At Harvard Law, Clark struck an uneasy truce between the professors over faculty appointments. CLS would be tolerated, but merely as an intellectual discipline. Still, scars were fresh, and feelings between men and women who worked in offices only a few feet apart remained bruised. CLS professors were leery about having their former nemesis Clark as dean.

Clark had other problems as well. Derrick Bell, Jr., the school's senior African-American professor and one of the country's leading scholars on civil rights, was into the second year of the leave of absence he had taken to protest the failure of Harvard Law School to have an African-American woman on its tenured faculty. The school was also defending an unprecedented lawsuit filed by a coalition of student groups claiming the school maintained illegal, discriminatory hiring practices. Race had replaced the ideological component of the CLS debate.

At the same time, a strong core of conservative students derided the efforts to seek a multiracial, multiethnic faculty. Students were becoming as polarized as their professors, and students on both sides of the political spectrum had lost confidence that they were getting the best legal education available.

The rupture had taken its toll at the *Harvard Law Review,* where all of these issues competed. The *Review* was mostly democratic and left-leaning, though there was a strong cadre of conservative students, many of whom were members of the Federalist Society. Even though a conservative was running the School, there was still a centrist stronghold on the faculty and in the student body. Thus, at the *Review,* on any issue of significance requiring a majority vote, the conservatives would lose. In that sense the conservatives felt as if they were oppressed. "There was a lot of political disrespect," said Ellen. "The fault lines are ideological, liberal and conservative, not man, woman, black or white." Coupled with having the 2L's do all the grunt work, the *Harvard Law Review* was "a difficult place to work," in Ellen's words.

Other editors agreed that with students judging each other by their perceived intelligence and already competitive with each other for masthead positions, choice assignments, and clerkships, sizing each other up along the political spectrum only added to an atmosphere that reemphasized divisions among people, rather than fostering cooperation.

Yet, despite this volatile climate at the *Review,* deciding to consider the piece Jerry Frug presented wasn't a difficult choice for Ellen. He realized that accepting the piece would represent a victory of sorts for liberal, CLS writing and the underrepresented voices of women. He figured it might upset some conservatives. But editors were considering other articles more to their liking, on topics such as law and economics, for future editions.

What he never anticipated was that the shocking, apparently random murder of Mary Joe Frug, the publication of her unfinished article in the *Review*, and the subsequent parody of it, would trigger a symbolic struggle for the soul of Harvard Law School and its prized *Review* greater than the conflict over CLS. In the process, the simmering battle between the proponents of CLS, often called "Crits," and the conservatives would be reignited and converge into a battle between the desire to promote a diverse faculty and student body and the need to protect speech, even if it disparaged that goal. The clash of ideology, power politics, and egos would threaten Harvard Law School and raise questions about whether the institution condoned sexism and racism. Harvard Law would be thrust into the national political correctness debate and exposed as fostering an atmosphere of intolerance and lacking moral leadership. And the world would wonder if, somewhere along the line, Harvard Law School hadn't lost its soul.

CHAPTER 2

MURDER AMONG US

The quiet, grassy neighborhood lined with clapboard homes of lawyers, bankers, architects, and academics, where New England School of Law professor Mary Joe Frug and her family lived, was also home to those who had inherited great wealth. A few blocks away, on Fayerweather Street, lived the governor of Massachusetts, William Weld. Members of the Rockefeller family had homes there. There people walked their dogs at night, jogged early in the morning, and greeted each other in passing. The Frugs' house, at 45 Sparks Street, was a red frame structure with white shutters, shaded by a large dogwood tree and a tall, broad evergreen.

The peace of this enclave was shattered on the night of April 4, 1991, when thin, red-maned Mary Joe left her house to walk to Sage Jr., a local grocery store six blocks away, to buy cookies for her daughter Emily. Having finished dinner, she dialed Judith Greenberg, another professor at the New England School of Law and one of her closest friends, and confirmed a date for breakfast the next morning. Then, at around 8:40 P.M., she walked out the door. She made it less than three hundred yards, just across busy Brattle Street, to the parking lot at the rear of the Armenian Holy Trinity Apostolic Church of Greater Boston. From behind a tall hedge, a man emerged wielding a

military-style knife with a seven-inch blade. In the glow of a
parking lot lamp he grabbed her and stabbed her four times,
slicing her twice through the left side of her chest and twice on
her upper thighs, then ran down a side street and disappeared.

Barely conscious, Mary Joe managed to flag down an ap-
proaching motorist. The driver stopped and ran into the church
to call an ambulance. Members of the church choir, inside practicing for an upcoming concert, raced outside to see what the
commotion was all about. Some of them mistakenly thought
Mary Joe had come to sing with them. The ambulance came to
take her to nearby Mount Auburn Hospital, but she never made
it. She died on arrival. She was forty-nine years old.

The shock of Mary Joe's savage murder reverberated through
Cambridge, Harvard, Boston, and beyond, for Mary Joe Frug
had been a vibrant, intelligent, dynamic woman, with strong
connections to various communities. Some people knew her
through her husband, Jerry, a law professor at Harvard; others
in Cambridge were familiar with her own work in feminism.
Still others in Boston had come to know her through her involvement in helping women in domestic abuse cases. From her
teaching post at New England Law School and the social network at Harvard, she bridged the gap between two very different cultures, working-class Boston and affluent Cambridge.
Some people merely knew her through her participation as a
parent at her two children's schools.

Four days after her death, more than one thousand people
gathered at her memorial service in Harvard's Memorial
Church. Friends and relatives came from around the country.
It was a tearful day and a somber service, interspersed with
some of Mary Joe's favorite music, such as the songs of Cat
Stevens. "Her smile, her wit, her unconventional intellectual
curiosity, and the clarity and connectedness of her friendship
attracted me instantly to Mary Joe," remembered Cynthia War-
dell, a friend from Mary Joe's freshman year at Wellesley College. "Mary Joe was indeed nature's therapist," said her friend
Mopsie Strange Kennedy, who is married to Harvard Law professor Duncan Kennedy.

Mopsie Kennedy told the grieving crowd that if the person

who murdered her friend had met her in some other situation, "if she, for instance, had been his lawyer, or come across him in some other comfort-giving venue . . . she would have been able to bring out his better side. And no doubt, this person would have ended up having a crush on Mary Joe, as all right-thinking people do." Her son, Stephen, added some levity, describing how his mother "ate the icing off the cake and left the cake."

Four months later, when Jerry Frug presented *Law Review* president David Ellen with the article Mary Joe was writing at the time of her death, many people were still mourning her loss. At holidays, people would leave bouquets of flowers at the fire hydrant near the corner of Sparks and Brewster, where she was killed. Several aspects of her death had left many people inside and outside of her social circle feeling uneasy. One unsettling facet of the event, especially to Mary Joe's women friends, was the prospect that Mary Joe's murder may not have been a random act, that she may have been killed precisely because she was a woman and an outspoken feminist. Her purse had been found on the sidewalk, undisturbed, with $33 still in her wallet. Nor was there any sign that she was sexually assaulted, though many people saw the stabs to her chest and thighs as violently sexual.

Members of the Cambridge Police Department considered it a strong possibility that she might have known her assailant. "I would think from the wounds that he confronted her," said Fidele Centrella, a detective sergeant in the homicide division of the Cambridge Police Department, choosing the word *confronted* carefully. If robbery was the motive, he explained, the murder was too unusual. "If I'm going to rob you, why would I stab you all these times under a streetlight?"

Moreover, said Centrella, a thirty-three-year veteran of the force, there were no signs that Frug resisted. "There were no defense wounds, such as a cut or stab in her hand as if she tried to stop him, which there probably would have been. It's a real nasty case." Another investigator familiar with the murder told the *Boston Globe*, "Whoever did it was loaded up on hate. But whether they hated women, or hated Mary Joe, or hated the person who crossed in front of them at that particular moment, or hated someone else and mistook Mary Joe for that person . . . we can't rule any of that out."

The police launched a massive investigation involving local, state, and federal agents, and conducted hundreds of hours of interviews with anyone Mary Joe may have known, including colleagues and former students. But other than the analysis of a footprint perhaps left by a white male in his twenties, approximately six feet tall, with brown hair, who had been seen at the time, the only physical evidence was the knife that the killer had left at the scene. The authorities had no leads. There was no suspect, and Mary Joe's case remained open, leaving women in Cambridge fearful of a murderer who was still at large.

Friends and others in the liberal community in Cambridge were upset by another angle, rumormongering that Mary Joe and her husband, Jerry, may have had an "open" marriage, something the Frugs' friends deny. The gossip began after police searched the room of a third-year law student who was close to Jerry, although they found nothing that would make the student a suspect. That Mary Joe was dynamic and sexy, a woman who "was determined not to abandon the feminine while becoming a feminist," as her friends remembered her, added to the intrigue. But the nasty gossip just hurt her family and friends further.

And beyond the Frugs' immediate social circle, in Cambridge's black intellectual community, people were troubled by a racial motive, "completely ignored by the papers," which they believed explained Mary Joe's murder. "It was no coincidence that she was murdered on April fourth, the anniversary of the death of Martin Luther King, Jr.," exclaimed Marthalene Donaldson, the owner of a national bed-and-breakfast business based in Cambridge. "I think her death was designed to send a message."

Suspicion of the police, innuendo, swirling rumors, racial undertones, and doubts about motives, were part of the climate in Cambridge, Massachusetts, from that spring of 1991 to the following year. At the Harvard Medical School, it was revealed

that Margaret Bean-Bayog, a Harvard-trained psychiatrist with an impeccable reputation, had had sexual fantasies about a young male Harvard medical student she had treated, who later committed suicide. An anti-gay diatribe in a conservative student magazine forced Harvard University chaplain Peter Gomes to declare painfully and publicly, that he was "a Christian who happens to be gay." Amid cries from conservatives for him to resign, gays defended the black conservative preacher, who had offered prayers at the inaugurations of Presidents George Bush and Ronald Reagan.

At Harvard Law School, where Mary Joe and Jerry were most at home, administrators, professors, and students were still suffering from the aftershocks of similarly scurrilous behavior. The ongoing battle between the faction of professors involved in Critical Legal Studies, in which Mary Joe and Jerry played important roles, and more-conservative scholars had opened a wide ideological gap between the left- and right-wing juristic camps, leaving few unscathed.

From its inception, Critical Legal Studies was an organization of lawyers, law professors, law students, and social scientists, preaching contempt for the status quo. The group was launched in May 1977 at a three-day conference in Madison, Wisconsin, where sixty academics met to present and discuss "critiques" written by eleven of them. These papers established the two fundamental strains of CLS.

The first line of thinking asserted that, contrary to how law was commonly taught and applied by judges, it was not a neutral body of rules that could logically be deduced from a series of cases. By "demystifying" the formal structures of legal doctrines "to reveal their latent social functions," one could see that the logic was "illusory." This was the "myth of legal reasoning." In fact, law was nothing more than "a wide and conflicting variety of stylized rationalizations from which courts pick and choose." This idea was a revival of "Legal Realism," a theoretical approach that had flourished in the 1920s and 1930s. The Realists saw that law didn't always work rationally, logically, or scientifically. Judges took other factors into account, such as economic and social realities, thus the name Legal Realism. Realism had started people thinking pragmatically about law and had laid the groundwork for the New Deal. But it had never gone beyond that.

The second strand of CLS was overtly ideological and political: law was simply "an instrument of social, economic, and political domination," furthering the "interests of the dominators" and "legitimating the existing order." This notion reflected the group's left-wing political tilt. The political bent of almost all of the presenters at the conference was not surprising. Most had been students or young professors in the 1960s and 1970s. Some had been involved in the civil rights and anti–Vietnam War movements. Others had lost faith in American government after Watergate.

As students, they were frustrated and enraged by the irrelevance of what they were learning. Indeed, law school tended to leave them bored after the first year, and in debt and uninspired after the third year. Many students in this generation pursued public-interest careers after graduation, but the majority were still willing to give up their ideals to spend their days in the service of large corporate law firms. Those who went on to teach law became hungry for an enlarged conception of a social view. They approached legal education by trying to solve the riddle of what was wrong with the way they had been trained and how they were teaching.

The birth of the conference was a crystallizing event. "It was pretty memorable, like the beginning of anything, when everything is kind of fresh and exciting," recalled Robert Gordon, a law professor at Stanford University. "We were mobilized just by the fact of getting together people who feel just like you do. Everyone at the beginning was at places where they felt politically and intellectually isolated."

From this weekend along the banks of Lake Mendota, these liberal academics agreed to keep the name "Conference on Critical Legal Studies," in an evocation of the Frankfurt School of Critical Marxism. Each year they would come together at an annual conference, at a mid-year regional meeting, and in "summer camp" sessions. More important, they would produce papers, network for jobs, and help members of this counterculture movement to win tenure.

The strength of CLS was that it left room for new ideas and that its agenda was inclusive, striving to make law, law schools, and society more open to diverse viewpoints. The downside was that CLS was "abstract, long-winded, obscure, and self-referential." Critical Legal Studies presented itself as a radical political philosophy, manifested not in action but in academic critique. It criticized law without totally rejecting it. Consequently, CLS professors could brilliantly manipulate legal doctrines, but they suffered from a failure of political imagination. Its message was too ivory-tower. And while its proponents attacked the illegitimate hierarchies of the world, the most active members often relished their positions at the pinnacle of hierarchy that was Harvard Law School.

Nevertheless, Mary Joe and Jerry Frug were drawn into this orbit. Like most of the professors in CLS, they had done exceptionally well in law school. Jerry graduated from Harvard Law in '63, where he was on the *Review*. He spent a year at the London School of Economics, and then a year as a clerk to Judge Roger Traynor, chief justice of the California Supreme Court. Mary Joe, two years younger than Jerry, went to law school at the George Washington University National Law Center. She graduated in 1968 in the top 5 percent of the class, earning Order of the Coif honors.

But they were also products of their time and interested in serving the public. In 1966, Jerry left private practice in San Francisco to become special assistant to the chairman of the Equal Employment Opportunity Commission in Washington. Mary Joe was in her third year of law school when the riots following the assassination of Martin Luther King, Jr., ripped through the District of Columbia, and demonstrators flooded the Mall. She was already working for Legal Services.

In 1970, when Jerry became general counsel of New York City's Health Services Administration, he and Mary Joe moved to Manhattan. He held that post for three years, and served as an administrator from 1973 to 1974. While Jerry was working for the health department, Mary Joe continued working for

Legal Services and began studying for her master's in law at New York University, under a Ford Fellowship in Urban Law. After receiving her LL.M. in 1972, she became an associate in law at Columbia University.

When Jerry accepted a teaching job at the University of Pennsylvania in 1974, they moved to Philadelphia. Mary Joe became an assistant professor at Villanova, and they each won tenure at their respective schools. Jerry spent the 1978–79 school year as a visiting professor at Harvard, and in 1981 he accepted an invitation to join the full-time faculty and moved his family to Cambridge.

By then, CLS was "on the map as something that was really developing," said Gary Peller, a secretary of the conference and a professor at Georgetown University Law Center. Other schools, like the University of Virginia, where Peller first started teaching, "wanted 'one.' " With three leading proponents and several younger newcomers like Frug on the faculty, no school was more identified with Critical Legal Studies than Harvard. Roberto Unger, a debonair, Harvard-trained Brazilian born in 1947, once described as "the smartest person in Brazil," was the primary intellectual force in the group's inception. His 1975 book, *Knowledge and Politics*, introduced a method he called "doctrinal deviation" to find "contradictory" pairs of values contained in legal principles. In it, Unger wrote that modern liberal theory failed to see that fundamental and inescapable contradictions made law radically indeterminate and produced opposite results in similar cases, depending on the outcome that a judge desired or that the system required.

For example, Unger and others showed how sometimes cases suggested that there should be clear, simple rules that left no room for discretion and no doubt about what conduct was lawful. On the other hand, many cases are decided on the basis that there should be flexible standards to meet particular situations. Similarly, some laws stress that only individuals can decide what they want and how much they are willing to pay for it. At other times, laws are based on the idea that it is appropriate to impose the community's sense of what it needs and what the fair price should be of fulfilling those needs.

CLS not only unearths these inherent contradictions in law, but shows that the legal system disguises the fact that there are really no guiding principles to determine when one set of contradicting values should prevail over another. Judges do have a choice in how to apply these values, and they have merely declared certain values privileged: the preference for rules, for individual estimations of worth, and for the idea that conduct is chosen. CLS is designed to promote "underprivileged" values, those most often associated with a left-liberal view of law.

Morton Horowitz, an elfin man then not even forty years old, gave the group a context. His massive history, *The Transformation of American Law 1780–1867*, described how in the nineteenth century the pervasive orthodoxy of law, in areas such as property, contract, and tort, as championed by formalists like Langdell, established the prevailing view of law as above politics and common-law principles. In terms of rules governing individual conduct, they were a neutral, natural body of laws.

Duncan Kennedy, just thirty-five years old at the time, was the group's magnet. Of the three, Kennedy was the most instrumental in helping to shape CLS into a full-fledged left-wing movement within law schools. A brilliant charmer, "Funky Dunc," as everyone called him, inspired ideas, and produced enlightening theories of his own. He never took the bar, however, and can only do in practice what a third-year law student can. Students joke that he is the only Kennedy in Massachusetts who will never be elected to anything. Still, he is an "inspired taunter." According to a CLS colleague—John Schlegel—Kennedy was a "cross between Rasputin and Billy Graham." He was at once "Machiavellian" and possessed "a gift for blarney that would make the stone get up, walk over, and kiss him." He could "work an audience or an individual with the seductiveness of a revivalist preacher."

Now in his early fifties, his hair thin on top and gray at the temples, he tugs at a mangy beard and glances out from above bifocals. He still wears his trademark denim jacket, now so faded it looks as if it is about to disintegrate. The proletarian uniform, though, is outmoded. After all, how much of a radical,

revolutionary law professor can one be if one is married to a
Boston socialite named Mopsie, has daughters named Fifi and
Kiki, and lives in a Victorian mansion in Cambridge? "In the
end, the critical techniques Kennedy employed to show the
gaps and internal contradictions in today's legal doctrine could
be redirected at him," wrote author and HLS graduate Richard
Kahlenberg.

But many students still admire his work on Boston housing
cases and his support for those interested in teaching careers.
"Duncan is often painted as a Crit with horns and a pointed
tail," says Keith Aoki, HLS '90, now teaching at the University
of Oregon School of Law. "He really does get down and dirty
and helps people." When he was younger, tall and lean, with
dark long hair, he exuded the aura of a rock-and-roll star. As a
young professor he cultivated the bad-boy image, loving to
astonish people with his rebellious ideas, such as proposing that
students be admitted to Harvard Law School and to the *Review*
by lottery (resurrecting professor Seavey's idea for selecting
students to work on the *Review*), and that law professors
should be paid only as much as custodians because they were
nothing more than society's janitors.

His radical zeal was genuine. It seemed to come from growing up in what he called an "upper bohemian" family. His father was a Cambridge architect and a member of the faculty of
the Massachusetts Institute of Technology. His father's style
was modern and avant-garde, Kennedy says. His mother was a
poet and painter who worked as a publisher's reader at Houghton Mifflin; she moved to New York after divorcing his father
in 1957. His maternal grandfather, a Harvard Law graduate and
corporate lawyer for the Hooker Chemical Company in Ni-
agara, New York, died when Kennedy was five years old.

Even though they "didn't really have a lot of money," education was important to the Kennedy family. Duncan attended
the private Shady Hill School in Cambridge. He attended high
school at Phillips Academy at Andover, Massachusetts, and in
three years he won almost every award imaginable: the Webster
History Prize, the French Department Prize, the English Prize,
the William Thompson Reed Memorial Scholarship, the Rob-

inson Cook Prize, the Katlin Prize, and the Poetry Prize. He was a National Merit Scholar, an honor-roll student, and a member of the Student Congress, the school paper, and the Contemporary Fiction Club. Moreover, he was an All-Club soccer player and a member of the Junior Varsity Tennis Team.

Harvard College accepted him easily. He graduated *summa cum laude* in economics in 1964. During his undergraduate days, he was involved in the National Student Agency, a group supported by the Central Intelligence Agency. But the organization didn't hold a lot of interest for him. He spent three years after college doing a year of graduate study in economics, living abroad, getting married, and starting a family. By the time he started at Yale Law School in 1967, he was a little older and more settled than most of his classmates.

At Yale, Kennedy became something of a celebrity. In his first-year class on property law, he attacked an experimental casebook that his professor, David Trubek, was using. Trubek, then only in his second year of teaching, had selected a book written by a former land developer named George Lefkow, who used the stages of land development to lay out the basic principles of the law on property. One day in class, Kennedy said to Trubek, "Look, what is this book all about? This is a pile of crap." And he started a devastating assault on the book. Trubek was flabbergasted. "I'm sitting there totally stunned," Trubek remembered. "But he convinced me that the book made no sense, that it was incoherent, that if there was some coherence to it, it had to be presented by the instructor. I had just made a terrible mistake by using the book." They soldiered through the rest of the semester using the book, and from that point on, Kennedy and Trubek remained good friends.

Having Kennedy in class was not easy. "He knew everything. He was very smart, he was not deferential, and he was there to provoke and challenge. Having somebody like him around is a little scary." Trubek recalled. "He was way at the top of the list of people with intellectual strength and breadth, I mean he knew about French structuralism, politics in Europe, and neoclassical economics."

But even with his reputation for being brilliant, rebellious, and difficult, professors found Kennedy terribly engaging. "He was remarkable, mature far beyond his years in terms of thinking of broad theoretical issues," reflected John Hart Ely, his former constitutional law teacher, later dean at Stanford University Law School. They liked the way he would undertake unconventional, often time-consuming projects. In a criminal law research seminar with Abraham Goldstein, a former dean of Yale Law School, Kennedy interviewed prisoners for his research project and "wrote a very sensitive piece, semijournalistic and psychological," Goldstein remembered.

Students rallied behind Kennedy when he published in his third year a polemic on "How the Law School Fails." In this intensely personal paper, he analyzed problems that still plague law schools, describing how law teachers transmit a "perception of hostility," deride students in class, fail to make themselves available afterwards, and stunt any academic creativity. The Socratic method of grilling students with questions creates a "degrading" master-disciple relationship that is very harmful, according to Kennedy. "In the long run there must be something deeply corrupting about the daily exercise of a license to inflict pain."

As for students, many are simply "brainwashed" in classes that are "boring or dead." No wonder students "turn off," going through the rest of law school as a kind of "half-man" or "half-woman." What made the law school atmosphere destructive was not the structure of the school, Kennedy explained, but the human relations that gave the structure its meaning.

He insisted that creating a more human atmosphere wouldn't diminish Yale Law School's "standards," or train students to think any less "analytically" or be less "successful professionals." Many classes "don't live up to their academic and intellectual pretensions" anyway, he said. Legal doctrines needed to be "challenged from a new direction, rather than confronted for the thousandth time with some well-known countervailing principle." A far more important objective was "to see that within their respective roles, students and faculty treat each other decently." If his ideas sounded like "legal hippieism," he wrote, then he was "a legal hippie." Two decades after he published his polemic, law school administrators were still trying to figure out how to make the second and third year offerings as interesting as the first, and how to make the whole process more humane.

After graduating from Yale in 1970, Kennedy clerked at the Supreme Court for Justice Potter Stewart, and worked briefly as an associate for a New York law firm before returning to academia. It was not an accident that Kennedy chose to be a professor at Harvard Law. This was where the Socratic method had been refined, perfected, and exported. Kennedy saw how Harvard had become a mechanism for controlling and deploying power. Since its founding, in 1817, the Law School had been "the major ideological transmission belt for conservative legalism in America," sending hundreds of students a year to the giant law firms that represented America's giant corporations.

Kennedy and his CLS colleagues understood that "to study law [was] one way to know power," wrote Jamin Raskin. They also knew that the traditional method of legal education didn't acknowledge any dynamics of power contained within it. That is why Critical Legal Studies found such "an easy target for subversion" at Harvard Law School. Kennedy's Yale polemic was just a launching pad for his unique brand of "syndicalism" or workplace politics.

Another article by Kennedy, "Rebels from Principle: Changing the Corporate Law Firm from Within," appeared in the Harvard alumni magazine, the *Bulletin,* in the fall of 1981. In that piece he described his own grandfather's acquiescence to unethical behavior by a client, a maker of poison gas for the War Department, among other things. The company had a factory in an elegant Victorian building near a river in upstate New York. Residents complained about noxious odors and that they couldn't grow anything in their gardens. To stave off lawsuits, the company planted geraniums in window boxes across the front of the building. But to make their "visual argument" work, every Monday at about 3:00 A.M., a grounds crew had to go around and replace all the flowers before they died. His grandfather knew what the company was doing, but never took any action. "He should have tried to do something about it," said Kennedy. "[W]e should ask of our students that in practice they try to figure out whether there are intelligent, more or less controlled risks they can take to put their careers behind their opinions."

It was part of his strategy for the "politicization of corporate law practice." Associates could sabotage the "hierarchy" of big law firms by doing something even as small as refusing to laugh at partners' jokes. "Blank expressions where the oppressor expects a compliant smile can be the beginning of actual power," he coached. (Naturally, dozens of alumni associated with law firms wrote letters to the *Bulletin* objecting to Kennedy's "guerrilla tactics.")

But Kennedy was just warming up. He circulated "Notes of An Oppositionist In Academic Politics," to urge his colleagues to try similar tricks. Finally he issued another "polemic against the system" in 1983 with his "little red book" entitled *Legal Education and the Reproduction of Hierarchy.* In this work, Kennedy asserted that the law reproduced hierarchy in three ways: by analogy; by legitimating the status quo; and by structuring law graduates into firms hierarchically.

His proposals were designed to make people think, to "reveal the hidden ideological presuppositions of institutional life," and were not necessarily meant to be adopted. But saying all hierarchy was bad and therefore illegitimate put him in direct "opposition" to the traditional notion of meritocracy. His ideas couldn't be dismissed as rhetoric because they directly challenged the status of Harvard Law School as the ultimate meritocracy.

When CLS emerged in the late 1970s, the first year of law school was a testament to the nineteenth-century glory of Harvard Law's first dean, Christopher Columbus Langdell, who refined modern legal education in America. The great legal institutions of western history—property, contracts, and torts— were taught the same way Langdell had taught them; professors used the Socratic method of thorough question-and-answer grilling, and urged students to deduce legal doctrines hidden in appellate court opinions. The second-year curriculum was effectively a tribute to Legal Realism and the statutory New Deal;

in it, students took welfare-state classes such as Taxation, Labor Law, and Administrative Law. The third year was marked by traces of Legal Process, a theory conceived in the 1950s by Harvard professor Henry Hart and former dean Albert Sacks; this approach emphasized that the outcome was fine if the process was fair.

As for the Harvard Law faculty, power was firmly in the hands of an older generation of professors hired in the 1950s and 1960s. They were white, male, *Law Review,* and liberal. Men like Abram Chayes, Andrew Kaufman, Albert Sacks, Frank Sander, Donald Trautman, and James Vorenberg had all clerked for the irrepressible Justice Felix Frankfurter. They were earnest scholars and advocates, but they were not firebrands like their senior colleagues, many of whom were their former professors, such as James Landis, Erwin Griswold, and Paul Freund.

That older group of mentor professors had been intimately involved in the New Deal—drafting and interpreting legislation, running new agencies, and enforcing the laws. Their experience had made them worldly and given them tremendous intellectual authority. From the 1930s to the 1960s, those professors were the moral force at Harvard. They understood why they had chosen law, how law should be used to uphold justice, and that Harvard's role was to lead the way. From the bench, for instance, Frankfurter frequently reminded Griswold, who served as dean from 1946 to 1966, that "the need of great teachers should be constantly in the foreground of the Harvard Law School." Seeking "to discover the potential Hamiltons, Jays, and Madisons" was perhaps "the rarest of all gifts of those who have the responsibility of headship of an educational institution." One should not merely follow those "who overvalue money as a factor in maintaining and advancing greatness in an institution," Frankfurter often counseled, concerned even then that Harvard was more interested in securing large grants than in providing the finest legal education available.

Without preaching to the rest of the faculty—almost without knowing it themselves—Landis, Griswold, Freund, and others of their generation simply transmitted to their offspring the same set of values about Harvard. But in the late 1970s and early 1980s, Harvard was no longer being run by that generation of older teacher-scholars. The last of the group, Lon Fuller and Henry Hart, were dead. Archibald Cox, the Watergate special prosecutor fired by Richard Nixon, and Paul Freund were retired. The surviving heirs to the Harvard fortune were good technicians and able craftsmen.

They weren't intellectual slouches, and each in his own right had played a significant role in advancing justice in the real world. Negotiator Roger Fisher, author of the best-seller *Getting to Yes,* brokered monumental deals such as the Marshall Plan and the Camp David accords, a settlement of the civil war in El Salvador, and a truce between the African National Congress and the South African Government. Mob-busting expert Nick Littlefield advised the government on breaking Mafia rings. Human rights advocate Henry Steiner sent twenty-five to thirty students a year all over the world to make habeas petitions for political prisoners and defend victims of state terror. Civil libertarian Charles Nesson defended Daniel Ellsberg in the Pentagon Papers case, and the residents in Woburn, Massachusetts, whose water supply was polluted by toxic chemicals dumped by a fertilizer company.

But there was a vacuum at the top, a lack of obvious leaders like those the preceding generation had looked up to. What kept them unified, though, was a common belief in Harvard as the paragon of legal education and the symbol of merit. "People valued the institution," said Archibald Cox. "You wouldn't want to do anything to hurt it." This loyalty created a cohesive faculty that valued civility and was perfectly content to be part of a legitimate hierarchy.

Even though he was the youngest dean appointed at the Law School, and later one of the youngest presidents in Harvard's history, Derek Bok embodied this tradition. Born in 1930, Bok was the grandson of the former editor of *Ladies' Home Journal.* He attended Stanford University and then Harvard Law School. He joined the faculty in 1958, where he taught former Massachusetts Governor and presidential nominee Michael Dukakis and Supreme Court Justice Antonin Scalia. A protégé of

Cox's, he became dean in 1968, and three years later was named president of Harvard University, at age forty-one.

Although he held a strong loyalty to the institution, Bok also saw the need for new ways of thinking. "I found the Law School, which I loved, very unified, and the faculty very together, but the whole definition of legal scholarship and what professors were about was strikingly uniform and probably somewhat too dull," he says, adding, "There were not schools of thought, there were not real opposing points of view. There were just lots of careful craftsmen putting together their views about how legal materials could be fashioned into an internally consistent, coherent body of law, which is very important."

Later, in the 1980s, he would issue a president's report criticizing law schools for "becoming the refuge of able, ambitious seniors who cannot think of anything else they want to do" and for directing graduates into careers that "often add little growth to the economy, the pursuit of culture, or the enhancement of the human spirit." To succeed him as Law School dean, Harvard selected Albert Sacks, a liberal sympathetic to the concerns of blacks and women demanding increased recognition on the student body and faculty. It was Sacks who helped attract professors such as Horowitz, Unger, and Kennedy.

The tenured core of CLS survived for two reasons: they enlivened the debate and intellectual fervor of the institution, and they shared an intellectual affinity with the men in Sacks, Vorenberg, and Chayes's generation, who also had a common ancestry in Legal Realism. The two generations differed only in their political style and ambition, the liberals identifying more with the Democratic Party than with the New Left. Given the strong liberalism at Harvard Law School, the majority of the professors were "committed to both academic freedom and intellectual engagement with CLS." CLS was just a generational extension of what they had been doing all along. They never saw it as "Cubism versus Impressionism," as one professor later described it.

But that was exactly what CLS was—it implicitly accused its predecessors "of teaching the legal equivalent of auto mechanics" and undermined their worldview. "What these guys do intellectually is say all law is bullshit, and that hits people where they live," a law professor told the *Chicago Daily Law Bulletin* in 1985. "[We] traditional lawyers have spent our whole lives saying it's not bullshit."

The CLS professors altered the content and dynamics of their classrooms. They disrupted the "Langdellian peace" of the first year by showing how "theoretically encased fields of law, such as Contracts, are historically responsive to social and political change" and reflected state power to advance certain ends. Jerry Frug, in his local government course, showed how cities evolved from chartered corporations with extensive economic and political power into constrained "public" corporations limited primarily to administering a town's public works. Horowitz tackled torts by teaching the actual historical development of the law of civil wrongs. In his property and housing law courses, Kennedy tried to show how ownership principles hid various social arrangements and advanced certain political ends. The beauty of it all was that students still needed to learn "black letter" law, the technical rules of law, and CLS helped enhance students' legal reasoning skills.

Critical Legal Studies also made "a formal inroad" into the first-year curriculum with the "experimental sections," in which two of the four first-year sections examined the law more critically and historically. The CLS professors also pressed for more clinical programs, allowing students to help prisoners, tenants, welfare clients, the homeless, and criminal defendants.

These changes would have been fine if this band of sixties leftovers hadn't decided to push for power. But that they would strive to do so shouldn't have come as a surprise. If they could change the law at Harvard, then they could change the law in America. Beginning in 1982, they blocked appointments, in one case thwarting a tenure offer to a woman because she was "not CLS." To eliminate the harshness of the Socratic method, they tried to institute a "no-hassle pass" in which students could "pass" in class without being penalized. Their plan narrowly failed. When the faculty, over their objections, instituted a policy allowing professors to raise a student's grade on the basis of class participation, the CLS professors urged students to hold demonstrations. The faculty was forced to withdraw the policy.

Members of the faculty, especially the more conservative ones, were furious. It was bad enough that CLS proponents preached ideas that were anathema to the legal system, i.e., dispersing power and reducing hierarchy. Now Kennedy and his "guerrillas with tenure," as he called his allies, were attempting to dominate the faculty, and even if they lost on certain matters, they were getting students to accomplish in the streets what they couldn't obtain by faculty vote. So much for Kennedy's pleas for brotherly and sisterly love.

The faculty became more bitterly and ideologically split than when Frankfurter had feuded with Roscoe Pound in the 1930s. Back then, Harvard Law professors prided themselves on being able to tolerate all bright people. Moreover, legal theory was not an issue. This struggle was different: theory was at the heart of it, and it had become marked by rudeness and discourtesy. The faculty was engaged in "vilification, name-calling, backstabbing, and character assassination," as assistant dean Charles Nesson described it. He urged the CLS professors to "be more open and generous to others, personally and intellectually," and at the same time tried to explain to other professors on the right that "the left is not a lethal threat to the future of the school." His peacekeeping efforts were to no avail. One professor told Calvin Trillin in 1984, in the first public exposure of the deep fissure at Harvard Law, that it had become "the unhappiest place." No appointments of professors from other schools were made from 1981 to 1985 because the faculty could not agree on a candidate, and where a "Missouri Compromise" was reached, candidates declined.

Given the country's shift to the right, it was only a matter of time before the empire struck back at Critical Legal Studies. In the second half of the 1980s, there was a tremendous institutional reaction, indicating that the law school would not change direction from its historical patterns. From its inception, CLS was on a natural collision course with HLS because the point of Critical Legal Studies was not to understand the law, but to change it and, in the process, to challenge the purpose and foundation of the Law School. Stanford's Robert Gordon explained why the Crits and their opponents at Harvard fought so furiously. "There's a peculiar kind of vanity or megalomania at Harvard, that the place is the soul of the American ruling class. Whoever wins the local institutional battles there thinks they will control America's cultural and institutional destiny."

Moreover, Harvard University has never been patient or kind to any academics or academic disciplines that have seemed "radical." In the early 1980s, the Economics Department abolished "radical" sections in the Economics 10 course, and fired all the professors to the left of John Kenneth Galbraith. Harvard's Government Department is dominated by hawkish conservative men such as Samuel Huntington and Harvey Mansfield.

The first public battle against CLS came in early 1984, when the conservative Federalist Society held a weekend symposium at Harvard to tell the public about "a growing crisis in the American legal system," manifested most notably in the Critical Legal Studies movement, which is "neo-Marxist" and "radical in outlook" and "seeks by its manipulation to effect a revolutionary 'utopian' change in American society."

That conference led to a Federalist Society–sponsored debate in May 1985 at New York City's Harvard Club, at which Harvard law professor Robert Clark for the first time publicly attacked Kennedy and the CLS professors. He accused them of being "engaged in a ritual slaying of the elders" and warned that "scholarship at the law school was deteriorating." A former seminarian with a Ph.D. in philosophy who taught corporate law, Clark was Kennedy's antithesis: reserved, controlled, and formal, compared with Kennedy's gregarious, casual, and almost reckless style. More fundamentally, Clark believed in legal positivism in contrast to Kennedy's view of law as indeterminate and incoherent. Clark had reached his limit with CLS. "I didn't like seeing science dismissed, denigrated, and what I saw was a knee-jerk bias against business, commerce, capitalism, and the legal profession, something nihilistic," he explained later.

Clark then led a ferocious assault against CLS in 1986 and

1987, eliminating four tenure candidates associated with CLS. With the support of a dozen conservative professors, Clark realized he could do what Kennedy had done—recruit a few professors from the "mushy middle" and prevent any candidate from obtaining a two-thirds vote of the faculty.

All he needed was one-third plus one, and he set out to build his coalition. In 1986, the first to fall prey to this strategy was Daniel Tarullo, an international law expert, who lost by a narrow margin. He was the first junior professor to be denied tenure at Harvard Law School in seventeen years. The same strategy was used on Ziporrah Wiseman, a professor of commercial law highly regarded for her teaching ability.

In the fall of 1987, Clark helped eliminate two more people who could have given the CLS faction of the faculty a competitive advantage. Clare Dalton, a darling of CLS, married to political economist Robert Reich, now U.S. Labor Secretary, seemed like a shoo-in. An assistant professor since 1981, she received the highest possible ratings for her work by twelve members of a fourteen-member outside review committee. But when it came time to vote, the faculty found that her work in nineteenth-century British law, then set to be published by Oxford University Press, and an impressive article on contracts in the *Yale Law Journal* didn't "meet the standards that we ought to have," Clark told the *Boston Globe*. Her work was subjected to line-by-line, word-by-word analysis by Professor David Rosenberg, a former New York litigator. As if he were an expert on British law, Rosenberg wrote an eighty-nine-page memo impugning her scholarship, despite the outside committee's glowing rating. One commentator called the opposition to Dalton "an academic smear campaign that resembled a drive-by gang shoot-out." Professor Lewis Sargentich told the *Harvard Crimson* that "a relentless attack was launched on her scholarship."

Dalton fell four votes short of the needed two-thirds vote of the faculty. President Derek Bok refused to intercede on behalf of the CLS professors, and the Dalton case quickly became a *cause célèbre*. Stanford's Gordon circulated a letter to all the nation's law schools denouncing the "red-baiting" and hysteria" surrounding CLS. His letter reminded the country's law teachers that "Harvard once defended [Felix] Frankfurter and [Zechariah] Chafee from conservative attacks, and was more resolute than most universities in resisting Senator [Joseph] McCarthy. . . ." More than two hundred law professors, responding to Gordon's letter, petitioned Bok to reconsider, and requested two national committees on academic freedom to investigate whether her tenure denial was politically motivated.

Harvard Law professor Derrick Bell, Jr., the school's first tenured African-American, staged a four-day sit-in to show solidarity with Dalton and to express his "disappointment and shame." He called the tenure denials a "threat to ideological diversity." Bok finally consented to the creation of a five-member outside review committee, but this group merely upheld the faculty vote. Dalton filed sex discrimination complaints with state and federal agencies, and asked the American Association of University Professors and the American Association of Law Schools to investigate the tenure process at Harvard Law School. Then she sued Harvard University for sex discrimination. The fact that Bok had turned her down, she told *Newsweek,* showed that Harvard didn't want "women who threatened the status quo too much." The whole affair, she said, reeked of "gender and political discrimination."

Also rejected in the spring of 1987 was David Trubek, Duncan Kennedy's first-year property teacher, who was a leading member of CLS. Trubek, a visiting scholar from the University of Wisconsin, was approved by a vote of thirty-to-eight for tenure. But this time Clark and other members of the right appealed to Bok, and Bok stepped in again. He convened an outside review committee and then vetoed the faculty's decision, rejecting Trubek. Trubek chose not to fight it and returned home to Madison, Wisconsin. "Divided? They were divided. They were armed camps already," remembered Trubek, whose description of Harvard as "the Beirut of legal education" rang true long after he departed. "The subtext of the 'Beirut' quote was the idea that people were committed to killing off the young of their enemies. They were after Clare because she was the young of CLS, the offspring," he explained.

Clark defended Bok's decision and the neutrality of the tenure process. He told *The National Law Journal,* "This place has become crazy to work at, there is an inbred notion of what's good scholarship, and it's about time somebody exercised independent review." His opposition, he said, "had nothing to do with ideology." Neither Dalton nor Trubek were "very good teachers" or "had demonstrated publishing excellence."

Harvard wasn't the only place where CLS professors were denied tenure or fired. It happened at Rutgers, New England, and the University of Pennsylvania. "It was a backlash. They scared the shit out of us," explained Kennedy. "Some people asked us how could we have let this happen. We were kind of amazed that we had gotten away with this for so long."

The civil war at Harvard, however, was fought harder and louder than at any other place because the stakes for each side seemed so much higher. There was a phrase around the law school at the time that conservatives wanted to "rule or ruin." The professors on the right would use savage tactics, such as destroying someone's career, to win. And they had powerful allies: the backing of the large corporations and law firms and the predominance of conservative ideologues in American government.

There were numerous casualties along the way. Paul Bator, a former deputy solicitor general under Reagan, who attacked CLS at the New York Harvard Club, defected to the University of Chicago, where he died shortly thereafter. Other professors wanted to leave, but couldn't give up the prestige. "It's difficult to go home and tell your mother that you're leaving Harvard, even if it's to go to Stanford," one professor told law columnist David Margolick. Professor Arthur Miller said he was "just absolutely shredded by this business," and stayed away from campus to avoid "the great debate and those noisy faculty meetings." After the Dalton debacle, the mood was even worse. Nesson told his second-year Evidence class in the fall of 1987 that after the faculty denied Dalton tenure, he "dropped out of Harvard Law School." He told his students, "I was alive somewhere else."

At every move in the conflict, Jerry and Mary Joe Frug were

near the center of things. While Duncan Kennedy was giving sound bites and quotes to the media defending CLS, Jerry and Mary Joe brought dinner to Derrick Bell's office during his sit-in protesting Dalton's denial. Jerry sat on panels at alumni reunions to explain CLS, and he wrote *Law Review* articles condemning the "McCarthyism" and "Red-baiting" at Harvard Law School. He was the left's representative on the faculty search committee established to help President Bok select a new dean of the law school at the end of James Vorenberg's term. And when Bok announced that he had selected Robert Clark, the factional leader of the right, Jerry denounced the decision as "a terrible choice for the school."

For her part, Mary Joe was both a CLS confidante and a real player. She and her family were close to the other families of the CLS professors at Harvard. Their kids attended the same schools, they cooked dinner for each other, and vacationed together. Professors such as Duncan Kennedy and David Kennedy, another Harvard Law professor active in CLS, came to her for support during the clashes with the faculty. Academically, she was among the first women to push CLS to embrace feminism. Despite its communitarian goals, CLS remained an old-boy, white male bastion, and almost caused the women in CLS to splinter off. Mary Joe helped establish a Cambridge-based women's study group, which included Clare Dalton and Harvard Law professor Martha Minow, and kept the women in CLS. The Cambridge "Fem-Crits" organized the ninth annual CLS conference in Boston in the spring of 1985.

Like Dalton, Mary Joe specialized in contracts and tried to deconstruct the way the law treated women. She wrote a groundbreaking article in the *American University Law Review* in 1985, examining how a well-used first-year casebook on contract law often portrayed women as naive victims of an agreement, and never as parties in sophisticated transactions. That article led other women professors to write similar articles examining the textbooks used to teach torts and property law. For many students, Frug was an inspiration during the drudgery of the first year, and her work was their first introduction to feminist jurisprudence and the realities of the legal world outside of the casebooks. Frug, like Dalton, also won a one-year fellowship at Radcliffe's Mary Ingraham Bunting Institute, which she was completing when she was murdered.

Her death left many of her friends at Harvard deflated. The appointments battles had worn them down, and now the gossip about her marriage was adding more pain. Jerry, Morton Horowitz, and Duncan Kennedy were in the midst of planning a CLS conference to be held in April 1992 at Harvard and Northeastern University. As many as five hundred people were expected, nearly the number of members CLS had at its peak in the early 1980s. Many of the panels were going to be led by the second and third generation of critical legal scholars Kennedy and the Harvard triumvirate had spawned. But Kennedy was heard to say that this was the last one he would organize. Other academics were asking whether this was the end of CLS.

Students, however, were still deeply interested in the ideas of CLS. Many could be found in heated debates with classmates at the student lounge in Harkness Commons or at lectures at which young minority scholars associated with strains of CLS were invited to speak. At the same time, through groups like the Federalist Society and the Law School Republicans, conservatives made sure there was always the presence of a counter position. The faculty's internecine politics had led to a kind of intellectual pluralism at Harvard Law School. The interests of students and professors now ran the gamut from CLS to moderate liberalism to legal process to law and economics.

But along the way the precious commodity known as trust was destroyed, and people at Harvard Law School no longer trusted one another. Congeniality and unity had been replaced by an ethos of scorn and suspicion. On the one hand, everyone—student or professor—thought he was right. On the other, part of the rigorous legal training that had made Harvard famous, which demanded that a lawyer be a dispassionate advocate, created just that, dispassion. CLS had proven, whether members of the faculty and student body were willing to admit it, that there was politics in law. They all understood that the law was not unbiased and that it could be manipulated. That was the reason for their existence. If the law couldn't be manipulated, giant corporations would not need to hire high-priced Harvard lawyers. Since various factions of the faculty had used their manipulative abilities to advance their causes, each was distrustful of anyone who claimed to be sincere.

That is why, in the fall of 1992, two seemingly routine decisions at the *Law Review*, over whether to publish and how to edit Mary Joe Frug's article, took on political and ideological meaning and became momentous events.

CHAPTER 3

FIGHTING WORDS

Still an unfinished manuscript, what *Harvard Law Review* president David Ellen had in his hands was far from the usual *Review* fare. Most *Law Review* articles were dry, academic analyses of judicial opinions, held together by long strings of footnotes to support an author's obscure legal theories. The article Mary Joe Frug had been writing at the time of her death read like a personal memoir about how law subjugated women.

In her first sentence she stated, "I am worried about the title of this piece," which she had nervously called "A Postmodern Feminist Manifesto." Why did it bother her? Because "postmodernism may already be passé, for some readers," she explained. "Like a shooting star or last night's popovers, its genius was the surprise of its appearance. Once that initial moment has passed, there's not much value in what's left over." On the other hand, she pondered, maybe the word *postmodernism* referred to such an "elaborate and demanding genre" that she would be opening herself up to "a flood of criticism" about what she'd left out, misrepresented, or mistaken.

Then there was the word *manifesto*, which was also troubling, not only because it evoked notions of Karl Marx's *Communist Manifesto*, but because it might make people think she was simply copying Catherine MacKinnon, whose seminal work was titled *Feminism, Marxism, Method, and the State: An Agenda for Theory.* Mary Joe kept the word "manifesto" anyway to link legal deconstruction with an actual political project: "What law (at least in part) constructs, law reform projects can reconstruct or alter." Her piece offered a serious challenge to conventional views of women, sex, and law review scholarship. Focusing primarily on "the relationship of law to the female body," she argued that even sex differences usually construed as natural or biological were in fact socially constructed. She drew on the style of Michel Foucault to explain "the constructed character of sex differences" and examined "the relationship between legal rules and legal discourse and the meaning of the female body." She concluded that "legal rules—like other cultural mechanisms—encode the female body with meanings." Moreover, she wrote, legal rules reinforced the terrorization, maternalization, and sexualization of the female body by failing to protect women adequately against violence, by perpetuating sexual stereotypes and by reinforcing economic inequality.

For instance, laws that made prostitution illegal, she explained, forced women to rely on powerful, sometimes violent pimps. The result was that these laws "allow and sometimes force" the "terrorization" of the female body.

Another of set of rules, such as those that reward women for singularly assuming responsibilities after childbirth, like legally sanctioned child-care credits and laws limiting abortion, essentially made "some women become mothers against their will," she added, thereby mandating the "maternalization" of the female body. Finally, those laws that criminalized certain types of sexual behavior and even sexual harassment laws, led to the "sexualization" of the female body.

At the end of the piece, she made several comments about marriage, sexual pleasure, sexual orientation, women's autonomy, and pornography. On the last point, she questioned the wisdom of antipornography ordinances that MacKinnon and Andrea Dworkin had helped write, and that had divided many feminists. "[I]t is a mistake to fear or avoid or condemn differences among feminists," Mary Joe claimed. She believed important lessons could be drawn from the failure of the campaign to enact antipornography statutes.

Those attempts to criminalize harmful pornography showed how important broad coalitions were to feminist law reform efforts. They had helped simplify and facilitate feminist political organizing, which could be helpful in the future. And they empowered women, she claimed. Personally, she would have liked to have seen advocates of the statutes try to "deconstruct" pornography, not just destroy it, but she understood their reasons. Overall, her article was squarely in the vein of Critical Legal Studies. By using the technique of deconstruction, she showed how rules that appeared "natural" effectively oppressed women, putting them at the mercy of pimps, into heterosexual marriages, and into maternal roles.

Despite the academic tone of her theory, her article was loose and informal. After all, as she said in a section devoted to style, "the medium *is* the message, in some cases." She cited an interview Madonna gave on "Nightline" where the rock star said, "Maybe I like dressing like the typical bimbo, but I'm in charge," to show that not all women see themselves as "walking embodiments of men's projected needs." She juxtaposed Madonna with MacKinnon, saying, "[I]t seems indisputable that Madonna's version of the female sexualized body is radically more autonomous and self-serving than MacKinnon's interpretation and significantly less troubled and less doubled than mine."

In addition to discussing Madonna's claim of sexual autonomy, she included discussions of a prostitute's rape and the pressures and dangers that confine women to monogamous heterosexual marriages. Perhaps the most provocative part of her piece was her analysis of the antipornography ordinances forged by MacKinnon and Dworkin. Frug agreed with MacKinnon that women were oppressed and subordinated through sex, but she criticized the ordinance campaign for not challenging people's attitudes about sex, saying that Mac-Kinnon and Dworkin "falsely simplified" what pornography was—that it wasn't what the ordinance advocates claimed it was. The definition of pornography could be expanded to include formula romances, lesbian and gay erotica, *The Story of O,* and articles from *Cosmopolitan* magazine, she wrote. "There are some pornographic works in which women fuck" and "some works in which the objectification of the ejaculating penis is not repeatedly depicted and valorized," she wrote, using a little "male talk" as she called it.

She footnoted a wide array of sources, ranging from first-person accounts of prostitutes in a book called *Sex Work: Writings by Women in the Sex Industry* to James Jones's *From Here to Eternity* to *The Story of O,* by Pauline Réage, to *Cosmopolitan.* Her frank talk about sex, her use of words such as *coitus, fornicate, cunnilingus,* and *orgasm,* and her references to pop icons and contemporary literature "didn't automatically rule it out" from being published, said *Review* President Ellen. "There was a history of law reviews doing some unconventional things." Indeed, the *Yale Law Journal* had devoted an entire issue to the television series "L.A. Law." With the birth of CLS, law review articles with a political bent had become vogue. The law reviews at Cardozo and Stanford universities had devoted entire issues to CLS. Other reviews, including the *Harvard Law Review,* had published articles written in the first person or in the form of allegories.

Jerry Frug gave Ellen a condition, telling him that if the *Review* wanted to publish the article posthumously, it would have to run as written, with absolutely no editing changes. Ellen didn't have a problem with that arrangement, he just had to decide whether the article deserved to be published in the *Review.* Even the *Harvard Law Review* gets "a lot of schlock," one former editor commented.

Ellen didn't dislike the article. Politically and intellectually, he understood the critical feminist point of view, and had been moderately intrigued with Mary Joe's theories about law and its relation to women. Its style and the fact that it was a draft created more of a problem. One solution was to run it in the "Books and Commentary" section because it was basically a comment on how the law affects women. He also had the idea of setting up the article as a tribute, to make it clear why an unfinished text was being printed in the *Harvard Law Review.*

In the *Review's* June 1991 edition, he had already dedicated a page in memoriam to commemorate the recent deaths of former Harvard Law School dean Albert Sacks and the murdered Mary Joe Frug. Through her husband, who was a Harvard Law professor, and through her own leading work in CLS and feminism, she was obviously a member of the Harvard Law School community.

He gave copies of Mary Joe's draft article to Janis Kestenbaum and Edith Ramirez, co-chairs of the "Books and Commentary" section, and to Mark Harris, one of the four supervising editors, to see what they thought of the piece and if they liked his idea about how and where to run it. Formal authority to reject or accept outside pieces rested with Kestenbaum and Ramirez, as the heads of the Books and Commentary office. "I thought it was a very original piece. It systematically examined the way legal definitions and the legal system assigned meanings to women," Ramirez reflected. "We were impressed with the substance of a lot of the ideas," added Kestenbaum.

But Ramirez, Kestenbaum, Harris, and Ellen had some nagging doubts about whether the piece was as good as Jerry Frug thought it was, and whether it made as "significant" a contribution to feminist legal theory as he felt it did. "We weren't sure it was the best thing she'd ever written, or if it was fit for a law review," said Ellen. "It was not as scholarly as a lot of the pieces we'd published."

Still, the co-chairs liked the idea of running the piece as a tribute. In the spirit of trying to make it work, they met with Jerry Frug again. He told them to give it another chance, and recommended they speak with Harvard Law professor Martha Minow. They agreed it was wise to solicit responses from other prominent feminists. Minow, a friend of Mary Joe's as well as a fellow charter member of the Fem-Crits, was persuasive. (Her own book, *Making All the Difference: Inclusion, Exclusion, and American Law,* published by Cornell University Press in 1991, discussed how law could accommodate unconventional ideas.) Minow thought Mary Joe's piece was "bold, original, provocative and fabulous." She liked the way Mary Joe had articulated and confronted the tensions within feminism and postmodernism. Her ideas were impressive and her piece was contributing further to legal feminism, Minow explained.

Mary Joe's unfinished manuscript would run in the March 1992 edition of the *Harvard Law Review*, and the editors would abide by Jerry's wishes not to edit it. "We recognized it was unfinished work and that the author was not around to correct it. So we knew we wouldn't make substantial revisions and we wouldn't have fully developed citations," said Kestenbaum. The two editors then selected three pieces that would accompany Mary Joe's manifesto.

Harvard University English professor Barbara Johnson was selected to write an essay on the "postmodern" in feminism. Ruth Colker, a Tulane University law professor who had taught briefly with Mary Joe at New England School of Law, would discuss a gap Mary Joe had left in her text where she had jotted a note to herself to go back and apply her analysis to the case of lesbians, who aren't necessarily "maternalized" by law. Colker would try to finish this section, to which Mary Joe had never had the chance to return. Finally, the editors asked Martha Minow to explain why she liked the piece so much, and in "an unsent letter" to Mary Joe, Minow offered some suggestions on how to strengthen and polish some of her arguments. In November, editors and citation-checkers were assigned to these three outside pieces. Everything had to be ready by the end of January 1992 to appear in the March issue.

School recessed for winter break, and when he returned to school in January, Ellen received Mary Joe Frug's article for his once-over. Even though it hadn't been substantially edited or changed and was going to run as a tribute, he still wanted to give it a final read. That's when he got a closer look at some of its more profane language. "I saw there was the word *fuck* and the word *cunt*," he recalled. "I had skimmed it before, but I didn't remember those two words. If I had, they just didn't register at the time. I felt certain that I hadn't seen them before."

The words appeared toward the end of the piece, where she suggested that the antipornography advocates should have "sought to deconstruct" rather than "destroy" pornography, and that pornography was just one part of a pervasive problem.

"In pornography women get fucked. . . . Now, women get 'fucked' in the workplace, too, where we do 'women's work' for 'women's wages,' working for male bosses on male schedules. . . . In addition, our past and present economic, social, and physical subordination makes us vulnerable to physical abuse at work, on the way there, and on the way back. We are raped at work and en route to work because of our sex, because we are cunts." That was an eerie sentence. As Ruth Colker noted in her companion piece, it evoked an image of violence and death, as if "Mary Joe were foreshadowing her own passing from this world."

To end women's oppression, people had to change the way they talked and acted about sex, she concluded. The antipornography advocates spotlighted a major medium in which women's oppression occurs through sex, but they themselves used and exploited traditional, stereotyped ideas and language regarding sex. They used stereotypically masculine attributes, typical of "male talk." She noted humorously that she'd done some of that herself. But her use of sexual slang was meant to forge a link between the overt sexual objectification of women in pornography and the cleaner, though still harmful, subordination of women in everyday life.

The resonance of her ideas was not lost on Ellen. But he finally understood why other editors, a few weeks before the break, had been telling him, "Hey, David, there's some stuff in here we need you to look at." As the article had circulated among various citation-checkers and readers preparing it to be sent to the printer in February, a number of people were bothered by the obscenities, the stridency, and the deal that had been struck with Jerry Frug not to substantively edit it.

Most perturbed was Carol Platt, the *Review's* managing editor. Although two women had served as president, Platt was the first woman to occupy the managing editor position. It was a difficult job. The managing editor was the taskmaster or "enforcer" of the *Review*, who distributed work to editors, saw that it was completed on schedule, and made sure a few people weren't doing all of the work. A native of St. Louis, Platt could have been Ellen's conservative twin. Like Ellen, her father was a doctor, and before law school she had also been a commentator, though in contrast to his work for *The New Republic*, Platt had written a conservative column for her college paper at Princeton, *The Daily Princetonian*. While David Ellen was applying for a clerkship at the U.S. Court of Appeals for the District of Columbia, with liberal judge Ruth Bader Ginsburg, she was planning to clerk for conservative judge David Sentelle. In contrast to his super casual and a bit sloppy "Woody Allen" appearance, Platt was dark-haired, petite, and wore stylish, tailored skirts and blouses and sometimes pants and jeans. She described herself as the only female conservative on the *Review*. Despite their differences, however, Platt and Ellen worked well together.

Platt and her boyfriend at the time, Patrick Philbin, one of the four executive editors, who also identified himself as conservative, were angry about the language Mary Joe had used in her article. They didn't think such profanity should run in a legal journal as esteemed as the *Harvard Law Review*. They decided to write a letter to the entire body to alert those editors who might not have known about the article. Another half-dozen editors signed on; Platt was the only woman. "We don't think we should be publishing language that a practitioner would be embarrassed to say out loud," they said in the letter, adding that they knew the article had already been accepted, and under specific conditions. If the language couldn't be deleted, they suggested, perhaps dashes could be put in the place of some letters in the most obscene words, or a disclaimer could be written saying that not all the editors agreed with the language contained in the article.

Janis Kestenbaum and Edith Ramirez, the "Commentary" co-chairs, as well as several other editors, were appalled when they read Platt and Philbin's letter. They felt strongly that the piece merited publication as written, even if it looked and sounded different from the average law review article. And they were planning to explain in an introductory passage why it was being published in this unusual manner. Moreover, as Kestenbaum explained, "Those words had substantive content. It wasn't an accident that Professor Frug used those words. The dashes proposal was ludicrous. It would have proven her point about the use of power in the law to shape and coerce women's lives and actions. It would have been pretty ironic."

Once again, deciding how to handle this article and which side to accommodate split along the same philosophical and ideological lines on which their professors had been divided for the past decade. The editors on each side, of course, thought their position was the right one. And at the center was the same tension that had existed in legal education since the late nineteenth century, between making law schools more representative, inclusive, and democratic, and keeping them elite. Here, as in the battle over CLS, the issue of including different voices conflicted with the desire to maintain a high standard of excellence.

As in the larger dispute, the division concerning what kind of articles to publish was political. Platt, Philbin, and their supporters, who took a traditionalist view that only "top legal scholarship" should be published, identified themselves as conservatives. Kestenbaum, Ramirez, and the other editors on the *Review* who wanted to see alternative forms of scholarship published considered themselves liberals. To them, it was important to help underrepresented voices gain the representation that had been denied them. This was clearly a political approach, and an outgrowth of Critical Legal Scholarship. They saw it as a privilege and an obligation to air voices traditionally excluded from legal scholarship.

Mary Joe Frug's article fit squarely into this realm. That was why merely agreeing to run it was a political act in itself, reflecting a choice of one direction—liberal—over another. Of course, the *Harvard Law Review* still published plenty of articles with a corporate or conservative law-and-economics bent; Lucian Bebchuk's "Federalism and the Corporation: The Desirable Limits on State Competition in Corporate Law," Victor Brudney's "Corporate Bondholders and Debtor Opportunism," and Daniel Fischel and David Ross's article "Should the Law Prohibit 'Manipulation' in Financial Markets" all ran during Ellen's command.

Ellen's predecessor, Baruch Obama, had worked hard to air

a "diversity of views." During his term as president, the *Law Review* had published "critical" articles by leading CLS-influenced academics, as well as pieces written in the law-and-economics vein. "Conservatives liked that because they wanted more conservative articles and liberals wanted more liberal articles." Everyone had gotten something, and a balance was struck between these two opposing viewpoints, though it wasn't easy, as the continuous feuding and mistrust between Harvard's two faculty factions indicated.

But Ellen didn't have time to waste. This was January, and he had the final deadline to meet. Among the people who most vigorously opposed Mary Joe's choice of words were two of his hardest-working editors, Platt and Philbin. As one of four executive editors, Patrick Philbin had the perhaps the most tedious and thankless job on the *Harvard Law Review.* Known as the "czars of the Blue Book," the executive editors usually had to work around the clock to make sure that every citation in each comment, note, and article conformed to the Blue Book style. Ellen couldn't afford to alienate one of his executive editors. He was in a bind.

Ellen understood that his conservative officers felt they were getting the article shoved down their throats, and that no matter how he handled the profanity in it, they would think it was done just to appease them. He thought that at least they deserved a chance to air their beefs about the piece—after all, they had done yeoman's work for him all year long.

Unfortunately, of all the things required of him as president, the one thing he hated was mediating disputes. So far, he'd only had to resolve a few almost ridiculously small things, such as stepping in when a student editor and a professor disagreed over whether to italicize a word, and accepting the blame for misidentifying someone as a "lawyer-lobbyist." His whole approach toward editing was to be as active an editor as possible, consistent with showing respect to the authors; "That's much more difficult than people realize," he commented. Until then, everyone had done pretty well at living together. He was sad that this last month of his term as president was heading toward a confrontation.

He decided that even though he wasn't disturbed by Mary Joe Frug's choice of words, his co-editors' concerns deserved to be addressed. "I felt that in some sense they were owed by the institution some kind of response, even though I didn't find it offensive," he said. "One of the most difficult parts of mediating disputes is deciding how to decide." He called a "full-body" meeting of all eighty-five editors to consider Platt and Philbin's proposals regarding the words in Frug's piece. Some action had to be taken, since there were only a few days left before the deadline to send the articles for the March 1992 issue to the printer. And most of the 2L editors were busy preparing for the upcoming officer elections the first Sunday in February.

January was usually a transition period for the transfer of power that was about to be given to the 2L editors. It was the time before the elections when the 2L's voted on ideas and recommendations, assessed the functions of the organization, developed their campaigns, and reviewed one another's work. With their energies directed toward the pending elections, most of the 2L editors were hardly aware of the simmering debate over the words in the Mary Joe Frug article.

Still, nearly all eighty-five members of the *Review* showed up for the body meeting on the evening of Tuesday, January 28, to decide whether to publish Mary Joe Frug's article intact, or to delete or revise the words that Platt and other conservatives felt might offend readers. They met in a classroom building since there were too many people on the *Review* to cram into the tiny rectangular lounge on the second floor of the *Review* offices at Gannett House.

It soon became clear that there was not enough support for deleting any parts or any of the words of the article. More than half of the editors agreed that under the circumstances, given Mary Joe Frug's murder and the fact that her article was still in draft form, the deal struck with Jerry Frug was reasonable, especially since the piece was going to be clearly marked "An Unfinished Draft" in the "Commentary" section. Moreover, as the editors had come to realize, it represented an interesting legal theoretical outlook. They voted to accept it as a matter of policy.

Even if none of it would be cut, Platt and her supporters wanted a compromise on the two words they felt might offend readers. As they suggested in their letter, they wanted either a dash or asterisks in the words *fuck* and *cunt,* making these words, "f—k" or "f**k" or "c—t" or "c**t." "We realized no one was going to agree to cut the words, but we thought that we should do something to denote the fact that we don't think this is just run-of-the-mill," Platt told her peers on the *Review.* That was ridiculous, responded Kestenbaum and Ramirez, who obviously had the most invested in the piece, and several other editors. She was just being a prude, they told her. Worse, they charged, she and her friends were simply trying to censor the article; this was also just another ploy to silence Mary Joe Frug. Indeed, they argued, Mary Joe Frug was consciously using the technique of taking words that oppressed women and reclaiming them to protest the harms that pornography and rape inflicted upon women. It was a common device employed in feminist writing.

The meeting was turning tense; people were edgy, angry. Law review editors can be opinionated people, highly confident in their own abilities. It was clear from the harsh accusations being flung about that their high confidence had turned into self-righteousness and disrespect. Having eighty-five people working in that little white house on intense deadlines was obviously a tinderbox, enough to cause something as small as an asterisk to explode into a major issue and to become a matter of pride. That is how out of whack matters had become at the Harvard Law School. Judging from the mood in the room, these students had lost some perspective. Then again, these 3L editors were the same students who had started their first year in Robert Clark's first year as dean. They had watched, listened, and apparently taken notes, as Clark and his adversaries on the faculty and the student body battled with one another. They were also getting on each other's nerves.

When the asterisk proposal looked as if it wasn't going to succeed, Platt and her allies turned to the idea of adding a footnote. The footnote would simply say that there were some words readers might find offensive, but that they had been left in because the article was being published posthumously. Nothing would even be done, by way of punctuation, to the words themselves. If they decided against a footnote, another alternative that would satisfy them was to add a similar statement, as a kind of disclaimer, in the preface to the article, where it would be introduced as a tribute. This would simply say that a few of the editors did not agree with some of the language contained in the article. Again, both of these suggestions were harshly attacked and shot down by several of the more liberal editors. "By this point there was no willingness to compromise," Platt recalled later. "They didn't want any compromise because they wanted to strike a blow for the cause. If it looked reasonable, something had to be wrong with it. That's how they dealt with our proposals and the footnote and the disclaimer."

Seeing how far apart and how riled some of his editors were getting, Ellen stepped in. He gave a speech supporting the idea of adding a sentence as a kind of disclaimer in the tribute. He explained to his co-workers that even though Platt, Philbin, and several of the other editors' politics were "very antithetical" to his own, "it was important to show them some appreciation for the work they put in." He told the editors of the *Review* that they should "compromise for the sake of compromise."

When the editors voted, none of the compromises was accepted. Even Kenneth Fenyo and Craig Coben, two conservative editors whom Platt and Philbin had been counting on, voted against their ideas; no dashes or asterisks would appear in specific words, and there would be no footnote, though Fenyo voted for the disclaimer. They certainly didn't like the article's crude language, or that its author was prominent in Critical Legal Studies, or that publication was conditioned on a deal made with Jerry Frug. But on First Amendment absolutist grounds, these two editors, as libertarians, believed the piece should run exactly as the editors had intended all along.

In the end, as a majority of the editors decided, Mary Joe Frug's "Postmodern Feminist Manifesto" would be introduced by a two-paragraph preface stating in part that "the Editors of the *Harvard Law Review* agreed that, under the circumstances, the preservation of Mary Joe Frug's voice outweighed strict

adherence to traditional editorial policy. For this reason, neither
stylistic nor organizational changes have been made, and footnotes have been expanded but not added."

Nothing would be said to alert readers that they might find
some of the language in the piece offensive, or that a minority
of the editors of the *Harvard Law Review* dissented from the
editorial board's position. That satisfied "Commentary" editors Kestenbaum and Ramirez. Their piece was saved, and they
and their liberal peers had prevailed over censorship and close-
minded conservative attitudes. They had succeeded in preserv-
ing the integrity of the piece, Mary Joe's voice, and important
ideas about women, language, and power. "We met as a body
and adopted as a policy that the language was preserved. We
easily won," said Kestenbaum.

Unfortunately, that didn't settle things between the editors
of the *Review*. As usual, the political became personal. Kestenbaum and Ramirez were angry at Ellen, believing he should
have defended them more forcefully. And they were incensed
at the conservative editors for trying to censor the piece and for
questioning their ability to decide on the matter. Although the
debate was mostly among 3L's, several liberal 2L editors were
also troubled because the incident seemed to reflect several conservative male editors' hostility toward women.

"On one level this whole issue was an argument over power,
over who has the power to make such an important decision.
And certainly Janis and Edith shouldn't have such power," explained Rebecca Eisenberg, then a second-year editor. "On another level it was an effort simply to block this kind of
scholarship. They didn't have to say, 'We don't want to publish
this piece.' All they had to do was say they wanted to change
parts of it, and that would be enough to get rid of the whole
piece because of the agreement with Gerald Frug."

But no one was more broken than Platt. "We were most
unceremoniously rejected," she said about the unwillingness of
the editors to concede anything. Moreover, they had impugned
her motives and called her a prude. She took it hard. Even her
allies Fenyo and Coben had disappointed her by switching
sides. "I felt personally betrayed by them," she added.

Ellen's attempt at dispute resolution hadn't stopped the fury. If it hadn't been January, with just one more issue to publish before the second-year editors took over, Platt, Philbin, and another conservative executive editor probably would have quit. Ellen was two weeks away from being done with his term, and his conservative officers were still irate. They felt all their work had been unappreciated, and once again, as conservatives, they had been under siege. He was disappointed things were ending sourly, "though I was glad I'd made it two inches from the finish line," he said. Some of Ellen's friends told him that he should have stepped in and acted unilaterally, saying, "We're going to compromise, period." But he told them, "It was not my place." This wasn't the last time he would be told he should have been more decisive. The next time, in less than two months, when he had another chance to prevent something even more harmful from being published, he would never forgive himself for not acting swiftly and deliberately.

In the meantime, relief for Ellen came on February 2, when the *Review* held the all-day election for his successor. The editors chose a woman named Emily Schulman. She was the third woman to be elected president of the *Harvard Law Review*. At Gannett House, as the mantle was transferred to Schulman, a few people clapped for Ellen, and several people congratulated him for a good effort. Leaving with a few of his closest friends, he was relieved it was over. "The weight of these disputes had just buried me," he said.

A few days later, after briefing Schulman about her responsibilities, he returned to a normal, slower pace. He began attending classes he'd been missing. As the weather grew warmer, he met his wife for lunch in the park. And he rarely went to Gannett House, except to duck in to get his mail. He stopped by once because he promised to show the people in the business office his wedding pictures. Having experienced enough of a controversy provoked by a few fighting words, he paid little attention to the eruption that Professor Derrick Bell, Jr., the students who had sued the school, and Dean Clark were about to cause on the Law School campus.

CHAPTER 4

RINGING HARVARD'S BELL

At about 5:20 P.M. on Sunday, February 23, Harvard Law School dean Robert Clark finally reached Derrick Bell, Jr., at his Greenwich Village apartment in New York City. Considered the leading black scholar in the country and a specialist in civil rights law, Bell had taken a leave of absence until Harvard Law offered tenure to a woman of color and she accepted. He was into his second year of protest, teaching at New York University, and he planned to stay away another year, even though Harvard University rules prohibited it.

Clark wanted to make it clear that if Bell desired to return to Harvard, where he was the first tenured black professor, the faculty would love to have him. Bell's prior indications that he would continue his protest leave would not be a barrier; the faculty could easily accommodate him in the teaching schedule. Please reconsider and rejoin the faculty, Clark told him.

Clark explained to Bell that he could do more good for the cause of diversifying the Harvard Law School faculty at the school than away from it. Progress was being made, Clark said, although the faculty hadn't made an appointment Bell wanted. Many students wanted him to return, and Clark urged Bell not to disappoint them. Finally he told Bell: You can have more influence on the next generation of *leading* minority (and other) lawyers at Harvard Law School than anywhere else. It had the best and the brightest—and the largest number—of minority students of any leading law school.

Bell thanked Clark for calling, and replied that what he had been telling him was all very nice. But his mind was made up. As usual, Bell was polite but firm. In his position, he couldn't really see coming back until a woman of color was appointed. Though that phrase could include Hispanic, Native American, Asian-American, or other minorities, Bell specifically intended an African-American. That an African-American woman still had not been offered tenure meant that he would have to stay on leave.

Clark reminded him about Harvard University's strict two-year limit on leaves of absence. He tried to make it clear that he could not waive the rule, and that Harvard's governing board was unlikely to do so as well. Requests for longer leaves were routinely rejected. Henry Kissinger was denied an extension while serving as United States Secretary of State. Charles Fried and David Shapiro had had to resign from the Law School to finish their terms in the Ronald Reagan Justice Department. The policy was designed to keep professors from staying in government or business positions indefinitely, thereby depleting the faculties of Harvard College and its various graduate schools. If, by June 1992, Harvard still had not tenured a black or minority woman, Clark explained to Bell, he would have to return to the faculty or else resign.

Bell told Clark he didn't think the policy ought to apply to him, because his leave was different. In the first place, it wasn't "voluntary"; the Law School's failure to have a single tenured woman of color on the faculty had left him no choice but to begin a "sacrificial financial fast" to draw attention to the problem. Second, nearly two years after he began his academic hunger strike, the situation that had prompted his action had not been remedied. Moreover, he planned to challenge the policy, and told Clark he would be sending a letter confirming his position.

Clark realized that Bell would go ahead with his own analysis anyway. Their phone conversation was just like previous ones they had had, before and during Bell's leave of absence. Nothing was going to change Bell's mind, short of the answer and resolution he desired. Despite his distinguished appearance, the blue, black, or gray pinstripe suit he wore almost every day, his gentle, lilting voice, and his fatherly demeanor, each of Bell's moves was calibrated and calculated. He was as much a needler and agitator as Duncan Kennedy was of the CLS faction—perhaps more so, because Bell was willing to give up his $120,000 salary, at least for two years. Bell was correct when he said that people always figured he was someone they could work with, because he looked so professional and so much like part of the establishment. He was no kente-cloth, fez-wearing, militant revolutionary. And they were often disappointed when they realized that he was a man who pushed back whenever he felt he was dealt with badly.

On February 26, three days after his phone conversation with Clark, Bell mailed him a formal response, confirming his stated intention to continue his leave-without-pay protest for the 1992–93 academic year. That wasn't all. Even if he was not granted an extension, he informed Clark, he would soon be filing a grievance against the Law School, challenging its faculty hiring and promotion policies. A suit brought by a coalition of nine student groups claiming that Harvard Law School's allegedly discriminatory hiring practices breached the school's promise to provide equal educational opportunities had moved up the appeals ladder. The case was set to be heard in just a few weeks by the Massachusetts Supreme Judicial Court, the state's highest court.

Bell's complaint would be on his own behalf as the first black tenured professor at Harvard Law School. His chief argument concerned the exclusion of women and minorities who might be exceptional practitioners and law teachers, but didn't go to elite law schools. Equating "teaching and scholarly potential with law school grades," these practices violated Harvard University's affirmative-action rules and probably violated state and federal laws, he warned Clark. Moreover, they personally denied him a right to be at a school that promised to be an equal opportunity employer. "The policies I am protesting violate my entitlement to hold a tenured appointment at a school that does not unfairly exclude persons with credentials, backgrounds, and experiences like my own."

He reminded Clark that in April 1990, when he first announced his intention to take a protest leave, he had been acting in support of students who had been urging the school to appoint not only women of color, but Asians, Hispanics, Native Americans, and others whose backgrounds and outlooks were not represented on the faculty. When the faculty had again failed to act, in the spring of 1991, Bell extended his leave another year. Now, after two years, the school still refused to provide "the diversity in our faculty appropriate to a law school to whom all in legal education look for leadership." For those reasons he felt he had to extend his leave.

He clearly understood that the university's rules limited voluntary leaves of absence to two years, but he said those "otherwise appropriate regulations" couldn't possibly have been intended to apply to his leave, which he considered "an exercise of academic freedom."

In his eyes, the Law School had consistently breached the commitment it had made to him when he agreed to become the first black professor at Harvard Law School, an assurance that he would not be a token black. Now, after more than twenty years, there were only two other black tenured male professors and not a single African-American woman on the faculty. That situation was slightly mitigated by the fact that there were three black males in tenure-track positions, and that 42 percent of all appointments since 1981 had been women and minorities. Still, Bell felt that the school's repeated rejection of his efforts to reform the school's hiring and promotion practices, forcing him into isolation, was nothing less than a way to seek his ouster from the school.

The worst part of it, he told Clark, was that he knew that in early March the faculty would be voting on an appointments committee recommendation to appoint a "slate" of four white males whose scholarship reflected conservative and CLS ideological positions. These appointments were being urged to break the gridlock of the faculty factions that had crippled hiring. This was the ultimate insult to Bell. Now, when it was convenient for Clark and his colleagues, the law faculty was apparently willing to depart from hiring strictly on merit. "It was, you will recall, the school's commitment to merit that was asserted as the reason we have no women of color on the faculty," he dug at Clark, reminding him of earlier statements in which Clark had said the "pool" of qualified minority women was too small.

Bell was planning to travel to Cambridge on March 3 to try to meet with Clark or another Law School administrator. The same day he arrived in Cambridge, the student coalition would be defending its discrimination suit against Harvard on appeal to the Supreme Judicial Court of Massachusetts, the highest court in the state. The next day, Bell would attend a rally on the steps of Langdell Hall to protest the lack of minorities on the faculty. Those events would electrify the Law School campus, but they would seem to be happening in a separate world from the *Harvard Law Review*. At Gannett House, most members were involved in the leadership transition, the transfer of power from the 3L's to the 2L's. Some *Law Review* members were supportive of Bell and the student activists. Former *Review* president Baruch Obama had addressed the press conference at which Bell declared his leave of absence. But for now, the bitter debate at the *Review* over whether to publish the views of underrepresented voices, albeit expressed unconventionally, seemed unrelated to the furor over hiring underrepresented individuals, however nontraditional their credentials or politics, on the faculty.

Clark was focusing on the latter issue, and he was not eager to experience the stir Bell was sure to cause. A strong-willed Southerner, Clark had ascended to the deanship on his stated desire to invigorate faculty scholarship. He had little patience for what he perceived as Bell's antics. When Bell staged his four-day sit-in to protest the faculty's failure to offer tenure to Daniel Tarullo and Clare Dalton, Clark carped to a reporter, "This is a university, not a lunch counter in the South." Clark claimed he was trying to say that Bell was turning the tenure denials into a case of racial injustice and using a tactic that should be reserved for a moral cause of the highest order. A faculty personnel matter was "not something one should go to the barricades for," Clark explained subsequently. Nevertheless, he apologized for his statement. But his comment continued to stand out as a symbol of his and Harvard's racial insensitivity. Though he was a former seminarian, Clark certainly exhibited the lack of compassion all too common at Harvard. Because he did not want to appear held hostage by Bell, Clark failed to negotiate a resolution, which at one time Bell was willing to reach. In many ways, Clark exacerbated a problem that could have been avoided.

As Clark said to Bell on the phone, he wasn't going to budge from strict enforcement of the university policy on leaves of absence, either. "The university rule is a good one. People should make a choice whether they are going to be at Harvard or not," he told *New York Times* writer Fox Butterfield, after news of Bell's February 26 letter began to circulate. Regarding Bell personally, his arguments were becoming like a familiar, hollow-ringing chorus to Clark. He told Butterfield, "In a sense we are just where we were two years ago, except time is running out for him." Moreover, "the faculty in general is not influenced by his actions."

Many in the press hadn't been convinced by Bell's actions, either. Columnists and commentators harshly criticized Bell when he announced his leave in 1990. The *New York Post* blasted Bell in an editorial headlined RACIAL ULTIMATUM AT HARVARD LAW, for wanting to lower standards in the name of completing the rainbow, and for trying to "coerce his colleagues." Columnist George Will accused Bell of "intellectual gerrymandering," interested in "carving out for blacks an exemption from competition." *The New Republic,* not always liberal on race issues, wrote, "Bell's solution is no solution."

But Bell wasn't playing to Clark or to the Harvard Law School faculty or to conservative analysts. He was coming from a different place, not as an individual, but rather as someone with a responsibility to the African-American population of the United States. From that perspective, Harvard Law School had changed only a tiny bit since it was founded in 1817. He was

part of the generation that had participated in the civil rights
struggles. In contrast to a younger generation of African-
American scholars, such as his Harvard colleague Randall Kennedy, or Yale Law School's Stephen Carter, who denounced
the "stigma" of affirmative action, Bell looked at affirmative
action merely as a desegregation tactic, a tepid, modest step in
a long, nearly unwinnable process.

That's why he didn't have much stomach for the appointments committee's reasons why the school couldn't take someone. To him there was a basic clarity and moral urgency about
it. His 1992 book, titled *Faces at the Bottom of the Well*, reflected his idea about the "permanence of racism" and white
people's "unspoken commitment to keeping us where we are,
at whatever cost to them or us."

His detractors—and he has made a habit of burning his
bridges behind him—have tried to cast him as a segregation-
ist and an apologist for extremists such as Louis Farrakhan.
Clark and others on the faculty have treated him like a pa-
riah. But Bell is simply a man who lost hope, and his book
is about his despair. As colleagues, former students, and
friends have described him, Bell was not a bigot. Yes, he
backed off from civil rights strategies he once advocated,
thereby alienating a segment of civil rights leaders who once
counted him as their friend, and yes, he knowingly insulted
his African-American colleague Randall Kennedy when he
said that at Harvard "the ends of diversity are not served by
people who look black and think white." But Bell was truly
color blind and humanitarian when it came to dealing with
people individually.

In *Faces,* Bell recalled an older black civil rights organizer
named Behona McDonald, from a small town in Leake County,
Mississippi, where Bell had supervised school desegregation
cases in the mid-1960s. White businessmen had threatened to
recall loans to McDonald's neighbors, deny them credit, fire
them from jobs, and kill anyone who tried to send his or her
children to a white school. In the face of those intimidation
tactics and the danger to herself and others, McDonald kept
signing up children to join the school cases Bell was handling,

and continued registering black voters. Bell once asked her what kept her going. She told him, "I lives to harass white folks."

Bell acknowledges that this may as well be his motto, too. He is one of those people put on earth to be a thorn in the flesh. It's the only way to move things forward, he believes. His leave of absence from Harvard was merely the latest in a series of defiant acts he had taken part in since he was a boy, each intended just for its harassing effect. Not all whites are racist, he admits, but he has no doubt that the oppression blacks have experienced is racial and has emanated from whites. That's what made his actions and words so potent. Like Behona McDonald, he never expected to topple his oppressors.

Some of his past defiances now have the tenor of lore, and his letter to Clark contained well-worn passages. But for Bell, confrontation was a way of life or, more appropriately, "a life calling" mounted with "sweet-tempered canniness," as *Boston Globe* writer Mark Muro noted. "All through my life, I've known confrontation makes history, that nothing gets done without pushing," Bell told Muro. "Contrary to usual belief, confrontations bring betterment, not just for others but for yourself."

Born in 1930, Bell grew up in a mostly black, working-class part of Pittsburgh. His maternal grandfather was a cook on a dining car for the Pennsylvania Railroad, and occasionally cooked for the president of the company. He was a native Pennsylvanian. It was his father's side of the family that originated in the South. Born in Dotham, Alabama, his father moved north as a young man and never went back. With no more than a sixth-grade education, his father worked as a janitor in a local department store. It was a good job, with regular pay. But after six years on the job, he developed narcolepsy and was forced to quit. Since he could work outdoors without getting sleepy, he started a hauling business. He had a few accidents going to sleep at the wheel, but D. A. Bell Hauling did reasonably well.

The business grew to a point where Bell's father could maintain four or five men on the payroll, and he moved his wife and four children to the top of Pittsburgh's Heron Hill district, a significant step upward in status for blacks. A few years later he would have enough money to buy a house. His father taught him an important survival lesson: whites always had the edge. "White folk are thinking and scheming while we black folk are sleeping and eating," Bell's father would caution. He never trusted whites.

From his mother, Ada, Bell learned the lesson of pushing back. It came after a stingy landlord kept neglecting to fix the back steps of the brick row house they rented. His mother, sweeping him and his brother up in her arms, marched into the rent office and waved the rent money at the landlord. She told him, "I have the money, but you don't get it until you come fix the back steps so my kids don't fall." The steps were fixed, and Bell saw his mother win, "by insisting and demanding." He would always remember that first confrontation with power.

Throughout junior high and high school, Bell delivered newspapers on a route that opened up a world for him. The customers in his eight-block territory covered a vast social spectrum. Most of the blacks were middle class, though some were unemployed. The last remaining whites in the neighborhood were upper middle class. They included doctors, ministers, and one judge. The whites "were always very warm and friendly and I got a lot of encouragement from them, but I could see the difference between their homes and ours."

Bell was lucky. He had an intact family, and the benefits of an extended family. He possessed a quick mind, something his family recognized early on. "They treated me like I was Jesus," he said. "I always had the feeling that I was fairly special." When he showed an interest in stamp collecting, his uncle, George Childress, bought him a big collection. When he developed an interest in records, the same uncle bought him a record player. Bell loved to sing, and has a brother who teaches music at Lehman College in the Bronx. When Bell wanted to try his hand at photography, his uncle bought him some dark-room equipment. And when he had hopes of becoming an aeronautical engineer, he bought Bell some model planes.

Childress, a bartender at one of the local black clubs and an official of the black musicians union, didn't have a lot of formal education, but he was dogmatic. John Foster Dulles was his hero. Childress made sure Bell had a lot of encouragement. It was because of this uncle's influence that Bell voted Republican in the first election he was old enough to participate in. To all appearances, Bell's was a conservative, proper upbringing, in keeping with the wartime days of the 1940s and the boom years of the 1950s. He was in the Boy Scouts in grade school and in the ROTC during high school and college. In junior high he met Jewel Hairston, the girl he would later marry. He was the first person in his family to go beyond high school, and he chose to attend local Duquesne University, where he could live at home and work for his father to earn money for tuition. Upon graduation, Bell got his commission to serve in the air force during the Korean War.

His first orders were to report to Sumter, South Carolina. His father didn't want his son riding in the segregated buses, so he gave him a car to drive. In a matter of days he came face to face with the harsh realities of the racism of the Deep South. This was 1952. On his way down to South Carolina, Bell took a white ROTC recruit with him. He knew they couldn't stay in white hotels, so he decided they would spend a night at a black rooming house in Richmond. As he and his friend entered the house, the woman who ran it shouted, "Get that white boy away from here," and subjected Bell to a tongue-lashing for being so stupid. Didn't he know how much trouble he could have gotten her into with the authorities? He took his friend downtown, dropped him off at a white hotel, and picked him up the next day.

When they got to Atlanta, Bell stayed in a black YMCA and his buddy lodged at a place for whites. During the day, he and his fellow recruit drove through the gorgeous areas in northeast Atlanta, where there were large houses with gates and circular driveways. He had never seen such wealth. At the officers' orientation, he was the only black officer. His driving buddy made himself scarce after they arrived, and they didn't see each other much.

As a second lieutenant, Bell was stationed at Alexandria Air Force Base in Louisiana, where he would stay six months before being sent to Korea. There he began a quiet, polite, one-man civil rights crusade of the kind that would become his trademark. First he complained to his superior officers about the segregation of the base buses as soon as they were outside the perimeter of the base. Then one Sunday he put on his dress uniform with its silver bars and went to the only Presbyterian church in town. It was a "whites only" church. Having been raised a Presbyterian, he asked if he could attend the service. Taken aback, the parishioners let him sit upstairs by himself. Unfazed, he went back a few weeks later to ask the minister if he could sing in the choir, as he had done back home in Pittsburgh. It seemed natural to him to sing in the choir if he wanted to sing. He was shipped to Korea before he could wreak any more havoc on the base or in town.

After completing his stint in the air force, he returned home to Pittsburgh, where he attended law school at the University of Pittsburgh. He graduated fourth in his class, and was the only black graduate. Already he was gaining a reputation for being opinionated. "Knows everything and wants others to know he knows everything," his classmates wrote about him in the law school yearbook.

His first job out of school was as a lawyer in the Civil Rights Division of the Justice Department under President Eisenhower. The only black among one thousand lawyers in the office, he quit after a year, when he was ordered to give up his membership in the National Association for the Advancement of Colored People. That was something he would not do; it was a matter of principle.

Fortunately, he landed a job at the NAACP Legal Defense and Education Fund, headed by Thurgood Marshall, joining the succeeding generation of lawyers who litigated the historic *Brown v. Board of Education* case. *Brown* ushered in thousands of lawsuits against schools, hospitals, restaurants, and polling places, and the six-lawyer staff at 10 Columbus Circle in New York City was embarking on the next round of cases in the post-*Brown* era that would forever change race-relations law in the United States. He worked closely with Constance Baker Motley, who later became a federal judge. They handled virtually all of the litigation in Mississippi, including more than three hundred school-desegregation cases, and flew there regularly because there were virtually no lawyers in the state willing to take civil rights cases. Later, LDF sent a full-time lawyer to Mississippi, Marian Wright, now Marian Wright Edleman, head of the Children's Defense Fund in Washington, D.C.

These were among the most difficult cases to litigate. Not only did they involve moral issues and public policy, but the civil rights lawyers had to be specialists in federal practice and procedure. They faced adversaries who used outrageous tactics and humiliating arguments, hostile judges who trotted out arcane rules to justify any technical or procedural way to avoid ruling for blacks, and local whites who threatened violence. "Nowhere else in the law did you encounter such resistance and intolerance. It was really a form of trench warfare. It was practicing law under the most extreme conditions," recalled Michael Meltsner, who shared a cramped office with Bell at the Legal Defense Fund. Meltsner later became a professor at Northeastern University School of Law.

It took unique lawyers to withstand the pressure. "They had to be masters of themselves, masters of the complexities of the legal situation, and masters of publicity and politics, in the sense that everything we did was in a fishbowl," Meltsner said. All of those skills would come in handy for Bell later on at Harvard.

One of Bell's first successes at the Inc. Fund, as it was called, came in 1962 when he helped James Meredith win admittance to the University of Mississippi despite the resistance of Governor Ross Barnett. Bell was in Mississippi during the famous "Freedom Summer" of 1964, as Bob Moses of the Southern Christian Leadership Conference proclaimed it. That was the summer when more than one thousand preachers, students, lawyers, and bankers came to register blacks to vote, and to open "freedom schools" and community centers. The previous summer, Medgar Evers, the NAACP secretary in Mississippi, famous for leading a massive boycott in Jackson, had been killed in front of his home in Jackson. Risking beatings, arrest, and their lives, the civil rights workers descended upon the hot, swampy Mississippi delta. They entered a place that comprised two worlds, a white culture and a colored culture.

Whites called it an invasion. The Association of Citizens Councils was formed to oppose civil rights and integration suits. These were composed of segregationists, largely bankers, politicians, and white business owners. They foreclosed on homes and fired workers suspected of being involved in civil rights activity. The state seemed at war with half of its own citizens.

In June of 1964, three young male civil rights workers were reported missing in the Mississippi backcountry. In July, Lyndon Johnson signed the Civil Rights Act. Another eighty civil rights workers were arrested, and more were beaten at strikes and rallies. It was especially dangerous for people working in isolated rural areas. On August 4, just days before the schools in the state were to be desegregated, the bodies of the three young men were found.

Bell had come to desegregate a school in Leake County, about fifty miles northeast of Jackson, where most of the violence and unrest was. On this case, Bell was a liaison to the Justice Department, whose lawyers provided support to the Legal Defense Fund. The Leake County school was in one of three districts that were still before the courts, almost ten years after the second part of *Brown* ordered the integration of public schools "with all deliberate speed." The plaintiffs lived in the small town called Harmony, where Behona McDonald, the woman who lived to "harass white folks," resided.

Harmony, Mississippi, is a unique place where blacks have had a history of sovereignty. In the 1840s, blacks were brought here from Alabama as slaves. They were not plantation slaves; they worked on small farms. After the Civil War ended, when the South was economically devastated, blacks were given a chance to buy the land they worked on. By the turn of the century, blacks owned about thirty thousand acres of land in Harmony. They maintained their land, though they were poor. This legacy of land ownership gave them an independence of spirit and made them tough.

Money from the Julius Rosenwald Fund made it possible to

build the Rosenwald School in Harmony in the 1930s, and the county then provided the teachers. The community had a lot of pride in this school, even though it had few supplies and was inferior to white schools. But in the early 1960s the county authorities had decided they were going to close the school. That was when the residents of Harmony turned to the Legal Defense Fund to try to keep their school. They were told that the NAACP was no longer bringing separate-but-equal cases, but could sue to integrate their school if they wanted. Following that advice, they sued and won.

The day before the schools in Leake County were to open as desegregated schools, just hours after people learned the civil rights workers had been killed, white businessmen distributed leaflets and went around the county threatening blacks that they would get fired and lose their mortgages if they tried to bring their children to a whites-only or desegregated school. Winson Hudson, whose niece was a plaintiff, remembered hearing whites say they would kill anyone attempting to walk into school. Hudson's house had been shot at before, when she let a white civil rights worker stay there.

It was dangerous to travel alone in the rural areas, but that night, Bell and Jean Fairfax, a community organizer assisting the Legal Defense Fund, drove into the countryside to tell people not to give up. They assured them they would uphold their constitutional rights. Fairfax had attended many hearings with Bell, and admired the way he had persevered under some of the worst conditions. She once saw him argue in a federal district courtroom in Jackson where a large mural depicting Mississippi showed blacks baling cotton or doing other menial work. All the whites in the picture were well-scrubbed, smartly dressed, and looked like they were going places.

Additionally, in that hearing, Bell had to listen to a lawyer on the other side tell a judge about a study showing that the brains of pygmies in the Congo were smaller than those of white people; according to the lawyer, this proved that blacks were intellectually inferior because they had less cranial capacity. Thus, the lawyer continued, blacks shouldn't be allowed to attend white schools because they lacked the intellectual resources to compete. "He had to sit through all of this stuff for days in front of this mural," said Fairfax, who moved to Arizona after retiring from the LDF in 1985. "I admired him for keeping his cool while doing this extremely difficult, personally humiliating work."

That tense night in Harmony before the schools were to open, Fairfax said, "I hauled Derrick all around the county. Through the night we sat on porches, under candles and kerosene lanterns, talking with people, reassuring them, crying with them. We were really afraid, not only of economic threats but of physical threats too."

The next day, one six-year old girl, Deborah Lewis, came forward to go to school. Federal marshals sent by the Justice Department arrived from several states. Bell, Fairfax, and the black citizens of Leake County were prepared for violence. As Bell and Fairfax, escorted by the marshals, pulled up in front of the school, hundreds of people were shouting threats. "That was the only time in my life I felt afraid that I would be in the middle of something violent," said Fairfax. They went inside and registered the little girl.

That morning was sunny and hot. Bell had taken off his suitcoat and put it in the trunk of the car. After they registered Lewis, he went to get his jacket out in case he needed to talk to the sheriff or other officials. But he couldn't get in the car. In the commotion, he had accidentally left the keys in his coat pocket and locked them in the trunk. People were shouting at him as he tried to pry open the trunk, and he was trembling. He and Fairfax ended up leaving in a police car. Once again, Bell was making another dramatic exit.

The police drove Bell and Fairfax to the home of Dovie and Winson Hudson, where the two sisters had prepared a congratulatory dinner of fried chicken, biscuits and gravy, rice, and peaches. "We were so hot and tired and dusty," remembered Winson Hudson, who, at seventy-six, almost thirty years later, was still active in civil rights. "It was a celebration. We laughed about Derrick and the keys gettin' locked up in the car. We think a whole lot of him. He was with us all the way through that terrible time."

Deborah Lewis went on to finish the school year. But her father lost his job and received threats that his house would be burned. A year later, after things had settled down a bit, Fairfax saw Lewis again. She was in the Legal Defense Fund offices in New York. Bell had invited her to attend the World's Fair. "He was very personally involved with the plaintiffs. This was not just a New York lawyer who breezed in and left," said Fairfax.

Bell stayed with the Legal Defense Fund until 1966, when he became director of the Office of Civil Rights at the Department of Health, Education and Welfare. His work in the South had left an indelible mark on his life. He had seen people take risks that some of his Harvard colleagues could never comprehend. But he also came away with a deep sense of failure as whites abandoned the schools he had supposedly integrated.

In future law review articles, such as "Serving Two Masters," published in 1976 in the *Yale Law Journal,* in his 1987 book, *And We Are Not Saved,* and then in *Faces,* Bell disavowed some of the desegregation tactics he and the Inc. Fund pursued in the South. He thought perhaps he had been wrong in advising the people of Harmony, Mississippi, not to retain their school but to seek to integrate it. In *Faces* he criticized black and white civil rights professionals as being "committed—to the point of obsession—with integration notions that, however widely held in the 1960s, are woefully beyond reach today." Naturally, comments like those soured his friendships with other people prominent in the civil rights movement.

But when he left Washington in 1968 to become the executive director of the Western Center on Law and Poverty at the University of Southern California, he was still a firm believer in the course set by the civil rights movement. He taught a course on civil rights law as an adjunct professor, and liked the classroom so much that he began applying for teaching jobs. He applied to Harvard Law School in 1964 and again in 1966, but was turned down twice.

During the 1966–67 school year, however, Harvard Law professor Charles Nesson invited Bell to lecture in his civil rights course. Bell still was not hired, despite his extensive experience in the area. Though he had served as associate editor-in-chief of the *University of Pittsburgh Law Review* and had graduated at the top of his class, in Harvard's eyes he had attended only a "regional" law school and had not clerked for any judge, let alone an appeals court judge or a Supreme Court justice, as most members of the Harvard Law faculty had.

Then Martin Luther King, Jr., was assassinated, and Harvard Law School's black students began pressing for a minority faculty member. They wanted someone who would be sensitive to the needs of African-American students at a predominantly white institution, someone who was "black." There was a concept of blackness, as opposed to someone who was liberal and white and had simply gone to the right schools. In 1969, Harvard invited Bell back for an interview and to meet with students. The faculty voted to hire him.

Harvard University president Derek Bok and the president of the Black Law Students Association, Robert Bell (no relation to Derrick Bell), flew to Los Angeles to offer him the job in person. "It was exciting, the prospect of having an African-American on the faculty of Harvard Law School," said Robert Bell, who became a state court judge in Baltimore. "I remember that Derrick explained to Bok that he would use this teaching position to continue his civil rights work. 'I don't want to be the token,' he told [Bok]. And Bok was emphatic about saying that was not our intention. We thought he would be the first of a long line," recalled Judge Bell.

Derrick Bell was given a two-year appointment as a lecturer at law, followed by a tenure decision. His first threat to resign came after he felt a decision on his tenure was being delayed, and within in a year, in 1971, he won what he called a "pioneering appointment," becoming the first black professor at Harvard Law School. He was an immensely popular teacher, especially for the black students now coming to the law school in greater numbers. He was an innovator in establishing the academic study of racism as a legal problem, and he developed the leading casebook in the area in 1973, which he titled *Race, Racism, and American Law.*

Soon his "willful arc of guerrilla theater," as the *Globe*'s Muro called it, would become a common scene in the halls of

America's legal establishment. Almost immediately after winning his slot on the faculty, he began complaining that the law school faculty needed to abandon its "traditional hiring criterion" and its overemphasis on academic credentials, in an effort to attract other minority professors and women. Persons without the most outstanding credentials could still do outstanding work, he claimed. Moreover, relying on the standard barometer to measure performance or potential was simply a subtle form of racism that needed to be eliminated. By insisting on the same old credentials, Harvard ensured that it would only hire more of what it already had: white, well-off, middle-aged men. He wanted the faculty to look at qualifications beyond grades, such as civil rights experience, to attract more minority professors, like himself, who maybe hadn't gone to the best law schools but had made a real difference in the world.

Again, in 1974, he told Dean Albert Sacks he was going to quit unless Harvard Law School moved faster to hire other black professors. A short time later the faculty recruited two more black law professors, Clarence Clyde Ferguson and Harry Edwards. Bell remembered that Sacks made a special trip to his office to remind him personally that his threat to resign, of course, had nothing to do with the appointments. And Clark Byse, then a member of the faculty appointments committee, has maintained that none of the appointments were made because of Bell's or student pressure.

But Bell could see through their veneer. One time, for instance, shortly after he received tenure, he went to a cocktail party at Dean Sacks's house. Talking to one of the guests, in a voice loud enough for everyone to hear, he said that to celebrate getting tenured he had gone out and bought a shiny black Cadillac, a beauty, with a red interior. As he was saying this, he saw other professors wince. Oh, no, the man they had just added to the faculty was one of those tacky, lower-class blacks, their faces read. Then, with a sly smile, Bell said he was just kidding; he still had his old Volkswagen. The point was made, however: faculty members did hold stereotypes about blacks. Once again, Bell had pricked their flesh.

By then, resignations, silent vigils, and sit-ins had become

Bell's modus operandi. In 1980 he accepted an offer to be dean of the University of Oregon Law School, the first black to become a dean of such a nonblack institution. Five years later he was out the door again, after causing a public stir there. The Oregon faculty had tenured a black woman, but passed over an Asian woman next in line after two white candidates dropped out. Bell resigned in protest. Some professors at Oregon have said Bell played the race card as a pretext to stepping down. The faculty had been seeking his resignation because he had become an absentee dean, spending more time on the lecture circuit than on campus, and he had refused to move aside. When he finally resigned, they resented it that he made them seem racist.

During the spring of 1986, on a stopover at Stanford Law School as a visiting professor, Bell generated another controversy. The school quietly began a lecture series after several students complained he wasn't teaching them enough real law in their constitutional law class. Bell's classroom lectures had been disorganized and marked by his political framework, they said.

Bell turned the incident into an example of the subtle operations of racism inside elite institutions. He wrote a long essay on the affair, and sent a copy to every law school in the country, asking professors to discuss the incident at their faculty meetings. "I publicized the incident in the hope that other minority law teachers would not be subjected to similar experiences," he said.

In the fall of 1986, he was reappointed at Harvard and started teaching again there. He soon noticed that Harvard had made few gains in fulfilling the promise to him that "he would be the first but not the last." Ferguson had died and Harry Edwards had long since left for his home state of Michigan. Edwards was later appointed to be a federal appeals court judge in Washington, D.C. Bell was still the only tenured black professor, though two assistant professors, Christopher Edley, Jr., and Randall Kennedy, were on a tenure track. There were only three tenured women professors on the faculty.

In June 1987, he held his four-day sit-in to protest the denial of a tenure offer to Clare Dalton and Daniel Tarullo. He was encouraged by CLS because its left-wing agenda supported the inclusion of minorities and women. His own scholarship, advocating "Racial Realism," was an offshoot of CLS theory. It had helped spawn a group of younger minority scholars, including Charles Lawrence, Kimberle Crenshaw, Patricia Williams, Lani Guinier, Mari Matsuda, Richard Delgado, and Gerald Torres, who wrote groundbreaking articles on race theory. Of course, since they took "critical" views, they were anathema at Harvard after the Dalton debacle.

During the summer of 1987, Bell dropped another bomb on Harvard, or at least wrote about an explosion at Harvard. In a report to President Bok on Harvard's affirmative-action record, Bell surmised that if all of Harvard's black faculty and staff were killed in an unexplained blast along with Harvard's president, the university would move aggressively to hire blacks and other minorities. Nothing short of such a tragic event would prompt swift action, he argued. He used the parable, he said, to illustrate the "crisis orientation" of most civil rights reform.

Although Bell had a point, Harvard Law School had been able to recruit black professors. The two most recent additions, Edley and Kennedy, were both highly promising scholars. Edley, hired as an assistant professor in 1981 and tenured in 1987, was a graduate of Harvard Law School and a former member of the *Harvard Law Review*. He also held a master's degree in public policy administration from the Kennedy School of Government. He had been an assistant to Stuart Eisenstat, domestic policy director in the Jimmy Carter White House, and in 1988 he was national issues coordinator for Democratic presidential nominee Michael Dukakis.

Kennedy, hired as an assistant professor in 1984 and tenured in 1989, graduated from Yale Law School, where he had served on the *Yale Law Journal*. He clerked in Washington, D.C., for U.S. Court of Appeals Judge J. Skelly Wright and then for Justice Thurgood Marshall. At Harvard, Kennedy had launched a popular academic journal on race called *Reconstruction*.

These two young African-American professors fit the Harvard mold perfectly. And three other African-American men who had been hired and were on a tenure track also seemed to possess the right stuff for Harvard. David Wilkins was a graduate of both Harvard College and Law School, and a former clerk to Justice Thurgood Marshall. Scott Brewer, a graduate of Yale and former editor-in-chief of the *Yale Law Journal,* had also clerked for Marshall. Charles Ogletree, a former director of the Public Defender Service in Washington, D.C., had also graduated from Harvard Law. He was the only one of the three who hadn't clerked for a judge.

But Bell still pressed for Harvard Law School to hire other women and minorities, even if they didn't have the *Harvard Law Review* or the *Yale Law Journal* on their résumés. He wanted the school to take a symbolic step, to send a signal that it was receptive to people from different backgrounds and truly interested in having a diverse faculty. Unfortunately for Bell, Harvard was unwilling to do this if it meant forsaking "merit," as the majority of professors defined it.

In the 1989–90 academic year, Regina Austin, an African-American professor from the University of Pennsylvania, was invited to Harvard as a visiting professor. Austin's résumé did not shine with Ivy League credentials. She had received her B.A. from the University of Rochester and her J.D. from the University of Pennsylvania. She had no law review and no clerkships to her credit, and had practiced law only briefly, as an associate with the large Philadelphia firm of Schnader, Harrison, Segal & Lewis. But she had established herself as an expert in torts, insurance, and product-liability law.

From the moment she arrived in Cambridge, Austin established herself as someone to whom minority women students could turn for guidance. At the annual fall dinner of the Harvard Women's Law Association, she told the students that was why she was there: "I'm not here to be the token woman or the token black, I'm here for the black women students." Her actions were consistent with her words. One of the things she did in her year at Harvard was to run a film group for black women, where they discussed the portrayals of women in films such as Spike Lee's *Do the Right Thing* and Melvin Van Peebles's *Sweet Sweetback's Badasssss Song.* The women loved being able to socialize and converse intellectually with their teacher. "She was so accessible to students," said Laura Hankins, an African-American woman student, then in her first year.

Bell saw how black women students gravitated to her the way they had to him, seeking her advice, her supervision on papers, and her job counseling. Then in his twentieth year of teaching, he realized that by not having a single tenured African-American woman on the faculty, Harvard was doing a great disservice to its minority women students. Of the student body at Harvard Law School, 45 percent were women and 22 percent were minorities. And of the 12 percent who were African-American, 55 percent, or 107, were women. Yet they lacked a single black woman professor to emulate. Bell became Austin's champion, sending memos to the appointments committee and encouraging students to speak out on her behalf.

But the appointments committee was unimpressed with her tenure piece, an article published in the *Stanford Law Review* that attempted to lay out as a legal claim the intentional infliction of emotional distress caused by racial discrimination and sexual abuse. On the grounds that the faculty could not consider the appointment of a visitor while he or she was still on campus—and could, in fact, do so only after the person had been away from Harvard for a year—the committee decided not to consider her a candidate. That decision sparked a student rebellion that included two all-night sit-ins in the dean's office, as well as class boycotts, petitions, and rallies. And it prompted Bell to announce that he had decided to give up his $120,000 annual salary to take an unpaid leave of protest until Harvard Law School had a woman of color on its faculty. The time had come for him to abandon being a mere bystander and to take a stand and join his students.

On the morning of April 24, 1990, *The New York Times* carried a story on its front page, telling the world that the first black tenured professor at Harvard Law School was declaring a leave of absence in protest of the school's hiring practices. Copies of the article were reproduced and posted everywhere. Signs all over campus announced that at noon Bell would make his dramatic statement. Bell was ready. At the appointed time, close to seven hundred students and supporters came out to hear him. Dozens of people pressed up against the windows of the Harkness Common, located at the north end of the campus quadrangle known as Holmes Field. Others stood on the concrete benches in front of the building. Bell stood confidently in front of the building, at a podium where microphones from Boston's five local television stations were set up. Students sensed that this was a culmination, and that someone whom they loved was taking a courageous stand.

He addressed the crowd for twenty-five minutes. In his steady though gentle voice, he explained why he felt he had to leave Harvard in protest: "Despite the good progress the Harvard Law School has made in hiring and promoting black men, I agree with our students who are telling us that without women of color in permanent positions, the faculty is as seriously unrepresentative now as it was before I became its first black member in 1969. . . . It is very sad but no less clear that black women must assume much of the future leadership burden in the racial struggle. It is thus imperative that we provide models and mentors."

At the end of the speech, Bell and the student leaders linked their arms and raised them in the air, symbolizing their resolve. *USA Today* captured the moment of what was one of the most dramatic events at Harvard Law School in several years. Students were the catalyst that led to his announcement, and Bell, with his call to "stand up and take risks," was the spark that would lead them to take further action and continue his crusade.

The decision was a difficult one for Bell, because at the time he was going through a personal struggle as well as a professional one. His wife, Jewel, was dying of cancer. She disagreed that Bell could not be a role model to black women students, and opposed his taking a leave of absence. In his true fashion, he did it anyway. But she also encouraged him to keep on teaching, and he followed that advice.

Jewel Hairston Bell died in August 1990. That fall, Bell remained on the Harvard Law School campus, although he was on leave from its faculty. He was allowed to keep his office and his secretary. Each Monday night, in a small basement class-room in Griswold Hall, about twenty-two students attended his seminar, "Civil Rights at the Crossroads," for no credit. "Her wanting me to continue teaching has really helped sustain me," he said.

In the 1990–91 school year, Harvard had twelve visiting professors on campus. Seven were women, and one of them, Anita Allen, was black. She had a "Harvard" resume: Harvard Law, a Ph.D. in Philosophy from Michigan, and tenure at Georgetown. She was petite and looked far younger than her thirty-eight years. To convey a more professional image, she wore her hair in a bun. She had many things in her favor. She was a civil libertarian, had a good teaching and publication record, and was nice. She was perceived as less radical than Austin.

But the appointments committee said that although her work in jurisprudence and privacy law, including a book, was good, her classroom skills were lacking. One-third of the students evaluating her first-year torts class complained that she focused too heavily on jurisprudence, philosophy, and economics, and talked too much. Also as a student, she had not won a position on the *Harvard Law Review*. Again the committee invoked the "year away" rule to delay a vote on her until she returned to her home school. The faculty was willing to consider her a candidate, though at a later date. It was a blow to Allen. "I had been an 'A' student since the third grade. Teaching evaluations have never been weighed that heavily. That has been blown out of proportion. Not being on law review was held against me," she said later.

To Bell, the fact that the school had passed over a second obviously strong black woman candidate was evidence of systematic exclusion, another attempt by whites to fix the rules to preserve their power. Angrier and more frustrated with Harvard, he accepted a visiting professorship at New York University for the second academic year of his leave, 1991–92. Ironically, his wife had wanted to move to New York before she became ill. She had never liked Harvard. "She hated the way they treated me, thought they were elitist," he said.

Now the second year was coming to an end. It looked

unlikely that Clark would consent to let Bell extend his leave.
Although Bell had staked out an extreme position, some compromise could have been reached. All he really wanted was a
commitment that over the next three to five years Harvard
would add women of color and other minorities to the tenured
faculty. But Harvard Law was not about concessions. Neither
the faculty nor the administration was willing to do anything
that would look as if they were caving in to his demands. As at
Oregon, Bell had also tarred some well-meaning colleagues as
racists, losing their support in the process.

It is understandable why Clark and other university leaders
wanted to go slow with Bell and not be pressured by a troublemaker as he often proved to be. But Bell's cause and recommended tenure candidates deserved to be taken seriously.
Egos again seemed to prevent progress.

But Bell had the benefit of something Clark and other opponents didn't: a galvanized student movement. Indeed, how
his struggle with Harvard Law School would be resolved rested
more on the efforts of a small student left than on his own pleas.
That same day in March 1992 when he returned to Cambridge
to discuss his request for an extension, his student advocates
were in court defending the discrimination suit they had filed
in 1990 against Harvard. Later in May, a month before graduation, they would have to defend their actions before a different
body, a disciplinary board, while another group of students,
who patently deserved to be punished, received unconditional
support. For now, the students' suit rested in the hands of the
highest judges in the state of Massachusetts. The court could
force the school to adopt a more vigorous affirmative-action
plan or affirm a lower court's order dismissing it. A lot de-
pended on the advocacy skills taught at Harvard Law.

CHAPTER 5

IF THE SUIT FITS, WEAR IT

Dozens of Harvard Law students and their friends and relatives began arriving at the thirteen-story courthouse in downtown Boston at 7:00 A.M. on Tuesday, March 3. Although the proceeding wasn't scheduled to begin until nine o'clock, they wanted to make sure they could get a seat in the first student-led discrimination suit against Harvard University ever to reach the highest court in the state. It was something of a feat to persuade Harvard Law students to leave the campus and cross the river en masse.

Predicting a large turnout, the judges selected to use the ceremonial courtroom for the 9:00 A.M. hearing. It is a stately room on the building's top floor evoking the art deco style of a courthouse erected in 1937. Royal blue carpeting adorned the floors, Philippine mahogany paneling covered the walls, and dark blue drapes hung alongside eleven-foot-high windows that overlooked the Charles River. The crowd of spectators and media quickly filled the elegant courtroom to capacity and spilled out into the hallway and a nearby attorney's lounge. In the frenzy, court employees scurried to set up loudspeakers to broadcast the hearing to those in the outer areas.

Caroline Wittcoff and Laura Hankins, two third-year law students, would be arguing for a coalition of six minority student organizations, the Women's Law Association, and eleven individual students who had sued Harvard for discrimination. It was entirely a student effort, in part because the students feared faculty members would hog the limelight and in part because no professor was willing to do more than offer occasional and informal advice. The students were appealing a lower court's decision to dismiss their case on the grounds that they were not the appropriate group to challenge the Law School's hiring policies in a lawsuit; they lacked standing to sue. On appeal, they were seeking the right to proceed to trial and to have discovery. They believed school records would show that the hiring process was secretive and discriminatory. When the suit was filed, in November 1990, Harvard Law School had sixty-two tenured professors. Of those, five were women and three were black males. There was no tenured African-American woman and no Latino, Asian, Native American, openly gay or lesbian, or physically disabled person on the tenured faculty. After 173 years, Harvard Law was still 92 percent male and 95 percent white.

This was the first case in which law students had sued their school for discrimination in faculty hiring. If they won this appeal, the case would be sent back to the Massachusetts Superior Court to address the hiring-discrimination charges. The Supreme Judicial Court had granted the students direct appellate review on January 22, allowing them to bypass the Massachusetts Court of Appeals.

Wittcoff and Hankins were seated at the counsel's table on the left side of the room, facing the judges. They would be on the judge's right as he looked down at them. Allan Ryan, Jr., a senior litigator in Harvard's legal department, and Daniel Steiner, Harvard's general counsel, were at the table on the right side of the room, the judge's left. In the row of seats behind the counsel's table were several lawyers from Widett, Slater & Goldman, a small Boston firm helping the students *pro bono*, counsel to three student groups from Columbia University and sixteen national civil rights organizations, including the Boston chapter of the Lawyers Committee for Civil Rights Under Law, the Center for Constitutional Rights, the Mexican-

American Legal Defense and Education Fund, the National Rainbow Coalition, and the LAMBDA Legal Defense and Education Fund. All the groups had signed on as *amici curiae*. The civil rights groups and several student groups at other schools were interested in this as a test case for other possible suits. Several lawyers from these various groups were also sitting "in front of the bar" in the attorneys' section. Behind them sat everyone else.

The panel of five white, middle-aged male judges entered the chambers shortly after 9:00 A.M., silencing the commotion in the room. There was a woman judge on the Supreme Judicial Court, but she was not on this case. The sight of these five white men seemed imposing to some people, a subtle reminder of the racial and ethnic underrepresentation these Harvard law students were complaining about. Chief Justice Paul Liacos, a gruff Bostonian and former adjunct professor at Boston University School of Law, was presiding over the hearing that morning. Liacos, who had commissioned gender, race, and ethnic bias studies for the courts, was at least aware of the impact of discrimination on the court system. Students hoped that would be a sign that he was receptive to their arguments about discrimination in legal education. The other four judges on the panel were Herbert Wilkins, Joseph Nolan, Neil Lynch, and Francis O'Connor.

Justice Liacos wasted little time with formalities and introductory remarks, offering only a sharp notice that he would tightly hold the Harvard students to their fifteen-minute time limit, or seven and a half minutes each, and Ryan to his allotted fifteen minutes. During each side's arguments, he did most of the questioning.

Caroline Wittcoff, who is white, rose to the podium. It was the first time she'd ever appeared in a courtroom. Except for a few administrative hearings she'd handled in one of her clinical courses, she had never faced a full-blown judicial panel before. She had practiced heavily in moot court sessions with supportive law professors and lawyer friends, and she knew the case law inside and out. Still, her task was difficult. She needed to show why a coalition of her Harvard Law School classmates, who were not employees of Harvard, as state law required, should be allowed to sue Harvard University.

Wittcoff was representing a student group known as the Harvard Law School Coalition for Civil Rights. Formed in the Winter of 1989 to promote a racially and culturally diverse faculty, it was a true coalition that brought together six student minority organizations and the Harvard Chapter of the National Lawyers Guild. They represented African-American, Asian-American, Native American, Latino, gay, lesbian and bisexual, and physically disabled students at Harvard Law. Together, via their 1990 suit and a series of sit-ins, protests, and rallies, culminating with Derrick Bell's protest leave, they had launched a student "diversity" movement. For three consecutive years they had kept the pressure on the faculty to hire women and minorities, and had kept public attention riveted on Harvard Law School. As the coalition had grown, so had the movement.

A certain amount of campus dissension is part of the tradition at Harvard Law. Despite the school's heavy corporate orientation, there has always been a strong countereffort by students, and the Coalition for Civil Rights was not unlike the student anti-apartheid group that pushed for Harvard to divest its holdings in South Africa, or the Third World Coalition, which led the charge for the appointment of Derrick Bell, or the Women's Law Association, which in 1972 unsuccessfully filed a complaint with the office of Civil Rights in the Department of Health, Education and Welfare.

In the 1972 complaint, which was phrased similarly to the wording of the current suit, women students charged that faculty hiring was being "done on the basis of an old boy network," and that the law school's practice of hiring predominantly Harvard Law School graduates excluded many qualified women. That complaint prompted the appointments committee to hire several women professors, including the first tenured woman, Elizabeth Owens.

But never had students filed a civil action against the university regarding the law school's hiring practices, and never had a group at Harvard been so organized, sophisticated, and highly mobilized. The coalition itself provided a lesson in political grassroots organizing and movement-building. The beauty of the suit was that it unified people whose backgrounds and interests were widely diverse. It connected the disability rights movement, the gay rights movement, the African-American movement, the women's movement, and the Latino movement.

As with Bell and his protestations, Harvard tried to dismiss the students' complaint as incidental, and the judicial system seemed to patronize them. Nevertheless, these students raised people's consciousness. They provoked the law school administration into establishing public-interest scholarships and minority teaching fellowships. And they further exposed the moral leadership deficiency at Harvard Law.

Caroline Wittcoff, Laura Hankins, John Bonifaz, Keith Boykin, and William Anspach, among others, were key movers behind the coalition and had helped draft the complaint filed in 1990. When the suit reached the state supreme court, in 1991, they were the group's leaders. When they had arrived on campus to begin their first year, they had seen the need to mobilize. Earlier in the summer of 1989, Robert Clark, in one of his first acts as dean, had eliminated career counselor Ronald Fox as the head of the Office of Public Interest Advising. In response to Clark's decision to ax Fox, more than eight hundred students signed letters protesting the action. They held demonstrations and established the Emergency Coalition for Public Interest Placement. Clark was forced to backpedal and reaffirm Harvard's commitment to *pro bono* and public-interest work. He appointed a faculty-student committee, chaired by Chris Edley, one of the school's three tenured black professors, to advise students seeking public-interest jobs. He reinstituted the post of Faculty Director of Public Interest Programs, and established a postgraduate fellowship for students working in public-interest jobs. For a long time afterwards, many students would recall a telling photograph of Clark that had appeared in the *Boston Globe,* showing him with his hands clamped over his ears, shutting out student demonstrators in the background.

That same fall, on September 1, at the start of classes, Clark had welcomed their class of 1L's with the message that "helping the wheels of commerce turn and helping business produce the goods and services needed by society" was part of the essential work of lawyers. "Do not let anyone convince you that you are 'selling out' in whatever career you choose," he advised them, adding, of course, that they must remember to think about "the ethical implications of the lawyer's role" and watch for the "ethical dilemmas and pitfalls" that "lie all along the road and in every corner of the profession." The thrust of his address was that corporate law was implicitly ethical.

But from the day he delivered his welcoming remarks and in his willingness to ax the public-interest adviser, these students in the first-year class, who sincerely hoped to find public interest jobs, had an adversary in Clark. His latest pronouncement merely bore out what they and 2L and 3L students and other faculty members, including Derrick Bell and Gerald Frug, feared would happen with Harvard in the hands of a conservative: that Harvard Law school would advocate nothing less than meritocratic heresy by seeking to pack its graduates into corporate boardrooms and fancy law offices in order to prop up the status quo.

Third-year and second-year students organized most of those fall protests. But in the spring of 1990, when the faculty declined to consider visiting professor Regina Austin for tenure, other 1L's joined the effort to fight the Law School administration. Two first-year students, John Bonifaz and Keith Boykin, quickly proved their mettle as masters of the press conference, the photo opportunity, and the news release.

By the time he arrived at Harvard Law School, twenty-three-year-old Bonifaz was a veteran activist. Thin, dark-haired, and fair-skinned, his boyish preppie looks belied the fact that promoting liberal causes virtually ran in his blood. His father, Cristobal Bonifaz, was an Ecuadorian immigrant who had come to the United States at the age of sixteen. A senior research associate at Du Pont during most of John's youth, he had later become a lawyer and moved with his family to western Massachusetts, where he set up a practice in Amherst.

While they lived in affluent Chadds Ford, Pennsylvania, his father became known for organizing farm workers, mostly mushroom pickers in the southeastern part of the state, and for founding the first Latino community center in that region. His mother, Deirdre, established and, for fifteen years, directed a nonprofit cooperative for low-income artists from around the country. Many of the unsung heroines and heroes of the civil rights movement came through his house to discuss grants and projects. "I would definitely attribute much of my education to them," he says.

In high school, at the Wilmington Friends School in Delaware, Bonifaz founded a peace group and led a student lobbying effort on Capitol Hill for disarmament. He graduated after three years and attended college at Brown University. In October 1983, a month after beginning his freshman year at Brown, he was organizing. The United States had just invaded Grenada, and he led about fifty students in a march on the federal building in Providence to protest the government's intervention. From there he went on to co-found the Brown voter registration project, signing up one hundred students for the 1984 presidential elections. He was a campus spokesman for Jesse Jackson's campaign. He also co-founded a campus anti-apartheid group and had the distinction of demonstrating with former President Jimmy Carter's daughter, Amy, a coed. In his senior year, he was brought before an administrative panel for "bearing witness" at a meeting of the university's trustees, and for a while he didn't know whether he would be suspended or allowed to graduate.

After receiving his degree, he worked for Washington mayor Marion Barry, Jr., and for Senator Edward Kennedy's reelection campaign. In 1988 he volunteered for Jackson's presidential election exploratory committee. Then he decided to go to law school. He was accepted at numerous schools, including Yale and New York University. Yale was too small for him, he thought. He was choosing between Harvard and NYU, weighing the level of activism at each school, and people's concerns about social issues. With the allure of CLS and the doors the school would open, he chose Harvard. It was students like Bonifaz who could restore the true glory of Harvard Law, which had been diminished by the venom, hatred, and blood-letting over faculty appointments. He was truly committed to pursuing a career in public-interest law. In the summer of 1991, he worked for Florida Rural Legal Services in Lake Worth, providing legal assistance to migrant farm workers. The summer before that, he had worked in New Mexico, offering legal help to people living on the Navajo Reservation.

If John Bonifaz was seasoned in rounding up students to demonstrate, Keith Boykin was a pro at drawing media attention. Taller and thinner than Bonifaz, Boykin was a former editor of the school paper at Dartmouth. He was a voice of reason as conservative students attacked students who had built a shanty on campus to protest apartheid in South Africa. After college, he worked as a schoolteacher and then joined the Michael Dukakis presidential campaign, which incidentally was being run by Harvard Law professors Chris Edley and Susan Estrich. He handled advance work and media. As a result, he had numerous press contacts, at the *The New York Times* and CBS News, among other places. Like their professors, these students knew how to manipulate public opinion.

That is exactly what they did in the spring of 1990, when Harvard passed over Regina Austin. First they organized an all-night sit-in at Clark's office, the first occupation of the dean's office in years. Then they helped Bell time and draft his statement demanding unpaid leave. The day before his announcement, they gave *The New York Times* advance notice of the story. They set up the press conference in front of Harkness Common and decided how television coverage would be pooled. Later that spring, they submitted a list of demands and met with negotiator Roger Fisher. They and others left a coalition meeting at the end of that school year with a mandate to sue. The idea had come from Linda Singer, a second-year student active in the coalition.

A suit was another way of keeping the pressure on the faculty and keeping Harvard Law School in the public eye. The media could easily follow a lawsuit story. The students in the coalition agreed to sue in state court because in federal court the law was more narrow and there were too many Reagan-appointed judges. They also decided to sue *pro se,* on their own, without

Bell as a plaintiff, or a leading lawyer or law professor as their attorney. "Frankly, we were afraid they might steal the show," said Boykin, who helped draft the complaint. And they decided not to ask for any monetary damages; they didn't want people to think they were just greedy Harvard law students.

On November 20, 1990, during the first year of Bell's leave, the coalition filed suit against the president and fellows of Harvard College, the governing body of Harvard University. It was a wintry New England morning, but the students held a press conference on the steps of the Middlesex County Superior Court in Cambridge. Reporters from the *Boston Globe* and the *Boston Herald,* as well as film crews from the city's five television stations, came to cover the event. "Today we use the only instrument of power Harvard Law School understands. Today we take Harvard to court," Bonifaz told the reporters. By notifying the media in advance, the students caught Harvard by surprise. When asked by the press for a comment, all Clark could say was that "we haven't seen the lawsuit," at least until he received a copy of the complaint a few hours later.

In their action, the Harvard students alleged that through a pattern of discriminatory hiring practices, Harvard Law School excluded a disproportionate percentage of qualified women and minorities for tenure and tenure-track faculty positions, in violation of Massachusetts state law. Those discriminatory practices, they claimed, denied students the benefits of integrated association and full and equal educational opportunity, fostered insensitivity and intolerance, perpetuated badges of inferiority, and reduced the business and professional opportunities that would flow from having an integrated faculty and role models. They also attacked the subjectivity of the hiring criteria, the secretiveness of the appointment process, and the lack of student input.

On December 21 the coalition filed notices with the court indicating that it wanted to depose former Harvard University president Derek Bok as well as professors Frank Michelman, Jerry Frug, and Martha Minow, and associate dean Louis Kaplow. The students hoped to gather information and to force these faculty members and administrators to answer questions

about the law school's hiring practices under oath. And they
wanted Bok to testify in the large Ames Moot Court Room in
front of the entire student body.

Harvard would have none of it. Immediately after the suit
was filed, the school moved to dismiss, arguing that the plaintiffs had no standing to sue under Massachusetts law. Even if
their allegations were true, Harvard's hiring practices had not
had a "disparate impact" as a matter of law on women and
minorities. Thus, the plaintiffs had failed to state a claim. The
university was going to play hardball to win this case if it had
to. One week before the students were to break for Christmas
vacation, the university filed motions to quash the notices of
deposition.

A hearing on the motions to quash was set for Monday, December 24, Christmas Eve. The students, in a letter, told Harvard's lawyer Allan Ryan that no one would be in Cambridge
then to fight it because of their vacation, and they asked if the
date could be moved. Ryan refused. Ryan replied that he was
planning to go to court that Monday, whether they were there
or not. If he had to work during the holiday season, why
shouldn't they? The students then drafted a letter to the court
objecting to Ryan's unwillingness to wait a week until they
returned. They told the court they thought it was out of line
for Ryan to try to quash those depositions on Christmas Eve.
A delay of one week, they said, would not harm the process to
which they had a right.

At 8:30 A.M. on the day of the hearing, Linda Singer faxed
the letter to the court clerk from Florida. Later that afternoon,
when Ryan arrived at the Middlesex County court at the Leach-
mere station stop in Cambridge, the court had already been
notified by the students' fax. The judge gave the students their
first courtroom win, postponing the hearing until January 2.
"We felt we had a significant victory when the clerk told us
that Ryan appeared and was denied," said Bonifaz. "He didn't
anticipate our fax."

Their glee was short-lived, however; their requests for depositions were quashed. They were denied the ability to unearth
evidence of any discriminatory hiring decisions until the court

ruled on Harvard's motion to dismiss. At 2:10 P.M. on Feb. 11, 1991, before a packed courtroom in the Middlesex County Superior Court, Ryan defended the school's motion to dismiss, telling Judge Patrick Brady that the statutes under which the students were suing did not apply to them because they were not past, present, or prospective employees who had been discriminated against. Even if they were, they hadn't suffered any harm directly as a result of discrimination. The state legislature had not intended to protect students when it wrote the laws. If the court denied the motion and allowed the case to proceed to the discovery stage, students would have the right to open people's records who weren't even in the case. "There is, I think, going to be a very deep intrusion into the records of people who are not before this court and who have not brought themselves before this court," he warned the judge.

Linda Singer and Pat Gulbis, third-year and second-year woman students respectively, rebutted Ryan. Singer had helped to conceive the lawsuit and knew the laws involved intricately. She quickly tried to disabuse the court of the idea that students couldn't sue because they were not in an employer-employee relationship with Harvard. "Courts have recognized repeatedly that when you discriminate in any aspect of education, you discriminate against the students that are being educated. And whether that's in a provision of facilities, whether it's in the composition of the student body, or whether it's in the composition of the faculty, that is discrimination in education and this is discrimination against students."

Gulbis argued that the students had a valid claim on which relief could be granted. "Harvard has not met its burden on its motion to dismiss, to show that there are no facts, as a matter of law, under which we could prevail, under which a court could find an inference of disparate impact. And so we ask that their motion to dismiss be denied."

But the trial court agreed with Harvard, and dismissed the suit on the ground that the students lacked standing. Such an action could only be brought by past, present, or future employees of Harvard Law School, not by students. Additionally, the harms alleged by the students were simply too indirect to give them standing to sue. Their argument that they had rights protected under law as intended beneficiaries of existing contracts with Harvard "seems to be quite a stretch," Judge Brady wrote.

That is not to say the students hadn't impressed the trial judge, or raised a close question. Technically, the students' claims on the merits were still open. In his ruling, Judge Brady went out of his way to applaud the students' efforts. "Whatever shortcomings Harvard Law School may have, if any, in failing up to now to provide a faculty sufficiently diverse to satisfy all students' needs, it does not appear to be failing in its obligation to produce first-rate lawyers. The written and oral advocacy of the students in this case has been commendable," wrote Brady, HLS '70, in his ruling dismissing the coalition's claim. "Having read approximately 109 footnotes in the several briefs filed by the parties and the *amici,* I feel entitled to submit just one," he wrote.

Brady's ruling came on February 22, 1991, just as the faculty voted to pass up a chance to appoint two visiting minority scholars, Anita Allen, an African-American, and Gerald Lopez, a Hispanic. Having their case dismissed deflated the members of the coalition, but these appointment decisions reinvigorated them. As they had done the year before, they organized another series of rallies, forums, and a blockade of the dean's office. They ended the blockade after four squad cars of Cambridge police arrived and officers threatened to arrest them.

Something else happened to renew their faith in their suit. Harvard's general counsel Daniel Steiner called a meeting in his office in Massachusetts Hall, located in the heart of Harvard Yard. Eight members of the lawsuit committee filed into a plush boardroom on the second floor. "We've asked you to come here because we want to see if something can be worked out. This phase of the litigation has ended," Steiner told the students. Apparently thinking that professors or outside lawyers must have been helping the students, which they weren't, Steiner added, "I don't know what your lawyers are telling you, but you clearly don't have a case on the merits, though you might win on the standing question."

That statement had the effect of solidifying the students' interest in pursuing the litigation. Standing meant that they could put the case into discovery and put people under oath. "It was enough to hear from Harvard that we had standing. It was an affirmation. However remote, they admitted there was this possibility," said John Bonifaz.

Ryan told Bonifaz and the other students at that meeting that he didn't know of any professors at the law school who were supporting them.

"Of course not," one of the students said. "We're suing them."

The meeting ended with the students telling Harvard's attorneys that they would not meet with the dean unless he presented specific proposals in writing to address the students' concerns about the hiring process to which they could respond. They made no agreement that they would stop the lawsuit; if further negotiations were successful, then they would withdraw it. They received no further word from Harvard until August 1991, when Steiner wrote the coalition a letter stating that Dean Clark would not be presenting any proposals and that there would be no meeting.

In the meantime, the students went ahead with the planning for an appeal. On January 22, 1992, the Supreme Judicial Court, with no explanation, granted their motion for direct appellate review. "[Harvard] misread our conviction and our commitment to this issue and what the student movement was about," said Bonifaz.

To the eager audience jammed into the state of Massachusetts' ceremonial courtroom for appellate argument that Tuesday morning, student advocate Wittcoff explained what the case was about: another fight in the continuing struggle for civil rights. "In *Brown v. Board of Education,* the United States Supreme Court recognized the invidiousness of discrimination in education and the serious and legally cognizable harm that students suffer as a result of discrimination in their schools. This case is the *Brown v. Board of Education* of the 1990s," she declared. "In Topeka, Kansas, in 1954, it mattered that a school stamped women and minority students with a badge of inferiority and denied them the benefit of an integrated association."

She was about to go on, when Chief Justice Liacos cut in to ask whether it made a difference in regard to the students' standing that in *Brown* the students were required to attend a school by law, as it was a public school, and in her case and the students' case, they were not. "I mean I could say that if you're dissatisfied with Harvard, you could voluntarily go to a *good* law school," he said, intending to add some levity with a deprecating reference to Harvard's preeminence. By the same token, his question raised the prospect that perhaps Harvard was no longer a "good" school. Still, it was a valid point, one that many observers had been asking. These students didn't have to attend Harvard Law School.

Wittcoff responded that it wasn't important whether a school was public or private. "What matters to student standing under [the law] is that students suffer direct and substantial harm as a result of discriminatory conduct. And those harms—"

"The suffering of harm in your mind, then, automatically gives you standing?" Justice Liacos pressed.

"There are two questions," she replied, without a trace of nervousness. "First is, Do students suffer direct and substantial harm? And the second question is, Are students within the area of concern of the [Massachusetts] statute?" The answer, she added, was that "the harms students suffered were direct and substantial, and they were the same harms that were suffered by students in *Brown v. Board of Education*."

As she explained, "When students at Harvard Law School sit in the classroom every day for three years and are never once taught by a single woman of color, or Latino, or Asian-American, or Native American, or openly gay or lesbian person, the discrimination that is the reason behind this long history of exclusion sends students a devastating message: that while we are good enough to sit in the classrooms at Harvard Law, we're not good enough to sit on the faculty, and that's a stamping of a badge of inferiority. It's the same stamping of a badge of inferiority recognized as early as *Brown v. Board of*

Education. The other type of harm [that] Harvard's discrimination inflicts on students is a denial of the benefits of association with an integrated faculty."

She cited several cases to support these arguments, ones used in previous briefs: a 1950 case involving a law school, in which the United States Supreme Court recognized that students could not learn law in a vacuum, isolated from the variety of life experiences, perspectives, and viewpoints that they would encounter as practicing lawyers; a case of neighbors who were denied the benefits of living in an integrated neighborhood; and a case involving co-workers who were denied the benefits of working in an integrated work environment.

Again the chief judge was unconvinced. "What is in this record that shows a direct harm to people in your position?" he asked.

What was in the record, Wittcoff responded, were affidavits of students claiming they were sent messages of stigmatization and denied the benefits of integration. Indeed, seven students from various underrepresented minority groups submitted affidavits detailing times when they heard sexist remarks in class or experienced insensitivity to minorities. In one affidavit, a woman student named Jennifer Green described how she was cavalierly dismissed by a professor when she tried to complain that a case he had assigned the class to read was sexist. Green also noted that an informal classroom survey she'd done showed that men were twice as likely as women to participate in class discussions. The women who did speak in class were derided by male students as "aggressive" or "bitchy." Those examples indicated "the problem of a sexist environment" said Green, who had only two women teachers in her three years at Harvard.

Similarly, Lisa Hodges, an African-American woman student, submitted an affidavit that she had been subjected to hurtful comments in class. She'd heard her classmates say that perspectives on the laws of slavery compared to perspectives on laws concerning cruelty to animals, that sometimes a woman asked to be raped, and that blacks have it easy because of affirmative action. A male professor in her first year explained the uncertainty of offer and acceptance in contract law by quoting a rape scene in a play. Another male professor failed to mention that the defendants in an important criminal case were black and that this fact may have influenced the outcome of the case. "While straight white males have their presence validated by people like themselves, I have no such support," Hodges submitted in her affidavit.

Harms like those were recognized and supported by law, Wittcoff told the panel. Indeed, the Massachusetts high court itself had recognized that environmental harms, such as feelings of degradation, stigmatization, and humiliation, were legally cognizable harms under the same statute on which the students were suing. Thus, as she went on to explain, even though students weren't employees or prospective employees of Harvard Law School, they fell within the area of concern of the statute because of their direct relationship and interaction with their teachers. Students had a much closer connection to the faculty than newspaper subscribers had to a newspaper or department-store customers had to the store, as Harvard had argued in its brief.

Additionally, the statute under which the Harvard students was suing was deliberately ambiguous, said Wittcoff. The legislature could have stated that "any employee or potential employee" had standing to sue. Instead, it stated that "any person claiming to be aggrieved by discrimination in an employment relationship" could bring suit. "If there were no students at Harvard Law School, it would be a research institute. And if there were no teachers, it would be a library. What makes it a law school is the interaction between the students and the professors." And with that she concluded.

Her classmate Laura Hankins, who is black and was also arguing her first case, picked up from there to argue that the eleven student plaintiffs in the suit had a right to challenge the law school's hiring practices because of the Massachusetts Equal Rights Act's promise of equal education opportunities. She had barely begun explaining how the students had a right to challenge the law school's hiring practices under the act when Justice Herbert Wilkins asked her about merit, raising the persistent idea that if women and minorities were hired, standards were somehow lowered.

"To what extent in your analysis of this is the quality of the particular professor or a potential professor encroached," Wilkins asked, "if in any degree the merits of the particular person to be hired are to be considered under your assessment of the situation?"

"Yes, Your Honor," answered Hankins, "the merits are certainly important in hiring. It is merely our claim that Harvard can't base its hiring decisions on something other than merit, on race or gender or sexual orientation."

The issue came back to the students' injury, Hankins said. "Harvard dismisses our injuries as aesthetic or perhaps even nonexistent. There are other injuries in history, which, when they were first voiced, were dismissed as nonexistent or intangible and therefore aesthetic.

"When Rosa Parks said she wanted to ride in the front of the bus, everybody wanted to know what she was complaining about. She got to ride the bus. She got to where she wanted to go. It is now clear that there was a stigmatization that occurred from not allowing blacks to move from the back of the bus to the front. Today, we say that we are allowed to sit in the back of the classroom, but we receive the message that we will never stand up front. It is the move from back to front that women and minority students are being denied."

It was a moving point. But again the judges wanted to know what was in the record to show that Harvard pursued a discriminatory policy in appointing and promoting faculty members. "Well, the complaint is allegations. Is there anything more than that?" Justice Liacos snapped.

Hankins wasn't intimidated. She said their complaint included statistics that showed a difference between the number of women and minorities at Harvard and the number at other schools nationwide. She was armed with figures. When the suit was filed, the tenured faculty had grown to sixty-two, but there were only five women (8.06 percent) and three African-American (4.84 percent) members. Harvard Law School was still 92 percent male and 95 percent white. At the same time, the number of women and minority students had grown substantially. Of the school's 1,620 students in 1990, 45 percent were women and 22 percent were minorities. As for the sixty-six "full-time" women and minorities on the faculty in 1990, which included tenure-track assistant professors, there were only five women (7.58 percent) and five African-American males (7.58 percent). In a 1991 survey of 175 law schools, the American Bar Association found that minorities represented 9.5 percent of all "full-time" professors, and that women represented 25 percent of the total. With a percentage of 7.58 "full-time" women, Harvard was woefully below the norm. And Harvard had no Latino or Latina, Asian-American, Native American, openly gay or lesbian or bisexual, physically disabled person, or woman of color.

"I understand that, but is there anything more than statistical evidence in this record? Do you have someone, for example, from the faculty committee that says, 'Look, every time a woman came up or a person of color came up, they were vetoed on that ground'? Or anything that comes even close to that?" Justice Liacos insisted.

"At this point, Your Honor, no, we don't," demurred Hankins.

But Justice Wilkins came to her aid. "It's your position, I take it, that procedurally you haven't gotten to the point where you have to make that demonstration?"

"That's right, Your Honor. We attempted to start discovery in the Superior Court and we were denied that opportunity. This is a disparate-impact case, in which we would need to show the significance of disparities in statistics between Harvard faculty and pools around the country."

"So your answer is that you ought to be able to proceed to try to demonstrate this?" interrupted Chief Justice Liacos.

"Yes," said Hankins.

Then Justice Joseph Nolan wanted to know if it made a difference whether the discrimination in this case was *de facto* or *de jure*, referring respectively to discrimination existing in fact or decreed in law, two legal principles established in *Brown*.

"We're not, at this point, charging that Harvard intentionally discriminates," replied Hankins. "We have been denied discovery, and so we don't at this point have access to any document that says whether Harvard intentionally discriminates. At this point, this is a disparate-impact case which says that Harvard's hiring practices have a disparate impact on the hiring of women and minorities, and that gets proved at trial looking at the statistics and whether the disparities between the statistics are significant, and that's a trial matter."

Justice Nolan was also interested in the students' contract claims under state law. He wanted to know what the students relied on to show there was a contract. "It is just the fact that you apply, you're admitted, and therefore you have certain contractual rights?" he asked.

"Well, there are cases that say our relationship as students at Harvard is a contractual relationship," Hankins answered.

Richard Kahlenberg, a former student, titled the memoir of his days at Harvard *Broken Contract*. Critical of the way hundreds of students arrived each year "to be Atticus Finch and leave as ["L.A. Law"'s] Arnie Becker," Kahlenberg wrote, "you could blame the institution, the Harvard Law School, for breaking its implicit contract, proclaimed on the walls of its buildings, that law is about justice, and then fostering an atmosphere where it is hard not to be a hypocrite." This was the same sentiment reflected in the students' complaint. Kahlenberg was a 3L when most of the plaintiffs were 1L's.

But Chief Justice Liacos wanted hard, not "implicit," evidence of a contract. "Was there anything in Harvard's policy statements or written materials that might indicate there was an expectancy that a student had a legitimate right to have a diverse faculty?" he wanted to know. After all, "You're coming from a law school that discriminated against women until 1951. Right? You couldn't be here in those days."

"Nineteen-fifty," Justice Wilkins, a graduate of Harvard College and Harvard Law School, class of 1954, chimed in. The other judges chortled.

"Well, I was there, whether it was 1950 or 1951," said Liacos, HLS '52; LL.M. '53. "You couldn't even be here [in this courtroom] in those days," he said to Hankins.

That exchange about the knowledge of Harvard history and the justices' association with the school indicated the power and reach of Harvard Law School. Naturally, the school would loom large in a courtroom, especially in one located in Boston. But that Justice Liacos felt compelled to show off his affiliation with the school made the students realize that the judges might be unwilling to allow a challenge to their cherished alma mater.

"Yes, Your Honor," she said sheepishly.

Recognizing that his statements about Harvard's earlier discrimination against women might have indicated that the students had a legitimate claim, Liacos quickly interjected, "I'm not saying that is the essence of the problem here." He said he just wanted to know what was in the policy statements that gave the students an expectancy on which to base a contract claim.

"Harvard, in much of its literature—in its catalogs, in the application, in their affirmative-action plan, which we attached to our first amended complaint—says, Harvard does not discriminate on the basis of race, gender, sexual orientation, creed, religion, and national origin."

"As to students?" Liacos asked.

"It says 'Harvard does not discriminate,' which we could argue at trial means—" Hankins said.

"Faculty as well," he said, finishing her sentence.

"Faculty as well," she reiterated, clarifying that whether the promises were contractually binding and part of a student's contract at Harvard would be a trial matter.

In closing, she gave some concrete examples of "what it means when we say students are harmed when Harvard discriminates in its hiring practices." It means, she said, "that in property class, when slavery is taught, only blacks are called on. It means that an environment is fostered which is intolerant of differences in race, gender, and sexual orientation."

She then gave a moving account of her own experience in a class she'd taken the year before with Professor Charles Ogletree, one of the three tenured black males at Harvard Law School. She told the judges how Ogletree often had guest speakers. One day he invited three black women lawyers he had worked with at the Public Defender Service in Washington, D.C., to address the students. "That class was the most moving class of my years at Harvard. One and a half hours later, when the class ended, those three black women walked out. I knew that, given Harvard's hiring record and its practices, I would likely never see any of those women teaching a class at the law school. One of those black women now teaches at Stanford Law School. Harvard dismisses our injuries as aesthetic. But the loss of those black women that day and their continuing absence due to Harvard's discrimination is a harm that I continue to suffer."

Then came Harvard's turn, and its lawyer Allan Ryan took his place at the podium in front of the judges. Before Ryan was given the go-ahead to begin, Chief Justice Liacos, obviously moved by the students' arguments, told him he had a tough act to follow. "Now I know I shouldn't say it, but these two young *pro se* advocates are going to put you to the test to see if you can keep up to their standards."

Ryan, smooth and experienced, would have no problem keeping up. His deference to the judges and his forceful presentation indicated that he had addressed countless judges and appeared before numerous magistrates. A member of Harvard's legal department since 1985, Ryan had previously worked as an assistant to the United States Solicitor General, and had been director of the Justice Department's Office of Special Investigations, in charge of hunting and prosecuting Nazi war criminals. During his career, he had argued eight times at the Supreme Court.

A sign that he was an effective litigator was the way he unnerved his student adversaries. He was the one who had waited until the week before the students were to start their Christmas break to move to quash the subpoenas they had filed.

Then, this morning of the appellate hearing, Ryan asked the coalition's Bonifaz to see if he couldn't get a couple of students to give up their seats so that his two children, aged ten and twelve, could watch the hearing. This was the first case he'd argued at the Massachusetts Supreme Judicial Court that his children were old enough to understand, and he wanted them to see their father at work. "You know," said Bonifaz, "quite frankly, I think it is just as important to these people as it is to your children. No, I'm not going to ask anybody to leave." Ryan then went and got permission from a court employee, who allowed his two children to sit in front of the bar with the attorneys. In the process, he had rattled Bonifaz, who saw the move as a another example of Harvard using its muscle at the expense of students.

"May it please the court. This case is not *Brown v. Board of Education;* Rosa Parks is not in this courtroom," Ryan said tersely, sending a chill through the room. It was a spontaneous comment, though he had spent a lot of time preparing. "I wasn't just winging it," he later said. "But I felt it was necessary to bring the judges back to the point of the case." And he went on to say, "What this case is about is a complaint that Harvard Law School is inordinately partial in hiring its faculty to those people who have compiled excellent records at first-rate law schools, who have served as editors of law reviews, or who have served as appellate clerks."

Ryan, not a Harvard alumnus, but a former clerk to Supreme Court Justice Byron White, added that "the eleven students who have brought this case allege that Harvard Law School is too male, too white, and too heterosexual to provide them with the perspectives, with the role models, and with the life experiences that they think all students should have," he said. "What these students seek in this case is the right to litigate any faculty appointment that in their view perpetuates what they feel is the school's disregard of perspectives that they think are important."

If the students' case went to trial, he said, there was nothing to prevent other groups of students, or other factions of Harvard Law School, from filing additional suits or counterclaims when they felt the school had gone too far in some other direction or was not paying enough attention in its course materials, in its perspectives, to what they felt was important, he told the panel.

But Justice Wilkins stopped him. "Aren't we basically dealing with a statutory principle? Some of these broader principles lie behind all this, but what did the legislature intend by the language it used? Are these people within the class that can bring the suit? That's the heart of this, is it not?"

"That is the heart of this case, Mr. Justice," replied Ryan. "And the answer to that question is absolutely no. The legislature did not intend that or anything remotely like that." Ryan reasserted a point from his briefs and the earlier hearing that there was scant case law holding that a student had the right to go to court to litigate alleged discrimination by a university against the faculty.

He cited a Massachusetts case in which the court denied standing to an independent contractor, and another case that denied standing to a car dealer, even though the case allowed a suit "by any motor vehicle dealer." Therefore, he argued, although the Massachusetts law in question said "any person aggrieved" could bring suit, the legislature intended that clause to be narrowly constructed.

So then, Justice Liacos wanted to know, "who has standing, in your point of view?"

"Standing to raise the grievances that are being raised here could come from any person who stood up and said, 'I was denied or passed over by the Harvard Law School for faculty appointment because of my race or my religion or my sexual orientation,'" Ryan replied. Then he went on to say that the students were trying to refashion their claim on appeal. "There is not an allegation in this complaint that the law school is treating any student differently from any other student because of race or gender or any other proscribed criteria. In fact, the whole emphasis of the complaint is that everybody in the law school suffers, white, black, man, woman, gay, straight. . . .When the Superior Court correctly concluded that their claim did not state a cause of action, these students on this appeal have tried to retool their claim and say, 'Well, wait a minute, women suffer more than others, minorities suffer more than others.' But that is not a claim that the law school is discriminating," he told the panel.

"It sounds to me that on that point the young lawyers are

learning very fast. Lawyers do that all the time, don't they?" asked the chief justice.

"Perhaps it's good training," Ryan said, without losing his pace, "but it's not good law."

"Well, I'd agree with that. But we hear it every day. Go on, Mr. Ryan," replied Liacos.

Moving on to the students' other contention, that Harvard Law School violated the Massachusetts Equal Rights Act, Ryan said that claim was also "quite untenable." The Equal Rights Act was designed to protect all the citizens of the state in the making and enforcing of their contracts, he explained. "These students are not being inhibited in any way, shape, or form in enforcing whatever contracts they might have with the Harvard Law School to pay their tuition, to study, and to receive an education." What they were claiming was something else, he said, explaining that they were saying that because they didn't see black women or Native Americans or Asian-Americans in their classrooms, they were being sent a message that those groups were inferior and therefore not qualified to teach. "That is a matter to be debated in the halls of the academy. It is not a matter that states a violation of the Equal Rights Act of this commonwealth. It's simply not a matter of contract."

Then, as any smart litigator would, he played up a weakness in the students' legal claim, although it was the strength of their effort. Because they had resolved not to disavow any disenfranchised group, they included groups of people with really no statistical disparity to justify a claim. For instance, the pool of people with disabilities, Native Americans, and open gays or lesbians from which Harvard could draw faculty members was minuscule. "It was very important for us to keep those groups within the coalition," said student plaintiff Boykin. "If the courts wanted to sever those claims, they could do so. But we weren't going to do it ourselves."

And since those groups were still in the complaint, Ryan capitalized on the small disparity between the number of professors in the country and the number at Harvard Law. He told the panel that in their own complaint, the students themselves noted that 3 percent of the law professors nationwide were women of color, fewer than 2 percent were Latino, fewer than 1 percent were Asian-American, and only eight, not 8 percent, were Native American. "If Harvard had hired one Asian-American or one woman of color in the last twenty years, then the statistical claim they bring would disappear like a puff of smoke."

Finally, as he had said before, allowing the case to go to trial would open the floodgates of litigation and allow students to delve into people's private records. "What these students are seeking is to be guardians *ad litem* for law professors who have not come forward in any forum," Ryan told the court, using the legal term for a person who is appointed to represent the interests of an infant or an incompetent in court.

Chief Justice Liacos, also a former law professor, thought that was funny. "I think there's no more likely group that needs a guardian *ad litem*, Mr. Ryan. Maybe [they need] a conservator too," he joked.

But Ryan wasn't there to quip with the justices. "If students are allowed to go forward to prove that of the 1.9 percent of Asian-American law professors in the country, Harvard does not have its share, and are allowed to put forward the records and qualifications of Asian-American professors who themselves had not come forward to vindicate whatever rights they might feel they have against Harvard Law School, then I submit the force of law in this commonwealth is moot," he ended with a flourish.

In less than an hour, the case that had occupied more than two years of at least twenty-five students' time, and given them practical experience they would never forget, had ended. As the students filed out of the courtroom, they were somber. They were worried that Justice's Liacos's dominating but not tough questioning might have proved Boston lawyer Nancy Gertner's warning to them at their last moot practice session that this was a "cold bench." And it was easy to see why some of the students felt they had been patronized by the judges.

They would have to wait close to six months, until summer, for an opinion from the court on whether or not they would be allowed to proceed to trial to prove their claims of faculty discrimination at Harvard Law School. But in less than two weeks they would learn something that would simultaneously shock and vindicate them. Dismissing their concerns and treating their suit as incidental, the faculty of Harvard Law School would vote to offer tenure to four white men.

CHAPTER 6

LET'S MAKE A DEAL

It was Friday, March 6, and nearly half of Harvard Law School's fifty-nine tenured professors were assembled for drinks and refreshments in the "faculty communal room," a long, glass-walled conference room decorated with Queen Anne chairs, a dark polished wood table, and soft carpeting, just off the main room of the faculty library on the fifth floor of Pound Hall. Few students ever see this private domain of the Harvard Law School faculty, because it is on a floor to which professors must have a special key. These late-afternoon gatherings were a ritual following each monthly faculty meeting. But never had there been so many professors present. Everyone was in a celebratory mood. Just minutes before, they had voted overwhelmingly in favor of the appointments committee's recommendation to make four tenured lateral appointments.

This was the highest number of offers made at one time to experienced laterals, professors from other schools brought in with tenure, as opposed to teachers hired as assistant professors and promoted to tenured full professorships after three to five years. Recruiting a professor laterally from outside was like a law firm recruiting a partner from another firm, though instead of bringing with him or her a large portfolio of clients, the teacher usually came with a long writing and publishing record, numerous contacts in academia, and a name in a field of law.

More significant was that this "slate" of offers represented the first time in years that the faculty could agree on individuals with such a range of intellectual leanings, from CLS to Law and Economics. The last person openly identified as a Crit to receive tenure was David Kennedy, in 1987. "There was a great feeling among us that this was a breakthrough on the intellectual-diversity front, and that we could now make the same breakthrough on the demographic front. We knew we could do it," recalled Paul Weiler, a ten-year veteran of the appointments committee and its chairman at the time.

The tenure offers were going to four respectable candidates. Joseph Weiler, a specialist in European law and common markets, no relation to Paul Weiler, had been a professor at Michigan since 1985. Harvard was interested in him to add luster to its European Law Research Center. Robert Mnookin, HLS '68, Fulbright scholar and former Supreme Court law clerk, was the director of Stanford Law School's Center on Conflict and Negotiation. He was being eyed to take over Harvard's Program on Negotiation upon Roger Fisher's retirement in June. Joseph Singer, HLS '81, taught property, conflicts, jurisprudence, and American Indian law at Boston University. He was married to Harvard Law professor Martha Minow, and adopted a CLS orientation in his writings. Henry Hansmann had received his law degree and Ph.D. from Yale, and taught corporations and Law and Economics at Yale Law School. Among the four of them, they covered every school of legal theory ranging from CLS to a traditional, doctrinal approach to a conservative Law and Economics outlook.

But there was something wrong with these prospective appointments. While Harvard Law School had invited nine women, including two African-American women, and a Hispanic man to be visiting professors over the last two years, none of them was offered a chance to become a permanent member of the illustrious faculty. Surely, if they were good enough to teach for a year, at least one was good enough to stay. Moreover, the professors changed the year-away or off-the-premises policy; that very policy had been the reason why, in the past two years, Regina Austin and Anita Allen, two African-American women, and Gerald Torres, a Hispanic, as well as white male professors could not be considered.

Harvard Law School's dean, Robert Clark, then in his third school year on the job, engineered the entire appointments package. For the past nine months he had met with professors one-on-one, lobbied for certain candidates, and built a consensus that a package deal was better than no deal. That the five members of the appointments committee represented the three principal theoretical positions held on the faculty—Duncan Kennedy and Randall Kennedy representing the left, Reinier Kraakman and Robert Clark representing the right, and Weiler representing the center—made it easier for them to win wider support. Clark was happy. He had broken the log jam that had "constipated" appointments, in the words of professor Daniel Meltzer.

As he had done in the past, Clark acted in spite of students, faculty, and alumni concerns about having a diverse faculty. Apparently, being an "academic traditionalist" meant that it didn't matter if the tenure offers were only going to white men or that it appeared that the year-away rule had been sneakily eliminated to help secure those appointments. Dealing with ideological differences was apparently more important than satisfying racial and gender differences. Maybe in the long run this would prove to be a good course of action. A larger faculty would lower the twenty-seven-to-one student-faculty ratio. The "pool" of highly qualified minority and women candidates was small, but there were exceptional minority professors at other schools. Their shortcomings weren't their academic credentials but their scholarship, which in many cases Clark and his allies found too radical.

The last thing Clark was concerned about was that these appointments were "politically incorrect." If Robert Clark stood for anything, it was the taking of actions that were "unPC." He had risen to the deanship by attacking the CLS faculty, lambasting them for "engaging in a ritual slaying of the elders" and for causing the scholarship at the Law School to deteriorate.

He had welcomed the Class of '92, in their first-year, by telling
them not to think it was immoral or unethical to choose a career
in corporate law, although insider traders like Ivan Boesky and
Michael Milken were even then burning in the bonfires of their
vanities, and Wall Street was drunk on leveraged buyouts and
mergers and acquisitions.

He was unapologetic about the decline in the number of Harvard students going into government, legal services, or public-
interest jobs: 6.4 percent in 1990, down from a high of 20
percent in 1970. In fact, 66 percent of the second-year students,
the Class of '91, would take jobs with law firms; 25 percent
would accept clerkships, which in most cases would lead back
to law-firm positions; 3.5 had government jobs; and 2.9 percent
would work in legal services and public-interest positions. Un-
troubled by this sharp fall in the number of graduates going
into public-interest jobs, he eliminated the Office of Public Interest Advising because he said it was not cost-effective to have
a full-time counselor when only 6 to 8 percent of the graduates
chose that field. He proposed halving the budget for Harvard
Law's clinical programs, citing complaints by students that they
received poor fieldwork supervision.

When he became dean in July 1989, he announced that he
wasn't going to try to "heal" the differences within the faculty;
instead, he would attempt to "manage" them. He reinstated the
position of public-interest adviser, set up a public-interest
scholarship, upped the amount of money that students taking
public-interest jobs could get to help repay their student loans,
and promised to hire twelve additional faculty members, a
bounty that would satisfy even the CLS faculty. The slate of
appointments voted on in March 1992 was just part of his way
of managing.

It wasn't a bad idea, and at any place other than Harvard
Law it might have worked. It looked as if the faculty might be
willing to put the tenure battles of the 1980s behind them and
recognize a diversity of opinions. But at Harvard, in the spring
of 1992, because of Clark's initial antagonism and the sharp
reaction against him, there was a wider gulf between the professors and a greater lack of respect for one another's views than

people acknowledged. The slate of appointments was hardly the panacea that Clark and others like Weiler thought it would be.

Most of the students learned about the vote several days later, when they saw in the *Harvard Law Record* a headline reading FOUR WHITE MEN OFFERED TENURE. The article also told them that the year-away policy had been quietly repealed. Many students were angry. Given the vociferous, persistent, and embarrassing case those in the Coalition for Civil Rights had made against the faculty for not including in their number any African-American women, Latinos, Asian-Americans, openly gay and lesbian, and physically disabled persons, the fact that these four tenure candidates were all white and all male, and that three of them were still visitors, was insulting. And the faculty had gone along with it.

They felt personally betrayed by Duncan Kennedy, the person who counseled students to "resist" hierarchy. Of all the people on the appointments committee, they thought surely Kennedy would stand by them. But Kennedy was like Clark, only ideologically opposite, in that he didn't push for every minority or woman candidate available; he had to like their politics. This time around, Kennedy had been lobbying for a woman named Kirsten Engel, a former staff attorney at the Sierra Club Legal Defense Fund in Washington, D.C., recently hired at Tulane. Because he and other professors from the left and center would not support a conservative Law and Economics male, professors from the right refused to back Kennedy's choice of Engel.

To many angry students and alumni, and a few faculty members, Harvard had again shirked its obligation to lead the way in opening the male-dominated world of legal education. Clark's claim of an ideological "breakthrough" seemed disingenuous. These appointments merely reinforced the notions about racism and sexism at Harvard that had driven the lawsuit against the school. They certainly gave greater clarity to the students' arguments made in the Massachusetts state supreme court just three days before the faculty vote about "systematic exclusion" of women and minorities at Harvard law school. And Derrick Bell's point in *Faces,* that whites would do anything to keep blacks and minorities down, at whatever cost, had a strange ring of truth, too.

Clark may have known the faculty was considering offering tenure to two white women and a black man, but the rest of the school didn't. A *New York Times* article about Bell's intention to seek an extension of his leave referred to this slate of appointments, but to activist students like Keith Boykin, the news "was a complete surprise." As Charles Nesson, an outspoken liberal on the faculty, later said about Clark, "He made the best deal he could make at the time. He thinks his heart is pure and the rest of the world will figure it out later."

But the students leading Bell's charge had been working too long and too hard to wait for the next "demographic" breakthrough. They had already been planning a series of rallies, demonstrations, and class strikes of the kind that, since Bell had announced his leave, were becoming an annual occurrence. Now they had a moral imperative. On March 11, five days after the vote, Reverend Jesse Jackson arrived on campus to speak at a rally sponsored by the Coalition for Civil Rights. During the late 1970s, when students fought to persuade Harvard University to withdraw its investments in South Africa, Jackson had appeared on campus to rally the students and rile the administration. He had spoken in the spring of 1990, the day Bell announced his leave. Now he had accepted the coalition's invitation to speak out against the appointments, and to urge continued support of Derrick Bell's protest. A forceful and dramatic speaker, he could articulate the sentiment that their lawsuit, their protests, and their fight for faculty diversity had not been in vain.

Judging from the crowd of nearly 450 students stuffed into the majestic Ames Courtroom, on the second floor of Austin Hall, students and sympathetic professors wanted to be inspired by the eloquent reverend. Jackson, looking lawyerly in a navy wool suit, starched white shirt and tie, peered intensely at the audience seated before him. He launched into an impassioned speech, heightened by his rolling baritone metaphors, analogizing the struggle at the law school to the struggle against apartheid in South Africa. Just as students had to fight apartheid there, so they must fight "apartheid in the Law School faculty" at Harvard. "Harvard is too high on the hill to cast shades of darkness when we need points of light. . . . It is beneath Harvard to do this." His voice rising, he said giving tenure to minorities and women at Harvard Law School was not only important to students currently at the school, but it was also encouraging to those who might never be able to attend a university. The position of tenured professor "gives aid and comfort to the lowest in American society, and it is more affordable than people think. It costs twice more to go to jail than to go to Yale," he said.

The next morning, on what students were calling "Zero Day," a group of about twenty students turned their attention to Clark, the person responsible for the faculty's insensitivity. It was a chilly day, with snow on the ground and still clinging to the trees. Beginning at 7:30 A.M., armed with hand-painted signs bearing statements such as "Academic Excellence Requires Diversity" and "Elitism, No; Excellence Yes," they walked to Clark's house on Irving Street, just a few blocks from the Law School, to surprise him at his doorstep. They waited about forty-five minutes, chanting, "No justice, no peace," before he appeared. "I was taking a shower and heard someone besides myself singing," he joked later, though it was almost as if he had been expecting their visit. He came out and greeted the students, and after listening to them for a few minutes, he offered to accompany them to the Harkness Commons, the Law School student union, where they could talk about the matter "over a cup of coffee."

Huddled at "the Hark," the students during this meeting were relentless. They blasted Clark for inconsistently applying the year-away rule and for not really caring about diversity. Members of the civil rights coalition called for the newly tenured four white men to decline their appointments. Clark admitted it was a "muck-up" not to have told students in advance about the appointments and the "suspension" of the policy regarding tenure offers to visitors. The students said they wanted to be represented on the appointments committee. Clark said that was highly unlikely. The ad-hoc breakfast adjourned at around 10:00 A.M., but Clark agreed to meet at a forum later in the day, after lunch. He also scheduled an emergency faculty meeting for that afternoon.

In the meantime, a crowd of students, organized by the student leaders and members of the Coalition for Civil Rights, marched in Langdell Hall. As many as one hundred students stood in the hallway of faculty offices and in front of the main reading room, where Harvard's extensive law library is located, chanting, "Diversity now, diversity now."

From there they moved to a large lecture hall in the northern part of Langdell Hall for the forum promised by Dean Clark. The student crowd thickened. Close to a third of the faculty, including several members of the appointments committee, also came out for the forum. Among the professors were Duncan Kennedy, Gerald Frug, Charles Fried, Christopher Edley, David Wilkins, Elizabeth Bartholet, Charles Nesson, and negotiator Roger Fisher. Also present was Sarah Wald, the Law School's dean of students. At their just-concluded meeting, the faculty had adopted the resolution sponsored by professors Edley and Fisher to reconsider all the women visiting professors in the last ten years, and to give the faculty as a whole a chance to consider minority candidates regardless of the appointment committee's recommendations. This was essentially the same resolution the faculty had defeated two years earlier. It took two years of concerted protest by Bell and other students and this apparently ill-planned announcement to convince the faculty how necessary this resolution was.

The forum lasted for three hours, moving like a circular dance, with the students and faculty members retreading old, familiar steps. Why can't we get involved in the appointments process? asked several students. That was a "terrible idea," answered two professors simultaneously. Other universities did that, and the result was a "stilted, inadequate critique of many candidates," offered tax professor Bernard Wolfman. Professor Frug disagreed with Wolfman, but noted that the idea would still be "overwhelmingly opposed," and that it was something the students really shouldn't push for too hard. Student involvement would undermine the legitimacy of the appointment process, said Charles Fried, because "the appointments committee must be taken seriously."

Edley told the crowd that politics was simply slowing down the process, and the small pool of candidates was not really the issue. "There is a large enough group who meet the threshold of political plausibility so that we can make deals," he said, but the problem was that "no one wants to support a minority candidate if that candidate is going to be charged to their account."

Wasn't the latest approach of hiring white men first, then white women and then possibly men or women of color in political deals among faculty groups obviously discriminatory? a second-year student asked. Professor Richard Fallon answered that having to make political deals and hiring a wave of professors was "lamentable, but not legally problematic."

And on it went, with students and faculty members retracing the same issues, but from different angles. Finally the students became exasperated at the repetitive rhetoric and repeated assertions that the faculty was committed to diversity. Clark continued to tell students that he couldn't say exactly when a female minority professor would be hired, but that he would keep meeting with interested students, and that he was receptive to ideas for ways to improve the hiring process. He would continue a dialogue, he told them.

But he was not going to veer from the decisions on which he had worked so hard to gain a consensus. He wasn't going to cave in to student demands just to become a "popular" dean. Not only wasn't that in his character, but he had become dean because he set himself apart from the pack. He was governed, he said, by an internal discipline acquired from boyhood, and a steadfastness in his own beliefs that often made him unpopular: "I'm pretty much driven by my own compass." His singlemindedness, however, has translated into bluntness, shortsightedness, and a tin ear. He himself once recognized that he had to watch what he said, because the words might come out too strong. A perfect example of that incaution was his "lunch counter" statement about Bell's protest. Ironically, he made that comment several days after he had asked Roger

Fisher to try to mediate a resolution between the Law School and Bell and the student activists.

Clark was forty-four years old when Harvard University president Derek Bok chose him to be the tenth dean of Harvard Law School. Many people said he looked too young for the job, one of the most powerful and influential deanships in the country. He had a full, amber-colored beard, flickering blue eyes that crinkled when he smiled, and a boyish peevishness. For someone whose mission was to spearhead the charge against tenure candidates Dalton and Trubek and against CLS, and who was seen as being able to restore law and order at Harvard, he was not a towering figure. Of average height, and compactly built, he spoke in a hushed, shy voice and often appeared stiff and standoffish in a group. He was hardly the showman or glad-hander that some of his colleagues on the faculty were. He looked as though he would be more comfortable wearing the black robe and white collar he had shunned earlier in his life.

He was essentially a composer, not a performer. As a hobby, he wrote neoclassical music on a synthesizer. His music blended Vivaldi and Bach with the jazz of New Orleans that he had heard while growing up. When he taught corporations law, before becoming dean, he had often given Friday-afternoon concerts at which he regaled his students with adaptations of the laws of insider trading, fraudulent conveyance, and tender offers, against a background of familiar tunes.

The synthesizer was a perfect instrument for Clark, because he was a synthesis of religious, philosophical, psychological, legal, and economic training. A Catholic, he had been a candidate for the priesthood, but had been more interested in philosophy than faith. He held a Ph.D. in philosophy, but applied it to behavioral science and psychology. He studied law at Harvard to broaden his philosophy training, but became fascinated by the organization of corporations and the application of economics to law. He is working on an opus tentatively titled *Laws, Markets, and Morals,* in which he compares little-examined religious and social systems with market and legal systems of controls. His goal is to "incorporate some of the techniques of religion in other spheres, the educational and the legal, rather than to have some global revival," he told *Boston Globe* writer David Warsh at the time of his appointment. He called it a "neo-Langdellian" approach.

Yet, if his style seemed low-key, more in keeping with the demeanor of his predecessor, James Vorenberg, his no-nonsense attitude fit the mold of past deans such as Bok, Griswold, and Pound, who had ruled Harvard Law School with an iron hand. He was a "no-bullshit dean . . . and this was the no-bullshit future," remarked a skeptical David Kennedy, following Clark's appointment. Kennedy, who called the appointment "out of step with the view of the majority of the Law School faculty," had been on the search committee. It was the first time such a committee had included an "ideological" sampling of professors. There were two professors from each main camp: Kennedy and Gerald Frug on the left, Bernard Wolfman and Clark on the right, and David Shapiro and Laurence Tribe in the center. Near the end of the nine-month search, Clark became a candidate, and he resigned from the committee. Bok announced his choice of Clark in February 1989, to be effective July 1, 1989.

Having served with Clark on the committee, and knowing how relentless he had been on CLS and on its tenure candidates Dalton and Trubek, Kennedy knew Clark would be a tough dean. Intellectually, his pledge to make Harvard "the best law school the world has ever seen" could be good for Harvard, bolstering its scholarly output, strengthening the school's waning reputation, and, it was hoped, increasing its endowment. But managerially, Kennedy, Frug, and others knew that because of his stubbornness and his abhorrence of the left, Clark could also be the most likely to widen the gulf between camps. Morton Horowitz called it "an outrageous appointment," and predicted that it would "polarize the faculty just at a time when we need a dean who [can] restore trust." He denounced Clark for having "regularly opposed minorities, women, and people with different views than his."

Even as a boy, Clark had been tough, placing nearly perfectionist standards on himself and others. Born and raised in New

Orleans, he was the second oldest of nine children. His father, William Clark, was a second-generation New Orlean whose roots could be traced back more than three hundred years, to Luther Clark, supposedly one of the first settlers in North-hampton, Massachusetts. The family moved to the gulf coast, where they worked on the Mississippi and Louisiana seaports. His paternal grandmother was from New Orleans; her family was French and spoke only Parisian French, not Cajun. His maternal grandparents were second-generation German and Scotch-Irish. Coming from Catholic families, his parents raised Robert and his siblings as Catholics.

When Robert was five, his father, an accountant for fruit importing companies, moved his young family to New Orleans East, to a house at 4701 Laine Avenue, an address he still re-members and which still stands today, off the Sheffman Tour Highway and not far from Lake Pontchartrain. A few years later his father built a larger house on the lot next door, at 4709 Laine Avenue, and Clark spent most of his boyhood there. That home also still exists.

Although the neighborhood he grew up in would become a suburb of New Orleans, when he was a boy it was semi-rural. Sections of swampy, undeveloped land were divided by resi-dential streets. The Clark house was located at the end of four streets. "It was in the city, but if you walked to the end of the street, about a quarter of a mile, what you found was 5,400 acres of cow pasture and swamp and woods and canals and bayous, which we used to hike around in," Clark remembers with characteristic precision. Although blacks lived one street away, Clark had little contact with them. "You didn't go there, they didn't [come] here," he offered.

Most of the neighbors had horses, cows, or other animals. For several years his mother, Edwina, raised chickens in their backyard to help ends meet. His discipline and respect for work began at home by helping his mother. With eventually nine brothers and sisters, Clark was always helping tend to the little ones. His mother and father gave him plenty of chores to do, too. Every Saturday morning he would sweep, mop, and wax all of the floors in half of the house. He also took turns with the laundry, and developed a system by which he could do all the laundry in ten hours. Sometimes he'd be in charge of the dishes, and sometimes he'd be responsible for cutting the grass. The Clark home was usually busy, bustling with kids, and serving as the neighborhood clubhouse.

All his siblings started working at chores in the house and at part-time jobs outside the home at a fairly early age, too. Clark got his first job when he was fourteen years old, as a plumber's assistant in a plumbing and heating company. At first he did office work, typing bills, estimating, and cleaning up the shop. Then he was permitted to work on construction jobs, helping to lay cast-iron drainage pipes and other heavy things.

In addition to an early work ethic, there was a serious, studious side to the family. Besides doing chores, everyone studied the Bible and went to church. "He had a family that was conducive to the idea that if you wanted to apply yourself, you could do it and achieve something," said George Stephen Hotz, a high school friend of Clark's, later an actuary in New Orleans.

At Cor Jesu High School, an all-boys Catholic school, later renamed Brother Martin High School, in New Orleans, Clark's intellectual curiosity and steely resolve were already evident. He was beginning to read the great philosophers, such as Immanuel Kant. He loved giving his friends synopses of Kant's arguments about *a priori* reasoning and what could and couldn't be proved. Then he discovered Socrates and syllogisms, and shared that with his schoolmates. Most of his friends weren't interested in such heady subjects, but they gave him an audience anyway. "He shared his interest in philosophy, but frankly it went right over my head," said Gus Cantrell, a friend from grammar school through high school, who still lives in New Orleans. "I gave him polite lip service. I didn't understand everything he was saying. But there was a certain respect he commanded. You knew he knew whatever book he was telling you about. There was a certain determination to him."

Clark was already mastering the skills that would serve him in later years. He had trained himself to wait until everyone in the house was asleep, or wake himself up in the middle of the night, to read for a few hours and then go back to sleep, just to see if he could do it and still function normally in school. "I remember he'd be reading while everyone was sleeping," said his brother Thomas, later a bank vice-president.

"I don't think Bob ever came home from school and said, 'I'm not going to do my homework tonight.' It was something he knew he had to do and he did it. I don't think 'Robbo' walked out of his house and took a walk without knowing what direction he was going," said Hotz. His friends nicknamed him "Robbo" after he came into school one day wearing a Scotch plaid sweater that made him look like he'd come from the University of Edinburgh. "He had that prominent chin and that professor look," remembered Hotz.

Even then, Clark had little patience for the mundane, and he was hard on others whose standards fell short of his. In physics, he needled his physics teacher by deliberately giving him the wrong answers. "Problem number one?" the teacher, a Mr. Wizard type, would ask one of the students. "Problem number two?" he asked the next student. "Clark?" he would call out, when no one else would answer. And Clark would give an answer he knew was wrong, to make the old man feel that even young Clark wasn't that smart. "Yes, he'd do his homework and he'd grasp the principles, but he would say, 'This is ridiculous, I have things to do,' He thought this physics class was a waste of time," said Hotz. "We would often be together, exposed to these social phenomena, Mardi Gras, a dance, watching television, a commercial or something, Bob would turn around with this mischievous smile and say to me, 'Big deal.' He just wasn't into wasting time."

Cantrell remembers how impatient Clark got once, during a Boy Scout outing, when the two were trying to earn a badge for cooking. Clark decided he would cook a whole chicken. He dug a hole, lit a fire, and buried the chicken in the coals. It was a cold day, and after letting it cook for hours, the chicken came out burnt on the outside and raw on the inside. "It was cold, it was late, I was hungry, and I ate it. Bobby complained the whole time," recalled Cantrell. "He was a perfectionist from the word go. He expected everything to be done perfectly. When we set out to cook chicken in the cold, he expected it to be perfect. Me, I was just hungry."

Both Hotz and Cantrell recognized something Clark's adversaries would take years to figure out—that he was not easily swayed. "If he's doing something he wants to do, then he's going to see it through, even if he's disgusted with it, and the only way you're going to stop him is to sit down and reason with him and convince him it isn't going to work," said Hotz.

Music and religion were perhaps the most important things in young Clark's life. He remembered lying awake at night, listening to the music floating into his window from a nearby black Baptist church. His father played the violin and the clarinet. One day he found his father's old clarinet in the closet and taught himself to play. His family didn't have money for him to take music lessons or to buy instruments. Another time, finding a broken piano on the street, he and his brothers dragged it into their tool shed and fixed it up. At night he would spray himself with mosquito repellent and go to the shed to practice. "I just wanted to play desperately, without anyone ever suggesting it, because I loved it," he recalled.

As a teenager, he saved up enough money from his grass-cutting jobs and plumber's assistant work to buy a piano. George Hotz's aunt, Olga Hotz, helped him find it. A pianist and sixth-grade teacher, she listened to Clark when he fooled around at the piano in their house. She saw his musical talent and recognized his deliberate attitude.

"Does he have a piano?" she asked her nephew one day.

"The kids pulled a piano from the junk and are working on it," Hotz said.

His aunt called Yetsie Koshada, a friend she knew was getting rid of some furniture at the time.

"Do you ever play that piano in the living room?" Olga Hotz asked. "Have you thought about getting rid of it? I know someone who could really use it. Why don't you sell it to the Clarks for three hundred dollars?"

She sold it to Clark, and he began to take lessons from a man in the French Quarter named Orval Klopp. Klopp had studied under Walter Gieseking, a German pianist, and had a flair for playing Debussy and Ravel. Clark practiced hard and moved far in a short time. "We took lessons from the same guy, and Robbo just sped right ahead. Orval would suggest things, and he'd do them," said Hotz.

He and Hotz discussed music the way other boys compared baseball team statistics. They would listen to Beethoven's fifth Symphony and try to figure out which other works were great. They moved Clark's stereo into the garage, where they spent hours listening and critiquing scores. Clark studied piano with Klopp for about a year and a half before leaving to enter the seminary. There, he still practiced and continued to write to Hotz about music. But religion had replaced music in his life.

None of his friends were surprised when Clark decided to join the Maryknoll Society. "I figured he'd be a doctor or a priest. There's a human side to him. I don't think you could come from that family and not care about people," said his boyhood friend Gus Cantrell. His family went to church regularly, discussed religion at home, and sent Clark to church retreats, giving him a sense that he had a vocation. Becoming a member of the Maryknoll Fathers, a mission-oriented order that advocated land reform in Latin America and ran agricultural schools and orphanages throughout the world, fit within that idea. Clark called it "a developed Catholic family's equivalent of the Peace Corps."

Father Eugene Kennedy could tell that this high school senior, sitting before him in the living room of a Garden District home owned by the Maryknolls, was someone special. Of the hundreds of seminary candidates Kennedy had interviewed, none had impressed him as much as Clark did, on this spring day in 1962. He had the feeling he might be talking to a future Thomas Jefferson or even a Mozart. "As soon as I met him, I felt that he was an extremely unusual young man—that he was singular, a very bright, highly creative individual. I felt the very great depth of his capacities, like feeling the underground spring of power yet unrealized, unprocessed, of someone who just had enormous creative ability," said Kennedy, who eventually left the priesthood and became a psychology professor at Loyola University of Chicago. "You could tell he observed and sensed the world in a different way. He was part of the last great wave of very gifted young men choosing to go into the church." From that day on, Kennedy decided he would do whatever he could to help this unusually insightful, soft-spoken teenager.

When Clark arrived at the seminary in Glen Ellyn, Illinois, a Chicago suburb, it was as if he'd been preparing for this highly structured environment all his life. He fit in easily, and quickly adapted to the rigors of study and work. Every seminarian needed to work, and Kennedy offered Clark a research job. But he also wanted to give him freedom to do his own "intellectual adventuring." Clark devoured the books in Kennedy's office. He taught himself to read Hebrew so that he could study the Old Testament in its original language. One day at lunch, instead of reading aloud from the Bible, as was the custom, he read from *Alice in Wonderland.*

Other students liked him, and elected him student body president in his junior year. But Clark declined the honor because he was struggling with serious doubts about a life in the church and his faith in God. He says he had read "too much philosophy," and could no longer accept the basis of the religion. For a year and a half he thought about nothing else. It was a painful and difficult time for him, but he was not ashamed to share his crisis with the rest of the students.

He was about six months away from graduating in 1966, when a teenaged postal carrier named Patrick Gunkel rode up to the seminary on his bicycle. Gunkel was a hyperintellectual. He had dropped out of high school because he thought it was excruciatingly boring, had taken a job at the post office, and spent all of his time reading and writing. Gunkel went up to the receptionist and told her, "I want to talk to the smartest person here." After thinking about it for a few minutes, Father Halbert, the dean of students, called for Clark. "I want you to meet this guy who just came in off the street and appeared at the door. See what you can do for him," he told Clark.

They went into a room, and the first thing Gunkel said, without saying hello or anything else, was "Why do you believe in God?"

"Well, actually I don't," Clark answered. It was the last answer Gunkel expected.

"You don't?" Gunkel said. "What are you doing here?" They talked for a long time about that, and have remained friends ever since. Gunkel became what many academics considered an eccentric genius. He wrote several unpublished books about what he called "ideonomy," the science of classifying ideas. The area appealed to Clark intellectually, and he became a constant source of encouragement for Gunkel, who moved to Texas.

By the time they met, Clark had already decided to leave the Maryknolls after graduation. "I thought the society—it's not an order—was a good group of people. I still think extremely highly of them. But I just couldn't see it. I didn't decide in one day, it was a process of one book after the other. That was that, I couldn't do it, live a lie, profess beliefs that I didn't believe."

If he had started out earlier in life, without his religious beliefs, Clark probably would have gone into music, his greatest love. But since he was not an accomplished player or theoretician by the end of his college career, it was a little too late for that. He liked philosophy, so he accepted a fellowship for the Ph.D. program at Columbia University. His plan was "to be a philosopher."

What interested him most at the time, and would stay with him after he moved into law, was the science of behavior. He went to Columbia specifically because Ernest Nagel, the author of *The Structure of Science,* was there. Nagel was part of the group of philosophers known as logical positivists, who came to the United States from Austria and Germany to flee the Nazis. According to logical positivism, anything that could be positively proven was true; simply searching for ultimate causes was immaterial. Unlike the seminary, Columbia was completely unstructured. All that Clark had to do was show up to take his comprehensive exams, write his term papers, and complete his thesis. Because he was more disciplined than most of the students, he took classes in psychology, sociology, and comparative social psychology, focusing on animal studies. It was a wonderful time for him, intellectually. He went hog-wild, reading whatever he wanted and auditing courses in any department. Socially, it was a good time for him too. In his second year he met his future wife, Kathy Tighe, the daughter of a Brooklyn postman.

At that time, Columbia was in an uproar over the Vietnam War. Students rallied and occupied buildings. Every day at lunchtime, someone would be at the sundial in the middle of campus with a bullhorn, leading a protest against the administration or the war. Clark opposed the war, but took a detached view toward the student protests. This was where his lack of sympathy for student protesters originated. He would go to some events and listen and argue with people. "But I wasn't for or against them," he said later. "I thought they were so silly that it was unimaginable, so unreasonable." When hundreds of police invaded the administration building to disperse students who had taken it over, Clark sat on a window ledge across the street on the eleventh floor of the John Jay Hall. He and a few philosophy department friends drank beer and argued about behavior theory as they watched the scene on the street below.

The entire student movement struck him as hypocritical. "The real motivating force was fear of going to Vietnam," he told a writer for the *Boston Globe*. He saw these students as merely assuaging their liberal guilt. That's why, nearly twenty years later, he thought Professor Bell's actions, the student demonstrations against the elimination of the public-interest coordinator, and the lawsuit against the school for not having a tenured African-American woman or other minority professors were counterproductive. The students' motivation, he believed, was simply to alleviate their guilt over going into corporate law.

As a graduate student, Clark saw himself as a rational scientist. He had become fascinated by the work of B. F. Skinner—not in its utopian aspects, contained in books like *Walden Two*, but in Skinner's animal studies. Skinner tried to prove that behavior was not inherited, but was molded by positive or negative reinforcement. Clark says his interest in Skinner was "idealistic," based upon his own general interest in science and the possibilities of human improvement. "My whole interest in behaviorism was how to improve the way people behave or how you educate people."

Reading Skinner's early works was "just like a revelation," he said; if he hadn't read *Science and Human Behavior* and *Verbal Behavior,* he probably would never have wound up a professor at Harvard Law School. Skinner's work gave him insight into how he could change his behavior and his environment so that he could produce papers and academic products. It offered him a framework for looking at himself that was different from the religious tradition he grew up with, which was more psychologistic. He selected Skinner as his thesis topic, comparing his work and ideas with those of the sociologist Talcott Parsons. He even mimicked Skinner by writing every night from 8:00 P.M. to 2:00 A.M. in his three-room walk-up apartment on Amsterdam Avenue, at the edge of Harlem.

While at Columbia, he was also intrigued by the "futurism" movement led by Alvin Toffler, and got a job as a researcher for Toffler, who was then writing *Future Shock.* Clark was interested in how new technologies might improve society, and in the ethical questions raised by such advances as biomedical engineering. From there it was just a short step to studying law, though when he entered Harvard Law School in 1970, he still envisioned an academic career in philosophy. All the great philosophers had another interest or occupation besides philosophy that they used as a basis for reflection. In the case of Kant, it was physics. Hume knew history. Aristotle mastered biology as it was understood then. It wasn't enough to study logic, methodology, and the debates about positivism and antipositivism that were going on. That was too sterile for Clark.

He thought the best thing to do was to learn about society and how it worked. He even thought about getting another Ph.D., in sociology or anthropology. Then, after talking to various people, he decided that studying law would be better, because "most of the sociological studies of organizations tended to be of the fringe, streetcorner society." Very few sociologists seemed to have had entree into large organizations, business, commerce, the things that really made society work. Three more years of school hardly bothered him. "Three more years?

What's three years if you're trying to write for the ages?" he thought. In a sense, he says, practicing law and becoming a law professor and the dean of Harvard Law School have been a giant detour.

About to earn a Ph.D.—only fifteen other students in his first-year law class had doctorates—and married, Clark had the air of an older, more mature law student. But in some ways he was a typically competitive Harvard Law student, not wanting to let on how much he was studying. "I found out through my wife, who talked to his wife, that he stayed up until four in the morning and went on as little as two hours' sleep," recalled Barton Fisher, one of his classmates. He wasn't doing that just for show; he was working doubly hard to finish his dissertation and to learn the new language of torts, contracts, and property law. His grades just missed qualifying him for the *Law Review.*

In Victor Brudney's corporations course, Clark found the window into the world of corporations for which he had come to law school. He wrote a paper on economic theory that was so insightful that Brudney footnoted it in his own 1972 corporate finance textbook. The paper was a far cry from Clark's first academic articles, published just a few years earlier, on the music of John Cage and Karlheinz Stockhausen.

But his transformation from philosopher to corporate lawyer was well under way. After his second year he applied for a job as a summer associate at the Boston law firm of Ropes & Gray. Partner Truman Casner interviewed Clark and assessed him as the best candidate he'd seen that day, if not in his entire career. "I as much as offered him the job on the spot," said Casner. Clark joined the firm as an associate after graduating from Harvard *magna cum laude* in 1972. He quickly proved his mettle as a lawyer by helping to plan a successful defense of Friendly Ice Cream, which was then being sued by a group of its store franchisees on antitrust grounds. He also helped Encyclopaedia Britannica, then over $100 million in debt, develop a refinancing plan to allow the company to complete a new edition.

After two years, however, Clark ached for the intellectual stimulation of academia, and started looking for a law professorship. The firm was not surprised by his decision. He was joining a long line of Ropes & Gray lawyers turned law teachers. The firm's founding partner, John Chipman Gray, an early lecturer, had been appointed the Story chair at Harvard in 1875. Two of the school's greatest professors, Lon Fuller and Archibald Cox, were associates at the firm. Former dean James Vorenberg had been a partner. When several partners found out that Yale had approached Clark with a job offer, they unsuccessfully tried to get Harvard to offer him a job. Unfortunately, though Clark had a Harvard law degree, he had not been on the *Law Review* nor clerked for an appeals court judge.

So, in 1974, Clark accepted the offer from Yale. There he became an exponent of the legal theoretical movement known as Law and Economics. This movement was a kind of legal behaviorism, seeing law as a way to fine-tune the free-market system. It was dominated by conservative academics and judges. Four years after he arrived at Yale, the same year he received tenure, Clark's former professor, Brudney, called from Harvard to see if he'd be willing to switch allegiances. Although Harvard was hiring new thinkers on the left, the faculty didn't want to miss the chance to catch the wave of conservative scholarship that was sweeping other law schools, including Yale and the University of Chicago.

Clark left Yale to start teaching at Harvard in 1979. He taught Corporate Law, and his classes were a big success, due in part to his Friday synthesizer recitals. He would later write a one-volume treatise on corporations law that would become the leading text on the subject. He began consulting for Fortune 500 companies on the side, as many professors did.

At first he seemed to want to win the respect of the CLS-identified professors, who were already a dominant intellectual force. For a committee on planning and educational development, he wrote a memo arguing that the school should change its goal from training legal servants for elite institutions to training lawyers interested in serving social justice. He recommended expanding clinical programs, and suggested that a professor's involvement in legal services, public-interest work, or legal reform activity be "a major, independent factor in appointments and tenure decisions." Those suggestions should have thrilled the CLS faculty. But the CLS professors advocated more-drastic measures, such as abolishing tenure and admitting students by lottery, to make Harvard more egalitarian. Clark's idea seemed silly to them, compared to those desires. Traditionalists, meanwhile, thought his ideas were too liberal.

To be taken seriously, Clark had to choose sides, and he concluded that Crits abhorred everything he admired, and vice versa. They hated hierarchy; he believed in the essence of it. He sought an objective approach to legal policy; they said law was subjective, nothing more than a rationale for the ruling class. Thus he repudiated any semblance of a moderate-liberal outlook that he might have had initially, and proudly identified himself as a traditionalist. He was a Democrat in the 1970s, but gave that up and became what he calls a moderate Republican. He said he believed in a smaller role for government, and in tight economic regulation, but he was more liberal on social issues. Academically, scholarship should be the overriding factor in appointments, and public interest was not necessarily more worthwhile than corporate experience, he decided.

His public attack on the Crits at the Harvard Club in New York City in 1985 was a declaration of war. His timing couldn't have been better. Ronald Reagan was in his second term as president, and the country was politically more conservative than it had been. Other conservative professors on the faculty, including Phillip Areeda, Louis Loss, Donald Trautman, Louis Kaplow, and David Rosenberg, gave him enough support that he could convince Harvard University president Derek Bok to veto the two-thirds faculty vote to tenure David Trubek, and to uphold the faculty's narrow rejection of Clare Dalton. Charles Fried, Solicitor General under Reagan, returned to the law school in 1989 and later became a staunch ally of Clark on appointments.

Bok had criticized the way Harvard Law students' career plans didn't "fit very closely with society's most pressing needs" and tolerated the Crits at first. But while he felt CLS created more intellectual ferment, he decided that the CLS faculty "had somewhat radical answers to give" and that they were "infusing a political element into something that ought to be much more neutral."

He liked Clark because he had a wide range of intellectual interests and was an academic traditionalist, bent on ivory-tower excellence. Bok wanted to send a message that Harvard was committed to scholarship. Clark was also an insider, as all Harvard law deans since Erwin Griswold had been. Most important, he knew the school would benefit from Clark's corporate connections. In February 1989, when Bok announced that he was naming Clark dean, effective July 1, plans were already under way to begin a $150-million capital campaign drive, five times larger than any previous fund-raising drive in the history of a law school.

The long-range planning process, started in 1987 by Dean Vorenberg, called for a new dormitory, a new legal services building, a new classroom and office building, the renovation of the library in Langdell Hall, and funding for twelve additional faculty positions. As a conservative former corporations professor who had the courage to stand up to the subversive element within Harvard Law School and could honestly say he had done it because he cared about the health of the institution, Clark could attract money from the school's affluent alumni. By December 1, 1991, a year after the Harvard Corporation formally approved the campaign, Clark had raised $65 million in pledges.

Clark had his own plans for the school, too. Almost immediately after taking the helm, in July 1989, he went to work to dismantle the power structure set up by the Crits. In addition to eliminating the public-interest counselor's position and suggesting to cut the budget for half a dozen clinical programs, he swept away the consensus style of his predecessor, James Vorenberg. Vorenberg had held faculty meetings every two weeks; Clark held only two in his first four months on the job. Vorenberg had been only an *ex officio* member of the appointments committee; Clark made himself chairman.

He also tried to gain the power to set salaries to alter the pay of the less productive professors. He wanted the leeway to entice people to Harvard, an effort often hampered by Harvard's rigid salary system. It wasn't a direct threat against the left, but it would give him leverage over that faction. Additionally, he set himself against the faculty by opposing offering tenure to Charles Ogletree, then a visiting professor, who as a criminal defense lawyer had once raised money for the defense of militant black activist Angela Davis in her 1972 murder trial. It would set a bad precedent because Ogletree wasn't a scholar but a practitioner, Clark said.

Eventually, Clark backpedaled on almost every politically incorrect action he took. His supporters say he learned fast. He helped establish two public-interest law scholarships, re-funded the loan-repayment plan for students going into public-interest work, oversaw the construction of a new building for the school's legal services program, accepted Ogletree's terms to put him on a tenure track, and reinstated monthly faculty meetings. This was not going to be a dean who would stand up against Senator Joseph McCarthy and defend the Fifth Amendment the way Erwin Griswold had, or initiate innovative clinical programs the way Albert Sacks had, or seek consensus the way James Vorenberg had.

Clark would act and then react. Everything he did would affect the tenor of the debate at the law school. The 1991–92 school year had been a period of "watchful waiting" for liberal and centrist faculty members. But he hadn't allayed their fears. In his hands, Harvard would move further rightward and stray far from the days when law was taught in a "grand manner." As the appointments slate of March 1992 showed, a deal could be struck at any time, and Clark would be happy to help negotiate it.

CHAPTER 7

THE IDES OF MAY

Judging from the two rallies in early March—the one addressed by Derrick Bell the day after students argued the appeal of their discrimination suit at the Massachusetts Supreme Court, and the other one by Jesse Jackson the day after school officials announced the appointment of four white men—plus the next day's morning surprise at Dean Clark's doorstep and the angry afternoon forum later that afternoon, it was clear that "Diversity Week" was starting early. "Diversity Week," or what sarcastic professors called "the Ides of May," had become a week-long spring ritual of teach-ins, sit-ins, class boycotts, and rallies to draw attention to the issue of the lack of minority law professors at the nation's elite schools.

The week culminated in a national "Strike Day" on the first Thursday of April, when students at schools throughout the country participated in a variety of events, often teach-ins, class strikes, and rallies. The idea originated with students at the University of California at Berkeley School of Law in 1989, and was taken up at Harvard in 1990 when students formed the Coalition for Civil Rights. Some Harvard professors, though, dated the spring rite of dissent to 1982, when students demonstrated against the faculty's decision to grade class participation.

One thing is certain: At Harvard, Diversity Week tied directly into protests over faculty hiring decisions. The first year that students fully observed the event, 1990, was the same year visiting professor Regina Austin was passed over by the faculty appointments committee and Derrick Bell declared his leave of protest. Many students had already organized protests over the elimination of the public-interest counselor's office the preceding fall, so they were motivated and mobilized to launch a series of rallies, silent vigils, forums, and two all-night occupations of Dean Clark's office.

The demonstrations and well-executed media strategy catapulted onto the national stage the issue of "faculty diversity" or lack of it at Harvard. The second year, 1991, when the faculty appointments committee voted not to offer tenure to Anita Allen, a similar outbreak of protest occurred. In addition to the scheduled class strikes, rallies, and forums, students again barricaded themselves inside the hallway and anteroom outside the dean's office. The occupation would have lasted through the night if the Cambridge police hadn't arrived and threatened to arrest any students remaining inside.

Clark hoped that by holding forums, as Derek Bok had done when he was dean of the Law School in the early 1970s to quiet student unrest, he could dissuade members of the coalition from attempting any sit-ins or takeovers of any buildings. But after the blockade of his office in the spring of 1991, he chose to take a tougher stance, and warned that any student who "interfered with the normal operations of the university" would be disciplined.

Clark was quoting from the statement of "Rights and Responsibilities" by which students as well as faculty and other employees of Harvard Law School agree to abide. It is a policy that spells out what kind of "academic community" Harvard Law School is to be, and where the lines of appropriate behavior are crossed. The code states that "interference with members of the University in performance of their normal duties and activities must be regarded as unacceptable obstruction of the essential processes of the University."

But the short, five-paragraph statement also recognizes that

Harvard is an "academic community" whose central functions are "learning, teaching, research, and scholarship." And that community, ideally, is characterized "by free expression, free inquiry, intellectual honesty, respect for the dignity of others, and openness to constructive change." Members of the community have essentially the same rights as other members of society; yet the university has a "special autonomy" in which "reasoned dissent" is vitally important.

Thus, all members of the university "have the right to press for action on matters of concern by any appropriate means," and the university "must affirm, assure, and protect" the right of members to "organize and join political associations, convene and conduct public meetings, publicly demonstrate and picket in orderly fashion, advocate, and publicize by print, sign, and voice." A "special emphasis" is placed on values such as "freedom of speech and academic freedom, freedom from personal force and violence, and freedom of movement." Thus, interfering with any of those freedoms is "a serious violation of the personal rights" on which the community is based.

It is the responsibility of all members of the Harvard community "to maintain an atmosphere in which violations of rights are unlikely to occur...." Failing to meet those responsibilities could be "profoundly damaging to the life of the University." Under the policy, all the members of the Harvard Law School community, "students and officers alike," are urged to uphold those rights and responsibilities, "if the University is to be characterized by *mutual respect* and *trust*." (Emphasis added.)

As far as these student activists were concerned, the events and their actions surrounding Diversity Week fit perfectly with Harvard's own stated desire to be a community open to "constructive change" and conducive to orderly political demonstrating and picketing. They never forced any teachers to stop teaching or cancel classes. Even Dean Clark was not prevented from working in his office, though dozens of students crowded the hallway and anteroom outside, carried signs, and sometimes sang songs or chanted slogans. Most of their demonstrations centered on Strike Day, always held the first Thursday in April.

Spring vacation in the 1991–92 academic year would begin on March 23, and student leaders of the Coalition for Civil Rights wanted to build more support and momentum for the upcoming Strike Day, scheduled for the first week after students returned. They decided to hold a silent vigil in the offices of former Solicitor General Charles Fried. To these left-liberal students, Fried was a political enemy. Although he was not on the faculty appointments committee that year, he was a powerful and influential professor adamantly opposed to what he thought was an attempt to force the school to adopt hiring quotas. He had fought against such quotas when he was the Solicitor General of the United States.

In the winter of 1985, Charles Fried left the teaching job he'd held at Harvard Law since 1961 to become deputy solicitor general during Ronald Reagan's second term, and four months later he was appointed solicitor general. He was a moderate, or a "fancy-pants neocon," as he called himself, compared to Attorney General Edwin Meese III and Assistant Attorney General for Civil Rights (later Counselor to the Attorney General) William Bradford Reynolds. But he eagerly accepted a role as a lieutenant in the Reagan Revolution. He says he shared "Reagan's gut-level dislike for the pretensions of government" and his "simple but understandable version of principles I believed in too." Those principles included a distaste for the "exaggerated faith in bureaucracy and government expertise" left over from the New Deal era and the "cynicism" and "self-hatred" resulting from Watergate.

Like Reagan, he wanted to see a strong nation with a "less intrusive government," and believed that the place to start was in the courts, to rein in the judges of the federal judiciary who felt their duty was to manipulate rules and expand the Constitution to redistribute wealth and remedy past wrongs. He relished the opportunity as solicitor general to begin this project of judicial restraint, to return the courts "to the position of neutral and modest arbiters . . . deciding cases according to known rules," even if that meant with a certain "wooden literalness." He saw himself in that role as the "David Stockman of the legal agenda."

Indeed, Fried looked like a lanky, six-foot-three-inch David Stockman, with straight graying hair parted to the side, a small round face with sharp features, and glasses. Often clad in Harris tweed sportcoats, starched oxford shirts, and striped ties, Fried exuded the air of a collegian, though when he was solicitor general he had looked the part of a pinstriped litigator, banker, or politician. There was little outwardly to reveal that he was born in Prague, Czechoslovakia, in 1935, under the name Karel Fried, or that his family, who were Jewish, had fled the Nazis in 1939, gone to London, and then settled in Manhattan. He looked, acted, and talked like an urbane Republican WASP. He had an undergraduate degree from Princeton, a master's from Oxford, and a J.D. from Columbia. He was invited to join the faculty at Harvard Law immediately upon completing a clerkship for Supreme Court Justice John Harlan. His specialty was philosophy of law, constitutional law, and ethics, and he also taught theory, contracts, labor, and trial advocacy. Yet he had never argued to a court before he accepted the appointment as deputy solicitor general. "I've probably taught more subjects and practiced less law than anyone who's been SG," Fried told writer Lincoln Caplan.

He quickly gained the chance to tackle the issues at the heart of the Reagan agenda: abortion and racial quotas. In the first major brief he filed as acting solicitor general, he argued that the Supreme Court should overturn *Roe v. Wade,* the case establishing a woman's constitutional right to an abortion. He called *Roe* a "symptom of a mistaken approach to judging" that "confused and threatened the ideal of the rule of law." It was "an extreme example of judicial overreaching," a "serious misuse of the Supreme Court's authority," and a "prime example of twisted judging." In Fried's opinion, no other Supreme Court decision provided such a stark example of how much the federal courts had become the political engines of the left-liberal agenda or offered such a great opportunity to set things "right."

In the first brief, and in a 1989 case, he returned to argue, Fried acknowledged that the right to privacy was a "correct conclusion from good judicial reasoning." The problem came with the court's trimester formulation, which the Court determined in *Roe v. Wade* as the periods when women could have legal abortions. He saw that as a gross example of judicial legislating, making new law in the name of doing justice. The Supreme Court had overreached and stepped into a domain that was reserved for Congress, Fried believed. A fetus was "potential" or "actual" human life; therefore, "whatever else is involved, [abortion] is not a matter of privacy." He drew that conclusion from the fact that the Constitution nowhere implied that a fetus was a person entitled to equal protection. If it had done so, outlawing abortions could easily be constitutionally compelled. But the constitution never said "a nonviable" fetus wasn't a person protected under the Constitution either. So that left a large space in which legislators, not judges, could choose. His brief in the 1989 case, arguing those points, was seen by many as the most strident ever submitted by a solicitor general.

As for the struggle against quotas and racial preferences "in the name of affirmative action," Fried played a central role there, too. Again, he was worried "about government taking over too many of the prerogatives that in a healthy, liberal society properly belong to individuals and to private institutions." He believed that federally mandated quotas or minority set-aside programs were a course of affirmative action that "dangerously aggrandizes government." Certainly, racial preferences helped make room for blacks and women in government and businesses, sometimes for the first time. But the underside of this was that affirmative action had made some of its beneficiaries feel inferior and somehow cheated the dominant group on "standards of excellence." Fried wanted government out of the "preference business" because the minority business enterprises and set-asides too often degenerated "into stifling political entrepreneurship and rent seeking." He wanted the government to enforce an antidiscrimination policy, but to impose race-related remedies only when someone had been shown to discriminate. Hard-liners like Reynolds and Michael Horowitz wanted Fried to go further and grant relief only to individuals discriminated against, a "victim-specific" and "color-blind" approach.

They had President Reagan on their side, and it was the

president's show, so Fried argued for the much narrower approach. After several attempts to persuade the court to adopt a victim-specific orientation on race preferences failed, Fried was able to pursue his strategy and prevailed. In one case involving mandating minority set-asides for city contractors, the Court severely restricted the government's use of minority preferences. Race-based preferences were justifiable only as remedies for past discrimination, and although they didn't have to be victim-specific, they could be used only when other, race-neutral measures had been shown to be ineffective. Another case held that employers were still liable for maintaining requirements and practices that excluded minorities under Title VII. The employer had to show why such requirements were reasonably related to his business, but he only had to justify those practices that had been shown to have an exclusionary effect, not ones that created a statistical imbalance or disparate impact.

Those may have been personal victories for Fried and political gains for the Reaganites, but the rulings reversed long-standing civil rights principles. In the name of judicial restraint, he persuaded the court to engage in its own brand of conservative legal activism. Not only did Fried turn the solicitor general's office into a propaganda machine for the Reagan administration, but the legal changes he advocated would have the harshest impact on women and minorities. In a panoply of Supreme Court cases, he and his legal team helped the Rehnquist court find ways to let government and private businesses and institutions off the hook, often at the expense of blacks, women, and indigents.

For instance, a municipal government can pass a law preventing the exercise of religious rituals if the law is not enacted for the specific purpose of restricting religious beliefs. In the court's decision, a city wanting to prevent followers of Santería, a religion involving animal sacrifices that is practiced by many poor immigrants from Caribbean countries, could legally pass a law prohibiting backyard poultry slaughters. The specific purpose of such a law wouldn't be to restrict religious beliefs, but it would have that indirect effect, and that was constitutional.

In another case, the court ruled that the police could destroy potentially exculpatory evidence unless officers intended to convict a defendant wrongfully. There aren't too many officers who will say they intended to convict someone wrongfully, but now they can destroy evidence that could help a defendant. And in a third example, police misconduct was not actionable if the officers "reasonably" believed their conduct was lawful. It is well established that those defendants against whom such misconduct might occur or whose exculpatory evidence may be destroyed are blacks.

Fried's involvement in procuring these and other rulings like them angered liberal activist students at Harvard, too. Additionally, Fried had been hostile to the far left and Derrick Bell, though Bell wasn't too keen on Fried either. Although Fried was in Washington while most of the tenure battles involving CLS proponents like Clare Dalton raged, his views on CLS and the law generally were well established. As solicitor general, he held a traditional, formalist notion of the law. Embedded in his books *An Anatomy of Values, Right and Wrong,* and *Contract as Promise* was the root of his philosophy of law: a belief that absolute commands of right and wrong are more important than utilitarian values, such as that one should do the greatest good for the greatest number of people. What mattered was the autonomy of the individual—which was what had attracted him so much to Reagan's ideology—and a feeling of being obligated to the law, which was an expression of neutral principles.

The ideal against which he measured the Supreme Court was a belief that "men of intelligence and reasonable goodwill can come to a fair measure of agreement about what the law is, and that our liberty is more secure when in the end it is to the rule of law that government power is responsible." As his Harvard colleague Philip Heymann said about Fried's vision of the law as quoted in Lincoln Caplan's 1987 book on the solicitor general's office, "For him the law is something that any right-minded lawyer can see."

Like Robert Clark, Fried also believed there was nothing immoral about doing a corporation's bidding. In a controversial article in the *Yale Law Journal* titled "Lawyer as Friend," he argued that a lawyer who chose to defend large corporations had as great a moral claim as one who practiced poverty law. Large corporations and the wealthy were "more victims than beneficiaries of the legal system," he wrote, adding that the middle class "gets quite enough legal services," and "the poor need other things far more urgently than they need lawyers." When questioned once about this view at a public forum, Fried replied that Harvard Law should teach more corporate law, not less. He noted that the Massachusetts Institute of Technology taught nuclear physics, but didn't teach its students how to repair toasters.

As he saw it, Harvard Law School's mission was to impart a certain intellectual rigor whereby students learned that arguments must be sound—and that rigor also applied to teaching and scholarship, through which students learned respect and knowledge of the law, truth and respect for an ability to reason, and how to take advantages of opportunities that were available. "It is not our job to channel them into any one place, but to make sure they are trained to deal with the regularities of the exercise of power," he believes.

Those views and comments naturally put him at odds with the left-liberal faction at Harvard Law and the Critical Legal Studies movement nationally. He regarded CLS as "one of the most important goads" to his own thought, and said he found the CLS professors "extremely clever, very hard-working, and very educated." He often exchanged drafts of articles with Duncan Kennedy and proudly hung in his office at Harvard a photo of Kennedy and himself, near a portrait of the Supreme Court justices on the bench when he was solicitor general, photos of himself with Reagan, and his appointment certificate, signed by Reagan. Lincoln Caplan noted that Fried's aggressive advocacy ironically proved the wisdom of CLS, by "choosing to question, rather than to reason from, the premises of earlier Supreme Court rulings."

Fried's biggest problem with CLS was that "they tried to colonize the law school. I think they did have disciples, they did have a movement. That's not a new phenomenon, it's not a deplorable one. I just don't have to accept it. It was also a situation where the disciples may not be as good as the masters." So on appointment and curriculum matters he usually lined up with the traditionalists on the faculty, such as Paul Bator, Phillip Areeda, and Clark. And like Bator, as events became more "disagreeable," he turned away from Cambridge and became more involved in national politics.

If Fried, as solicitor general, was a shadow Supreme Court justice—or the "tenth justice," as Caplan regarded him, he became "shadow dean" at Harvard Law School after he returned from Washington. Unlike the reticent Clark, who often seemed cold and distant when talking to students, faculty members, or alumni, Fried "schmoozed" easily. He could work a cocktail party, banter with the most conservative or the most radical students, and smooth whatever feathers Clark ruffled. He had a way of saying things that made his ideas seem valid, rather than coming out badly or offensively as even Clark's well-intentioned statements often did. And he was willing to speak out on controversial issues.

He faced a unique situation at Harvard. A number of faculty members, the most prominent of them being premier constitutional law professor Laurence Tribe, had opposed him in several cases when he was solicitor general. Professors Susan Estrich, Martha Minow, Kathleen Sullivan, and Tribe, as lead counsel, filed an *amicus* brief against him in the abortion case *Thornburgh v. American College of Obstetricians and Gynecologists,* when the administration first proposed overruling *Roe v. Wade.* One of the most outspoken critics of Reagan's legal strategy, Tribe attacked Fried for using the solicitor general's office in such an overtly ideological way, saying the government's abortion plea was "unprincipled," "divisive," and "dangerous." Fried, Tribe told reporters, was "hardly a friend of the court." Tribe squared off against lawyers from the SG's office under Fried's watch in the 1986 case *Bowers v. Hardwick,* in which Tribe unsuccessfully challenged a Georgia law that punished sodomy as it applied to consensual, adult homosexual activity. And they directly confronted each other, again unsuccessfully for Tribe, in *Schweicker v. Chilicky,* a 1988 separation-of-powers case involving the wrongful denial of social security benefits.

Fried and Tribe and the CLS professors tried to show mutual respect as good advocates and legal theoreticians, but because they were so far apart fundamentally in terms of the role of the law, it was hard for them not to be suspicious of one another. Fried's tendency to be impulsive, obdurate, and willing to cause a flap sometimes fed the fire.

He was unyielding, for instance, when it came to acquiescing to any of Bell's demands and ideas on hiring women and minorities. Part of that may have resulted from the fact that Bell had sought a faculty vote to deny Fried's reappointment because "his record on civil rights was deplorable," Bell said.

And Fried regarded Bell's protest as deplorable too. Bell, Fried thought, was simply "engaging in spin-control to the point of dishonesty." Claiming that Harvard was at fault for not having appointed a "woman of color" was bogus. "I'm sympathetic to his claims that a black woman's experience historically is different, that they have greater responsibility in the community. But I think the black woman category is a phony category. It's not in any governmental plan as an affirmative-action category. To acknowledge that a group in the population has suffered doesn't mean that it has to be represented in the faculty. That doesn't mean that courses pertaining to them shouldn't be taught, but they don't have to be taught by them. The merits of his case were arguable, but they were wrong. All things being equal, I would be glad to have black women on the faculty, but his claim is way overdrawn and the merits of his protest were defective."

Bell's request for an extension of his leave of absence and his constant harping on the issue was, Fried said, just another way of playing to the crowd, "to make a martyr of himself and preen." Fried got angry just talking about Bell. "It's self-advertising. If you're a victim, the rules don't apply to you. He's pumped up and misused it in the wrong way. His arguments take leave of the ground and take a life of their own. In fact, to continue speaking like this is to forfeit the right to be taken seriously."

Not only did he have no patience for Bell, but he was resolute about punishing students whose protests on Bell's behalf disrupted the campus or trespassed in the dean's office. "His tactics were not admirable—urging students to violate rules. It's become a standard rhetorical trap which one simply should not cave in to."

It was not surprising then that students would feel provoked by Fried, or that Fried would be livid that day in March when students walked into his office to protest the school's willingness to package appointments politically and its seeming unwillingness to offer tenure to minority candidates, male and female, who were qualified to teach at Harvard.

At noon on Wednesday, March 18, just three days before school recessed for spring vacation, a group of about fifteen student activists gathered in front of the door of Fried's office, located on the first floor of Langdell Hall. The door was closed, though the light was on, and they could see that Fried was inside. He was preparing for a class he was teaching later that afternoon. They opened the door and walked in. It was a large, rectangular office with floor-to-ceiling wooden bookcases lining the side and back walls. In empty spaces on the wall hung his photos of the justices of the Supreme Court; himself with Reagan, and with Duncan Kennedy. There was also a court artist's rendering of him arguing in front of the Supreme Court, and a poster of the Metropolitan Opera's performance of Verdi's *Simon Boccanegra,* a complex opera about politics and the rulers of medieval Genoa, Italy. In 1965, twenty-five years after it had last been taught, Fried reintroduced Roman Law as a course at Harvard. Opposite the door was a large, double-wide window looking out on to the shady grassy area known as Holmes Field.

Fried was sitting at his desk, which was at a ninety-degree angle from the window, facing a wall of bookcases. His long, skinny legs were propped on top of the desk, and his face was buried in a book. Hearing and seeing the door open, he lifted his head and saw more than a dozen students moving silently along the bookcases facing him. "Hello. Can I help you?" he said, trying to engage the students in conversation. But they sat down to begin a silent vigil. One student held up a sign reading, "Don't talk to us, talk to Dean Clark." Fried said that was when he realized they were there simply to be "disagreeable." Agitated and flustered, he was willing to talk to them, but otherwise he wanted them to leave. Now he had no idea how long they'd be there.

He hurriedly dialed Dean Clark's office. When Clark's secretary told Fried that Clark wasn't there, Fried asked to talk to Vice-Dean David Smith, and she transferred his call to Smith. "I have students in my office. Come and get them out of here," he bellowed. Smith immediately called Sarah Wald, the dean of students. Wald was on her way to lunch, but agreed to meet Smith right away at Fried's office. Fried was standing in the hall, waiting for them to arrive. Meanwhile, the students remained sitting quietly in the office, wondering what was going to happen.

As soon as Fried saw Smith and Wald, he began yelling, "You get them out of here. If they're not out of here, I'm calling the police. I'm going to report these students to the bar authorities too." He wanted Smith and Wald to guarantee that these students would be brought before the school's Administrative Board, the body that hears disciplinary complaints, of which Wald was a member. "I want you to assure me that the Ad Board will deal with this. If not, I'm calling everyone. I'm going to go to over your head to the university," he roared to Smith and Wald, his face turning red and puffy.

"I can't guarantee you anything," said Wald, who then suggested that Fried let her talk to the students alone for a minute. She closed the door and told them, "Some of you are third-year students. If he goes to the bar authorities, that could be hell for you with regard to being admitted into practice." She told them he was serious and that she would give them a few minutes to think about whether they wanted to stay. She also told them that she and Vice-Dean Smith were going across the hall to call the Harvard police. After a few minutes they returned. The students were gone; they had quietly filed out of the office.

But Fried was shaken. Now he was more determined than

ever to have these students disciplined. They had been getting away with disrupting the campus for too long. Apparently "individual autonomy" stopped at his office door. "It was intended to be offensive. It is a kind of trespass on your space. And because it is an offense, it should be made clear that it's not acceptable. If I accept it, they're just going to do this in someone else's office," he said, describing why he decided to bring charges against the trespassing students.

Indeed, the next day, students walked into the office of Reinier Kraakman, a professor on the appointments committee who taught corporations, corporate finance, and corporate theory. Born in 1949, Kraakman is a sociologist and an expert on corporations, in the mold of Dean Clark. He received his undergraduate degree from Harvard, began his graduate study in sociology on a Fulbright fellowship at Harvard, and completed his Ph.D. and law degree from Yale, where he served as editor of the *Yale Law Journal*. Following law school, he clerked for Judge Henry Friendly of the U.S. Court of Appeals for the Second Circuit, and then joined the faculty at Yale, where he taught before being recruited by Harvard in 1987. He is an expert on takeovers, directors' and officers' liability, shareholder derivative suits, and third-party enforcement strategies.

Kraakman, with his light straight hair parted to the side, his square jaw, and his round glasses, looked like a younger, fairer Fried. However, he dealt with student protesters much more calmly. At noon on Thursday, March 19, a group of fifteen students, some of whom had sat in at Fried's office the day before and some of whom were newcomers, filed into his office, tucked in a small corridor on the third floor of Langdell Hall. When they came in, Kraakman was preparing for a 2:00 P.M. class. He knew instantly why they were there, but instead of confronting them, he told the students that if they weren't going to talk, he would leave. He said he needed to prepare for class, and calmly walked out of the room. The students only stayed about a half hour longer.

By Friday, March 20, the day before spring break, the students in the Coalition for Civil Rights achieved what they had wanted. They had made these professors, heavily involved in making hiring decisions, feel uncomfortable. In Fried's case, they had made him explode in a rage, and in Kraakman's they had driven him from his office. They had sent a message that they were serious about their call for change. That morning, posters appeared referring to a remark Fried had made to the *Harvard Crimson* after the sit-in, suggesting that although sit-ins were proper when someone was doing something unlawful, the demonstration in his office was wrong because Harvard wasn't doing anything unlawful. The poster repeated part of that quote, attributing it to Fried. Below that, it said "Do the Proper Thing." Someone had pasted one on Fried's office door. Flyers alerted students, faculty members, and employees to up-coming class boycotts and rallies scheduled for Strike Day, April 2, the first week back from vacation.

Word was slowly getting out about their sit-ins in Fried's and Kraakman's offices. Some professors and administrators believed the students had handled themselves well, conducting the silent vigils as they intended, and resisting the temptation to get into a verbal altercation with Fried. Others felt that fac-ulty offices were sacrosanct; they couldn't have students just barging in on them. The two sit-ins seemed threatening to fac-ulty members. Still, the students succeeded in keeping the pres-sure on the school regarding the recent appointments.

Then the campus quieted considerably by the end of the weekend of March 21, as most students left Cambridge for va-cations in warmer parts of the country, or went to visit their families. The library was virtually empty except for the few students who had stayed behind to finish their third-year pa-pers or wanted to begin studying for final exams. Hardly any professors were working in their offices, as they often did on Saturdays and Sundays. But Fried hadn't settled down; he was still fuming about the students' intrusion into his office the past Friday. He decided he would do what he had been wanting to do since the spring of 1991, when some of the same students had taken over Clark's office: he would seek to have those stu-dents disciplined by the school's Administrative Board.

On Monday, while most of the student body was away, Fried delivered a letter to the secretary of the Administrative

Board requesting that the students who had come into his office be identified and charged because they had interfered with the performance of his duties and hindered his ability to prepare for class. He didn't know who the students were, and he interrogated Wald to see if she could name them. From mediating protests over the past three years, Wald knew who some of the students were, but she was reluctant to identify them. A week later, once classes resumed, four students would be identified, one erroneously, and the Administrative Board would begin considering whether to initiate any disciplinary action against them.

While students were away and the same day Fried complained to the Administrative Board, *U.S. News & World Report*'s annual issue listing "America's Best Graduate Schools" appeared on the newsstands. For the second year in a row, Yale Law School ranked as the number-one school in the country. Harvard's ills were beginning to affect its standing. Yale, of course, was Harvard's longtime rival, and it already enjoyed a public-relations advantage over Harvard. With only 150 students per class, no grades in the first semester, greater access to professors, and a reputation for imbuing students with a sense of serving the public interest, Yale was perceived as a kinder and gentler alternative to boot-camp Harvard. This year, Yale was more in the news than usual as two of its graduates, Clarence Thomas and Anita Hill, fought bitterly over Thomas's nomination to the Supreme Court. Two other graduates, Bill and Hillary Clinton, were already exploring Bill's run for president.

In the *U.S. News* survey, Yale received a total score of 100 points, and Harvard earned only 94.9. In rating how selective the law schools were in admitting students, Yale ranked number one, and Harvard took the number-two spot. Harvard had slipped in that category from the year before, when it took first place and Yale took second. Also, the survey showed that while Yale's median LSAT score was 46, Harvard's was 45, suggesting that the caliber of students Yale took was higher. And Yale was pickier. Its acceptance rate was 6.2 percent, compared to Harvard's 10.8 percent rate.

Perhaps a greater measure of Harvard's decline was that Yale far outranked Harvard in faculty resources—calculated by measuring such things as expenditures per student, the number of volumes in the library per student, and the student-faculty ratio—in which Yale rated first and Harvard came in fifth. And in placement success, Yale was first and Harvard was sixth. That number was measured by analyzing the percentages of the class of '91 employed upon graduation and then six months later; the ratio of on-campus recruiters in 1991 to that year's graduating class; and the class of '91's average salary. In academic specialties, though, Harvard ranked number one in international law, a field the school was reemphasizing, and number four in tax, a category in which Yale did not reach the chart.

Those annual beauty contests didn't usually matter to Harvard students, faculty members, administrators, or alumni. But this year's survey, reported on the front page of the *Record* with the headline YALE #1 AGAIN!!, confirmed for some students that while Harvard might be in the "right" hands (like Clark's), the school was losing ground.

During the Coalition for Civil Rights' litigation over discriminatory faculty hiring, a group of conservative students made a similar claim, though against the left. Fifty conservative students, including white men and women, a Hispanic, and a black man, filed a motion to intervene on Harvard's side because they felt the coalition's suit was tarnishing the reputation of the school and diminishing the value of their education. As a sanction against the students for taking on this litigation, they sought punitive damages. At the same hearing in February 1991 when Harvard defended its motion to dismiss, those students appeared prepared to argue their motion. When the judge called on them to proceed, though, they told him they would stand by their filing rather than address the court at that time. Their motion was eventually denied, and they never appealed.

That same week, during spring break, another article appeared in the national press, applauding Clark for engineering the latest package of appointments. HARVARD LAW SCHOOL FINDS ITS COUNTER-REVOLUTIONARY, read the headline above L. Gordon Crovitz's "Rule of Law" column in *The Wall Street*

Journal. Known as a conservative law columnist, Crovitz hailed Clark for breaking the grip of "the establishment of tenured radicals" at Harvard. That the majority of professors could agree on four new hires "could signal the end of an era when ideological deadlock meant that numerous scholars were turned down for being too conservative or even too moderate," Crovitz wrote. He failed to note, however, that numerous scholars were rejected because they were too far left.

Because of the "courage of Clark's convictions" at Harvard, "it's safe again to appoint faculty on merit," Crovitz noted. Disavowing any inroads made by Critical Legal Studies, he acknowledged what the *U.S. News* survey confirmed: that "for more than a decade, [Harvard] has earned a reputation for divisive politics, not incisive scholarship." A gleeful Clark told Crovitz the appointments were a "tremendous achievement," something many of the students didn't understand because they just saw four white men. What clouded the students' judgment, Clark suggested, were their own doubts and guilt about the affirmative action that had led to their being at Harvard. "The minority students need a sense of validation and encouragement, with the fundamental problem being a need for self-confidence that plays itself out as, 'Why doesn't Harvard Law School have more teachers who look like me?' In a sense we're dealing here with one of the symptoms of affirmative action. This means this debate could be a recurring theme through the 1990s or until we get to some equilibrium."

Many students read Crovitz's column when it appeared, though others in the Coalition for Civil Rights learned what Clark had said about them when they returned to campus on Monday, March 30. These students, who constituted the bulk of the minority population at the school, were outraged. Not only were Clark's comments dismissive, but, as student leaders later pointed out, they sounded too similar to the Supreme Court's reasoning in the infamous 1896 case of *Plessy v. Ferguson*, which had upheld the doctrine of "separate but equal" to justify the enforced separation of blacks and whites. In that case the court had suggested that the plaintiff only imagined that segregation stamped him with a "badge of inferiority." The court wrote: "We consider the underlying fallacy of the plaintiff's argument to consist of the assumption that the enforced separation of the two races stamps the colored race with a badge of inferiority. If this be so, it is not by reason of anything found in the act, but solely because the colored race chooses to put that construction upon it."

Once again, Clark patronized and offended them. "People were furious about what he said. It was, 'These students are crazy, they're insecure, and those of us who are secure and know we're smart don't pay any attention to them.' This was not the spirit of cooperation that was supposed to be going on at the law school, that 'we're going to work together on solving what these issues are,' " said Laura Hankins, the student advocate who earlier that month had argued in court that minorities "are allowed to sit in the back of the classroom" but "receive the message that we will never stand up front."

Clark knew Strike Day was three days away, set for Thursday, April 2. Remembering the past two years, in which overnight sit-ins had taken place in his office, he wanted to avoid another such occupation. Fortified by Fried's action, Clark issued another threat to students. On Tuesday, March 31, he wrote an "open letter to the law school community" expressing his "dismay" at the protests that had taken place the last few years over discrimination in faculty hiring. "I'm sorry that some students have chosen to test the limits of appropriate behavior," he said, indicating that he would institute disciplinary action against the student activists if they continued disrupting the school. He encouraged "opportunities of communication," such as meetings and forums, saying, "Open discussion—even heated discussion—is far more likely to lead to mutual understanding and effective advocacy of well-founded views." Like Fried, Clark had waved the stick of disciplinary action at students before; now he was prepared to use it.

But this was not moot court, where "effective advocacy of well-founded views" or a debate on non-neutral principles prevails. This was about change—about changing the clubby nature of the faculty, and about the larger struggle against racism. For that reason, the students seeking diversity could not turn back. They knew the risks, and they believed their cause was right. They were still going to proceed with their plans.

On Wednesday, April 1, the day before Strike Day, four students—John Bonifaz, one of the originators of the Coalition and the lawsuit; Julia Gordon, an active member of the Coalition; Raul Perez, a second-year student active in La Alianza, the Hispanic law students' association; and a third-year student named Ashley Barr (who, it turns out, was not one of the protesters)—were informed by the Administrative Board that it was considering bringing disciplinary charges against them for having sat in at Fried's office. Bonifaz, who had faced a similar situation in college at Brown, was dismayed. "If anyone was unruly, it was Fried," he said.

Then came Strike Day, Thursday, April 2. The morning began with a class strike in which more than four hundred graduate students throughout the entire university—including the Kennedy School of Government and the Harvard Business School—walked out of their classes to denounce the recent Law School appointments. In the past two years, the Coalition for Civil Rights had urged professors to hold a teach-in on that day, to discuss issues of minority recruitment and faculty hiring. Some professors, such as Randall Kennedy, cooperated. Others didn't. This year's strike had a surprisingly large amount of support from beyond the confines of the Law School. All of the students involved wore red armbands. Posters bearing slogans like "The Issue Is Discrimination, Not Self-Confidence," referring to Clark's *Wall Street Journal* comment, were plastered around the Law School campus, on walls, doors, trees, lampposts, everywhere.

The Coalition for Civil Rights rallied around its four members, whom they dubbed the "Fried Four." They set up a table on the first floor at the Harkness Commons, perhaps the busiest spot on campus, where all the student mailboxes were located and where students congregated. More than one hundred students signed a statement saying that they, too, participated in the Fried sit-in and should be charged. The Coalition also asked students to endorse a no-confidence vote against Dean Clark on the issue of faculty diversity. Three hundred and thirty students voted to reject Clark on the issue of faculty hiring, and thirty-eight voted in favor of him. The day ended with pickets, a vigil, and a rally in the afternoon. More than one hundred students attended the demonstrations and the rally.

The day certainly met the expectations of the school officials, proving to be another celebration of the "Ides of May," and they were happy the students had chosen not to test "the limits of appropriate behavior." But the leaders of the Coalition were disappointed. Despite the student support they received, Strike Day had been anticlimactic, and they felt they still needed to do something confrontational, something more dramatic that would again force the school and the public to focus on the discrimination in faculty hiring at Harvard Law. They spent the weekend of April 4 planning their next step, one that in the eyes of school administrators would cross the boundaries of appropriate behavior and surpass the "trespass" in Charles Fried's office. Those students didn't know that as they were preparing their next move, a group of conservative students on the *Harvard Law Review* were unveiling their own statement about the state of affairs at Harvard, something that would cast over the school an even darker shadow than its failure to have a faculty that looked like America.

CHAPTER 8

CRUEL AND UNUSUAL
LAW REVIEW HUMOR

When the 1,780 students at Harvard Law School in 1991–92 began their week-long spring break and the campus seemed quiet, inside Gannett House, at the offices of the *Law Review*, life was not calm. Editors were busy readying articles and features for future publication. New 2L leaders were steering their first few issues on their own. Other 2L and 3L editors were tech-citing, proofreading, and revising articles. They were working intensely, but they were also tense. Editors were still upset over the manner in which the unfinished manuscript of slain Professor Mary Joe Frug had been handled, the suggestions that had been rejected, and the way the issue had mushroomed into a controversy for the full body of editors to address. Some third-year editors felt the whole issue had been a waste of time. "Why did we even run it at all?" one editor was heard asking.

Now the explosive matter of faculty appointments and faculty affirmative action was seeping into the *Review*. Some of the more conservative editors had grown weary of watching the students hold one vigil or rally or forum after another to protest the lack of faculty diversity. They saw Bell and his student supporters, their classmates, simply trying to satisfy quota-like demands and attempting to portray Harvard Law School as inhospitable to minorities. People on the *Review* felt "PC'd to death," another editor observed. *Wall Street Journal* columnist Crovitz had assessed things correctly, they thought.

On the other side of the political spectrum, numerous editors were involved in the student-led diversity campaign, had supported the lawsuit against the university, and were active in other liberal law groups such as the National Lawyers Guild, the Women's Law Association, and some of the minority law student organizations, such as the Black Law Students Association and La Alianza.

This created a rift between editors, though the friction was only partly the result of ideology and the CLS-versus-traditionalist split that divided the law school. It was also due to the muddle of race and gender politics generally, which, during the 1991–92 year, seemed extraordinarily confused. After all, law professor Anita Hill charged that she had been sexually harassed by Supreme Court nominee Clarence Thomas; William Kennedy Smith was acquitted of date rape; and boxing champion Mike Tyson was convicted of raping an Indiana beauty contestant. Those incidents made women and men unsettled.

At the *Review,* at least, 3L editors—liberal, center, and conservative alike—had a built-in, institutional, and usually humorous mechanism for venting their frustrations. It was the journal's annual mock issue, known as the *Harvard Law Revue,* pronounced "Review-ie." The *Revue* was essentially the *Review*'s April Fool issue, and it was the traditional souvenir of the *Law Review*'s annual spring banquet, held the first weekend in April. The earliest *Revue* dated back to 1940, the first year on record of the spring ritual. It was hardly an "official" *Review* publication, but it was published under the *Review*'s aegis. It received financial support and endorsement from the Law School, as did the annual spring show put on by the Harvard Law School Drama Club, or the *Harvard Law Record*'s spoof issue, *The Rectum.*

Most colleges and universities have a tradition of parody. It provides students with a way to blow off steam, and the hidden grains of truth in the humor often help to deflate egos, reduce the pomposity of people and institutions, and offer constructive suggestions for improving campus life. Even in this regard, Harvard University is a leader. The *National Lampoon* satire magazine, launched by a group of Harvard College students, is an outgrowth of the *Harvard Lampoon,* which is part of the campus's collective being.

At the Law School, the student left and the CLS faculty long enjoyed the political and social benefits of parody. CLS professors distributed four issues of a mock newspaper called *The Lizard* at a national law teachers' conference in 1984, which disrupted the normally staid event, of course. *The Lizard* looked like a takeoff on tabloids like the *National Enquirer, The Weekly World News,* and *The Star,* with screaming headlines like OH, MY GOD, IT'S ALIVE, and articles such as "Annals of Academic Freedom" and "Notes from the Margin," all making fun of themselves.

In the late 1980s, students published an underground paper called *The Reptile,* drawing on the name *The Lizard.* "We were making fun of them as much as anything else," remembers Luke Cole, class of '89, who penned cartoons for *The Reptile* and the school paper, the *Record.* Cole and his classmate Keith Aoki later published a book of their scathing satiric drawings, cartoons, and poster art, entitled *Casual Legal Studies.* As student activists, sympathetic to the left (Duncan Kennedy wrote the introduction to the book), their pieces were irreverent, "oppositional," and deliciously funny. They engaged in a fair amount of left-bashing, sparing no one, student or professor. But they hit the right harder. "While we tarred the left and the right, we had a clear political mission which was to point out the very real damage that the right was doing to the school," says Cole. Through this satire, these two students clearly captured the pressures of law school, the careerism that flourished at Harvard Law, the hypocrisy of some professors, and the shamelessness of the faculty's power struggles.

Cole dubbed Harvard Law School and his weekly comic

strip in the school paper "HLS, Inc.," where "the latest line is the bottom line." One of the strips, "I Do This So I Can Represent Poor People," ribbed Alan Dershowitz, who said he took celebrity cases so he could do *pro bono* legal work, too. The first frame of the Dershowitz cartoon opened with the narrative, "The Law School is buzzing—it seems that Phil Donahue Professor of Law Alan Dershowitz is moonlighting again." Below that caption was a drawing of a familiar scene: Dershowitz appearing on "Nightline," telling interviewer Ted Koppel, "That's right, Ted, I'm opening a deli." The next frame read, "Yes, it's Harvard Square's latest overpriced eatery, drawing its cuisine from former clients," and pictured below that was a building with a giant sign, "Dersh's Deli, and Legal Service to the Rich, Famous, and Book-worthy." Indeed, many Harvard Square restaurants were too pricy for students. Dershowitz in fact opened and later closed a Jewish deli at the Square, and he was chided for choosing high-profile clients like socialite Claus Von Bülow, whose story he turned into the bestseller *Reversal of Fortune,* which was made into a popular motion picture. The succeeding four frames showed what was on the menu: "the Harry Reems foot-long hot dog," referring to the porn star Dershowitz had defended, and "the Von Bülow: caviar and insulin" sandwich, in honor of Von Bülow, whom Dershowitz successfully defended against charges that he attempted to kill his wealthy wife. "And just like in class, you get a little bit of baloney with every order," read the caption in the last frame, below which a curly-topped, mustached, bespectacled Dershowitz was shown saying with a smirk, "Well, it's no secret that I wrote this decision—er, recipe."

Then there was "Faculty Affirmative Inaction at Harvard: 20 Years of Progress," showing two charts of the faculty's hiring. On one side of the page were drawings of the symbol for males, all in white, one for each of the fifty-two members of the Harvard Law School faculty in 1968. The other half of the page was a similar chart of arrows of the male symbol, one for each of the fifty-four males on the faculty in 1988. At the bottom of this chart were two black male symbols, representing the two black tenured men, and five arrows of the female symbol, in white, representing the five white tenured women at the time. It was a stark illustration of the little progress that had been made. Duncan Kennedy hung a copy of the chart, in poster size, on his office door.

Students suffered at the hands of Cole and Aoki's brush, too. One time he drew a mock advertisement. "Are you: Obsessive? Anal Compulsive? A Neurotic Over-Achiever? Competitive? Greedy? Masochistic? Paranoid? Generally confused? Then a promising career as a LAW STUDENT could await you!!! Mail coupon today!!!" A fake coupon was included at the bottom of that side of the page. On the other side of the page was another ad saying, "Are you: Egotistical? Arrogant? Smug? Self-Important? Sadistic? Convinced of Your Own Total Moral and Mental Superiority? Generally incoherent? Then a career as a LAW PROFESSOR is for you!!! Mail coupon today!!!"

Michael Anderson, another student in the class of '88, produced a film titled *Trade School*. A Cole-drawn poster advertising a screening read: "You've seen *Paper Chase*, you've read *One L* . . . Now, see the first movie to tell it like it really is . . . The Anarchist Film Festival's TRADE SCHOOL."

Professors got into the act, too. David Shapiro wrote "The Death of the Up-Down Distinction," for an issue of the *Stanford Law Review* devoted to CLS. This three-page piece was a spoof of an earlier article by Duncan Kennedy in the *University of Pennsylvania Law Review* titled "The Stages of Decline of the Public/Private Distinction." Shapiro cleverly and good-naturedly tweaked the jargon-filled, self-referential style of CLS writing by categorizing the history of "up" and "down" into such stages as: "primitivism," "post-inquisitional de-absolutizing," "pretending-the-problem-isn't-there-icism," "Re-absolutifying-ism-ization," and "Poopification." Kennedy often divided his articles into theoretical stages. And CLS, with its antihierarchical framework, analyzed the world by making "up-down" distinctions. Just as CLS professors tried to debunk the apparent logic of legal rules, Shapiro wrote that "up" was not really "up"; it was actually "down" because "if you go up long enough, you will end up by going down. For example, to get to the sun from here, I have to start by going up, right? But if I keep on going, when I get near the sun I will be going down, right? So the up-down distinction stinks, and if you don't believe me, take a trip to the sun. Only you had better wear something cool."

For the 3L editors on the *Harvard Law Review*, writing a *Revue* of their own was a chance they eagerly awaited. Reserved for third-year students, this would be their last hurrah. Each spring, as the second-year students took command of the *Review* and the last few issues for the year, 3L members turned to the *Revue*. The *Revue* looked exactly like an issue of the *Harvard Law Review*, with the same thick tan cover, the same paper stock, the same typefaces, and the same layout. The *Revue*, however, mocked articles that had appeared during the preceding school year, especially the driest, longest, most erudite, or technical. Those articles served as hooks on which to hang footnotes. Just like a normal issue, the *Revue* was loaded with footnotes. Only these footnotes were fictionalized, and they contained mainly inside jokes and spoofs of editors' idiosyncrasies, pokes at the Law School and professors, and some political barbs. "It is meant to be a pinprick at the bloated balloon of *Law Review* pretensions," observed David Von Drehle, Boston correspondent of *The Washington Post*.

During the 1992 spring break, third-year editors were putting the finishing touches on several *Revue* articles. Although any third-year editor could participate in writing the *Revue*, it was obvious from who and what had been selected to be parodied that conservative editors were dominating the exercise. And it appeared that retribution was what they wanted. For example, they had selected Professor Charles Ogletree, who had written in the Supreme Court issue, apparently to get back at him for his role as counsel for Anita Hill; and Richard Kahlenberg, an alumnus whose book *Broken Contract* criticized Harvard Law School for preparing students to be corporate lawyers. And they elected to write a takeoff of Mary Joe Frug's piece in retaliation for having to abandon "traditional editorial policy" for a piece of feminist propaganda containing profanity.

Other 3L editors weren't surprised that Mary Joe Frug's article was picked to be spoofed. Janis Kestenbaum remembered someone at the planning meeting for the 1992 *Revue* saying, "Oh, we have to do one on the Mary Joe Frug piece." "We almost expected it because of the fact that it was controversial. At the meeting, a lot of people talked about it," relishing the jokes they might want to spin off it. Once the ideas were agreed on, interested editors were assigned to write various articles, and went off and did them. Then a computer file was opened for 3L editors to write a footnote or two or three, or to edit or add something to an article. It was all done quickly, mostly from the end of February to the end of March.

Carol Platt also vividly remembered that planning session, an open meeting on February 13 for any 3L editors interested in working on the *Revue;* it was her birthday, but she stopped in on this meeting to find out what her co-editors had in mind for the *Revue.* She didn't like what she saw. She was willing to live with articles and footnotes that had a little sting. She understood that the nature of the *Revue* was "sort of like *Mad* magazine," but she thought some of the things that were being suggested were too hurtful. What was supposed to be a well-meaning way to poke fun at people who tended to take themselves and everything else far too seriously was turning into a forum for angry men to express their hatred venomously and antagonistically, she remembered.

Other liberal editors, however, such as Books and Commentary chiefs Edith Ramirez and Janis Kestenbaum, seemed willing to live with what jabs the conservatives gave if the conservatives didn't touch what they wrote. Platt left the meeting unhappy because the editors had tacitly agreed on an "I won't touch your dirty stuff if you don't touch mine" attitude. "I think there is a difference between pinpricks and a sledgehammer. Poking fun is one thing, deliberately stinging is another," said a disgruntled Platt. But she let the matter rest because enough other editors, far more liberal than she, were willing to go along with writing the *Revue* under those terms.

Second-year law student Rebecca Eisenberg was in Gannett House on those late nights during the spring break, when the 3L's were putting the last flourishes on the *Revue.* At three o'clock in the morning she used to hear them banging on the floor and laughing hysterically in the room above her. She was worried the editors were getting out of hand. Because she was at the *Law Review* constantly, she got to see who was writing the *Revue*. When she saw that the authors included several of the most outspoken conservative 3L males, she feared she might be one of their targets, and she was right. Eisenberg had irked a number of the conservative editors. Then again, she felt they had hurt her, too.

To the conservatives on the *Review,* Rebecca Eisenberg was a California "valley girl," a princess who whined and was intellectually a lightweight. Actually, the only thing "California" about her was that she had gone to college at Stanford, in Palo Alto, just outside of San Francisco, and had majored in psychology, a subject area not perceived as rigorous as, say, political science, history, or philosophy. In fact, she was a Phi Beta Kappa graduate who hit home runs on her LSATs.

A stocky woman with bleached-blond hair and a gravelly voice that rose to a high pitch on certain words, Eisenberg exuded a carefree style. She rode her mountain bicycle everywhere, dressed casually, and didn't seemed to study very hard. Compared to many of the other women students at the law school, who wore crisp, neat outfits, like those in the catalogs of L.L. Bean or Talbot's, and had a refined New England air about them, Eisenberg seemed out of place.

"I'm no fool," she would tell skeptics, and at Harvard Law School, she found that she frequently needed to remind her classmates of that. Her first year was a great disappointment for her. She saw from the cases she read, the opinions written almost exclusively by men, and the few women teachers she had, how small a voice women had in the legal profession and in the law, and how little law had anything to do with her experiences and her life. She felt that few of her peers took her seriously or considered her intelligent because she was a woman and because she was blond. She was shocked; she'd always taken pride in her accomplishments and had never considered herself an unintelligent person. She was someone to whom other people often listened. "I don't think I was ever thought of as anything but highly intelligent until I got here, when I felt that people were just dismissing my point of view constantly, based upon the way they stereotyped me," she recalled.

She was so discouraged with the law school that she almost didn't try out for the *Law Review* at the end of her first year. But then she decided to dive in, and she made it. Her attitude might explain why the percentage of women who applied for the *Review* was lower than the percentage they made up of each class. For instance, at the time, 45 percent of Harvard Law students were women, whereas only 25 percent of the members of the *Review* were women. In the 3L crop of editors, the class of '92, ten out of forty-four editors were women, approximately 23 percent. In her class of '93, fifteen of forty-one editors, or 37 percent, were women, an improvement.

Once on board the *Review,* however, her situation didn't improve; it seemed to be a repetition of her negative experience in her first year. She overheard deprecating comments about women. At the January meeting where the language in the original Mary Joe Frug piece was debated, she heard one male editor disparage the women editors' outspokenness by saying it was "the best argument against the Nineteenth Amendment [he had] ever seen." He eventually apologized publicly to the staff. Another editor once remarked that "rape was the price that women pay for freedom." Several men on the *Review* told her "that rape is something women make up," she said. Other male editors disregarded her editing suggestions. And even though she received an A in the law of corporate taxation, perhaps the most difficult course in the Law School curriculum, younger editors sought out other male editors in her class for advice on how to do well in the course. She felt that a lot of the work she put into the *Law Review* was simply disregarded. On the other hand, she wasn't an angel to be around or to work with. She had a temper and liked to make excuses for why she couldn't do something, which annoyed some of her 3L editors.

Little by little, as those incidents mounted, Eisenberg was becoming a staunch feminist, something she had never before considered herself to be. She had been assigned to edit professor Ruth Colker's accompanying piece to Mary Joe Frug's article, which critiqued the work from a lesbian perspective. She found working on Colker's piece challenging. It prompted her to venture into the feminist library of the Women's Law Association, and in the comfortable environment of feminist novels, cookbooks, and works of art, she painstakingly checked sources, analyzed arguments, and tightened prose. She had also enrolled in a class in feminism, and reading Susan Faludi's 1991 feminist work *Backlash: The Undeclared War Against American Women* inspired her to want to review the book for a future issue of the *Review*.

As her consciousness rose, however, she too experienced a backlash. Thinking that she might want to teach law someday, she applied to clerk for several California federal district and appellate court judges, almost a prerequisite for the job. She interviewed with fourteen judges and made several trips to California. By March, nothing had come through for her. A friend told her why. It seemed that certain male 3L editors had called clerks of judges with whom she'd interviewed to tell them not to hire her because she was a feminist. One conservative editor told her no one had called those clerks to "expose" her as a feminist and to sabotage her chances. What had happened, this editor said, was that someone had merely overheard a male editor talking to a friend who was a clerk to one of the judges to which Eisenberg had applied; when the clerk had asked the editor what he knew about Rebecca, the editor had told him she was a liberal.

Indeed, she had applied to clerk for some politically and judicially conservative judges, and several conservative editors thought she was being disingenuous. But Eisenberg was not a "liberal" or a "conservative." Yes, she was a feminist, but in no way was she an unabashed liberal. She didn't favor short prison terms for people who committed violent crimes. In fact, she was in favor of long terms. She didn't completely disapprove of the death penalty, although she thought it was administered unfairly against blacks. She wasn't absolutely pro free speech. Those so-called liberal stances she just didn't agree with. For that reason, she applied to some conservative judges. "I didn't, like, feel it was that big of a deal to uphold a huge sentence. To some people that would be a big deal, to me it really wouldn't

be. Certainly, I'm also very tough on issues like sexual harassment that a lot of conservative judges aren't," she said later.
The judges she really wanted to clerk for, such as federal appeals
court judges Patricia Wald and Ruth Bader Ginsburg, usually
had their pick of editors-in-chief and high-ranking officers of
law reviews not only from Harvard but from Yale, Stanford,
Columbia, Michigan, and other top schools.

Whether the editors "called" the judges or simply "told"
judges' clerks about her when asked, she believed that she was
the victim of a "clerkship conspiracy," as she and some of her
women friends called it. It distressed her gravely. "I personally
didn't want to believe it, and I still don't want to believe it,"
she said, noting that she had investigated the matter and talked
to other editors who had specifically overheard those phone
conversations. Something else depressed her: the way an editor
assigned to oversee her book review of *Backlash* fought against
her. She and this editor, Adrian Vermeule, who was also vice-
president of the conservative Federalist Society, didn't get
along. On this project, specifically, he disagreed with her desire
to contribute to feminist scholarship, and with her method. She
resented having to persuade him the book was important from
a "legal standpoint." She wanted to write about "theory"; he
wanted her to write about "law." She wanted to discuss "policy"; he wanted her to talk about "cases." Determined to write
something publishable, she stayed at Gannett House day and
night, even through her spring break, working on her book
review.

Of all the editors she saw working on the *Revue* while she
was holed up at Gannett House, she most disliked a supervising
editor named Craig Coben. Coben wasn't a crazy right-wing
ideologue, but he held strong conservative views and had a deep
libertarian streak. On the *Law Review,* where he was one of
the hardest workers, he supported the publication of the unfinished manuscript by Mary Joe Frug and did not vote for the
suggestion that a disclaimer be added to warn readers that they
might find some of the language offensive. He had opposed
Emily Schulman, the second-year editor elected to succeed David Ellen as president of the *Review,* and the third woman to

ever hold that position. Mostly, he was seen as a kind of insensitive, tactless, "I'm going to be master of the universe" kind of male. "He's a bull in a china shop," said one editor.

Dark and handsome, with thick, brown, curly hair and furry eyebrows, Coben had spent part of his youth in Livingston, New Jersey, where his father was a partner with a predominantly Jewish law firm. Education was important to his family. Both of his brothers had graduated from elite colleges, Harlan from Amherst, and Lawrence from Harvard. Harlan was the author of two novels, *Miracle Cure* and *Play Dead*. Craig had attended high school at Phillips Exeter Academy and had gone to Yale for college. At Yale he had been on the lightweight crew team in his freshman year, but had devoted more time to the debating association. He was also a member of Hillel, a Jewish students' association. In his senior year, his father had died at age fifty-nine, but Craig had still managed to graduate Phi Beta Kappa.

When he reached his last semester at Harvard in the spring of 1992, he faced a bright future. He had won a highly coveted clerkship to Judge Douglas Ginsburg (no relation to Supreme Court Justice Ruth Bader Ginsburg) of the prestigious Court of Appeals for the D.C. Circuit. And he would be graduating *magna cum laude*. Now he could sit back, relax, and have fun on the *Revue*.

As Eisenberg witnessed those late nights at Gannett House, the self-selected editors who decided to write the 1991–92 *Revue* acted as if they owned the *Harvard Law Review,* as if it were their playhouse. They felt they were free to get back at everyone—the liberal 3L's, the "PC" editors, the whiny 2L's—and to brag about how smart, macho, and destined to be great lawyers they were. Eisenberg peeked at a few footnotes and was dismayed at how mean-spirited and juvenile some of the things being said were.

One night, Eisenberg confronted Coben about the *Revue.* She had read old issues, and had concluded that the tradition was cruel, unnecessary, and a waste of *Law Review* time and money. She expressed that to Coben, saying she didn't think that kind of humor was funny, and that she wasn't alone; a couple of other people who had seen some of the *Revue* were also worried they were being too malicious. Coben didn't say much. Then, a few days later, he pulled her aside, into the treasurer's office. "Rebecca, I know you're really upset about the *Revue*. Let me just tell you that you're not the only one who gets ripped upon, everybody gets ripped upon," she remembered Coben saying to reassure her.

"Well, Craig, I just want to let you know I disapprove of what you're doing. I don't care if it's only ripping upon me or ripping on everyone but me—I think what you're doing is a lame waste of *Law Review* money that's only going to be harmful when it comes out. That's my point of view," she retorted.

"I think you might be unhappy with the final result," he conceded. But that hardly consoled her.

"If I'm unhappy with the final result, I'm not going to be quiet about that. You'll hear about it," she promised him. Eisenberg was good at throwing fits. She'd thrown them before and was more than willing to do so again. Before graduation came, she would have a chance to make good on her threat.

She didn't see the final product, though, until the first weekend in April at the spring banquet.

Carol Platt planned to tell the males contributing to the *Revue* to tone down their cracks, too. But she saw that some of the liberal, "feminist" women 3L's were laughing at the jokes, including those about the Frug piece, so she decided not to say anything. "If everyone, including the women who were committed to getting the original [Mary Joe Frug] piece published, thinks it's okay, then I am just being a prude," she thought.

A male editor named Mark Harris also had qualms about the *Revue*. Just before classes recessed for vacation, Harris called outgoing president David Ellen to ask him to read galley proofs of the *Revue*. Harris, a friend of Ellen's, had worked on some of the spoof articles, and he wanted David to read it to make sure the inside jokes weren't too hard on anyone. The condition was that Ellen could only offer feedback; he couldn't step in and make revisions. Ellen had stayed away from the production of the *Revue* because he understood that as president of the volume of the *Review* being spoofed, he was going to be the butt of at least one of the articles. He figured he would be teased about his "slightly casual attire" and his "hyperactive" editing. Getting roasted in the *Revue* was just another part of being president of the *Harvard Law Review*, and he would take his lumps.

Still, he agreed to read a draft of the *Revue*, and took it with him to Montana, where he spent his spring vacation. Some of the jokes and spoofs offended him, though when he returned to Cambridge, he called his friend Harris back and suggested only a few minor changes. He had agreed he wouldn't intervene, and didn't assert himself further. Like Eisenberg and Platt, he didn't see the *Revue* again until April 4, the night of the spring banquet.

Although Ellen was no longer in charge of the *Review*, he says he had the moral authority to warn, "If you publish this, you're committing a crime against humanity." He never said that. Others whose instincts told them some of the editors were going overboard didn't forcefully try to stop it either. And those editors were concentrating on the footnotes, not the spoof articles, to protect their own reputations. Yet knowing how opposed some of those editors were, the editors in command of the *Revue* went ahead with it anyway. It wouldn't be until after the banquet that people inside and outside of Gannett House realized how damaging the 1992 *Revue* issue really was.

Of all the receptions and dinners hosted at Harvard Law School, the *Harvard Law Review* spring banquet was the most celebrated affair of the year. Like so much at Harvard and at the *Review*, the banquet itself was filled with traditions, rituals, and a rich history. Except for the dinner commemorating the *Review*'s one hundredth anniversary in 1987, all the *Review* banquets since 1949 have been held at the Harvard Club, in downtown Boston. All have been black-tie affairs, and with a few exceptions, they have occurred on the first weekend in April, a time when Cambridge springs into bloom. It is a dinner in honor of the changing of the guard, to celebrate the elections held earlier in February, when few people want to brave a New England winter to venture to Cambridge. It was the outgoing president's evening, at which the baton was formally passed to the new president.

What made this such a distinguished event was that over the years some of the most esteemed and distinguished members of the bench, the bar, Congress, business, and even the media have attended or addressed the banquet: most came from the roster of the *Review*'s former members. Therefore it was not unusual to see or hear at the banquet Supreme Court justices, federal appeals judges, congressmen, senators, diplomats, writers, and entertainers. Each 3L class looked for the biggest name in law it could draw to be the keynote speaker. And they voted on a member of the faculty to be the toastmaster, in effect the emcee, whose remarks were supposed to be humorous. This was supposed to be a light, festive occasion.

Richard Goodwin, outgoing president in 1958, invited Vice President Richard Nixon to be one of the speakers. In a letter to Nixon, Goodwin quoted Louis Brandeis, one of the *Review* founders, who said it was the purpose of the *Review* to serve as a "force for the fruitful development of the law." Goodwin went on to describe Nixon, as "a man who is engaged in contributing toward developing an environment in which the rule of law can flourish." Nixon declined the invitation, and, of course, history proved Goodwin wrong. But Justice John Marshall Harlan and Senator Hubert Humphrey gladly accepted the honor that year. Justice Earl Warren had attended the year before; William Brennan, Jr., attended the following year; Hugo Black attended in 1961; and Felix Frankfurter was the toastmaster in 1962, his last year on the bench.

Speakers were usually chosen because they were important figures of their time. A panel at the *Review*'s eighty-second-anniversary dinner, on March 15, 1969, included professors Phillip Areeda, Richard Cooper, Lewis Sargentich, and William Kunstler, defender of the Chicago Seven protesters at the 1968 Democratic convention in Chicago. That same year, 1969, wives and dates were invited for the first time. Until then, the event, like much of the *Review*, had been an all-male institution.

Ken Kesey, the author of *One Flew Over the Cuckoo's Nest*, gave the keynote speech in 1980, a few years after the film version of his book, starring Jack Nicholson, won major Academy Awards. The following year, the *Review* was supposed to get actor Walter Matthau for the banquet. Managing editor Edward Schallert's father was the president of the Screen Actors Guild and had made the arrangements. But Matthau was filming a movie at the time, and had hurt his back. So actor William Windom, who later became a regular on the television series "Murder, She Wrote," stood in for Matthau. "We were all looking forward to seeing Walter Matthau, and when we saw William Windom, everyone was asking, 'Who is he?' " recalled a member of the *Review*'s business office. Speakers in the early-to-mid-1980s included Massachusetts congressman Barney Frank, class of '77; Massachusetts Senator Paul Tsongas, and Yale Law School dean Guido Calabresi.

No previous banquet had been as grand as the one hundredth anniversary dinner, held on April 11, 1987, at the Copley Plaza hotel in downtown Boston. More than nine hundred people attended. Justice William Brennan, Jr., was scheduled to deliver the keynote address, and the eighty-year-old justice was at the banquet. But he was unable to deliver his address because of a bad cold. Paul Freund, Harvard's senior constitutional scholar, gave the opening remarks, and a panel of five prominent *Review* alumni addressed the guests.

On that panel were Erwin Griswold, former solicitor general and Harvard Law School dean; William T. Coleman, former secretary of transportation in the Ford administration; Elliot Richardson, former secretary of HEW, secretary of defense, and U.S. attorney general in the Nixon administration; Joseph Flom, founder of one of New York's premier mergers and acquisitions firms, Skadden, Arps, Slate, Meagher & Flom; and Susan Estrich, a professor at the Law School and the first woman president of the *Review*. Professor Lance Liebman was the toastmaster.

That night, the panel dealt with a serious topic too. From their comments, it was clear the panelists were echoing a concern that *Law Review* alumni were not making enough of their experience on the *Review*, that they were being caught up in the money game, and that they had an obligation to do great things in life, to devote themselves to public service and to carry on the tradition of the *Review*. Someone even suggested that the publication's influence and quality had slipped. William Coleman called on members of the *Review* to work in the public sector. "We need to make sure that the *Law Review* once again has the ability to produce leaders. . . . Washington needs you. Stop asking for $80,000 and go to public service." Elliot Richardson, president of volume 60, class of '41, said lawyers must have respect for the legal profession as "larger than oneself."

Raj Marphatia, the president of the one hundredth volume, urged older alumni not to be influenced so much by the fact that a person was an "editor" of the *Harvard Law Review*. "You, the greatest lawyers in the country, should be concerned with honesty, integrity, sincerity, and compassion. Show that they matter by going beyond labels," he implored. The next day, friends and alumni were invited to an open house at Gannett House, where a huge, nine-hundred-dollar cake, made to look exactly like Gannett House, detailed down to the bike rack in front, was waiting.

Although the 1992 banquet was much more low-key than the hundredth-anniversary dinner, it was still a snazzy affair at the Harvard Club. Everyone shone in their tuxedos and gowns. The evening started off smoothly, with cocktails in the Massachusetts Room beginning at seven o'clock. Places had been guaranteed for 145 people, including the outgoing 3L editors, the 2L's, faculty members, their guests, and numerous illustrious past *Review* members. The conversation was lively, cocktails were flowing, and people happily reunited with their former classmates.

At 8:00 P.M., the students, faculty members, alumni, and guests moved into the Harvard Hall for an elegant spring dinner of broccoli soup, mixed green salad, and an entree of roasted potatoes and chicken Monterey—a chicken breast stuffed with spinach, sun-dried tomatoes, and Monterey jack cheese. The only signs of the charged atmosphere on campus or within the *Review* were the red armbands and red ribbon pins nearly three-quarters of the editors were wearing. Renee Jones, a 2L editor, had distributed the armbands as part of a silent symbolic statement in protest of the recent tenure offers to four white males. "We knew that alumni and faculty would be at the banquet, and we wanted to show them that members of the *Law Review* supported faculty diversity," Jones told the *Harvard Law Record*. "It's not like it is supported by only a fringe element of the student body." A number of the guests didn't really know what it was about, and others wrote it off as more of the usual constant student needling.

As they progressed to the vanilla-raspberry ice cream truffle dessert and selected after-dinner drinks from roving cordial carts, Charles Fried welcomed the guests and began the program. Treasurer Bruce Spiva announced that the members of volume 105 of the *Review*, on behalf of outgoing President David Ellen, had donated $250 to Stone House, a shelter for battered women in Boston. Each year the *Review* made a charitable gift on behalf of the outgoing president. David Ellen had a close friend who worked at the shelter, and this was his preferred non-profit organization. The editors agreed it would be a good place to make a contribution. Then Ellen rose to accept the gift and introduce his successor. He made a few self-deprecating jokes about his editing, and lamented that he was missing the NCAA college basketball playoffs being broadcast on television that night. On the serious side, he plugged the *Review* and emphasized how important it was that law reviews continue to be student-run. That year, George Mason University in Arlington, Virginia, had proposed replacing its student-edited law review with a partially faculty-run one. The idea had generated tremendous outcry, and the school eventually adopted two hybrid student and faculty-run reviews. Then Ellen turned the floor over to the toastmaster, Charles Fried.

The tall, gangly, silver-haired former solicitor general, who had returned to the faculty at the end of the Reagan administration, tried to make light of the red-ribbon demonstration. Pinning a red ribbon on his lapel, Fried said he felt as though he "needed protection from diversity protesters," and analogized the ribbons to the red blood of the Paschal lamb, which Jews in ancient Egypt had put on their doors so that the Angel of Death would pass over their homes, an event now marked by the holiday called Passover. It was understandable why he felt he needed protection: it was only three days earlier that fifteen students held a silent sit-in at his office singling him out for having argued against anti-affirmative action while SG.

Fried then turned his sarcasm on the *Review*'s incoming president, Emily Schulman. "I have to tell you, I've never met Emily Schulman before this evening, but she really scares me," he said, going on to describe her as a "threatening, powerful, and formidable person." Why? Because, as he recounted, with her "soothing speech" and "gentle approach," she had told him that he was not chosen to write an introduction to a recent edition of the *Review*. He thought he was "making progress" during dinner, Fried told the group, until the food came and he noticed that she had ordered a vegetarian meal, one of only four ordered that night. With that, he introduced the new president of volume 106, Schulman.

Fried was being purposely flip, in the usual manner of toastmasters. But several people thought his analogy of the ribbons to the origins of Passover was anti-Semitic and degrading. "I found his reference to the Paschal lamb offensive. He was making light of what many people regard as a very serious issue. . . . My sincerity and depth of conviction were being cast aside. I found that upsetting," said 2L editor Sam Bagenstos to the *Harvard Law Record* the following week. Others said Fried's references to Schulman reflected how men have undermined women in power by considering them scary and threatening, and the irony was that she was only the third woman elected president of the *Review* in 105 years.

Born in 1957, Schulman was older than most students, and had taken time off during college, causing her to receive her undergraduate degree two years later than her freshman classmates. Like her predecessor Ellen, Schulman had attended college in Cambridge, graduating from Radcliffe *magna cum laude* in 1985. She was gracious about Fried's comments, and didn't respond to them. Instead, she tried to poke a little fun at herself too. Partially gray-haired, she talked about how the job was already making her prematurely gray.

Then Fried introduced Erwin Griswold, the keynote speaker. There was perhaps no one who loved the *Review* more than Griswold. President of the magazine in 1928, Griswold received the first issue directly from the printer each month. After every issue for decades, he sent a letter, affectionately know as the "Grizzer-gram," to the *Review* president, complimenting the editors if the issue was distributed on time, and chastising them for any mistakes or if articles were too long and boring.

At eighty-seven, the man who had stood up against McCarthyism, fought for desegregation, led Harvard Law School for twenty-one years, and, as solicitor general, recommended against publishing the Pentagon Papers, a decision he later regretted, was still going strong. That year he published his memoirs, he served as titular head of the Law School's $150-million capital campaign drive, and still went to his office every day at the Washington branch of a major Cleveland law firm, where he lent advice on Supreme Court and appeals court cases. He and his wife, Harriet, still owned a house in Belmont, Massachusetts, just outside of Cambridge, and they had both come up from Washington for the banquet. As he told the students in his gruff, scratchy voice that they should think of law as being a noble cause, not just a business, everyone could hear how much he loved the *Review*.

Unfortunately, later that night, when the guests left and the editors went off to their post-banquet party, the souvenir they carried with them showed how little respect some editors of volume 105 of the *Harvard Law Review* had for their peers, for the hallowed institution of the *Review,* and for Harvard Law School. In the thirty-four pages of the *Revue* were dozens of mock footnotes and four satirical articles ranging from the tasteless to the vile: there were numerous references to male anatomy and the editors' sexual and intellectual prowess; attacks on the liberal editors; praises for conservatism; bragging comments about the male editors' entitlement to clerkships and fancy jobs; and denigrating comments about women editors. What the "pets" of Harvard Law School had produced was shameful. Given the malicious, self-serving drivel in this issue, including how Griswold himself was portrayed in it, his plea to the editors to regard law nobly had come far too late. Those editors most involved with the *Revue* had clear contempt for their co-editors and for the world at large—a rather disconcerting thought, considering that directly after graduation they would be writing opinions and recommending judgments in federal cases that would affect the lives of women, minorities, and people far less able and privileged than those they so easily ridiculed.

The editors of the *Revue* made their intentions known from the first page, a takeoff on the *Review*'s normal table of contents. One of the things purportedly inside the edition was a section titled "In Memoriam: USSR," which alluded not only to the death of communism in Russia, but also to the demise of Critical Legal Studies. A list in italics of those being memorialized included Harvard's Duncan Kennedy and Morton Horowitz, Fidel Castro, and Leon Trotsky. At the bottom of the page, in small print, was a tiny disclaimer that said it all: "Right-wing copy © 1992 by THE HARVARD LAW REVUE ASSOCIATION" and the statement, "*WARNING: Contents are highly insensitive.*" Just inside, on the page that normally lists the board of editors, were three groups of names. Parodies on the 3L editors' names were in the group headed "Philosopher Kings." The 2L editors' names were in the "Non-Rigorous Bozos" category. This, apparently, reflected the esteem in which the 3L writers of the *Revue* held themselves, and the loathing with which they viewed everyone else. Listed in a group at the bottom of the page were the "Technocrats," an insulting reference to the business staffers, perhaps the most loyal and dependable workers of all.

That was just the beginning, however. The footnotes accompanying the four main articles hit individual editors. These footnotes appeared as a reader would find them in a regular issue of the *Review,* a reference to a book or article cited in the text. Footnotes adhered to a highly technical citation form and style. In the *Revue,* the footnoted sources were imaginary, and the titles of books and articles were barbs or plays on words about various people. They were written in the usual footnote format. Some editors were teased for being "corporate cog wannabees," others for being "academic wannabees" or for their "noblesse oblige" for wanting to work in the public interest. The *Revue* tweaked editors for "brown-nosing," "back-scratching," and "feather-bedding."

As she had expected, 2L editor Rebecca Eisenberg was referred to in at least five footnotes, and was ridiculed especially hard. One footnote read:

See Eisenberg, *Have the 3Ls Been Telling the Judges I'm Liberal??!,* 105 J. IMAGINED CLERKSHIP CONSPIRACIES 746 (1992). . . .

Another said:

See Eisenberg, *Gee, Judge Kozinski, This Poker Stuff Is Neat!,* 105 J. PEROXIDE AND EMPTY SPACE 42 (1992) (providing His Honor with immediate inspiration for a rousing round of "dumb blond" jokes).

Almost all the women editors mentioned in footnotes were described in relation to their looks or clothes or watching TV:

See Riles, *Every Day is Halloween,* 105 GHOULISH GARB L.J. 100 (1992) (scaring little children away from Gannett House).

Compare Riles, *Yes, I Did Pay for This Dress,* 105 ALLSTON BEAT $13.95 (1992) (voted best dressed by Popular Mechanics magazine) *with* Platt, *Yes I Did Pay a Lot for This Dress,* 105 HERMES $459.99 (1992) (shopping where her mother does).

Compare Riles & Eisenberg, *We're Not Revue Geeks,* 105 J. FASHION DON'TS 746 (1992) *with* Platt, *Dressing to Impress,* 105 WHAT WORKS FOR MARGARET THATCHER L. REV. 934 (1992).

Janis Kestenbaum and Edith Ramirez, who fought against the proposals to delete the expletives in Mary Joe Frug's commentary, were criticized for their stridency. They were the subject of many footnotes:

> *See* Ramirez & Kestenbaum, *The Books Office is Committed to Quality*, 105 CHRYSLER L. REV. 60 (1992) (getting whipped by the competition). . . .

> *See* E. Ramirez, FROM QUIET 2L TO RABBLE-ROUSING BOOKS CHAIR (1992).

The footnotes about Kestenbaum not only ridiculed her personal politics but were humiliating:

> *See* Kestenbaum, *I Can Take a Joke,* 105 AS LONG AS IT'S NOT ABOUT MY NOTE, MY CLOTHING, MY CLERKSHIP, MY OFFICE, OR ANYTHING ELSE IMPORTANT TO ME 288 (1992) ("Try me.").

> *See* Kestenbaum, Note, *Gender Discrimination is Really Bad,* 105 WASTE OF FINE WHITE PAPER L. REV. 98 (1992) (going where others have gone before).

Kestenbaum was "untamed," Ramirez was "Al Haig," Eisenberg was a "Hellcateye," Renee Jones was "Taxing"; but Erik Corwin was "distilling," Jeffrey Hoberman was "Grace Under Pressure," Michael Imbroscio was "Party On!" Mark Popofsky was "Power Tool," and Michael Rosenthal was "The Natural." In all of these footnotes and characterizations, the women editors were pains in the ass, but the men described in the footnotes, with the few exceptions who took "naps" or registered for "gut courses," were strong, virile, highly intelligent, and crafty. The *Revue* applauded the guys' "late-night wanderings" and "drunken rantings." Although the *Revue* writers could brag about their own brainpower or their own status as "self-appointed power brokers," they didn't tolerate other editors with ego.

For instance, the footnotes written about 3L editor Paul Clement criticized him for having an inflated ego:

> *See* Clement, *I Can Explain Anything with a Graph,* in THE ANALYSIS IS EASY ONCE YOU ASSUME AWAY THE HARD STUFF 54 (1992) . . . *See* Clement, *Renaissance Man: Self-Proclaimed Debate King, Econ Scholar, Stud,* in GOD, I'M GOOD 32 (1966–?) (injuring elbow while patting himself on the back).

Other footnotes about 3L males praised their virility and power:

> *See* Coben, *Team Sports, Tight Shorts,* 105 WHEN YOU REALLY WANT TO SEE THE ACTION AT COURTSIDE 256 (1992) (really showing his "stuff") . . . *See* Coben, *I'm So Smart My Head Hurts,* 105 J.L. & Solipsism 655 (1991).

Outgoing president David Ellen was let off relatively easy. The writers of the *Revue* chose not to center an entire article around him, and razzed another student instead. But they still chided Ellen for being one of those "sensitive new-age guys" and for tending to rewrite articles while claiming to respect authors' voices. One footnote, for instance, comparing him with his predecessor Obama, said: "*Don't Compare* Ellen, *No One Writes as Well as I,* in AUTHOR'S VOICE? WHAT AUTHOR'S VOICE? (E. Schulman ed. 1992) with B. OBAMA, KNOW WHEN TO SAY WHEN (1990)." Other criticisms about him, laced in several footnotes, were more serious jabs at his leadership. One item referred to his "waffling" in decision-making. Another item reflected editors' doubts about his claim that he hadn't seen the explicit language in the Commentary by Mary Joe Frug: "*See* Ellen, *I Really Had No Idea Such Blasphemous Language Was in the Frug Commentary,* in *REVUE CLUELESSNESS* 35 (M. Milnes, N. McCullough, J. Hoberman & S. Lev. eds. 1992)," this footnote read.

His successor, Emily Schulman, was not as gingerly treated

in the *Revue*. Numerous footnotes referred to her as "authoritarian" and the "equivocator." Two footnotes, casting her as dictatorial, read, "*See* Schulman, *Perhaps the Books Office is More to Your Liking*, 105 J. REVUE MANIP. 12 (1992) ('If I pick all the articles, we won't even need to form an office.') and Schulman, *It's About Time We Raised Our Standards Around Here*, 105 J. AUTHORITARIANISM & BAD TIMING 81 (1992) ('Look, I didn't want to publish Frug either.')"

Running through the pages and pages of footnotes in the *Revue* was a sense of anger and disgust over having run Mary Joe Frug's commentary, and vengefulness against liberal editors. Anywhere they could, the principal writers of the *Revue* used words like "f**k" or "s**t" to dig at the proposal to soften the impact of expletives in the Frug commentary. A few of those sorts of footnotes follow:

> But let's not forget that "women are fucked in the workplace because they have cunts." Frug(ed), 105 HARV L. REVUE 1077, 1091 (P. Philbin ed.).

> The author of this piece is not dead. Nonetheless, the use of this profanity may shock and amaze some readers.

> *See* Coben & Meron, *Conservative Men in Conservative Times*, CHAMELEON L. REV. (1980–?) *But see* P. Philbin, THE REAL THING (forever).

> *See* C. Coben, DOMINANCE, HARVESTING CONSERVATIVE PIECES FROM LIBERAL 2LS (1991). . . .

One editor was called a "Chameleon Federalist" because he apparently was a liberal and a member of the Federalist Society. Another footnote referred to the editorial process "evolving from EE read to PC [political correctness] read." And another claimed that an editor's note would come through "because he's been working so hard," and "he's white, male and conservative."

The articles themselves, which the footnotes merely accompanied, comprised five spoof articles: a takeoff on Charles Ogletree's article in the Supreme Court issue; on Mary Joe Frug's commentary; on Griswold's memoirs; on a book by former Harvard student Richard Kahlenberg; and on 3L editor Dan Meron. Given the subjects of the parodies, the 1992 *Revue* read like a bad joke, the butts of which were a black, two Jews, a woman, and a WASP. The *Revue* also contained a mock memo from a fictitious Supervising Editor to a "Hopeful Note-writer."

The satire on Ogletree was titled "Hill v. Thomas: A Comedy of Harmless Errors." In it, Ogletree contemplates whether to accept the assignment of a *Law Review* article he considers boring and doesn't have time to write. Instead, he chooses to write about the Thomas confirmation hearings, where he played a pivotal role as Hill's lawyer. Then he describes what it was like opposing the nomination, by a "crafty Bush" of "this natural law loon-bin Thomas." He notes how Senator Edward Kennedy initially decided not to consider Hill's charges because "after all, he may have propositioned her, but he didn't drown her." Ogletree says that "sensing the presence of television cameras," he "rushed to the scene." At the end, the fictitious author equivocates about who was most credible. He complains that the editors have reduced his piece to five pages, but realizes that he has nothing to worry about, "as long as I have a publication for my tenure file." Overall, it casts Ogletree as a media-hungry professor with little writing ability, who managed to publish an article in the *Harvard Law Review* so it would look good for his tenure case.

The *Revue* also included a parody of a review of Griswold's memoirs, here titled *Ould Man, New Scorn: The Personal Rantings of the Only Guy Who's Known Every President of the Revue,* a play on the real title, *Ould Fields, New Corne: The Personal Memoirs of a Twentieth Century Lawyer.* In this piece, the reviewer asks himself whether Robert Keeton should have been selected to write about the book. "I didn't think much of the idea. He's just as much of an old windbag as Grizzer. . . . So in the spirit of high-level academia, I stabbed him in the back, pushed him down the stairs, bashed his brains in, and stole his ideas—metaphorically speaking, of course, and all in the spirit of good fun." The imaginary reviewer explains why he's the only one who can comprehend Griswold: "If my p***s were as big as my br**n, it would be me that Clarence Thomas watched on all those videotapes. I am that brilliant. Just ask my mother." One footnote referred to the book as Griswold's "cornball memoirs."

On page 13 of the thirty-four-page *Revue*, tucked between the spoofs of Meron and Kahlenberg, was the worst piece in the *Revue*. Titled "He-Manifesto of Post-Mortem Legal Feminism" (parodying her original title), this was the spoof of Mary Joe Frug's commentary. A preface, replicating the one originally written to accompany her article, read: "The following Commentary was pieced together from scraps dictated to Eve X, a telekinetic feminist from beyond the grave. The Editors of the *Law Revue* have agreed to rewrite and re-edit the entire piece, in strict adherence to the traditional editorial policy. The names have been changed to protect the innocent." The author, supposedly dictating from her grave, is "Mary Doe," the "Rigor-Mortis Professor of Law, New England School of Law, 1981–1991" and "wife of Gerald Frug, Professor of Law, Harvard Law School."

Running through the piece is the double image of a scholar and professional worthy of attention only because of who her husband is, and of a sex-starved woman yearning for a man. As in the original, "Mary Doe" begins, "I'm worried about the title of this article. 'He-manifesto' is derived from 'he-man,' and I love men with big muscles." This male-obsessed Mary Doe recalls, "When I was a pre-woman, my family used to take me to Coney Island and I would gaze upon the men in the tight Speedos. It was then that I realized how phallocentric society had become. Yet I would eat Coney Island hot dogs at Nathan's. I ate those dogs with a lot of relish. I still do."

In this piece, the asterisks win the debate. "Men f**k wom*n every day. The male reader may think: 'Mary Doe, you're talking about it as if it's a bad thing.' But I don't mean f**k in the carnal sense. This is f**king scholarship, and my unique voice expresses itself through words such as f**k to convey images and meanings that other words just couldn't convey. If you don't like it, well, f**k you."

Mary Doe reflects on "the irony that I, a postmodern feminist, am being published because of my husband's tenure here." And the authors embrace the stereotype that feminists cannot take a joke. Their Mary Doe writes, "Postmodern feminists represent a diverse group of people. Some of us are intellectuals. Many are politically committed. Most of us are disillusioned. Others are just plain horny. But there is one thing that we have in common: we have no sense of humor."

The piece goes on to tell the story, still in this Mary Doe-qua-Mary Joe voice, about how, like all "postmodern feminists," she liked to "go out at night to hunt down some hunky men and rip their clothes off." This portrayal of Mary Doe and feminist friends (Harvard Law professor Martha Minow among them) out on the town reinforces the stereotypes about the way women treat men and about men conquering women.

Mary Doe admits their late-night adventuring is "degrading," but says she and her friends "all carefully selected wimps for husbands. Like Jerry." She recounts how "one night Kitty MacKinnon, Andie Dworkin, Buffy Minow, 'Nita Hill, Gennie Flowers and I went out for a feminists' night on the town. First, we picketed the local brothel, just like Operation Rescue. Kitty views prostitution as exploitation. I see things differently; like most pro-lifers and feminists, I simply don't like to let anyone else have a good time.

"Then we went to Bob's Big Boy restaurant, and we were having a meaningful discussion on the sexual politics of meat. Our waitress seemed sympathetic to our views: we asked her to join us. Kitty said, 'Take off your apron.' The waitress looked at her with raised eyebrows. Kitty went on: 'Waitress is a sexist diminutive. Come join our cause. Come sit on my lap.' The waitress hopped aboard."

The piece ends with Mary Doe at the Pearly Gates, trying to get into heaven. She is greeted at the gates by Frankfurter, Brandeis, Marshall, Harlan, Black, and Pitney, who apply the Harvard tenure process to see if they should let her in, asking, "Is the applicant white?" "Does the applicant teach in an abstract, formalistic, and utterly incomprehensible manner?" "Is she a man?" Then Al Sacks raises his hands, announces that the admissions policy should be open to everyone, and proclaims, "It's the person's heart and not the hair under her arms that counts." The men hugged her, ushered her in, and gave her a beer. "Things were definitely looking up," she says at the end. Although this piece was written from a conservative perspective, its critique of the hiring process at Harvard Law School closely approximated Bell and his supporters' claims of discrimination.

It was in the footnotes where the editors most clearly revealed their stereotypes, and intolerance toward women. "Sources" cited included: *"I'll Sleep With Anything That Sits Down to Take a Pee,* from the UNSHAVEN ARMPITS LAW REV"; "*I like Wimmin Fine,* from IN THE KITCHEN AND THE BEDROOM"; "SOME GIRLS STILL COOK L. REV."; "WHAT'S A GAL GOT TO DO TO APPEAR IN THE HARVARD LAW REVUE? (threatening to hold her breath until she turns blue in the face)"; and "IN SEARCH OF THE ELUSIVE M.R.S. DEGREE CANDIDATE."

Past editors of the *Harvard Law Review* have made offensive comments in the *Revue,* and have criticized co-editors perhaps unnecessarily harshly. But never before had the editors maligned a woman who had been brutally murdered. Even worse, the *Law Review* editors responsible for this issue of the *Revue*—with its parody of a loved and respected woman scholar—had chosen the night of April 4, 1992, to distribute their spoof—the exact one-year anniversary of Mary Joe Frug's death. Her husband, Jerry, had been invited but had not attended the banquet. If he had, this was what he would have found served up at his plate.

When some editors read what their peers had written about them, they were angry. As soon as possible, they would tell the leaders at the *Review* how upset they were. But none of the editors thought the 1992 *Revue* would go any further than the inner circle of Gannett House. Because of the "insular view we all had of the *Revue*," no one expected that more than a limited audience would see it. "None of us think of it as a public document," said one editor. It would take a few days before the *Revue* sunk in and seeped out.

CHAPTER 9

CAUSE AND EFFECT

Rebecca Eisenberg finally saw a completed copy of the *Revue* on the night of the banquet, which was a negative experience for her anyway. She had worn a red ribbon to show solidarity with the students opposing Harvard's tenure process and in protest of Charles Fried, the toastmaster. During the cocktail hour, she and Fried spoke briefly. He asked her why she was wearing a ribbon, and she politely told him it was to protest his views on hiring women and people of color. He said that to do so would necessarily require Harvard to compromise its quality and the qualifications of its faculty. Even though theirs was a friendly exchange, she wanted to teach someday, and knew that saying something like that to an important professor was taking a risk. But if that meant not teaching, "so be it"; she wanted to tell him how she felt.

But then, hearing Fried describe Emily Schulman, a woman who had broken the barrier that had produced only two women presidents of the *Harvard Law Review* in 105 years, as someone who "scared" him and who was "threatening" was too much for her to bear. In the middle of his speech, she got up and walked out, taking her copy of the *Revue* with her. She went on ahead to the traditional post-banquet editors' party. There, she thumbed through the issue, looking for references to herself, and she also noticed the remarks about some of her women co-editors. A lot of the footnotes bothered her, yet they didn't necessarily surprise her. She remembered how some of the male editors on the *Review* had treated her earlier in the year, attempting to expose her as a liberal to conservative judges, disregarding her editing suggestions, and dismissing her concerns about the *Revue*.

When she got home to her Somerville apartment late that night, she showed the *Revue* to her roommate. He was the one who noticed the parody of Mary Joe Frug's commentary and pointed it out to her. But she was too tired that night to read it. The next day, Sunday, April 5, she went to Gannett House to work on her book review, though she couldn't concentrate. She was upset and hurt and couldn't get anything done. She went back home and read the *Revue*, especially the footnotes, this time carefully. She started to analyze it—what it said about all the other women and what it had said about men, the biases it contained, such as the way men's sexuality was associated with power and women's sexuality was associated with incompetence, and the lack of respect it showed. In effect, she deconstructed it. She went to her computer and stayed up until 4:00 A.M., pounding into the keys her feeling that the *Revue* displayed the sexism and gross discrimination against women that she had experienced at the *Review* all year.

It seemed odd to her that at the same time she was writing her review of Susan Faludi's magnificently insightful book, *Backlash*, she was the target of an apparent backlash in the *Revue*. Then again, perhaps it was not so strange; Faludi's point is that whenever women appear to be making strides, efforts are made to set them back. As Faludi asserts, there has always been hostility to female independence, and backlashes against women's advancement are reactions to progress. Faludi claims that the so-called progress for women in the seventies and eighties was a "myth," but that backlashes occur whenever women are believed to be on the verge of a breakthrough. Here too, the *Harvard Law Review* was celebrating the election of its third woman president. The death of a prominent feminist legal scholar from its own community had awakened many people at Harvard to the reality of violence against women. And the politically motivated hiring of four white males, coupled with the vigorous and constant pressure from students, illustrated the unfairness of the school's hiring practices to women and people of color. For a group of 3L editors to use the *Revue* to vilify those women and to denigrate efforts to eradicate apparently discriminatory hiring was consistent with the sort of backlash that Faludi identified.

The *Revue* contained the same "dime-store moralism of yesteryear" (women "in search of the elusive M.R.S. degree," girls "who still cook," and "wimmin" in the "kitchen and the bedroom"), "glib pronouncements of pop-psych trend watchers" (Eisenberg's "person-dependent" view of time), and "frenzied rhetoric of New Right preachers" ("harvesting conservative pieces from liberal 2Ls") commonly deployed in the backlash of the 1980s, according to Faludi. Those editors wanted to push women and outspoken co-editors and scholars alike backward into the role of good little girls.

Faludi writes that when "feminism itself becomes the tide, the opposition doesn't simply go along with the reversal: it digs in its heels, brandishes its fists, builds walls and dams. And its resistance creates countercurrents and treacherous undertows." This was what the editors did in the *Revue* and how the administration would defend them once others outside the tight *Law Review* circle discovered their parody.

In the meantime, it accused Eisenberg of imagining a clerkship conspiracy and reawakened the doubts about her own abilities that she had experienced in her first year at Harvard, all in an effort to break her political will. The women targets and victims of backlash often mistakenly personalize the situation, giving the offenders even more power.

On Monday, April 6, when the editors returned to Gannett House after the banquet weekend, Eisenberg posted a memo, the one she had stayed up half the night to write, discussing her feelings about the *Revue*. "Although I had been vocal on the *Law Review*, I hadn't done anything to set myself apart," she said. She was taking another risk. She felt "terrified about the consequences" of her memo, though at first no one responded to her. "I was waiting for people to confront me. But no one really did anything. They just ignored it." This lasted for just a short time, however.

Meanwhile, that same Monday, other students were taking their own risks, not in reaction to the *Revue,* because few people outside of Gannett House knew about it, but as part of their ongoing protest over faculty hiring. They were embarking on what was to become a twenty-four-hour sit-in at the dean's office suite in Griswold Hall, their third in three years. Even though Dean Clark had sternly warned that he would file disciplinary charges against students if they continued to "test the limits of appropriate behavior," the leaders of the Coalition for Civil Rights believed a sit-in made the most dramatic statement about their goal. It evoked the sit-ins in the South for civil rights, and the student activism during the Vietnam War.

They felt their protest was "appropriate" because it confronted an unjust hiring record, one in which the faculty was still 95 percent white and 92 percent male. The students were frustrated by meetings, resolutions, and debates that had produced only tiny, halting steps. Earlier that spring, Clark had told them he and the faculty were committed to the "general" goals of hiring more women and minority men and women, and that he wanted to open the lines of communication with students like themselves. But then, in *The Wall Street Journal,* he had contradicted himself and provoked the students he wanted to mollify. Given what he had said to columnist L. Gordon Crovitz, those students were not about to concede the moral high ground to Clark—not even with the specter of disciplinary action looming over them.

Clark's office is on the first floor of Griswold Hall, a boxy, five-story glass-and-steel building constructed in 1969. Hardly anything about this structure suggests that its architect, Cambridge's Benjamin Thompson, also designed and rehabilitated Quincy Market, at Boston's waterfront, into a bright, lively festival mall. After entering Griswold Hall, one goes up a small flight of stairs into a square lobby, sparsely furnished with a couch, a table, and a glass display case exhibiting the faculty's latest publications. A portrait of Erwin Griswold, to whom the building is dedicated, hangs prominently on a center wall. To the left is an elevator, and to the right are two double doors leading into a narrow corridor. The corridor connects Griswold to Langdell Hall, and the dean's office suite and other faculty and administrative offices lie off of this hallway. A visitor to the dean's office enters an outer area, where the dean's two secretaries' desks are located. Their office can be seen from the corridor through a glass panel. Behind their desks is another wall with a doorway in the center, leading to the dean's private office.

It is a spacious rectangular office, with enough room for a small round conference table at one end. Reflections of Harvard's past are everywhere. Hanging on the walls are portraits of Harvard's nine previous deans, starting with Langdell. A stand-up writing desk that once belonged to Harvard alumnus Oliver Wendell Holmes, Jr., rests in an alcove. And Clark sits at a carved wooden desk built for Justice Joseph Story, one of the school's first professors. None of the sit-ins have occurred inside this inner office. The students have always remained in the narrow entrance hallway, or in the lobby and entryway of Griswold Hall.

Between 11:45 A.M. and noon on Monday, April 6, 2L Lucy Koh and 3L William Anspach waited in the basement of Austin Hall, at the offices of Harvard's Labor Law Project, a clinical program. Fifteen students active in groups that were part of the Coalition for Civil Rights had agreed to hold this sit-in at the dean's office, as had been done each spring for the past two years. Only five students arrived who were actually willing to do it, even though when they had originally planned the sit-in they said they would proceed only if they had fifteen people.

They walked through the underground tunnel from Austin to Griswold Hall, took turns using the bathroom, and walked up a floor to the corridor of the dean's office. A *Crimson* reporter and photographer followed behind. When they got to the corridor, they discovered that the door leading to Dean Clark's office suite was locked. They had wanted to enter Clark's office and remain there until they were forcibly removed, but now they decided to remain in the corridor. They sat down on the floor and began studying. Each student was dressed in a dark, long-sleeved shirt or turtleneck and wore jeans or dark pants. Each of their faces was masked by an enlargement of the black and white sketch of the bearded Clark that had run in Crovitz's *Wall Street Journal* column.

Once in their places, the students declared that they weren't leaving for twenty-four hours. "Twenty-four hours of excluding the Dean from his office pales in comparison to 175 years of systematic exclusion from the faculty," they said in a statement. In addition, "The Dean can take no comfort in the University Statement of Rights and Responsibilities, which asserts that 'interference with members of the University in performance of their normal duties and activities must be regarded as unacceptable obstruction of the essential processes of the University.' There is nothing 'normal' about discrimination; the 'essential processes' of the law school cannot be served by the exclusion of women and minorities from the legal academic community."

From inside the office, Dean Clark's secretaries could see the protesters through the glass wall separating their area from the corridor. Other students joined the original few. At their peak they had fourteen students sitting in. The secretaries left and reentered the dean's office suite, passing easily through the demonstrators sitting in a circle on the floor. Vice-Dean David Smith left and came back with his lunch. His office was located on the corridor, opposite the dean's suite. It was not a serious and intimidating atmosphere.

But after about two hours, the students announced they were not going to let anyone but the security police and the clerical staff enter the dean's office. Professor Charles Fried, who had stopped by the dean's office earlier, returned to get coffee from a dispenser in a pantry located off the corridor. The students turned him away. One of Clark's secretaries came and left several times, each time escorted by a member of the building maintenance staff. The last time she tried to enter the office to reach her desk, she seemed shaken, scared, and on the verge of tears. Having to keep walking over the students seemed to unnerve her. Several demonstrators told the building manager that the protest was not aimed at the staff; they were free to come and go.

The building manager, seeing how rattled this secretary was, got angry, slammed the door of the dean's office, and walked away. Other people, however, were moving freely in and out of the corridor, including Professor Paul Weiler, chairman of the appointments committee, some uniformed security guards, and a mail carrier. Other students came and sat with the protesters for brief intervals. On the outside of the doors leading from Langdell to the corridor and from the main entrance of Griswold Hall to the corridor, the protesters posted signs saying the dean's office was closed. Vice-Dean Smith tore the notices down. A cameraman from a local television station filmed the scene until a member of the law school's public relations office who was there observing ordered him to leave.

At about 2:30 P.M., Dean Clark came into the corridor from Langdell Hall. Four of the demonstrators, who had taken off their masks by then, went to talk with him. The rest of the students remained in a tight formation in front of the door, with their masks on. For about forty minutes Clark discussed faculty diversity with them. One of the protesters, later identified as Charisse Carney, a leader of the Black Law Students Association, asked him if he had been quoted correctly in *The Wall Street Journal*, and if he meant what he had said about students' insecurities regarding affirmative action. He told her the paper had accurately reported what he had said, and that he had been speaking from his experience with affirmative action.

When he finished talking with the group, he walked toward his office and asked to enter. The students in front of the door sat stiffly, not moving. He didn't try to push through and enter, but merely turned around and left. Several other students also left. But the sit-in continued with a core of nine students. The students were disappointed to learn that Clark still stood by what he had told *The Wall Street Journal.* "We had all been hoping that he would say he had been misquoted or that he didn't mean what he said. But he didn't. We were even more angry after he came in," another protester said subsequently.

While the masked demonstrators sat in the hallway, facing

off with Dean Clark, another twenty students demonstrated in front of Griswold Hall to show their support. To maintain an element of surprise, the organizers had only told a few people about their decision to hold a sit-in. Yet, once it began, word spread quickly around campus that they were occupying the dean's office.

Inside, at about three-thirty, Vice-Dean Smith warned the students they had to leave or face possible charges by the Administrative Board, or even arrest. He let the students talk among themselves for about ten minutes. Seeing that they weren't going to leave, he squatted down and quietly gave them the same warning again. A few minutes later he locked the corridor doors, and no longer allowed the students to exit to use the bathroom or to receive food from supporters outside, though each time he or a security guard entered or left the corridor, protesters standing outside the doors would throw in a bag of Goldfish crackers, some cheese wrapped in a ball of aluminum foil, and other snacks. At around that time, one of the Harvard police snapped several pictures of the student demonstrators.

Professor Frank Michelman appeared at the corridor at about 4:00 P.M. He said he wanted to speak to the students. As a Harvard fellow, Michelman held one of the most prestigious positions within Harvard University. Far less visible than professors like Alan Dershowitz, Laurence Tribe, and Arthur Miller, and less confrontational than Bell or Duncan Kennedy, Michelman had emerged as a strong ally of the students. Having appeared at almost every rally and forum, he seemed to care deeply about their concerns. The security guards refused to let him in. A Boston legal aid lawyer named Leo Goldstein, acting as an adviser to the students, also wanted to speak to them. Michelman finally persuaded Vice-Dean Smith to let Goldstein meet with the students inside the corridor. Based on what Goldstein told the students about other protests and arrests at Harvard, the students thought they were going to be arrested too.

The year before, students who had blocked the corridor had received warnings all day from school officials that if they weren't out of the hallway alongside the dean's office area by the end of the day, they would be arrested. At 4:00 P.M. that day, they had received a final alert, and four Cambridge police squad cars had arrived in front of Griswold Hall. The students, deciding not to risk arrest, had ended their sit-in. But they had managed to block passage into the dean's office for a day, and had gotten the scene of the police cars pulling up to the building covered on the evening news.

This year, Clark told them he was raising the stakes, and they expected—even hoped—to get arrested. They had already received two warnings. Goldstein told the students inside that if Harvard was going to arrest them, it would be after 6:30 P.M., so the sit-in would not get mentioned on the local evening news. Although the students had originally decided they would stay until five o'clock, they agreed to stay until six-thirty. Nine students huddled together tightly on the floor and waited for what would happen next.

At around 7:00 P.M., a security officer told the students they would be arrested before midnight. They said they would wait it out. After about 8:00 P.M., the students decided they were not going to let the security police leave and reenter Clark's office. Later they said that they would let the police leave and enter Clark's office freely if they could leave the corridor to use the bathroom, located just off the lobby area, and receive food, pillows, and blankets from their supporters outside.

The protesters inside were communicating via a two-way radio with several other students operating out of a command center at the labor law office. Other students, situated on the outside of the doors at each end of the corridor, had brought blankets, sleeping bags, pillows, and books. Everyone was preparing to spend the night, either inside the corridor or on the concrete floor in the lobby of Griswold Hall. A group of students were still clustered together in front of the building.

At about 9:00 P.M., Daniel Steiner, Harvard University's general counsel, arrived at Griswold Hall. Steiner, Harvard College '54 and Harvard Law School '58, was quite familiar with the activities of the Coalition for Civil Rights, from their prior acts of civil disobedience and their spring ritual of Strike Day, and from having to defend against their lawsuit. Students outside the building had been negotiating over whether to let a university official go inside. They finally agreed to let Steiner enter.

Steiner and a security guard arrived in the hallway. One of the security officers sternly told the students that two other students outside had threatened an officer guarding the doors at the end of the corridor leading to Langdell Hall. He told them that both of the students had been taken to the security department's main office, and that Steiner was there to talk with the officers about this incident. Steiner walked into the dean's private office, and stayed there for about forty-five minutes. There had been a scuffle between two guards and a student who was peering in through the window of one of the doors leading into the corridor. The guards had thought the student, the newly elected president of the Black Law Students Association, was trying to force his way into the corridor. They had opened the door and argued. The campus police had escorted the student to the security department's offices, in another part of the university. The students in the corridor worried he had been arrested. They didn't find out until later that he had been detained and released. He would also face possible disciplinary charges.

While Steiner was conferring with the other guards, another security officer allowed the students to use the bathroom one at a time. Some students also ate food and changed into T-shirts left for them in the bathroom. Then the guards locked the main doors of Griswold Hall, leaving the nine students in the corridor and still others camped in the building's entryway on the other side of the double doors leading to the narrow hallway. The students in the interior corridor stayed there through the night, trying to sleep. They listened as a Kennedy School student in the lobby area played "diversity" songs on his guitar. As they tried to sleep, security officers again took pictures of them. And in the morning they took another set of photographs.

From the command center and makeshift press office in Austin Hall, students there had called the local and national media to cover the sit-in. And they were communicating with the occupiers inside to draft a list of demands. At seven o'clock the next morning, close to seventy-five students joined in a demonstration in front of Griswold Hall. At that early hour, the media was already arriving. The student occupiers inside agreed to let four sympathetic faculty members come in to talk with them: CLS guru and appointments committee member Duncan Kennedy; Michelman; Christopher Edley Jr., one of the school's three tenured African-American professors and a strong ally of Bell's; and David Charny, a popular, newly tenured professor.

The professors advised them on what would happen if they were charged with trespassing or other violations, and helped the students draft a list of demands, including a call for a special faculty meeting to be held to adopt a more diverse package of candidates for tenured positions. The students also wanted the faculty to rescind the appointments offered earlier that spring to four white men. Such a dramatic reversal was unlikely, given that the faculty as a whole would never want to admit it had made a mistake. Besides, Clark, the members of the appointments committee, and ultimately the faculty had already decided that breaking the log jam between the professors on the left and those on the right was more important than promoting minorities or women to the tenured faculty. Most of the faculty did not want to do anything that would be seen as caving in to Bell's or the students' demands. They would move at their own pace, and had passed a resolution stating that they were going to make hiring more women and minorities their next priority.

When Vice-Dean David Smith, whose office is across the hall from Clark's arrived for work that Tuesday morning, the students blocked the entrance to his office and he could not get in. "The office is closed," they chanted. Preventing Smith from going into his office may have been their fatal mistake. This time it could be argued that they had "interfered" with a member of the university in the performance of his "normal duties," and had given the school grounds to discipline them.

Indeed, as that was happening, the school's Administrative Board, the body responsible for disciplining students, had called an emergency meeting upon Clark's request. On the 1991–92 Administrative Board were three members of the faculty, former dean James Vorenberg, David Shapiro, and Arthur Miller; three students, Juan Zuniga '92, Dorothy DeWitt '94, and Barry Langman '93; and two administrators, dean of students Sarah Wald and registrar Sue Robinson. At this meeting, professor Richard Parker was sitting in for Miller.

The Administrative Board generally presided over cases of plagiarism, cheating on exams, theft, or vandalism. Not since 1987, when students held demonstrations against South African apartheid and Harvard's financial holdings in companies that did business in South Africa, had the Administrative Board considered disciplining student protesters. Now it was contemplating whether to bring charges against protesters in two instances: the Fried sit-in and this overnight takeover of Clark's office. The latest protest raised more serious questions, since Vice-Dean Smith hadn't been able to get into his office to perform his "normal duties."

It didn't take long that morning for the Administrative Board to reach a preliminary decision that it could "issue charges against the individuals involved, that if sustained could lead to reprimand, suspension, expulsion, or dismissal." Within ten days, all nine of the protesters would voluntarily come forward, and the Administrative Board would vote to charge them all with violating the university's Statement of Rights and Responsibilities. They would defend their charges in an unprecedented two-day hearing in early May, a month before graduation.

As the Administrative Board was preparing its response that Tuesday morning, supporters of the remaining nine protesters organized a rally heralded by hastily drafted notices which appeared on campus that morning. At noon, after their stated twenty-four hours, the nine students ended their occupation of Dean Clark's office. Tired and drained, they walked out of Griswold Hall and joined the demonstrators out front. Though their futures were in jeopardy, they had succeeded in creating a confrontation. "We have reached our goal today," Charisse Carney, president of the Black Law Students Association, told

a crowd of cheering supporters. "We have successfully esca-
lated this struggle."

At the *Review* that Tuesday morning, the reaction to the
Revue was also beginning to escalate. Renee Jones, a 2L editor,
following Eisenberg's lead, posted a memo saying she felt the
environment at Gannett House was especially harsh on her as
a black woman. Jones had organized the red-ribbon protest
against Fried at the banquet, and had been called "taxing" and
"paranoid" in the *Revue*. Tom Joo, another 2L editor, wrote a
memo stating that he agreed with Rebecca and Renee, and that
what the *Revue* had said about Mary Joe Frug demanded an
apology to Gerald Frug, to everyone else at the journal, and to
the school. It was only after reading Tom Joo's memo that Eisenberg went home and read the parody of Frug's commentary
more carefully. In her memo she had focused on the personal
attacks on her and other women editors contained in the footnotes.

"When I went home and read it, I was really sad.... What
horrified me was how inconsiderate they were.... The Mary
Joe Frug parody so very much imitated the Mary Joe Frug article. It starts the same way. And there is no way they could
not have known it was going to be distributed on the same day
as her murder," said Eisenberg. The date of Frug's murder was
written in the preface to Frug's commentary, and that issue was
already in print. "The fact that they couldn't have noticed it
really made me wonder. I thought maybe they did notice it,
maybe on some level they chose not to notice it, acting in willful
blindness," Eisenberg recalled.

The next morning, in the seminar on "Feminism and Gender
Discrimination," taught by visiting professor Kathryn Abrams
from Cornell, several women asked Eisenberg if she had put a
copy of the front cover of the *Revue*, the page indicating the
banquet program, and the first page of the parody of Frug's
commentary in their mailboxes, with the most offensive passages highlighted in pink. Eisenberg told them she hadn't leaked
those excerpts of the *Revue* though just about anyone could
have. After all, the banquet had been a quasi-public affair attended by 145 people, including students, professors, and their

guests. The women didn't know whether to interpret this action as an effort to reveal the contents of the *Revue* to the rest of the school or as a threat to themselves, as they were some of the most outspoken women on campus. One thing they realized: the *Revue* as a whole, and the parody of Frug's commentary in specific, rubbed the work of a highly regarded feminist from the Harvard community in their faces.

The more they studied it, the angrier they became. To them it was clear that the *Revue* was an attack against many students' efforts, both inside and outside of the *Review*, to improve Harvard Law School by eliminating racism and sexism and by diversifying the faculty and student body. "I think it would be impossible to say that what happened with the *Revue* had nothing to do with other things going on. Everything has an effect on everything else," Eisenberg reflected. The women arranged to meet later that night to prepare a response, and Eisenberg accepted their invitation to attend. That evening and into the next day, eleven third-year women drafted a six-page statement titled "We Will Not Laugh, We Will Not Be Silent: A Response to the *Harvard Law Revue*'s Attack on Professor Frug." It included short essays by five women expressing their outrage about the parody of Mary Joe Frug's Commentary.

The banquet and the *Revue* "celebrated violence against women at the expense of the memory of a noted feminist scholar who died by an act of misogynist violence," wrote 3L Andrea Brenneke. Additionally, said Brenneke, the initial debate over the words in Frug's original commentary, Fried's comments about the new female leader of the *Law Review*, and the *Revue* itself, were all "acts of retaliation leveled against women for entering into positions of authority within traditionally white, male, and privileged institutions." Overall, she was "shocked and appalled" at the "spitefulness and misogyny" of some members of the *Review* and the "complicity" of others.

In a second essay, Brenneke repeated horrifying and often-cited statistics of violence against women, such as information from 1990 and 1988 FBI reports that 30 percent of the 4,399 women identified as murder victims in 1990 were slain by their boyfriends or husbands, and that a woman was battered every fifteen seconds and raped every six minutes. That might explain why she and her classmates "had no sense of humor," as the writers of the *Revue* described feminists. "Violence against women is not funny; the murder of Mary Joe Frug was tragic and should serve as a reminder that no one is excepted from the hatred visited upon women. To parody this situation is not only childish and insensitive, it is a perpetuation of the forces that killed Mary Joe Frug.... We will not laugh. We will not be silent," wrote Brenneke.

Marilynn Sager noted that it was "terrifying" that a year after Mary Joe Frug's brutal murder, "her memory had been raped by those who could not face the challenge inherent in her bold words." Kate Nicholson and Laura Adams discussed the paradox of humor, "the power of jokes to undercut," and the power it gives the joke-teller to "say in the guise of fun what would never be acceptable in straightforward discourse." No matter how they are expressed, "hatred and hostility simply are not funny.... It just isn't funny to ridicule a woman who was brutally murdered, or to take cheap shots at her family and friends." Publishing the parody on the anniversary of her death "is not humor, it is an outrage."

Nicholson and Adams also noticed that perhaps the deepest irony about the parody was that in the very piece it mocked, Mary Joe Frug had discussed the use of humor and parody in postmodern discourse. In her original piece, where she noted that "[t]he medium is *the* message" in some cases, Mary Joe Frug added that "[w]hen style is salient, it is characterized by irony and wordplay that is often dazzlingly funny, smart, and irreverent. Things aren't just what they seem." But then she repeated Andrea Dworkin's phrase, "the circumstances of women's lives [are] unbearable," and added that that was "[h]ardly appropriate material for irony and play." Neither was her death appropriate material for irony and wordplay.

On Thursday, April 9, as those women students were drafting their statement and essays, each of the nine students who had held the sit-in at Dean Clark's office received an overnight-delivery letter from the Administrative Board.

They were informed that they had been "tentatively identified as participating in the incident" and that the "Administrative Board will soon be considering whether to issue
formal disciplinary charges." On Friday the four students
identified as having participated in the sit-in at Charles
Fried's office received similar overnight-delivery letters from
the Administrative Board. All thirteen students were notified
they had until 5:00 P.M. Monday, April 13, to submit a statement before the Administrative Board proceeded further
against them.

Friday was a day of confusion, rising anger, and growing
campus turmoil. In the lounge at Harkness Commons, students
were rallying around the "Fried Four" and "Griswold Nine"
protesters, as they had been dubbed, circulating petitions urging
the Administrative Board not to proceed against them. In the
case of the Griswold Nine, the name resonated with a reference
not only to the Chicago Seven anti-Vietnam protesters charged
in connection with disturbing the 1968 Democratic convention
in Chicago, but, more fittingly, to the "Little Rock Nine," the
nine black students who attempted to desegregate Central High
School in Little Rock, Arkansas, in 1957.

The campus was split over the students' acts of civil disobedience, their reasons for it, and the way the administration
should respond. Robert Arnold, editor-in-chief of the Law
School newspaper, *The Record,* wrote an editorial praising the
Griswold Nine "not only for their politics but simply because
of their activism." Considering how apathetic most students
were, Arnold wrote, the Griswold Nine should be "commended, lauded, and celebrated" because their lock-out showed
"they actually care about this community."

An unsigned, one-frame cartoon on the editorial page also
applauded the student's efforts. Depicted was a classroom
scene, in which smiling, apparently eager students sat in all the
seats of one of the amphitheater-shaped classrooms. Crouched
behind a podium at the front of the room were two male professors: a tall, skinny one closely approximating Fried, and a
shorter, bearded one slightly resembling Clark, though they
could have been any number of professors.

The two professors are shown expressing panic at the number of alert, eager students in the room.

"What the hell can you do?" the first one asks.

"Well, there are only two choices, either we give 'em diversity or—I shudder at the thought—we have to . . . teach!"

"Oh . . . the inhumanity!" replies the first one.

Running below the entire frame is a caption reading, "The diversity movement comes up with a *really* effective form of protest for 2L's and 3L's."

In a letter to the editor, two spokespersons for the Coalition for Civil Rights, Camille Holmes and Jeffrey Lubell, both 2L's, demanded a public apology from Dean Clark regarding his comments in *The Wall Street Journal:* "The struggle for diversity at HLS is not about an imagined crisis of self-confidence but about the empowerment of traditionally disempowered communities to help share in the development of the law, the expansion of perspectives and backgrounds represented on the HLS faculty, and the resulting increase in excellence of HLS as a leading educational institution," they wrote. "But we will not stand for your insulting dismissal of our thoughts and feelings as 'symptoms of affirmative action.' "

There was hardly unanimity on the issue, however. In the *Record* alone, one Harvard College alumnus wrote to say he hoped that "diversity would include professors chosen simply for excellence." Otherwise, diversity might as well include "People of Russia who may be indispensable for the future; English Professors upon which our common law rests; Transvestites; Former felons who mastered jailhouse law; Third-world lawyers from India and Pakistan; Arab Fundamentalist lawyers." A Law School alumnus wrote that Bell should say good night and not return. Bell's original demand that the faculty grant tenure to a woman of color was "unworthy of the law school that many of us still respect," this graduate said. "Had Bell demanded that a person of color not be hired, he'd be seen as a racist. To demand a hire on that basis is no less a rabble-rousing stance. Bell is simply appealing to a different rabble."

In the same April 10 issue of the *Record,* a comic strip titled

"Liabilities," penned by student Paul Taylor, also criticized the student left's commitment. The cartoon drove home two ideas: that students could always go to another law school if things were really that bad; so far, none of them was really willing to give up the cachet of a Harvard law degree. The first frame of the cartoon shows an earnest student with one fist in the air and a microphone in the other, leading a chant: "We need more diversity at this law school!" The crowd enthusiastically agrees. The leader then asks, "So how can we empower ourselves?" The crowd responds: "Boycott Clark!" The leader continues, "And if the faculty isn't diversified, we'll take the ultimate stand—*we'll* leave this school in protest and attend another law school!" In the final frame comes the students' answer: "Not really."

A student in the lounge that day met with petitions to sign about the Griswold Nine, posters, flyers, and copies of the *Record* with letters and commentaries about the lack of women and minorities on the faculty. In each student mailbox, the women angered by the *Revue* put a copy of their statement and packet of essays. This was the first chance the rest of the student body had to learn about the *Revue* and to see how badly it treated women in general and Mary Joe Frug in particular. To many students, the insensitivity to women displayed in the *Revue* was closely connected to the issue of discrimination in hiring that students, allied faculty members, and Bell had been complaining of for the past three years. That is exactly what students like Andrea Brenneke hoped people would conclude. In compiling their statement, she and her allies "wanted people to look at the *Law Review* and the Law School as an institution and how it adds to a hostile environment to women and minorities. We have a silent administration and a dearth of internal mechanisms to deal with these issues." The appointments in February exemplified the problem. "The faculty, because it is mostly white men, focused on the ideological battles between them versus the larger issues of the community," she said.

But now the "larger issues of the community" were surging to the forefront. As the day progressed, students and several faculty members were saying it was unfair that the Griswold

Nine and the Fried Four should be disciplined when nothing was being done to acknowledge that the authors of the *Revue* had "tested the limits of appropriate behavior." *Law Review* president Emily Schulman saw that the *Revue* was beginning to affect more people than just Eisenberg or the other editors who had initially voiced their concern about it. Politically, she considered herself a feminist and a liberal. She not only found the parody of Mary Joe Frug's commentary offensive, but she herself had been the brunt of several footnotes echoing stereotypes about the threat of women in powerful positions. Although the parody was produced by the outgoing 3L leaders of the *Review*, it was published on her watch. Because the *Revue* carried the *Harvard Law Review*'s imprimatur, and the misjudgments of some 3L editors had been so glaring, she decided the *Review* had to respond. She called a meeting of the full body of editors for later that Friday at 4:00 P.M.

Nearly all eighty-five members of the *Harvard Law Review* gathered in the large lecture hall, known as Langdell South, in the southern wing of Langdell Hall, because the staff was too big to hold a body meeting at Gannett House. Unlike her predecessor David Ellen, Schulman was decisive and took command of the meeting, telling the editors that the *Review* had to issue some kind of apology for the *Revue*. Other 2L women, like Eisenberg, Jones, and Annalise Riles, as well as other 2L and 3L men and women, wanted even more accountability. Wounded by various footnotes describing them as concerned about "shopping, napping, and soap opera time," they demanded an explanation and an apology. In addition, their feelings had been hurt, a highly regarded professor had been maligned, and the entire body was going to have to shoulder the responsibility for a small group of misguided individuals. They wanted to know who had written the Frug parody, the other articles, and various footnotes. They also wanted to know how it could have been written without anyone's oversight and over the objections of individual 3L editors.

But not everyone saw the harm in the *Revue* articles, the footnotes, and the Frug parody. Eisenberg, Jones, Riles, and others tried to explain why it was hurtful, how it degraded women, glorified violence against them, and perpetuated typical stereotypes. Still, there were some who failed to see the indecency of mocking someone who had been brutally murdered, and demeaning her husband, her friends, and her work, precisely on the anniversary of her death. A frustrated Riles read the Frug parody aloud. Even then, some people said that it still didn't offend them, and tried to dismiss any pain the parody may have caused. Eisenberg was infuriated. She stood up and said, "This might not offend *you*, but why don't you care that this really violates *me*?" It was that kind of intolerance and callousness—if it didn't hurt them, it couldn't be harmful—that angered her most.

What she was addressing was a common problem for women and women's rights advocates involving the definition of harm. Indeed, to many, the law defines certain things as harmful, according to who makes the laws. The biggest challenge of feminist jurisprudence is to create causes of actions and legal recognition for harm to women in areas the law doesn't account for. Convincing the Supreme Court that a "hostile work environment" was a "harm," a legally actionable form of discrimination against women, was a crowning achievement for legal feminists like Catharine MacKinnon. But there are many areas where the law does not recognize harm to women. Street harassment is one instance. That behavior hurts a lot of women, frightening them and even making them feel violated, but it is not recognized as hurtful by law. A lot of men say it isn't action but speech, and claim that women are flattered when hissed and jeered at.

Another bitter point about the parody was that in her original commentary, Mary Joe Frug had recognized "what a hard time women have had in communicating our situation." Again, as if foreshadowing the events that would transpire, she cited a heartbreaking passage by Andrea Dworkin that made that point.

The accounts of rape, wife beating, forced childbearing, medical butchering, sex-motivated murder, forced prostitution, physical mutilation, sadistic psychological abuse, and other commonplaces of female experience that are excavated from the past or given by contemporary survivors should leave the heart seared, the mind in anguish, the conscience in upheaval. But they do not. No matter how often these stories are told, with whatever clarity or eloquence, bitterness or sorrow, they might as well have been whispered in the wind or written in the sand: they disappear as if they were nothing. The tellers and the stories are ignored or ridiculed, threatened back into silence or destroyed and the experience of female suffering is buried in cultural invisibility and contempt.

To the dismay of women like Eisenberg, since the majority of people on the *Law Review* didn't define the mock issue as harmful, the fact that it really harmed a minority of people on the journal didn't make it harmful. "Most of the people weren't hurt by it, so it wasn't hurtful," she reflected in disgust. As the Friday afternoon meeting progressed, and after doing a lot of explaining, the editors were beginning to realize that they should accept some institutional blame. Everyone who had joined in the fun, taking a few minutes to add a footnote or two, or even to read parts of the parody, shared some complicity. So did the people whose instincts had told them the parody had gone too far, but had failed to act. Some members admitted various levels of culpability, and the two principal authors of the Frug parody identified themselves. The *Review* as a whole began considering a resolution authorizing Schulman to write an apology on the *Review*'s behalf to disseminate to the rest of the school.

But before a vote was taken, as the editors were in the midst of this intense self-evaluation, a group of about forty men and women, mostly middle-aged, burst into the Langdell Hall room where they were meeting. The intruders had come from Pound Hall, a few hundred yards away, where registration had been taking place for a weekend-long "Crit Networks Conference" sponsored by the Conference on Critical Legal Studies. More than five hundred law professors, activists, and social scientists had come from all over the country to attend the group's largest conference in years. Scheduled were three days of events, split between Harvard Law School in Cambridge and Northeastern Law School in Boston. Panels, lectures, and plenary sessions would cover a wide range of topics, including gay and lesbian issues, workers' empowerment, progressive legal practice, Eastern Europe, corporate law, violence against women, Canadian critical legal theory, third-world legal issues, housing and homelessness, native rights, reproductive rights, race consciousness, feminist legal theory, legal history, and workplace oppositionism.

Coincidentally, the first session on Friday night included a lecture on domestic battering, a panel on right-wing minorities, and intersectionalities in domestic violence of race, gender, culture, and sexuality. One of the panels set for Saturday was to discuss sexual harassment, and that night a ceremony in memory of Mary Joe Frug was planned at Northeastern. On Sunday afternoon, a panel discussion on political correctness was scheduled, as well as a discussion on "students, diversity, and CLS."

During Friday night's registration at Harvard, 3L Marilynn Sager passed out copies of the women students' statement about the parody. The parody played right into the hands of Mary Joe Frug's closest allies and the people most likely to wage a political and ideological offensive. Many of the conferees were learning about this incident for the first time and, as expected, they were incensed by what they read. After all, having been a charter member of the Critical Feminists and married to a fellow Crit, she had been one of their own. Sager and a group of about seventy-five people were planning to hold a silent protest in front of Gannett House that evening. When they learned the editors were meeting at Langdell South, the group decided to go to the meeting instead, and stormed in.

"*Law Review, Law Review,* what's wrong with you?" chanted the meeting-crashers, barging in on the meeting. Emily Schulman stepped forward. In an eloquent and reasoned fashion, she told the conferees she understood how they felt, and said that on behalf of the *Review* she regretted what had appeared in the *Revue.* "We are trying to resolve this ourselves," she assured them, and told them it would be best if they left. A conservative and a liberal editor, who had been on opposite sides of much of the debate, got up on their chairs and ordered the intruders to leave. After about fifteen minutes, the Critical Legal Studies people exited. Sager, who had followed the CLS people in, was optimistic about the way Schulman would handle things. It was clear that she had "courageously undertaken a difficult leadership role at the *Review*," Sager said.

The editors' meeting ended at 10:00 P.M., after six hours of discussion. Following much explanation, the editors agreed the *Revue* was offensive, and expressed their remorse for the pain it might have caused Mary Joe Frug's family and friends, and members of the *Law Review* staff. They voted to let Schulman write an apology to the rest of the school on the *Review*'s behalf. But many issues remained unsettled. Eisenberg and Riles and several other editors believed other editors had a hand in writing the Frug parody and they wanted to know precisely who they were. From her late-night sessions at Gannett House, Eisenberg had a pretty good idea who it might have been; she and her allies felt they were owed a full explanation and, most of all, retribution. Other editors wanted to see the *Revue* discontinued. And still others thought the *Review* should not distribute any more copies of the mock issue. They agreed to resume the meeting at 9:00 A.M.

On Saturday, when the editors gathered again, the mood had changed. Women like Eisenberg, Riles, and Jones were angrier than the night before. Other 2L's were also joining their side. It was clear that liberal 2L's, women and men, were making this a crusade to get back at the conservatives for the things they had said in the parody. For them, the issue was "analogous to the Contras versus Daniel Ortega in Nicaragua," one editor observed. The personal was political and conflict was inevitable. It "wasn't the 3L's eating their own," this editor added. Still, the 2L's had a "purge mentality," said another 3L editor. "People said things like 'We want the people who wrote it' and 'We demand that they step forward and take their punishment.' "

Not surprisingly, the majority of 3L's closed ranks, further angering the 2L's. "What makes you so morally pure?" a 3L asked. "You're taking yourselves too seriously," said another editor. "You are destroying our community," a third charged. Others felt that CLS professors from the outside were using the left-liberal editors to wage battle against the conservatives. And some people blamed the 2L's for creating the controversy in the first place by leaking the *Revue* to students.

"Certain conservative editors hurt these women's feelings, but some people just genuinely didn't like some of these women," said outgoing managing editor Carol Platt. "No one wanted to do more than cause a pinprick or two to people who had been under their skin all year. It was more thoughtless than calculatedly cruel. Mary Joe Frug was brutally killed. It should have been so clear. These people were young and thoughtless. But there was no grand conspiracy. It was the slings and arrows of everyday life made into this grand scheme of evil."

To Platt, the *Revue* reflected the culture of the *Harvard Law Review,* where people are disconnected from one another and from others' feelings. "Every piece has an author, a primary editor, and an executive editor. Different parts are being read and edited by different people. So when we're editing, we'll say, 'Do you have the Frug piece?' It's disembodied. We've lost the sense that there's a human being behind the words. It's dehumanizing, it's wrong."

That the *Review* was not as much of a community as others liked to believe was clear. Even if the majority of editors were not sexist or hostile to women and the *Revue* was merely an aberration, Platt's acknowledgment of the disembodied structure of the *Review* indicated that there was a climate ripe for abuse. Moreover, she revealed something perhaps more troubling about how Harvard was training its best and its brightest and the kind of lawyers they would grow up to be.

On Saturday, the editors voted not to distribute any more copies of the *Revue.* They agreed to discontinue the *Revue* in 1993 and donate to a local charity the money it would have cost to produce it. It was an idea outgoing president Ellen offered the night before. They also agreed to form a task force to investigate the status and treatment of women on the *Review.* But the 2L editors were still not satisfied. They wanted names, or "heads," as one editor said. If no one else came forward, they were going to petition the Administrative Board to investigate the *Review,* something some people wanted anyway, and seek to have these editors censured, kicked off the *Review,* and expelled from school, if possible. Most of the pressure was on the 3L editors Craig Coben and Kenneth Fenyo, who had identified themselves as the authors of the Frug parody. Coben spoke briefly, saying he really respected women, he respected his mother.

Even then, the 2L's wanted to determine the punishment for those two authors and other 3L's involved in creating the *Revue.* They proposed a resolution to exclude the 3L's from voting on how they would be disciplined. None of the 3L's voted for what was suggested by the 2L's. The 3L's would participate, and they would not let their co-editors be kicked off the *Review.* But the situation was still frightening. Some people feared that anything they said would be misinterpreted. Moreover, everyone had a friend on the line, and they didn't want to see their careers torpedoed. "There was just so much hysteria," recalled Platt. "It seemed like we were all going to be burned at the stake. There was just such ugliness. I thought, 'This is like the Cultural Revolution [in China].' It was just a scene from a nightmare."

Schulman was making liberal and conservative 3L's hang together; she wanted them to assume collective responsibility. She decided, and a majority of editors finally agreed, that everyone who had some involvement in the *Revue* should write a separate letter of apology. And the two authors of the Frug parody would write their own. Platt was willing to live with that arrangement. But she didn't want to see Coben's and Fenyo's careers ruined. "Craig and Ken are happy-go-lucky cynical types. They are not *Dartmouth Review* bitter, conservative ideologues. They did something wrong, and this got out of hand," said Platt.

Other conservatives didn't think there should be any separate letters in addition to the *Review* letter from the president. Indeed, they felt that Schulman had sold out the conservatives. On the other hand, some of the liberals felt that she hadn't gone far enough for them. "I was very angry at her for allowing the 3L's to vote on their own fate," said Eisenberg. "It was unreasonable, unjustifiable. You can't let them vote on whether they're going to be punished or not. I thought that this was an issue for the 2L's, regardless of what the 3L's thought. I thought it was their problem they gave to us. Emily could have supported our motion to exclude them from voting on their punishment." But Schulman didn't go with any one group. Although she was a liberal and was upset by the sexism displayed in the *Revue*, she was driven by institutional loyalty. As events would unfold, she may have made a critical mistake by not establishing her own power base.

At 3:00 P.M., after a total of twelve hours of discussion, the editors ended their meeting. Shortly thereafter, Schulman issued the *Review*'s statement and returned press calls. The women students' packet of essays had reached the news media, and it naturally piqued reporters' interest. On Sunday, Schulman went to the Ropes & Gray room in Pound Hall, where the CLS conferees were lunching, and read her statement aloud. "On behalf of the *Harvard Law Review*, I want to express my deepest apologies for the offense and pain caused by the recent publication of the *Revue*." She characterized the *Revue*'s parody of Professor Mary Joe Frug as "vicious and indefensible." Neither the Mary Joe Frug spoof nor the *Revue* reflected the "official" views of the *Harvard Law Review*, she said.

She said that the editors were "ashamed" of publishing the *Revue*. She described how troubled she was that the *Harvard Law Review* "was capable of producing such an appalling piece of work and that institutional mechanisms were not in place to quash it." The editors specifically responsible for the *Revue* would be issuing their own apologies, she informed the gathered conferees.

The editors' decision not to distribute additional copies of the *Revue*, she said, was not a cover-up, but rather a reflection of the harm the *Revue* had inflicted on Professor Mary Joe Frug's memory. Further dissemination would only perpetuate that harm. She also informed them that publication of future

*Revue*s was being discontinued and that the money that would have been used to produce them would be donated to a charity honoring the memory of Professor Frug. She also indicated that the *Review* was establishing a task force on women. "At its best, the *Revue* reflects an understanding of the need to confront and deflate the arrogance and elitism that *Law Review* culture breeds and rewards. At its worst, the *Revue* harnesses that arrogance and elitism to attack and demean others. Unfortunately, it is the latter that occurred this year."

Schulman had bravely faced up to an enormous responsibility. It was a horrible way to have to start a term. For her predecessor, David Ellen, though he was not in the center of the controversy, it was a painful time too. He was at the Friday session, but could not attend the Saturday meetings because he had chosen to use that weekend to hunt for an apartment in Washington, D.C., where he would be beginning his clerkship after graduation, and he had nonrefundable tickets. A friend of his called him there to tell him that some third-year editors with knowledge of the *Revue* were going to write a group letter of apology. They would be meeting on Sunday to draft their response. Since he had read it before publication, he agreed to add his name. He decided to return in time for the meeting on Sunday.

When he arrived back in Cambridge, he found a message on his answering machine from a Boston reporter asking him to confirm that "You were president at the time that the *Revue* was conceived, written, and published, and that you were directly editorially responsible for its contents." He knew from the sound of the question that he was getting dragged into what was becoming a public scandal. But he hadn't been president at the time; he had already turned over responsibility to Schulman, and the *Revue* had been written by a self-selected group of third-year members. Like other presidents before him, he had stayed out of the way of the *Revue* because he knew that by tradition he would be a target. He never spoke to the reporter. At the Friday meeting, he contributed only a few comments.

"The meetings were uncomfortable. . . . I felt like it was a very hostile environment," he said. He was one of the editors who suggested abolishing the *Revue* and donating the money for it to charity. The preceding Monday, in response to Eisenberg's memo, he had told a few editors who asked him about his role how he had stayed out of it and had only cursorily read the *Revue* before it appeared. He had watched the tension build all week, and said he was "a wreck in Washington."

A pain gnawed at him. He knew he had made a crucial mistake in failing to act in the face of what he called "a grave injustice." Even though he would be signing a public letter of apology, he felt he had to explain his inaction at least privately to his peers on the *Review*. He was feeling badly about the *Revue*, and, given the message on his phone machine, he worried that others were going to come after him. On Sunday, April 12, to set the record straight and offer "a fuller explanation" of his exact role so that would be there "no misunderstandings," he penned one of the most honest and painstaking letters he'd ever written. "I read the piece while on spring break in Montana, found much of it offensive (beyond but including the Frug parody), and called the editor, who had asked for my opinion, to offer my two cents. Unfortunately, what I did not do—and what I should have done—[was to violate] the condition on which I was shown the *Revue* and [demand] that the presses be stopped. I also knew that, while I had no formal authority to actually stop the presses myself, such a demand may well have worked. But again—partly out of some misguided unwillingness to feel myself in the role of 'censor,' partly out of weariness after a full year of sometimes contentious editing, and partly out of plain cowardice (it's not the first time I have been accused of such)—I did not do that. . . . I am terribly and deeply sorry for this and, if I could have a chance to show the courage I lacked that day in late March, I would. Nothing can remove the pain this has caused others and nothing can relieve the sense of shame I will always feel."

Unfortunately, David Ellen would never have a chance to redeem himself. That Sunday, as he was confessing his omission, and Schulman was reading the statement of apology on behalf of the *Review* to the CLS conference, Laurence Tribe, Harvard's most celebrated liberal professor of constitutional law, was invoking Ellen's name, castigating him and every one of the editors of the *Harvard Law Review*.

CHAPTER 10

TRIBAL WARFARE

While outgoing president of the *Harvard Law Review* David Ellen was writing his deeply sad letter of apology for not having done more to stop the *Revue* from being published, and while Schulman was appearing in front of Mary Joe Frug's closest friends and colleagues at the CLS conference, Laurence Tribe was in another room at Pound Hall, denouncing the *Review*. He was speaking at a bagel brunch sponsored by the Harvard Law School Jewish Law Students Association. He had been planning to discuss "hate speech," a timely topic in light of the parody. In fact, the *Review* had given Tribe its final copy of the *Revue* so he could study it for his remarks. Having read it, he altered his topic to focus exclusively "on the ongoing events in the murder of Mary Joe Frug and the *Harvard Law Review*'s idea of what is funny."

He titled his speech "A Tale of Two Cities." One city was Los Angeles in 1984; the other was Cambridge in 1992. The story in L.A., he said, began with a man whose company, called Truth Missions, was established with the express ideological purpose of denying the Holocaust. The story in Cambridge began with a group that was involved in putting out a spoof version of the *Harvard Law Review*, known as the *Harvard Law Revue*. Their mission was less clear, but operated in a strikingly similar way. The parody of slain Professor Mary Joe Frug was, "to put it kindly," he said, "a piece whose thesis is that the hatred of women is a hoax perpetrated by paranoid feminists. . . . The *Law Review* might have well danced on Mary Joe Frug's grave for what they did . . . they made a decision to desecrate her memory with verbal knife-stabs . . . a rape in all but biological reality."

Everyone could see how distraught he was over the *Revue,* especially the parody of Mary Joe Frug. What most people didn't know was that it had made him want to resign, and in the days following this speech to the Jewish Law Students, he would come close to walking out on Harvard. "It was sickening," he said later, explaining why this had affected him at a deeper level than anything else involving the school had in the past. "It touched a raw nerve. Though I didn't know her that well, Mary Joe Frug was one of the most vivacious, life-affirming, and energetic people I knew. I'd see her out on the jogging trail and she'd smile and it just filled you up." As Mopsie Strange Kennedy had said at the memorial service for Frug, all "right-thinking people" eventually got a crush on her; apparently she had charmed Tribe too.

The parody of Frug and her work was another example of hate speech, he said in his talk. The editors were not only akin to Holocaust revisionists; they bore a resemblance to the Ku Klux Klan because the Klan and the *Review* both adhered "to a code of silence." The authors hid in anonymity just as KKK members wore white hoods to shield their identities.

He questioned whether he and his fellow professors at Harvard should be cultivating the skills and intellects of students who could have written such a hurtful thing. "What is the point of teaching?" he asked. "I'm sharpening their knives to stab innocent victims." The fractious atmosphere at Harvard and the message that the student left had been sending about the lack of a diverse faculty had contributed to the making of the parody. He acknowledged the absence of women role models and reminded the audience how much more had to be done.

Having talked for forty-five minutes, he opened the floor for questions and comment. Knowing that Tribe had asked to study the *Revue,* several *Law Review* members, including Rebecca Eisenberg, Marilynn Sager (one of the eleven women students organizing the protest of the parody), and Wendy Thurm (outgoing editor-in-chief of the *Civil Rights-Civil Liberties Law Review*), came to hear him. Reporters from the *Harvard Law Record* and the *Harvard Crimson* were also covering the event. The comment session opened a torrent of emotion and debate. Several women said the parody made them feel further alienated from a school already dominated by men. "We just don't belong here as women," one of the women students said.

Then came an obvious question about the First Amendment: Wasn't the *Revue* protected under free speech? a student wanted to know. Tribe, whose career has been built around defending the First Amendment, suggested that when speech is part of a pattern of deliberate harassment or intimidation, such as where pornography is used to harass women in the workplace, it might be sanctioned or may constitute part of the evidence of a claim of gender or race discrimination. Genuine issues of sex discrimination cannot simply be swept under the rug of the First Amendment.

The free-speech argument wouldn't prevent an investigation into the incident, he said. "If we believe that laws against racism and sexism are consistent with the First Amendment, then I think it does follow that even if HLS were an arm of the government and fully subject to the First Amendment, it would be consistent with the First Amendment to launch an official investigation into the existence of racial and sexual harassment on the *Law Review.*" People inside and outside the *Review* were calling for a further investigation of the circumstances surrounding the writing of the *Revue* and the Frug parody, and Tribe seemed to agree there would be a basis for such an inquiry. The parody authors were still publicly unknown.

Tribe also suggested that perhaps women should boycott the *Review,* saying he knew "a great many students who have refused to become part of the *Harvard Law Review.* . . . It wouldn't be an inappropriate response for a very large number of students to boycott the *Harvard Law Review.*" Eisenberg strongly disagreed with that idea. She told Tribe his approach was wrong. Women shouldn't leave it; they should try to take it over. "There is value to working within the system," said Eisenberg. "What we want is more people who are willing to put themselves on the line." Tribe said he understood how she felt, but "a number of us [had] been part of the Harvard faculty for twenty years thinking things like that," and it hadn't worked.

Marilynn Sager also spoke up, disagreeing that a boycott was the answer. "Although this incident has made a lot of us feel like we don't belong here, I want to back up what Rebecca said. I do not want to lead a boycott of the *Law Review* by 1L's." Reconsidering what he said and commending Emily Schulman for the way she had handled the situation, Tribe said they were right, maybe a boycott wasn't such a good idea.

A man at the brunch said he agreed the *Revue* was obviously offensive and disgusting. But analogizing the *Revue* authors to revisionists of the Holocaust, "while powerful," didn't apply in the case of the *Revue*. Sager responded that for her, as a woman and a Jew at the school, "this is the same kind of pain." Jennifer Taub, a 2L, agreed with Sager. "Did you walk around in fear on this campus [after Professor Frug's murder]? . . . You can't tell me this isn't the same thing as the Holocaust." Another 2L, Gail Javitt, told the group that she had once heard Eli Wiesel say there shouldn't be competition among sufferers. Everyone in the room applauded.

Wendy Thurm lashed back at the man who had criticized Tribe's Holocaust analogy: "Women are killed every day . . . let's not kid ourselves." Tribe reminded the group that it was useful that as lawyers they could make distinctions, but that people denied violence against women existed simply because it was ubiquitous. "There's a kind of slow-burning Holocaust against women all the time. We cannot allow ourselves to be silenced. Much, much more needs to be done," he said, encouraging students to do more than just complain about the parody. He urged them to respond in "uninhibited counter-demonstrations."

Students turned to the issue of the Griswold Nine and the Fried Four. Tribe said he was concerned that so much energy had been used to prosecute those students, but that no action had been taken in response to the *Revue*. "If the law school takes the sit-in more seriously than they take this, I think that would be sick." And before the group adjourned, Tribe assured the gathered listeners, "I have no intention of limiting this discussion to this room."

When the question-and-answer session ended, the Jewish Law Students Association broke with its custom of not commenting on political issues and decided to issue its own letter condemning the *Revue* later in the week.

For Tribe to speak out on a political and contentious issue was not unusual; some would say it was his trademark. While he is not as omnipresent or as sanctimonious as Alan Dershowitz, his rival on the faculty for celebrity status, Laurence Tribe is an orator extraordinaire, a preeminent congressional witness, and a popular television commentator. Not a single major Supreme Court decision goes by without him giving his analysis of the case's impact and ramifications. That's because he is usually on one side or another, as the principal Supreme Court advocate or as an interested party, known as an *amicus curiae*, or friend of the court. Five years after he received tenure, *Time* magazine in 1977 named Tribe one of the nation's ten most outstanding law professors. In 1988, *The New Republic* called him "the premier Supreme Court litigator of the decade." And the *Northwestern Law Review* wrote: "Never before in American history has an individual simultaneously achieved Tribe's preeminence both as a practitioner and as a scholar of constitutional law." The Ralph S. Tyler, Jr., Professor of Constitutional Law, he holds the only chair in constitutional law at Harvard and is popular among students.

The author of the country's leading constitutional law treatise and a brilliant scholar, he has been a highly respected and influential faculty member, too. A traditional civil libertarian liberal, Tribe was often the token centrist on faculty matters. He was perceived by most on the faculty as being not as far to the left as Critical Legal Studies proponents, and he did little by way of his scholarship to associate with CLS. He once wrote a letter to *The New York Times* to correct an assertion that he was affiliated with CLS. "Particularly since my own treatise, much of my other writing, and my work as a Supreme Court advocate have at times been disparaged by 'Critical' scholars as too conservative and mainstream, I can hardly be suspected of undue sympathy to the critical cause."

Yet, because of his liberal bent, he often sided with them on faculty matters and appointments, and in the same letter to the *Times* in which he distanced himself from CLS, he said that history would record the struggle over CLS as "progress to new and deeper understanding of law and commitments to justice." The first time he publicly criticized a tenure decision to the press was to express his dismay over the denial of tenure to CLS-affiliated contracts professor Clare Dalton. "If a young, relatively conservative male unconnected with Critical Legal Studies had written the same book [that Dalton did], I am morally confident that person would have been given tenure," he told the *Crimson*. The three tenure denials in 1986 and 1987 were clearly ideologically driven. "Anyone who believes [those decisions] are a coincidence has more faith in the neutrality of the tenure process than I can muster," he told *The National Law Journal* in 1987.

Looking back on his comments about Dalton's tenure denial, Tribe was concerned then about underlying sexism in the faculty's hiring and the conservative faction's willingness to sack prospective professors because of their ideology. Because of his outspokenness on those matters, he was named chairman of the faculty's six-member search committee to find a replacement for then-outgoing dean Vorenberg and to balance representatives of the left- and right-identified groups. He worked hard to find a candidate for the deanship who could bridge the division within the faculty. He was dubious of Bok's choice of Clark as dean, though he didn't think there was anyone capable of calming the professors, and he said so publicly. "Given the diversity of the Harvard faculty, the search for a dean who would both demonstrate strong leadership capacity and please every group within the faculty would have been futile," he remarked to another reporter for *The National Law Journal*.

Tribe generally preferred to play a key behind-the-scenes

role. But whether he was out in front or in the background, they were some who called him a judicial and academic opportunist. His advice to the Senate Judiciary Committee on the confirmation hearings of Supreme Court nominee Robert Bork and his three-hour testimony against Bork (one of twenty-seven appearances before congressional panels), his writings (more than ninety articles and fourteen books), and the Supreme Court cases he selected were all seen by critics as part of an intricate and carefully laid plan to one day become a Supreme Court justice. During the Reagan era, Tribe was considered a Democratic president's likely choice for the Supreme Court, making it easy for people to consider him the leading justice-in-waiting.

Unfortunately, his visibility on Supreme Court confirmation hearings, his high-profile cases, and his charged criticisms of the Rehnquist court and Reagan's legal revolution "overexposed" him, dampening his chances to win a nomination. Too many conservatives were salivating at a chance to "Tribe" him the way he had helped to "Bork" Bork. And a Democratic president faced with making the first nomination for his party in more than twenty years probably wouldn't (and didn't) risk it. Others said that since he realized he wasn't ever going to secure a judgeship, he had set his sights on the deanship, or if not to succeed Clark, then to wield as much power on the faculty. By publicly condemning the *Harvard Law Review* and Harvard Law School, Tribe was seizing a political opportunity. Though, at a place like Harvard, there were few people not willing to capitalize on opportunities to advance their own agendas. And what he said he feared about the recent sit-ins—that more energy would go into prosecuting them than into disciplining the authors of the Frug parody—is precisely what happened.

Tribe's critics have loved to point out that he charges more per hour than the highest-paid Wall Street Lawyers, suggesting that he is just another egocentric, money-grubbing attorney. And his consulting arrangements and corporate cases are lucrative and plentiful. It is not money, however, but his passion and emotion for people like Mary Joe Frug that guide his underlying concern for federalism, his zeal for the separation of powers and the separation of church and state, and for civil rights. That is what has made him a champion of women, blacks, gays and lesbians, and other underrepresented individuals.

Laurence Tribe doesn't look as formidable an advocate as he is. The morning at the Jewish Law Students brunch he appeared lawyerly, wearing a dark suit and tie; but in the classroom he usually wears khaki slacks with a crewneck sweater and running shoes. His soft, reddish-blond curls, gray at the temples, clear blue eyes, pear-shaped body, and deliberate, almost pained, manner of speaking, make him appear cuddly, not cunning. Of course, he can be calculating, but he wins because his intellect far surpasses that of most of his opponents, and he has an accurate sense of right and wrong. He has earned his reputation as one of the country's most vigorous defenders of the Constitution and as a liberal advocate for change in the real world. While he is of the same generation as the more radical oppositionist Duncan Kennedy, he is more like his older liberal colleagues and mentors Archibald Cox and Paul Freund, going beyond the ivory tower into the heart of what America should be.

His commitment to individual rights is a by-product of his heritage. His grandparents fled Russia to escape the czar's pogroms, and went to Shanghai, where he was born on October 10, 1941. When he was two years old, his father was interned in a concentration camp by the Japanese, who had occupied that part of China. "It might have something to do with my sympathy for people who are on the receiving end of unjust exercises of power," he said to writer Andrea Sachs.

Released from the camp by American liberators at the end of the war, his father took his young family to San Francisco in 1946. Like other recent immigrants, his father had little money. He struggled as a car salesman, and lost what little he made on bad business deals. Life in the new country was not easy for Tribe, a "fat little kid" who spoke more Russian than English. At the San Francisco public schools his parents sent him to, the other kids ostracized him for not being athletic. He retreated into painting and studying, and wanted to become an artist. He still paints as a hobby, and many of his pieces grace his Cambridge home. His son, Mark, is an artist in San Francisco.

At sixteen, Tribe was winning awards with his pastels, and he was taking college-level calculus courses by mail. He graduated early and accepted a full scholarship at Harvard. There he found an intellectual heaven. After his freshman year, he ranked second in a class of 1,100. He joined the debating society, and his team won the national championships in his junior year. Even if his family had been able to afford to fly him home for the holidays, he probably would have preferred to stay at Harvard.

He realized it would be hard to make a living as an artist, and thought about becoming a doctor. Then, intrigued by what he says is the intricate structure of truth embedded in mathematics, he switched from medicine to math. By the time he received his undergraduate degree, he had a *summa* in his major and had finished all the course work needed for a doctorate. Winning a National Science Foundation grant, he entered Harvard's graduate program in math and planned to spend the next year after graduation writing his thesis and receiving his advanced degree. But that year, Tribe made another sudden switch; he decided to become a lawyer.

He says he realized he wanted to do more than spend the rest of his life "communing with a blackboard on problems that were aesthetically very intriguing but just not very relevant to the world." He found math beautiful, and loved the ultimate and profound truths experienced when a theorem was proved. But he wanted to do something more connected with real life and with social concerns. The law dealt with justice and was also intellectually challenging. Several former college friends said another reason he switched to law was that he didn't want to be overshadowed by another prodigy, named Saul Krioke, who became a renowned mathematical philosopher at Princeton. If he moved into another field, Tribe could avoid having his contributions always compared to Krioke's.

He was accepted at Harvard Law School, where his first-year grades, while in the top 10 percent, were just shy of qualifying him to win an invitation to join the *Harvard Law Review.* He says he could have worked a little harder, and it took a little longer before he "felt comfortable with the inevitable indeterminacy and malleability of legal argument." His grades got better, and professors Cox and Freund noticed his intellect and encouraged him to excel. In 1966, at the age of twenty-four, he graduated from Harvard *magna cum laude.* After law school, he returned to California to clerk for state supreme court judge Mathew Tobriner. In 1967, Tribe moved back east, accepting an offer to clerk for Supreme Court Justice Potter Stewart. Tribe left his mark on several opinions he drafted for Stewart. "The Fourth Amendment protects people, not places," he drafted for *Katz v. United States* (1967), a case holding that electronic eavesdropping is a form of search and seizure even though there is no physical trespass.

In 1969, at age twenty-seven, he returned to Cambridge to teach at Harvard Law, turning down a competing offer from Yale. Three years later, at thirty, he won tenure. Ten years after arriving at Harvard, he published his groundbreaking, 1,700-page treatise, *American Constitutional Law,* the first systematic examination of constitutional legal doctrine in close to a century. In it he combined legal analysis with new theoretical and historical observations. Rather than dividing the book into chapters by doctrines, he combined the chapters into what he called "models" to better explain the structure of the Constitution. The book reflected his overriding liberal philosophy, but was regarded as "fair-minded" and "thorough in exploring alternative viewpoints." Revised in 1988, it is used by nearly every law student in the country to study constitutional law; now in its thirteenth printing, it has been cited more than 1,365 times by state and federal courts. "It may well be that no book . . . has ever had a greater influence on the development of American constitutional law," said Erwin Griswold.

Not surprisingly, the eminence he won from his treatise soon drew people to hire him to argue cases at the Supreme Court, where he became known for his dazzling oral argument. He began his secondary career as a Supreme Court advocate by winning three cases in a row. His first case, in 1978, presented what would become his pet legal issues: free speech and the separation of powers. In it he persuaded the Court to hold that state courts may not prohibit free speech by a municipality. His second case, in 1979, on behalf of the National Organization for Women, established him as a defender of women's rights. The Court ruled that federal courts may not interfere with Congress's time extension for the passage of the Equal Rights Amendment. He argued the third case in this hat-trick in 1980, ten days after his father died. This case established the right of the press and the public to attend criminal trials.

From 1978 to 1992, Tribe argued twenty cases before the Supreme Court, winning fourteen and losing only six, a record unmatched by any other private practitioner. He successfully defended a Berkeley, California, rent-control law, California's moratorium on nuclear power plants, and the right of states to limit bank mergers. He persuaded the Court to hold that the Department of Labor could not limit migrant farm workers' federal suits as authorized by Congress, that the Commerce Clause could not be used to bar municipal hiring preferences, and that the First Amendment protected gay-rights advocacy in public schools. Those cases represented tremendous gains for the poor, for environmentalists, for women, blacks, gays and lesbians, and for liberal interests generally. They are especially significant considering the decisions were made against the backdrop of a fervent religious right, a conservative majority on the Supreme Court, and a dominant group of Reagan-Bush ideologues at the Department of Justice.

The case he is proudest of is one he lost, *Bowers v. Hardwick*, a 1986 decision against the rights of homosexuals to engage in private sexual conduct without fear of prosecution. In a narrow five-to-four vote, the Court held that states may criminalize consensual sex acts between adults in their own homes. The defendant in the case, Michael Hardwick, was convicted of practicing sodomy with a male partner in his own bedroom. Working with the American Civil Liberties Union as lead Supreme Court counsel, Tribe wasn't sure he could persuade the Court to rule that a constitutional right of privacy existed to declare Georgia's sodomy law unconstitutional. But he was sure such a constitutional basis existed. He told the Court in oral argument, "The issue is not what Michael Hardwick was doing in his bedroom; the issue is what the State of Georgia was doing in Michael Hardwick's bedroom." Of Tribe that day, Hardwick said, "He was incredible. I've never seen any person more in control of his senses than he was."

The Court refused to adopt his expansive notion of privacy. "It was one of my biggest disappointments," said Tribe. But four justices indicated they would be willing to find that such a right existed. And he felt further vindicated when, in addition to the four dissents and the public's hostile reaction to the decision, Justice Lewis Powell, part of the majority, later declared he had voted the wrong way.

Like most advocates, Tribe sometimes disagrees with the nature of his clients' businesses. In some cases where the client is unpalatable to him, he has asked that charitable contributions be made in lieu of his fees. In 1989, for example, he was faced with a dilemma. Congress tried to abolish adult telephone services, known as "dial-a-porn," by criminalizing all obscene telephone messages. Companies naturally challenged Congress, and Tribe believed an important issue of free speech was at stake. But he said, "I didn't necessarily want to keep their money. I mean, it's not my favorite industry." He arranged for his client to contribute whatever money it owed him to shelters for abused women and children, and to children's television advocacy groups. Tribe won when the court held unanimously that Congress violated the First Amendment by criminalizing "indecent" phone messages, along with more obscene ones. By a vote of six-to-three the Court upheld the ban on "obscene" messages.

Before Tribe agreed to defend a $400,000 jury award for Rose Cipollone, a woman who, shortly before she died of lung cancer in 1984, sued the company that made the cigarettes she smoked, a cigarette company involved in the case offered Tribe $1 million to take their side. It wanted Tribe to argue that congressionally mandated warning labels on cigarette packages preempted federal suits. Tribe declined to represent the cigarette maker. "My family didn't want me getting rich off of

blood money," he said. But he felt that the constitutional principle of federalism was at risk, so he decided to represent Mrs.
Cipollone instead. "I also didn't think the government should
be able to get off so easily simply by putting a warning on a
package of cigarettes." He won a seven-to-two decision holding
that suits against cigarette companies were not preempted by
the warning labels.

Even though most of the outside cases he takes are *pro bono*,
he works for hire, and is one of the highest-earning lawyers in
the country. He pulls in $1–3 million annually, charging be-
tween $775–1,200 an hour, according to the *American Lawyer*
magazine. At Harvard, professors are not allowed to devote
more than twenty hours per week to outside consulting or litigation; there is no limit, however, on how much they can earn
for those twenty hours, and no requirement that they report
how much they earn from their outside work. He won a dramatic court victory for Pennzoil in its $10-billion battle with
Texaco, earning $3 million in the process. And he counseled
the law firm defending convicted securities manipulator Michael Milken. He also worked as a consultant to Hoylake Investments, led by Sir James Goldsmith, in its $21.1 billion
pursuit of B.A.T. Industries PLC.

Embarrassing details about his fees first emerged in the aftermath of a 1982 case. In that case, *Larkin v. Grendel's Den*,
Tribe successfully urged the Court to declare unconstitutional
a Massachusetts law that allowed churches to veto liquor li-
censes awarded within five hundred feet of the church. He
asked for $264,206.25 in fees, plus expenses, a request the Com-
monwealth of Massachusetts challenged. Tribe was seeking
$275 an hour, more than what most senior partners at major
firms at the time billed. Moreover, the state said that he kept
poor time records and that an associate of his charged $625 to
write a one-sentence letter. Tribe was never charged with any
wrongdoing. The evidence supported him on every important
point, and the court awarded him about half the amount he
sought. However, one of the documents in the case revealed
that he had charged other outside clients as much as $525 an
hour since 1981. That case won him the moniker "Larry Tribe,

P.C.," suggesting that he might as well be running his own professional corporation.

Whether he defends indigents or corporate barons, all of his Supreme Court cases have fit within his view of the law. Tribe's legal philosophy is that the Constitution was written so that principles of liberty and equal protection and opportunity could grow as the nation evolved. In his view, a justice's job is to interpret the charter, and that makes it necessary for the court to take stands on complex, socially sensitive issues. He is especially concerned about privacy as a constitutional concept, and has written extensively that there is a way to justify a constitutional right to an abortion. But he has criticized *Roe v. Wade,* the landmark abortion decision, as flimsy.

Those views were most sharply articulated in his 1985 book, *God Save This Honorable Court: How the Choice of Supreme Court Justices Shapes Constitutional Choices.* There he advanced his notion that the Constitution is an incomplete document, one in which "nearly all of its most important phrases are deliberate models of ambiguity," which "*compel* the Supreme Court to put meaning *into* the Constitution." Concepts of original intent and other variants of strict construction are "inconclusive" and abdicate responsibility for the choices that judges interpreting the constitution "necessarily" make. Because of the power the Supreme Court has over "the basic ingredients of our day-to-day lives," the Court's balance is a legitimate issue.

He debunked the myth of what he called the "surprised president," the mistaken idea that justices, once they are on the bench, usually surprise the presidents who appoint them. On the contrary, he argued, presidents usually got exactly what they wanted from a nominee. And the idea that the Senate merely rubber-stamped appointments and was essentially "spineless" was also a myth; over time, the Senate has rejected one out of every five nominees to the Court, he wrote.

A majority of the justices were over seventy-six years old when he was writing his book. He knew that the aging of the Court signaled "a potential constitutional revolution in the making." Hence, it was the Senate's job to determine whether a nomination would be good for the court and the country at the time. His observation in the prologue, that the "lull" of a "gray" court was "only the calm before the constitutional storm that surely lies ahead," was prescient in that it predicted the vicious fight two years later over the nomination of former appeals judge Robert Bork, during which Tribe became the Senate Judiciary Committee's star adviser and witness against the nominee. *God Save This Honorable Court* was the intellectual blueprint for liberals against Bork, and Tribe succeeded in affecting the direction of the Court.

But as Tribe himself noted in his influential book, "he who lives by the crystal ball must learn to eat ground glass." And like Bork, wrote nomination chronicler Ethan Bronner, Tribe was also "oddly naïve about the long-term effects" his publicity at the hearings would have. From the moment Tribe appeared to testify against Bork, conservatives began lying in wait to do to him what he did to Bork. In the meantime, they have been filling their arsenal with evidence that Tribe is the Bork of the left. *Benchmark,* a legal journal published by the conservative Virginia Law Center for Judicial Studies, devoted an entire issue to tarring Tribe as an unprincipled liberal activist.

With articles entitled "The Many Faces of Laurence Tribe," "God Save This Honorable Court—And My Place on It," "Tribe on Legalized Abortion: Where There's a Will There's a Way," and "Pettifogger of the Year," the Tribe edition of *Benchmark* read like an issue of the *Revue.* But this wasn't supposed to be a spoof. The authors were serious about making a preemptive strike for a "Stop Tribe" movement. "One would think Tribe spends almost every waking moment of his life campaigning for the high bench," wrote *Benchmark*'s editor, James McClellan. "The worst kept secret around Washington is that Tribe not only wants, he wants desperately, a seat on the Supreme Court. . . . Every article, every interview, every speech, even every brief and pleading, seems crafted with an eye on how the written or uttered word will enhance [his] chances of becoming Mr. Justice Tribe," railed William Bradford Reynolds, formerly of the Reagan Justice Department.

Tribe tried to brush off the attack. "If I didn't know better,

I would think that much of it was humorous because it was such a caricature," he told reporter Andrea Sachs. He has never denied that he wouldn't want to be nominated to the Court. "Who wouldn't? I mean, why not?" he told Sachs, but added it was not an obsession for him. If it were, he said, "I certainly would have been more cautious about the positions I took," and he would "not have testified against Robert Bork."

Tribe's work was an easy target. After all, he did write extensively about how the Constitution protects sexual conduct between consenting adults (read "advocates homosexuality"), and had analyzed the arguments on both sides of the abortion debate (read "believes in abortion rights for children"). Even for some liberals, he had made too many appearances on "Nightline," had been brought in too many times to testify before congressional panels, and had become too controversial because of his behind-the-scenes work to thwart Bork's Supreme Court nomination. Many people complained that Tribe had tacked back and forth in an apparent campaign for a seat on the Court.

There is no doubt, however, that even off the bench, Tribe has continued to affect the direction of the Court. The reach of his ideas has already begun to extend beyond the United States. He has helped write the constitutions of the Marshall Islands, Czechoslovakia, and the Republic of Russia. But he is grounded in his teaching, his first love, where he is always drawn back to the Constitution.

It was because of his prominence and intelligence that the force of his statements and ideas about the *Revue* and its parody of Mary Joe Frug were so powerful. Some cynics called that the effect of the "Golden Larry Tribe Rule." If Larry Tribe says it, it has instant respectability, and it must be important. Indeed, his comments were discomforting; the authors at first had hidden under the veil of anonymity, and they had perpetuated the harmful notion that hatred against women is a hoax perpetrated by paranoid feminists. But were they guilty of genocide? Were they cross-burners? His analogies to Holocaust revisionists and Ku Klux Klan members applied in one sense, but seemed far-fetched in another. Yet they indicated how serious a breach the editors had committed, and they influenced many students at the brunch to continue to speak out against the Frug parody and the *Law Review*. He touched off a such a firestorm over the *Revue* that, by week's end, students would call for Dean Clark's resignation.

Later that Sunday, following his remarks, several *Law Review* editors still felt unsatisfied with the way the *Review* had responded to the parody. These included the same three 2L women, Eisenberg, Jones, and Riles, 3L Marie Milnes-Vasquez, and 2L male student Kunal Parker, who pressed unsuccessfully to have the authors of the parody formally censured or thrown off the *Review*. Inspired by Tribe's statement to take their disgust public, they wrote an open letter to the school expressing their disappointment about the meetings of the *Law Review* editors earlier that weekend—the way their views had been disregarded and the way the *Law Review* had failed to hold the offending parties responsible. "What transpired at a meeting supposedly intended to redress the harm that has been done and to rebuild a sense of 'community' at the *Review* left us feeling just as victimized as we did the first time we read [the parody].... We were appalled by the manner in which many of you treated those of us who demand greater individual accountability for the article," they wrote.

On Monday, April 13, students returning to class found their Harkness mailboxes stuffed with letters of outrage and apology. The Battered Women's Advocacy Project, a clinic that assists women who are victims of physical, emotional, and verbal violence, denounced the *Revue* for making fun of violence against women.... It was the fault of Harvard Law School for "failing to educate students about the realities of violence against women."

Wendy Thurm and Michele Kalstein, co-editors-in-chief of the *Harvard Civil Rights–Civil Liberties Law Review*, wrote that the "community must get tough on hate—especially hate directed toward women and minorities" and in light of the fact that the attack on Frug, her family, and the women at Harvard Law School had occurred as "thirteen students faced reprimand or suspension for their nonviolent protest against what they perceived as an atmosphere of hostility toward women and minorities." Nor should the silence of the majority of the faculty and the administration after the *Revue* was disseminated be ignored. In a letter on behalf of the Women's Law Association, co-chairs Marie-Louise Ramsdale and Elizabeth Moreno (Moreno also wrote a humor column under the pseudonym "Alysse MacIntyre" for the *Record,* and was one of the Griswold Nine) wrote that the "pain and anger" caused by the *Revue* and the general attitude toward women and minorities expressed by the authors "reflects and reinforces a campus climate that simply cannot be tolerated and must cease."

In a memo to "the law school community," Dean Clark also condemned the parody. Many students and faculty members, like Tribe, were angry that Clark had waited nine days after the *Revue* was distributed at the *Law Review* banquet to respond. Stories about the parody were already appearing in the Boston newspapers. He issued his letter in response to press inquiries. "The piece offends all standards of decency and I deeply regret that members of the community have been subjected to it. . . . The article displays a gross insensitivity to the feelings of others," he wrote, and added that he would wait for the completion of the *Review*'s internal examination before considering what additional steps he would take.

The next day, Tuesday, April 14, Craig Coben and Kenneth Fenyo, the two *Law Review* editors who had confessed to writing the parody of Mary Joe Frug, weighed in with their own letter of apology. But theirs seemed grudgingly written. They admitted that what they had written was "in poor taste and offensive," and that they had "caused distress to members of the community and most especially to Professor Frug and his family" and had apologized personally to Gerald Frug. But they noted they weren't the only ones involved in the parody, reminding the school that a group of ten editors had agreed to lampoon Frug. Several of them had seen the parody and had not objected. The two editors conceded writing the parody was "wrong," and said they understood now why it was "inappropriate." They had "never intended to hurt anyone or condone violence against women," and did not realize that the banquet was on the anniversary of Mary Joe Frug's murder.

Eight other editors, saying they were "involved to varying degrees with the production of the *Revue*," issued a separate letter saying they were sorry that none of them had tried to stop the Frug parody from being published. They admitted that they were each "in a position to take greater steps to prevent the publication of the offending material." Among those "deeply sorry for not doing so" were ex-president David Ellen and former Books and Commentary editors Janis Kestenbaum and Edith Ramirez. Each of the five other editors also held a position of authority: Mark Harris and Sean Lev, former supervising editors; Robert Niewyk, former executive editor; and Paul Clement and Andrew Fish, former Supreme Court Office co-chairs.

Kestenbaum and Ramirez issued their own *mea culpa,* saying they had "made a serious mistake by failing to protest the initial decision by others to parody the Frug piece." They were the ones who had initially decided to publish Frug's commentary and had fought to "preserve the integrity of the piece" when other editors wanted to change the language, and they had also worked on the *Revue.* They offered their explanation of how they, of all people, could have let the Frug parody slip through: they had assumed everyone else involved in the project would exercise good judgment; they also knew that the Frug parody was an effort to criticize their decision to publish her commentary in the March issue. For those reasons, they had not even read the text of the spoof.

The professors received copies of those letters too. And a group of five, mostly liberal faculty members—Elizabeth Bartholet, Daniel Meltzer, Todd Rakoff, Tribe, and James Vorenberg—wrote a one-paragraph letter to the *Review* telling the editors that those apologies weren't going to keep them from speaking out against the parody. "Receipt of those communications does not affect our desire to have our views and those of our colleagues known," they said in their letter. And forty-seven out of fifty-four tenured professors signed a statement addressed to the *Review,* saying they believed the parody in the *Revue* about Mary Joe Frug was "contemptible and cruel."

Three third-year *Review* editors, Bruce Spiva, former treasurer Lori-Christina Webb, and Charlie Robb (no relation to Virginia senator Charles Robb), fired back a response defending the *Harvard Law Review* from attack. Hoping to correct the misimpression left by the letter Eisenberg and her supporters—Riles, Jones, Vasquez, and Parker—had distributed earlier in the week, that the editors were not willing to take individual responsibility for the Frug parody, they explained why they had voted against motions calling for individual editors to apologize publicly. The *Revue*, they said, was the "work of many hands: some editors helped write it; more helped to edit it; some knew the titles of the individual parodies; others read parts of it; others were completely ignorant of its contents; virtually everyone in the 3L class could have participated. As much as is possible at a place like the *Review*, this evil was institutional evil." They noted that the *Review* was taking "forward-looking measures" to address the "systematic sexism which made this tragedy possible."

But they berated Tribe for seriously distorting the situation to increase public pressure on the editors responsible for the *Revue*, saying that comparing the *Revue* authors to Holocaust revisionists and Ku Klux Klan members ". . . belittles the horrors perpetrated by Hitler, the Klan, and those who apologize for them. . . ." Tribe should "understand as well as anyone the way oversights and omissions can lead to great harm and public controversy," they added, recalling how he had once signed a petition to keep a school for blacks out of his neighborhood. Then, saying he had not been told all the facts, he had sought to have his name struck from the petition. "Good people can do bad things," these students wrote. "We must condemn their actions. But we should hesitate to damn their characters on the basis of a single error."

It was too late to spare the *Review* and the two editors who admitted to writing the horrendous spoof. The matter was out of their hands and in the public arena. Tribe had set the tone; others were capitalizing on momentum he had generated, and the controversy was escalating. On Wednesday, April 15, "wanted" posters of Craig Coben and Kenneth Fenyo, the parody authors, appeared all over campus, taped to classroom walls and hallways. Below a black-and-white yearbook photo of Coben, the poster read: "Spring 1992: Harvard Law School. Fall 1992: Clerk for JUDGE DOUGLAS GINSBURG, D.C. Circuit, JUDGE NOT AND YOU SHALL NOT BE JUDGED." The poster of Fenyo bore the same wording, except for the name and address of the judge, J. Clifford Wallace, of the Ninth Circuit Court of Appeals, for whom Fenyo was to begin clerking after graduation.

The posters were a reminder that those two men would soon be writing the opinions of some of the nation's most powerful judges. Nine out of the ten editors who confessed to having been in a "position to take greater steps to prevent the publication of the offending material" had clerkships lined up to start in the summer after graduation. Paul Clement, one of those editors, had already been selected to clerk for Supreme Court Justice Antonin Scalia, beginning in 1993, a year after graduation.

It was ludicrous that a group of students who were calling for an end to discrimination were facing the possibility of suspension or expulsion while another group of students who had participated in the degradation of women were on their way to clerk for the country's most prestigious judges. Professor Christopher Edley was urging his colleagues on the faculty to withdraw letters of recommendation for clerkships they may have written for those *Law Review* editors. Some students said they would write to the judges, and report the editors to state bar associations. Others suggested that the two editors primarily responsible for the Frug parody should work in a shelter for battered women. Many students were pressing for an investigation of the *Review* and the writing of the Frug parody.

Tribe continued to speak out against the *Review* and the spoof issue. He seemed more certain than he had been when he spoke to the Jewish Law Students that the making of that grotesque piece stemmed from the Harvard Law School itself: from the faculty's inbreeding and from its failure to hire more than a handful of women and minorities on the faculty. The student left's message was hitting home. "It starts with the faculty, our own process of self-selection," he explained to *Boston Herald* columnist Margery Eagan. "Over twenty-three years I've watched with growing dismay as an almost completely male bastion has remained. We keep talking about broadening and including in our ranks a greater diversity, but in the end we still have a small handful of women and minorities. . . . It may be that the qualities we look for in students are insufficiently connected to decent character. Combine that with the way we choose faculty, and it's not surprising that the atmosphere is one where some can think [this] is humorous. It's a big mistake to think this is the responsibility of a few bad apples. The apple is rotten."

He also believed the *Revue* and the parody could be viewed in the context of sexual harassment. "If speech is part of a pattern of deliberate harassment or intimidation," one cannot simply hide behind the First Amendment, he said to the *Boston Globe*'s Anthony Flint. For instance, when pornography is used to harass women in the workplace, "the First Amendment's objection may be less decisive." He said "careful inquiry" was needed to assess allegations being made by others that the parody of Mary Joe Frug was part of a process of harassment of women on the *Law Review*.

One thing was clear: the denials, apologies, *mea culpas*, finger-pointing, and name-calling, in the wake of the of the distribution of the *Revue* and the leak of the first page of the Frug parody, renewed concern over illegal discrimination and the homogeneity of the faculty. There was new impetus to restart the decade-long battle over the political content of legal scholarship and legal education, and an apparent leadership crisis at Harvard Law. In the aftermath of the parody, more questions about what had really happened regarding the *Revue*—who had edited it, who had read what parts, who had worked on the layout, and so on—remained unanswered. Moreover, it was obvious that the *Review* had collectively ducked those questions, except for the two editors who were willing to confess. By deciding not to distribute additional copies of the *Revue*, the editors had effectively prevented the public from seeing how rotten the *Revue* and the *Harvard Law Review* really was.

"This has got to be one of the lowest points in Harvard Law School's history. It has hit rock-bottom on the scale of morality," said third-year student John Bonifaz, a member of the Coalition for Civil Rights. For Bonifaz and other students involved in the left-diversity movement, the parody was an affirmation of everything they had been fighting against for the past three years. A school that had only three black men and five women on its tenured faculty of fifty-nine, a ten-to-one ratio of men to women, and an eighteen-to-one ratio of whites to minorities created a perfect breeding ground for racist and sexist attitudes. "An issue like the *Revue* can only come out in an atmosphere that makes such tasteless statements conceivable and palatable," said second-year student Camille Holmes, coordinator of the Coalition for Civil Rights.

And the problem started at the top. Through his initial attempt to eliminate the office of public-interest advising, his "lunch counter" statement about Derrick Bell's leave of absence, his remarks about minority students' insecurity in the *Wall Street Journal,* and his upholding of the appointment of four white men, Clark had fostered an environment where students could think racist and sexist stereotyping was funny. On Thursday, April 16, the Coalition for Civil Rights called for Clark's resignation. A hundred students and supporters attended a noon press conference. "What do we want? Resignation! When do we want it? Now!" they shouted. A representative of each of the student groups within the coalition stated why Clark had to go. The students read a letter from Jesse Jackson supporting the Griswold Nine. Keith Boykin, a leader of the coalition, organized the event. He believed Clark had made a bad situation worse. "Look at what happened after the nine students had a sit-in. The dean did everything in his power to expedite the prosecution," Boykin asserted.

In deciding to assemble the leaders of seven student organizations to press for Clark's resignation, Boykin drew on his experience as a student at Dartmouth College, when conservative students had attacked shanties other students had built on the campus to protest South African apartheid. "There were trials and counter-trials, demonstrations, and counterdemonstrations, and the president was always the center of attention," Boykin remembered. "By the end of the year he was gone, he had resigned." That spring of his third year at Harvard, "things were getting worse, converging into the parody, and I thought it was important to pull all these different strands together and demand some sort of accountability in terms of leadership."

Peter Cicchino, a third-year student who, like Clark, had once studied for the priesthood, wrote an impassioned letter explaining why Clark had to resign: "Sued by its own students, increasingly more segregated in its already segregated faculty; further embittered by ideological strife; venue for the most vicious and obscene attacks on women; this is the place we have become, the place which you have—however unintentionally—helped us make.... I plead with you now, in the midst of this terrible crisis which afflicts this institution, to realize...that your strengths could best be deployed elsewhere. Resign your deanship. Let another person—someone who might heal this place—be appointed. And for your part, continue to do what you do best: teach, research, write, and build the financial support which this institution needs and which someone other than a dean is more capable of achieving."

On Friday, April 17, the *Harvard Law Record* published Cicchino's plea. The same day, the Administrative Board officially charged the nine students involved in the sit-in at Clark's office with obstructing access to the dean's office, interfering with the freedom of movement of people working in his office, refusing to leave when asked, and acting in a manner that served to intimidate the dean's staff. Clark held fast to the reins, and Harvard's creme-de-la-creme *Law Review* continued to be attacked. Clark called an emergency faculty meeting to talk about the parody and to attempt some damage control.

When the day was over and the weekend began, Tribe found himself at a new low. With each press interview he granted, each statement he made, and the anger and determination he saw students exhibit, the less he wanted to be associated with Harvard Law School. He seriously wanted to resign, and had thought about it all week. On Saturday he telephoned his colleague and friend Christopher Edley at home. Edley was one of the school's three tenured African-American professors, and a strong ally of Bell and the students. One of the students facing disciplinary charges for participating in the sit-in at Clark's office a week earlier was a research assistent of Edley's.

Tribe told Edley he was considering offering his resignation as a form of protest, as Bell had done two years earlier. "That's terrific," Edley answered Tribe. "I wish I had the financial wherewithal to do it." But Edley talked Tribe out of it. Edley understood how having one of the school's giants, like Tribe, quit in protest would strengthen the claims being made that Harvard Law School was inhospitable to women and minorities. Yet he also saw that such a move might cause more turmoil. "I don't think this is the most constructive way to respond to the situation," Edley counseled Tribe. "It's not a now-or-never stratagem. Why don't you talk to some more people to find out what they think?"

Tribe took Edley's advice and talked to about a half-dozen people. The next day, Sunday, April 19, Tribe held a strategy meeting in his office on the third floor of Griswold Hall. In addition to professors Edley, Frank Michelman, and Alan Stone, most of the Critical Studies professors were there: David Kennedy, Betsy Bartholet, Morton Horowitz, and Gerald Frug. It was hardly unusual for the CLS crowd to be caucusing, but Tribe was rarely among them, although he often voted with them. Now he was in front of the pack. For several hours they considered whether they should call for Dean Clark's resignation, demand changes on the appointments committee, or ask for an investigation of the *Law Review* by Harvard University president Neil Rudenstein.

By day's end, they had drafted a harshly worded, three-page letter implicitly requesting all of the above. Tempers at Harvard Law School were at an all-time high, and the business of legal education had hit an all-time low.

CHAPTER 11

DEFENDING THEIR RIGHT, STARRING ALAN DERSHOWITZ

On Monday, April 20, after his Sunday meeting, Laurence Tribe and fourteen other professors released their three-page letter condemning the climate at Harvard Law School as "misogynist" and "sexist." It was a harsh denunciation of the school and the *Law Review* by a large portion of the faculty, and it was most sharply directed at Dean Clark. "There is good reason to believe that the *Law Review*'s publication of the April 1992 *Revue* is a symptom of a much wider problem. . . . Harvard Law School has done far too little to address issues of sexism and misogyny . . . a deeply rooted and long-standing pattern of systematic exclusion," they asserted. "A central factor in that hostile environment is a faculty whose composition, and whose processes of self-replication, profoundly undervalue the contributions that a more genuinely diverse group of teachers and scholars could make."

They called for the entire faculty to condemn the "institutional sexism and misogyny" that had produced the *Revue*, and to recognize "the prejudices that infect" the faculty's "continued failure to appreciate" the need for diversity and the capacities of members of diverse groups in society. Most significantly, they demanded the transformation of the Law School as a "white male preserve," and asked the dean and faculty to dissolve the current appointments committee and replace it with members who could begin taking immediate action to increase women and minorities on the faculty. They also requested Dean Clark to appoint a "special committee" to conduct an inquiry into the facts of the *Revue* incident and other related matters involving the treatment of women, and to report its findings to the dean, faculty, and students, and to the Administrative Board.

"We know that many of our colleagues think it is mistaken to draw a connection between the grotesque violation of Mary Joe Frug's life and death and the nature and priorities of this institution, including its hiring practices. But we are convinced that failure to see this connection is itself a significant part of the problem." Tribe and these fourteen other professors were condemning both the faculty and Dean Clark. They were reacting in part to the way Clark had responded to the parody "so dispassionately" and in so "low key" a manner. "There was a leadership vacuum," said Tribe.

Five professors smelled a possible mutiny and wrote their own letter, agreeing with the sentiments of the other fifteen but disagreeing with some of their recommendations. They concurred that "what happens in law school classrooms has an effect on the surrounding culture, including the legal culture of the nation as a whole . . . the *Law Revue* raises disturbing questions about the culture we inhabit and help to maintain." A more "genuinely diverse group" of professors should be an "urgent institutional priority."

There it was. A third of the Law School faculty—professors Elizabeth Bartholet, Gary Bellow, David Charny, Abram Chayes, Christopher Edley, Jr., Martha Field, William Fisher III, Charles Haar, Morton Horowitz, David Kennedy, Duncan Kennedy, Frank Michelman, Richard Parker, Lewis Sargentich, Laurence Tribe, William Alford, Richard Fallon, Charles Nesson, Henry Steiner, and Alan Stone—connected the parody to

Harvard's hiring practices and admitted that Harvard Law School was a "hostile environment." They represented not only the school's liberal wing, but some of its most senior and centrist faculty members, like Chayes, Stone, and Fallon.

None of the professors was asking for the Administrative Board to discipline the students responsible for the parody; they recognized that the issue wasn't the personal shortcomings of those budding young Republican jurists, but the culture of institutional sexism that made the vulgarity of the parody acceptable at Harvard Law. "This is the first time that a significant number of the faculty have collectively criticized the institution as a whole for what they see as a major failing," said Tribe. "It's a third of the established core of the school saying that the place is in serious difficulty because it has approached the issue of gender in the wrong way."

Indeed, it was a major confession of fault, and a vindication for the students who had sued Harvard University for discriminatory faculty hiring at the Law School. Even if the students lost their case against Harvard, which was still before the Supreme Judicial Court, they had succeeded in discrediting the fallacious argument that the pool of highly qualified minority and women professors was too small to draw from. Those two letters indicated that a substantial number of professors believed they could create a more diverse body without sacrificing academic excellence. And they acknowledged that students were injured by a discriminatory hiring process. That kind of recognition was a diversity-proponent's dream. Caroline Wittcoff, the third-year student who had argued the law students' appeal at the state supreme court earlier in March, was elated. It was a "public admission on the part of some of the defendants that there is discrimination going on in Law School hiring," she said, adding that if the court allowed the case to go to trial, those letters could be crucial in proving discrimination.

That same Monday, students found in their "Hark boxes" a copy of a three-page complaint from one professor, David Kennedy, to the Administrative Board, formally requesting it to investigate and press charges against the students directly responsible for writing and causing the *Revue* to be published and distributed, as well as outgoing president David Ellen and members of the masthead "responsible for maintaining a working and academic environment hostile to women." He urged the board to investigate those students in connection with their moral fitness to practice law, and in the context of sexual harassment at the *Law Review.*

Moreover, he told the Administrative Board of "troubling reports" that women had been intimidated from running for an office at the *Review,* and that women were afraid to work alone at Gannett House or leave the building alone at night, "not because of random street crime" but because of "the climate of harassment" at Gannett House. He had learned from *Review* member Rebecca Eisenberg and others about the phone calls that were made to judges she had applied to for clerkships, and about the other incidents that had occurred during the year at the *Law Review.* "For these men to laugh like this at the vicious murder of a prominent feminist is terrifying—and may well be terrorizing." His words sounded frightfully similar to what Mary Joe Frug had written in her original feminist manifesto, which had been so cruelly ridiculed. It was another small victory for her.

That Kennedy's complaint resonated with the sound of Mary Joe Frug's ideas was not surprising. He was a close friend of the Frug family. He had read a copy of her original feminist manifesto almost a year before Jerry Frug called it to David Ellen's attention. He had even discussed it at her memorial service in April 1991. In retrospect, his words to the 1,000 mourners gathered in Harvard's Memorial Church were foreboding. He had foreseen the impact her own words would have. "I think we'll find her last work truly amazing," he said. "Her insistence on the play of patriarchy, class division, racial conflict, and gender prejudice in our lives, our fantasies, our work . . . Mary Joe's scholarly project was a crazily ambitious one—a project in many ways just begun." Those were exactly the complex and conflicting issues surging to the forefront in the wake of the parody, and the controversy was far from over.

The letters and the complaint once again put Robert Clark

on the defensive. Almost before the ink was dry on them, he wrote his own letter to "the Law School Community." Considering that he was coming increasingly under fire, his tone was self-assured and reasoned, but he ignored the Tribe group's demands. He said he respected the colleagues who had signed the two open letters, and shared their basic concern that Harvard Law School should provide an "accepting and supportive environment" for everyone. "But to state that the parody reflects misogynist attitudes shared by many is unfair. Indeed, the fact that virtually everyone here deplores the parody suggests that a rather different attitude prevails."

Replacing the current appointments committee would be a setback, he asserted, noting that the committee had been working to develop recommendations for the appointment of outstanding scholars and teachers. Moreover, he disapproved of the call for disciplinary action against the authors of the parody, saying that the school placed a premium on freedom of expression. Finally, he urged caution in "generalizing" this incident for political purposes.

Clark had a powerful ally in Charles Fried. In a "letter of one" to the faculty, Fried said it was "incorrect," "illogical," and "unfair" to link the parody to Harvard's hiring practices. The appointments committee had "done an excellent—though not perfect" job in helping the school "move ahead more vigorously in refreshing our faculty." The addition of two women to tenure-track assistant professorships, announced in the two weeks since the parody had come to light, would "offset the disparity between men and women faculty members" and there would be more appointments to come, he promised. It was "unfair to use the deplorable episode of the *Law Revue* parody as a stick with which to beat the dean." He responded to the charge by the Group of Fifteen that those who failed to see the parallel between the parody and the predominantly white male composition of the faculty were part of the problem. "There is about as much connection between the *Revue* and our hiring policy as there is between members' overdrafts in the House [of Representatives] bank and the budget deficit." (Voters, however, didn't think the connection between their representatives' personal spending habits and the country's were so far-fetched; many of the rascals were not reelected.)

Fried believed the authors of the parody should not be punished. Although what they had written was offensive, it should still be protected as free speech. The First Amendment rights of those editors were not really being threatened, but Fried and others of the right wing latched on to the banner of free speech. By putting hate speech and speech against hate on the same moral plane, Fried and other political conservatives could avoid having to acknowledge the racism and sexism seeping from the walls of Harvard Law School.

The First Amendment was intended to cover things that are in bad taste, and courts have historically protected the most vulgar and offensive speech, Fried explained to one reporter. He cited a 1988 Supreme Court decision upholding *Hustler* magazine's right to lampoon preacher Jerry Falwell, regardless of how "slashing and one-sided" the satire was. "If we claim, as we do, that we are bound by the principles of the First Amendment, you don't punish someone for protected free speech," he said. He acknowledged that a friend and colleague's memory was "sacred," but feminism or any other political doctrine was not, and could certainly be parodied. "I am afraid this deplorable incident will be abused to confuse the two," he said.

Harvard's chapter of the Federalist Society also weighed in with its defense of the *Law Review* editors responsible for the parody. Neil Glazer, president, and Adrian Vermeule, vice-president and also a 3L editor on the *Review*, criticized, among other things, the "anonymous accusations of vaguely defined sexual harassment" and the "systematic campaign of libel addressed to the future employers of *Law Review* editors." To call the parody an act of "violence," merely "trivializes the horrifying act of Professor Frug's murder." They blamed "some radical elements" at the Law School for having "seized upon the attenuated metaphor of violence" to politicize the incident.

Thus far, Alan Dershowitz, Harvard's celebrity professor, had sat quietly through all of the posturing, hand-wringing, and finger-pointing surrounding the Frug parody. At first he thought the public condemnation of the parody and the *Law*

Review editors who confessed to having written it would end the matter. That's the way it should be; it's what he believed properly happens in the "marketplace of ideas." But having read letter after letter and listened to speech after speech denouncing Harvard as "misogynist" and the parody as a "symptom" of sexism and racism at the Law School, he could not contain himself any longer. His blood was boiling. He was dismayed that David Kennedy was seeking disciplinary charges despite the fact that no rule had been violated. And the "Special Committee" called for by the Group of Fifteen smacked too much of an "un-Harvard Activities Committee" to monitor politically incorrect offensive speech.

But he was angriest at Tribe. "When he calls my students the equivalent of rapists and Klansmen, I just think that's not appropriate." As he saw it, "Larry was one of those who was kicking these students in the balls when they were down, and he should know better." And he interpreted Tribe's and the far left wing's condemnation of the editors as a thinly veiled power grab. He decided to take matters into his own hands.

"HARVARD WITCH HUNT BURNS THE INCORRECT AT THE STAKE" was the headline the *Los Angeles Times* put on Dershowitz's nationally syndicated column on April 22. In his editorial, Dershowitz charged that those attacking Harvard for failing to do enough for women and for seeking an investigation of the parody had created "the atmosphere of a McCarthyite witch hunt." Calling the parody "somewhat" offensive and the apologies from the responsible students "profound," he cast the entire issue in terms of political correctness and a double standard for offensive speech.

"The overreaction to the spoof is a reflection of the power of women and blacks to define the content of what is politically correct and incorrect on college and law school campuses throughout much of the nation. . . . Women and blacks are entirely free to attack white men (even 'dead white men,' as they do in describing the current curriculum) in the most offensive terms. Radical feminists can accuse all men of being rapists, and radical African-Americans can accuse all whites of being racists, without fear of discipline or rebuke."

"But even unintentionally offensive parody of women or blacks provides the occasion for demanding the resignation of deans, the disciplining of students, and an atmosphere reminiscent of McCarthyism. . . . There is something very wrong at Harvard Law School, but it is not sexism or racism. . . . What is wrong at Harvard is that for too many radical professors and students, freedom of speech for those who disagree with them is 'just not their thing.' "

If the country hadn't known how sorely split Harvard Law School was in the wake of the parody, they knew it now. This was vintage Dershowitz, the contrarian, the mouthpiece, defender of last resort to the rich and infamous and the most unsympathetic victims, who, like the authors of the parody, were hardly victims. In fact, at the time, Dershowitz was representing former heavyweight boxer Mike Tyson on the appeal of his conviction for raping beauty contestant Desiree Washington in Indiana. No wonder he was blasting radical feminists for accusing men of being rapists; to some on the left, he was surreptitiously trying to influence public opinion with regard to his client. He had already charged that his client's accuser had led Tyson on and was just after his money, an unproven accusation he had no trouble making.

It was just a matter of time before Harvard's celebrity professor found a way to intervene. He loved taking unpopular positions, couldn't resist a flap, and had a knack for fanning the flames of controversy. But he usually did all that outside the context of Harvard Law School. He says he's "apolitical" when it comes to Law School affairs; his life is not in the day-to-day administration of the Law School, and he doesn't find Law School politics gratifying. "If I'm going to be in the political world, I'd rather be in a more important political world outside. I'm so confrontational on the outside, I like to work in an environment that is warm and supportive." On the other hand, he asserts, "I'm not going to let other people play politics and sit back and not respond."

Most Americans have seen Dershowitz, with his bushy, reddish brown hair, thick mustache, and metal aviator glasses, in the glare of the klieg lights, hurriedly escorting an embattled client—former boxing champion Tyson, convicted of rape; hotel executive Leona Helmsley, the "Queen of Mean," sentenced to jail for tax fraud; and socialite Claus Von Bülow, acquitted of twice attempting to murder his wife—up a set of courthouse steps and into a packed courtroom to tell a judge why his client has been wrongly charged or convicted. Often he puts the government on trial for violating his clients' constitutional rights. Afterwards, the lights go back on, and Dershowitz is seen fielding questions from a pack of reporters outside the courtroom or on the courthouse steps, usually as incredulous lawyers from the other side cringe at the sideshow.

Bright, engaging, and an exceptionally capable advocate, he is usually brought in to join a team of lawyers after a defendant has been convicted of a crime or after he or she has been sentenced. His focus is to rally public opinion to win a reversal on appeal, and if that means being obnoxious, so be it. He will rely on the inflammatory rather than the intellectual, which is why he is sought after by the persecuted and reviled by the "respected members" of the bar.

Many practitioners like to say Dershowitz is overzealous, a demagogue, and mainly interested in enhancing his superstar status. He has represented Soviet dissidents, U.S. Nazis, pornographers, fallen televangelist Jim Bakker, "Green Beret" doctor Jeffrey MacDonald (convicted of bludgeoning and stabbing to death his pregnant wife and two daughters), Jonathan Pollard (convicted of selling American military secrets to the Israelis), in addition to Tyson, Helmsley, and Von Bülow. He has made more than two dozen appearances on "Nightline," has written three best-selling memoirs, and has been portrayed in a major motion picture, adapted from *Reversal of Fortune*, his popular account of the Von Bülow case. All of the above have made him more than a legend in his own mind. He puts himself out there, demands what is due, says what he feels, defies tradition, challenges authority, and raises eyebrows, everything that defines the word *chutzpah,* the title of one of his books.

He sees himself as a crusader for justice, whose mission is to fight the "cheat elite"—the police, prosecutors, and defense attorneys who doctor facts to produce the results they want—

the sleazy deals by prosecutors or their quick dodges to avoid deals, and attempts by appeals courts to manipulate facts and the law to save face and pervert justice. If he must, he will go close to the line of ethical conduct to accomplish his objectives. He is a liberal Democrat, but because he defends civil liberties, he is seen by many as being on the far left. Still, because he has represented U.S. Nazis and pornographers, he is seen by many on the left as being a supporter of the right. Inside Harvard Law School he is considered a centrist or right of center, depending on the issue. He has a long history of angry, inconclusive, public confrontations with judges, prosecutors and politicians. He turned on Tribe and the professors allied with him because he felt they had begun a witch hunt.

Dershowitz could easily have gone to Tribe's office to discuss his disagreements with him privately. It would have required walking about thirty paces across the hall from his office on the third floor of Griswold Hall to Tribe's. They were both the eldest sons of Jewish families touched by the Holocaust, extraordinarily effective advocates and defenders of civil liberties, teachers, authors, and commentators, yet a wide gulf separated the two professors, in style and substance.

Tribe's office, for example, is quiet, like a comfortable law firm library where partners and associates work solitarily. He works with his door slightly ajar or closed, and doesn't like to be interrupted. There is little by way of memorabilia to indicate the breadth and depth of his advocacy. A few spare copies of his books sit on the shelves; a poster of Vaclav Havel, whose constitution for Czechoslovakia he helped write, hangs on one wall; and a small metal balancing sculpture stands behind his desk. Everything seems neatly arranged and organized.

Dershowitz's office, by contrast, is noisy, busy, and messy, like an understaffed and overworked office of a public-interest advocacy group. Stacks of paper cover the top of his desk. Piles of folders and papers are spread across the floor. Two plastic crates filled with letters to him—mostly hate mail, the choicest of which he tapes to his office door—sit on the floor. He constantly stops to take phone calls: from production assistants from television talk shows asking him to appear on an upcoming day, from co-counsel for outside cases confirming strategy, and from groups inviting him to speak to their members. (He pulls in $15,000 to $20,000 for speeches to groups who can afford to pay.) His secretaries breeze in and out with letters for him to read and papers to sign.

In terms of decoration, his office is a living shrine to its occupant. On a wall of shelves behind his desk are dozens of copies of his own books, *Taking Liberties, The Best Defense,* and *Chutzpah,* even a package of audiotapes, in case anyone happens to call for one. On the far side of his office, opposite his desk, are numerous caricatures of him, the kind of cartoons often done at bar mitzvahs and weddings. A singed Israeli flag sent by an anti-Semite, and dozens of letters, saying things such as "Die Jew" and "JEWS ARE YOUR ENEMIES COCKROACHES AND PARASITES! WAKE UP AMERICA!" are pasted on his office door.

On the door is also a movie poster from *Reversal of Fortune,* showing Glenn Close, Jeremy Irons, and Ron Silver, who played Dershowitz. Directly behind his desk is another souvenir from the movie, a black and white clapper saying "Scene 175X, Take 2." Hanging behind his secretary's desk in the office across the hall is a front page from the *New York Post.* Its huge, four-deck headline reads, "Lawyer: CLAUS WILL WIN, New Evidence Uncovered, Not Presented at Trial, Complete Story on p. 5." Beside this full-page headline is a large photo of an evil-looking Von Bülow. In his office he keeps a bound copy of the screenplay for *Reversal of Fortune,* bound copies of all the pleadings in all of his major cases, and bound volumes of all his columns. Everything is saved for posterity.

There are a few signs that Dershowitz has some intellectual pursuits. He has copies of *On Liberty* and *Libertarianism* by John Stuart Mill on a bookshelf, and other books about criminal law, such as *Where the Law Ends* by Christopher Stone. But Tribe is the more academic and intellectual one. He wouldn't be caught dead on talk shows like "Geraldo," "Morton Downey," and "Donahue." Dershowitz, smug and combative compared to the sweet, boyish, pristine Tribe, relishes opportunities to appear on such shows so that he can spread his civil-liberties gospel to as wide an audience as possible. Tribe usually wins his cases, and Dershowitz usually loses. Then again, many of Dershowitz's clients are guilty scoundrels.

Dershowitz and Tribe share some characteristics. Both decide whether or not to accept cases based on how "pissed off" they are. For Tribe, it is whether he feels a constitutional principle has been violated; he pursues corrupters of the Constitution. Dershowitz challenges corrupters of "the system"; he will sign on if he feels that someone has received an excessively long sentence or a conviction based on illegally proffered or admitted evidence. He agreed to represent Leona Helmsley because he felt the government was trying to "scapegoat" her.

Both men are highly compensated. Dershowitz is known to receive five hundred dollars an hour and Tribe seven hundred dollars, in addition to their $140,000-a-year-plus salaries. (Dershowitz earns more from speaking and royalties, and receives larger book deals, than does Tribe. Tribe, though, appears to earn larger fees on cases.) People say Dershowitz is as obsessed with being a celebrity figure as Tribe is with becoming a Supreme Court justice. And just as Tribe says he has never deliberately taken a case or written anything in the hopes of gaining such a nomination, Dershowitz maintains that notoriety alone never lures him to a case. Both are hypersensitive when it comes to anything critical written about them, and they are quick to demand a retraction or a correction when something they said may have been misquoted or misrepresented.

Personally, they were cordial, but not close. Dershowitz always felt that Tribe was one of those professors who snubbed him for not being "scholarly" while secretly being jealous of all his media attention. Tribe says they just never had time to develop a relationship. In a letter he wrote to *The New York Times* to correct the impression left in an article that he was among those who "politely but pointedly distance themselves from Dershowitz," Tribe defended Dershowitz, saying, "Not only is Alan a friend of mine, but I have enormous respect for the important work he does." In the acknowledgments to his book, *God Save This Honorable Court*, Tribe thanked Dershowitz for putting him in touch with his editor at Random

House, Rob Cowley. Their friendship didn't go much further than that. And Tribe didn't enjoy being called a McCarthyite and a fascist any more than Dershowitz liked his students being described as the moral equivalent of rapists, Klansmen, and Holocaust revisionists.

Dershowitz's mistrust of Tribe may have stemmed from the fact that Tribe blended in as if he were a refined, gentile, Cambridge WASP, while Dershowitz always stood out as a "bigmouth Jew." But Dershowitz takes pride in his Brooklyn street smarts and in his religious upbringing. He says his Jewishness is always with him, both "consciously and unconsciously," and calls it the "permanent chip on his shoulder." It is a combination of being committed to Jewish causes and some religious observance. What he describes as a "Holocaust" mentality keeps him constantly alert to any potential persecution—of Jews and other underdogs.

In many ways he is carrying out the work begun by his paternal great-grandfather, who emigrated from a shtetl in Poland in 1883. Like most immigrants, Zecharia Dershowitz worked in a sweatshop in Manhattan. If he hadn't been home on the Sabbath, he might have been killed in the great 1911 fire at the Triangle Shirtwaist Factory, where his shop was located. He decided two things after that brush with death: his children would never become factory workers, and they would never work on the Sabbath.

In 1911 he was among the first wave of Jews to move from Manhattan to Brooklyn. From the front of his house, "Reb Zecharia," as he was called, ran a small family synagogue, called a *shteeble,* and there was a pocketbook workshop in the back. During the late 1930s and early 1940s he ran a kind of underground railroad for Eastern European rabbis to escape the war, claiming they were "needed" for the new immigrant community in the States. Dershowitz's grandfather, the cantor in the family temple, worked as a printer and a box maker. His father, Harry, was born in 1909. He and a partner eventually opened a men's work-clothes store that sold "wholesale" during the week and "retail" on Sunday.

Alan's maternal grandfather, Naftuli Ringel, came to America with the second wave of Polish immigrants in 1907. He left behind three brothers and dozens of relatives. All but one brother were murdered along with seventeen thousand other Jewish residents of their town by the Nazis, despite a strong defense by the Jewish resistance fighters. His grandfather first settled in Scranton, Pennsylvania, but later moved to Manhattan, where he worked to earn enough money to send for his wife and three children still in Poland. Alan's mother, Claire, was born after Naftuli was reunited with his wife; two other children died of diphtheria. Claire Ringel and Harry Dershowitz were married in 1937. Two years later, Alan was born, followed by his brother, Nathan, two years after that.

The Borough Park section of Brooklyn, where his mother has lived for the past fifty-six years and where Dershowitz was raised, is a step back to prewar Poland. In this neighborhood, still predominantly Jewish, men wear long wool coats and broad-brimmed hats, and almost all have beards. The young men grow their sideburns long until their bar mitzvahs. Married women keep their heads covered with wigs. They tend to their children while the men pray and study the Talmud. All of the stores on Thirteenth Avenue, the main commercial thoroughfare, cater to the strict Orthodox Jewish life. There are kosher butcher shops, kosher restaurants, kosher pizza parlors, stores that sell silver candelabras, menorahs, and wine cups, stationery stores that sell only cards in Hebrew, stores that sell baby bottles, dolls, and toys with Hebrew lettering, and on Sundays the street hums with the activity most cities and malls experience on Saturdays.

Not all the Chasidic sects now living in Borough Park get along with one another, and they look down on the more secular residents, like Mrs. Dershowitz. She, in turn, feels that the neighborhood has gotten too crowded. The yeshiva where Alan and Nathan attended high school has been razed. But the Borough Park YM-YWHA, Young Men's and Young Women's Hebrew Association, at 4912 Fourteenth Avenue, where Alan played basketball and hung out with his friends, still exists and is still heavily used. As a boy, Dershowitz was much more interested in skipping school, playing basketball, or going off to

Brooklyn Dodgers games or movie openings at Radio City Music Hall than in studying.

Throughout his school days at the yeshiva, Dershowitz was a rebel and a gadfly. He always wanted to question, question, question, challenging the rabbis, asking, "Why not?" and mocking them. He was suspended from religious class for the last six months of high school for "lack of respect." His mother, from whom he inherited his untamable reddish hair, strong nose, and defiance, refutes Dershowitz's "troublemaker" reputation: "He was good. They just picked on him for no good reason. If something happened, they'd say, 'Dershowitz did it.' They didn't even want to give him a chance. He probably didn't want to take all the guff they handed out to him."

The idea of becoming a lawyer was planted by the principal of his school. "You got a good mouth on you, but not much of a Jewish mind. You should become either a lawyer or a conservative rabbi," his principal advised. But his father, a quiet man, also encouraged debate and dialogue in his home. During dinner-table conversations, he would ask, "Is it fair?" "How would that help the underdog?" "Would that be the right thing to do?"

Dershowitz didn't choose to become a lawyer until his second year at Brooklyn College. There he began to blossom academically. He earned top grades and was elected president of the student government. He went on to Yale Law School, where he was first in his class and editor-in-chief of the *Yale Law Journal*. After graduation he clerked for Judge David Bazelon and then for Supreme Court Justice Arthur Goldberg. Harvard Law School hired him at age twenty-five, and at twenty-eight he became the youngest full professor in the Law School's history.

In 1964, when Dershowitz accepted an offer to teach at Harvard Law School, "he was one of these, you know, shorthaired, professorial types that they have up at Harvard who don't know the first thing about practicing law," his brother, Nathan, explained. "I mean he was writing these scholarly works when he first got out. Stuff that maybe seven or eight of us had read. He produced some books, certainly, not much in the way of generally available things."

At the time, Alan sported cropped hair and wore horn-rimmed glasses, fitting his brother's description. A young, bright professor, he quickly established himself as a scholar in the nascent field of Law and Psychiatry. Being almost the same age as the students, he was highly accessible and popular. "Classes were fun, something unusual at the law school," one former student of his commented.

Nathan, four years younger than Alan, was the one doing criminal appeals in Manhattan. It wasn't until five years after he was tenured that Alan began working on criminal appeals and took "the case that changed my life." And the case came to him through his brother. Sheldon Seigel, a guy Nathan had known since they were kids in camp together, was arrested for planting a bomb in the office of Sol Hurok, the impresario who booked Soviet performers at Carnegie Hall. The bomb had killed a woman in the suite, and this ex-camper and others of the Jewish Defense League were being charged with her murder. Seigel had been indicted on first-degree murder. On Nathan's recommendation, Sheldon's sister called Alan to see if he could defend her brother. She wanted him represented by "Alan Dershowitz of Harvard Law School," to give her brother's defense more credibility. Dershowitz accepted a leading role in his first of many high-profile, often untenable criminal cases.

That first case easily appealed to him because it touched his Jewish nerve. He also couldn't understand why Seigel, who admitted to Dershowitz that he had made the bomb, wasn't being more actively prosecuted. Dershowitz later learned that Seigel was a government informer, and that he had secretly taped most of his conversations with the detective to whom he was feeding information on the JDL. Seigel claimed the detective had coerced his cooperation and had promised he would never have to testify against his JDL friends.

However, he didn't have tapes to support that assertion. At a pretrial hearing, Dershowitz cleverly filled in this gap during his cross-examination of the detective. First he read from transcripts of the taped conversations he did have—evidence the detective could only contradict if he perjured himself. Then he went on to "read" parts of other conversations supporting Seigel's claim. The detective believed that Dershowitz was reading from statements that had been caught on tape, and confirmed what Seigel claimed. The judge in the case admonished Dershowitz for playing what he called a "reprehensible" trick. But neither Seigel nor his co-defendants, whose cases couldn't be made without Seigel's testimony, were ever tried.

The violence, corruption, and double-dealing in that case gave Dershowitz a healthy contempt for "the system." From it he developed the following thirteen "Rules of the Justice Game" that he lived by and also taught students. Rule 1: "Almost all criminal defendants are, in fact, guilty. Rule 2: All criminal defense lawyers, prosecutors, and judges understand and believe Rule 1. Rules 3 through 12: For police, prosecutors, and judges, it is easier to violate the Constitution to convict guilty defendants than to comply with it. Most police will lie about whether they violated the Constitution. Many prosecutors encourage the police to lie, and many judges pretend to believe police officers who they know are lying. Most appellate judges pretend to believe the trial judges who pretend to believe the lying police officers. Nobody believes members of organized crime, drug dealers, career criminals, or potential informers. Rule 13: Nobody really wants justice."

He also created a course in legal tactics and ethics. At the heart of it is a sliding scale of tactics and ethics. Lawyers have a range of possible ethical standards from 1 to 5, with 1 being the least ethical and 5 being the most. On the other side of the equation is a similar scale for the range of tactics available, the most hardball of these being to badger a rape victim about her sexual history. Tactics and ethics, he tells students, are the basic trade-off that must be made between any criminal lawyer and client. "Very often, if you want a T-5 [toughest tactics], you're going to have to go to an E-3. If you want an E-4, sometimes you're going to have to settle for a T-2."

In the Seigel bombing case, he scored a 5 for tactics, 1 for ethics. But "an E-1 is still legal, still ethical." He doesn't encourage sneaky, marginally ethical behavior at any cost. "Qualms is good," he likes to tell his students. Though he acknowledges that "lying works," he says, "I wish it weren't so. . . . The job of a defense attorney is usually to keep the truth from getting out." Constantly alert for signs of any potential persecution—of Jews and other underdogs—and adept at maneuvering the balance between tactics and ethics, Dershowitz began to build a lucrative practice representing some of the country's most ruthless criminals. Another motivating factor was a brain tumor his son Elon had developed, and the cases offered a way to finance the boy's treatment. Also, his scholarship was being overshadowed by the more far-reaching work being done in Critical Legal Studies by people like Duncan Kennedy, Roberto Unger, and Morton Horowitz.

One case seemed to lead to another, with many referrals being filtered through his brother in New York. Nathan also provided backup on cases. By the mid-1980s, Dershowitz had a client roster that included convict-essayist Jack Abbott; Rabbi Bernard Bergman, for his involvement in a major nursing home scandal; the famous Jewish Soviet refusenik Natan Sharansky; and *Deep Throat* star Harry Reems. By writing newspaper columns about his cases and regularly appearing on radio and television to talk about the injustices his clients faced, Dershowitz fed his own public-relations machine.

He reached true celebrity status when he masterminded the successful appeal of Claus Von Bülow's conviction for attempting to murder his heiress wife, Sunny. People like convicted spy Jonathan Pollard, Jeffrey MacDonald, who was convicted of murdering his family, Leona Helmsley, "the tax scapegoat of 1992," boxing champion Mike Tyson, and O.J. Simpson, charged with the murder of his former wife and her friend, flocked to him for his legal counsel and media savvy.

About fifty percent of Dershowitz's cases are *pro bono* ones, like the representation of the Tison brothers featured in *Reversal of Fortune,* who smuggled weapons into prison to help their convicted-killer father and another murderer escape, and then watched the convicts shoot and kill a family of four in Arizona in order to steal their car to get away. In the movie, their last name was switched from Tison to Johnson and their race was switched from white to black, factual changes that Dershowitz was willing to forgive. In 1992, Dershowitz helped get their death sentences reduced to life terms.

His other portion of outside work is for clients who don't want it known they are being represented by Alan Dershowitz: individuals charged with such crimes as money laundering, cocaine distribution, and fraud. He says he accepts this rather "lowbrow" work because they are cases in which the courts are most tempted to take shortcuts.

Meanwhile, the more attention Dershowitz got in public, the more his colleagues at Harvard Law School bristled. A number of professors whom Dershowitz had disappointed when he turned away from "scholarship" found his behavior unseemly. Others were just plain envious. So he left them alone and hoped they wouldn't bother him. Certainly, internal faculty politics was not nearly as much fun as debating William F. Buckley and Patrick Buchanan, or taking on a Rhode Island judge who banned him from his courtroom because he disliked something Dershowitz had written in *Reversal,* or trying to open Mavin's Kosher Market, a deli in Cambridge's Harvard Square, amid picketing by a group called Women's Alliance Against Pornography protesting his representation of porn stars and his columns in *Penthouse* magazine.

Dershowitz has never wavered from his guiding principles. He will represent despicable characters because he says that "the true test of liberty is our willingness to grant it to those who would deny it to us." He often quotes H. L. Mencken, who wrote that "fighting for freedom requires the defense of some of the worst people." His pet cause is the First Amendment; anything that smacks of censorship is fair game, as he believes that "the voracious appetite of the censor is never satisfied." He believes that women who file false rape charges are villainous and should be exposed. He found a cause he labeled "Free Speech for Me," and described it as the "thoughtless rhetoric of the extreme left" that is helping to define what is "politically correct" and "incorrect."

To get his adrenaline pumping on that issue, all he had to do was look outside his window on the campus of Harvard Law School. From the day Bell stood outside of Harkness Commons to declare that he was taking a leave to protest the lack of minority women and men on the faculty, saying that others who "look black and think white"—understood to refer to Harvard's Randall Kennedy—hurt the cause, Dershowitz disapproved of the student left movement. He wrote a column after Bell made his announcement, in which he defended Kennedy and criticized Bell for attempting to impose a "political litmus test." Bell, he said, did not want the "widest possible diversity among the blacks or women on the faculty"; what he wanted was "a relative uniformity of viewpoint."

Two years after that rally, Dershowitz still felt that the diversity campaign by students was a sham. "I don't think anybody genuinely wants diversity. The true test of diversity for me is would people on the left vote for a really bright evangelical Christian who was a brilliant and articulate spokesperson for the right to life, the right to own guns, nonintervention in South Africa, anti-gay approaches to life, anti-feminist views? Would there be a push to get such a person on the faculty? Now, such a person would really diversify this place. Of course not. I think blacks want more blacks, women want more women, and leftists want more leftists. Everybody thinks diversification comes by getting more of themselves, and that's not true diversity."

In the furor over the mockery of Mary Joe Frug, Tribe's outspokenness fed into Dershowitz's contempt for "guilty white" academics who "caved in" to every demand made by minorities and women. The "current student body is only one constituency," he said. "We cannot kowtow to their every wish." Tribe's problem was that he "was speaking out of both sides of his mouth," said Dershowitz to writer Peter Collier. "At Harvard he panders constantly to the students with his radical rhetoric. But then, in the outer world, he is 'Laurence Tribe, national figure,' who has to pull back from and rationalize these positions."

But for the present, Tribe wasn't pulling any punches, and this battle of the legal titans continued to escalate. On April 23, the day after Dershowitz's column appeared, Tribe wrote a memo to the faculty about the op-ed piece. (Their relationship had apparently deteriorated too far for Tribe to walk down the hall and settle his differences privately.) It was a mistake for Dershowitz "to perceive a spirit of censorship or a demand for 'political correctness' " in his and other faculty members' desire to "talk back loudly when some students have made a sick joke of the mutilation and murder of a member of the community," he wrote. He attacked the "dismissive and trivializing tone" of Dershowitz's editorial. Dershowitz's view of political correctness, in fact, was a "crazy mirage," he said.

Tribe added, "In the name of courage and iconoclasm, Alan repeats a conventional wisdom that seems to me all convention and little wisdom. . . . Does Alan really think that only he has a sense of proportion, and that all of us who take this whole episode in a very different way are simply too weak-willed to live by our First Amendment principles when matters hit close to home?" Strongly denouncing the parody and calling for further inquiry did not put "into the air a chill that is inconsistent with the society of the dialogue that Alan and I would both celebrate."

Of course, Dershowitz had to fire back with his own memo pointing out that Tribe had once used the same idea of a publication being " 'merely' in somewhat poor taste" when Tribe defended *Hustler* magazine's parody of a drunken Jerry Falwell in which the evangelist was depicted as having engaged in incestuous relations with his own mother in an outhouse. Dershowitz did believe Tribe was weak on the First Amendment. After all, he also noted, Tribe had advised Congress with regard to a flag-burning amendment, and defended an overturned Minneapolis ordinance that would have criminalized pornography as sexual harassment. Dershowitz and Fried also wrote a letter to the Administrative Board asking it to "reprimand" David Kennedy for requesting an inquiry.

Meanwhile, riding the momentum generated by Dershowitz, a group of twenty-one mostly conservative professors decided to file their own response to Tribe's earlier suggestion that, by not realizing the parody in the *Revue* was a symptom of a larger

problem in faculty hiring and the failure of the faculty to include more women and minorities, they were part of the problem. "Such conclusory accusations neither help the community
to deal with a painful situation nor assist it in identifying particular ways the school can be made more open, civil, and welcoming for all of its students," they asserted. Defending the
hiring process, they wrote, "Although much remains to be
done, the appointment process here has for some time given
significant weight to minority status and to gender."

With fax machines and copiers now whirring at full speed,
Professor Betsy Bartholet wrote a memo in response to the
letter, Dershowitz's article, and statements by other professors.
"First, what I see some of you doing is belittling and trivializing
the incident. . . . Second, what I see some of you doing is mocking, marginalizing and condemning those of us who take the
Revue incident and related matters involving charges of sexual
harassment seriously."

Tribe and Dershowitz—indeed, the entire faculty—had
taken the debate over the *Revue* out of the *Law Review* editors'
hands. Tribe and the liberal bloc tried to fill in for the leadership
void they felt existed at the school. Dershowitz and the traditionalists had sent up a smokescreen to cover up the immorality
of the *Revue*'s publication in the first place; in the process, they
made the authors the victims and wrote them off with a simple
"boys will be boys" or "sophomores will be sophomores" dismissal.

If anyone was guilty of the "Free Speech for Me" syndrome,
it was Dershowitz himself. The harm of being called a rapist,
even if the person accused is not guilty, is not comparable to
the harm of being raped. Nor is being accused of discrimination
the same as being discriminated against because of gender or
race or religion or national origin or sexual orientation. Dershowitz may have had to fear getting beaten up in his neighborhood, and he recognizes discrimination against Jews. He
feels he's been a victim of cultural prejudice against Jews, he
once said he did not want to teach in a place that would not
appoint a Jew as dean, and he helped secure Albert Sacks's appointment as dean of Harvard Law School. But he didn't seem

to recognize that in the United States, millions more people have been attacked and killed on the basis of gender and race than on the basis of religion. He's never had to fear walking alone on a street at night. The parody had set off an unprecedented volley of attack and counterattack because it touched not just on the question of harm or free speech or political correctness, but on the issue of power. To make men monitor their speech is to take away some of their power.

It was easier for Dershowitz, Fried, and other professors on the right to deride something as "politically correct" or to hide behind the mantle of free speech. By accusing Tribe and the more liberal professors of trying to politicize the situation— and denying that they were engaging in politics was also political—they were maintaining the status quo, snuffing out debate, and covering up the hostility to women and minorities at Harvard Law and the poor way it was training future lawyers.

For that reason, the battle continued to rage; especially as the trial of the nine students charged in connection with a nonviolent sit-in at the dean's office moved forward.

CHAPTER 12

TRIAL AND GRAVE ERROR

As Dershowitz, Tribe, and most of the rest of the faculty continued to trade memos and letters, returning one almost as quickly as another was issued, the Administrative Board announced that it would not be bringing charges against three students identified as having participated in the sit-in at Charles Fried's office in March, and that a fourth student had been misidentified. This decision came after the three students, John Bonifaz, Julia Gordon, and Raul Perez, wrote a letter to the board saying they understood that their activities had "crossed a boundary between offices, in which professors have a privacy interest, and other areas of the Law School." They had not "meant to disrespect" Fried, but had chosen him "because of his prominent role on the faculty and the interest he has consistently demonstrated in addressing the issue of faculty diversity." Still, they were not waiving their right "to protest the lack of progress toward achieving a diverse faculty," and referred to the school's Code of Rights and Responsibilities, which clearly states that "reasoned dissent plays a particularly vital part" in the Law School community and ensures that students are entitled to "press for action on matters of concern by any appropriate means."

For that reason, the board only issued the students a

reprimand, which would be placed in their files, along with their letter. But the matter would not be reported outside the university, to bar officials or potential employers, "so long as that individual engages in no further violation of University or Law School rules during the rest of his or her term as a student," the Administrative Board announced on Thursday, April 23.

But the other case—involving nine students who had been photographed and identified as having prevented Vice-Dean Smith from entering his office—was set for May 4, a little more than a week away and three days before final exams started for three of the students. For the first time in the history of the Administrative Board, the students were exercising their right to a public hearing. In this case, "public" was being defined as open to the "Harvard Law School Community," meaning students, professors, employees, their relatives and guests, and the *Harvard Crimson* and the *Harvard Law Record*. No cameras, videotaping, or audio recording equipment would be allowed.

The nine students were being represented by Peter Cicchino, the articulate 3L who had eloquently called for Dean Clark's resignation, and by Professor William (Terry) Fisher III, the only professor of those whom the students had asked for help who hadn't turned them down. Fisher, a legal historian, was hardly a litigator, but the students didn't have much choice. Bemis Professor of International Law Detlev Vagts, a senior member of the faculty, agreed to act as the prosecutor for the administration. Vagts would present the school's case first, and he would be followed by the defense. The students were expected to testify on their own behalf, and each side had the right to cross-examine witnesses.

The school was still in an uproar over the Frug parody, the Administrative Board proceedings, and the faculty appointments earlier in the year. The administration was receiving angry letters from alumni as well as from students and professors at other schools, writing to voice their disappointment with Harvard; and the school was becoming the subject of numerous, mostly critical, editorials in the local and national press. To try to quiet the campus, Clark scheduled a forum for

Wednesday, April 29, four days before the Griswold Nine hearing.

In the late afternoon of the twenty-ninth, close to 200 people filled the maple-paneled, hull-shaped Ames Courtroom, on the second floor of Austin Hall. This had been the site of the previous forum in March, following the announcement of the appointment of the four white men, and it would soon be the location of the Griswold Nine hearing. "How to Build a Sense of Community at Harvard Law School" was the title of this afternoon's forum, a title that, despite all the "open letters to the law school community," indicated that even the administration recognized there was no community at the Law School.

As they entered the mock courtroom, each student, faculty member, and observer received a copy of a worksheet prepared by negotiating expert Roger Fisher. It described the "symptoms" of the problem: the pain caused by the *Revue;* the Law School climate, which had made many women feel marginalized; the institutional failure of Harvard Law School to hire a sufficiently diverse faculty; and the problem of free speech being restrained because of a fear of the consequences. Fisher's chart listed some prescriptive ideas and courses of action.

Charles Ogletree, the popular black professor best known for representing Anita Hill in her charges of sexual harassment against Supreme Court nominee Clarence Thomas, and a subject of the *Revue* himself, was the moderator of a panel comprising Clark; professors Todd Rakoff, William Alford, and Elizabeth Bartholet; students Shelley Simms, a second-year student who was a member of the *Law Review* and the Black Law Students Association, and Jim Bowen, also a second-year, who was the former president of the Harvard Law School Republicans and incoming editor of the conservative *Journal of Law and Public Policy;* and Dean of Students Sarah Wald, who was also a member of the Administrative Board. Almost every constituency of Harvard Law School, except alumni, was represented. "We won't spend a lot of time talking about the past," Ogletree announced.

Clark was the first panelist to speak. "I see myself as here basically to listen . . . I want to collect ideas for all of us to consider. This is not *the* meeting—it's the beginning of a whole series of endeavors. I see a lot of tension in this community, and some of it is caused by witting and unwitting things we do to each other," he said. And he admitted he was one of those who had increased the tension by doing something unwittingly—telling *The Wall Street Journal* that students who benefited from affirmative action were insecure. "I'm very sorry for talking to *The Wall Street Journal* reporter and saying things that struck many students here as very offensive. It was wrong for me to say it . . . I didn't mean to be dismissive towards any of our students. . . ."

"I'm someone who likes to come to work, and what I've felt this spring is that I don't like to come to work," lamented Todd Rakoff. His feelings had started with the faculty appointments and then had been intensified by the *Revue*. "But I must admit that over the past few weeks, I find myself reacting more and more to the reactions of those events . . . this seems out of control to me."

"We have to treat other people with respect," said Jim Bowen.

For the next two hours, each panelist talked about his or her disillusionment, and recommended such things as an independent committee to examine the quality of community at Harvard. Students in the room urged Clark to drop the charges against the Griswold Nine, to take responsibility, and suggested that if a community were to exist, it must be built on a presumption of inclusion. The forum had the air of a giant group-therapy session. "I don't feel that Harvard Law School is a community," said Professor Christopher Edley, Jr. "It's a job. I don't like being here, and I spend as much time as possible away from Harvard Law School, a privilege Harvard law students don't have."

"Why are we so focused on reactions and not on what actually happened?" asked Rebecca Eisenberg, who had become one of the more outspoken women about the *Revue*. Indeed, her co-editors were furious that she was speaking out and talking to reporters. *Review* rules state that only the president speaks for its members. "It's ridiculous to punch me and then criticize me for saying 'ouch,' " she added.

Throughout this exchange, Dean Clark was bent over a pad of paper, taking notes. Raul Perez, who had participated in the Fried sit-in, started directing his comments to Clark, then stopped. "Goddammit, look at me," Perez shouted at Clark. "You see, he is always in a state of denial," Perez told the spectators. "He has been more of a divider than a healer. I hope that in the future you'll be a little more sincere in both your comments and your actions."

Peter Cicchino told Clark, "You have an opportunity to do something dramatic . . . and all it takes is words . . . issue a statement saying you want Professor Derrick Bell to come back . . . and why not, as a gesture, ask the Ad Board to drop persecution of the nine students? Why don't you do it?" Most of the students and faculty rose and gave Cicchino a standing ovation.

"Pardons are not in my power," answered Clark. Still, he had found the power to take four important, albeit reactive, steps to improve the situation at the school. He had established a working group to develop a policy on sexual harassment, had recommended that the appointments committee focus on recruiting women professors, planned to name more women to key faculty committees, and was going to begin monthly exchanges with the appointments committee and students.

When the forum ended, some people felt better for having been able to air their feelings. Others were unenthusiastic and didn't expect much to change. There was an unusual backdrop to the meeting: at about the time it was beginning, a state jury in California acquitted all of the officers charged in the beating of motorist Rodney King. And by the time the meeting adjourned, fires were burning throughout South Central Los Angeles. The verdict wasn't addressed directly at the forum, but over the next few days, as the Griswold Nine prepared for their disciplinary hearing, the newscasts, playing the videotape of the beating over and over, and the footage of broken store windows, smoke billowing from warehouses, and looters running with television sets and other goods in their hands, would be a constant metaphor for the unfair treatment endured by blacks, women, and minorities. It was a reminder that the harm caused by the parody and the discrimination that had led the nine students to sit in at the dean's office were real.

For Derek Honore, one of the nine students facing possible suspension, the rioting in Los Angeles touched him personally. His family lived in South Central. He had a brother on the L.A. police force. Smoke had entered his family's apartment. And he was unable to get letters of recommendation from a school he had attended because it had been closed. Elizabeth Moreno, the humor columnist for the Harvard Law School newspaper and one of the Griswold Nine, was also affected by the riots. Her mother worked in South Central, and during the rioting, someone threw a Molotov cocktail through a window of her mother's office building. "It was really hard personally because several people were affected by the events in L.A.," said Lucy Koh, another of the Griswold Nine. "It made it difficult for some of us to decide whether to stay on and go through the trial or not."

Deciding whether to go through with the hearings was not easy. There were many considerations. Most of the defendants were not activists and had never before been involved in such a serious act of civil disobedience. Now they were facing the possibility of suspension. They were committed to seeing a diverse faculty at Harvard. But was a trial going to help or hurt the cause? Would the publicity be positive or negative? Would it be worth it personally for each of them? In the few days before the hearing was to begin, they held a meeting with their counsel, Cicchino or Fisher, almost every day.

At 7:00 A.M. on Friday, May 1, all nine defendants met at Terry Fisher's office to continue working on their defense. Fisher and Cicchino had something else to discuss with them. Two other professors, Alan Stone and negotiator Roger Fisher, who had begun to act as a liaison between the administration and the students, had presented several proposals, which, if the students accepted them, might end the matter and spare the Law School further publicity. For instance, they suggested that the students write letters as the students who sat-in on Fried's office had done, apologizing for any disruption caused by their sit-in, and that they send flowers to Dean Clark's secretaries for having made them feel uncomfortable by their presence.

The meeting lasted for four hours, with the students eventually moving to the Black Law Students Association offices when Fisher had to leave to teach a class. They discussed whether the proposals would work to settle the matter and prevent the Nine from being suspended. They had no guarantees from Dean Clark or the Administrative Board. The majority of the students didn't *want* to settle. "This was not about FTD, this was about diversity," said Koh. But several other students were not as sure about continuing. Charisse Carney, a 3L, was facing a heavy workload and had to complete several papers so that she could graduate. If she was suspended or expelled, she might not graduate at all. Elizabeth Moreno was having serious doubts, and given the magnitude of the L.A. riots, participating in an all-night sit-in at the dean's office no longer seemed worth defending. Jill Newman, a close friend of Moreno's, was also uncertain. And Derek Honore was still worried about the wreckage from the riots at home. Moreno decided she would accept Roger Fisher's proposal and try to reach a settlement with the administration. "I don't care about the rest of you, I'm sending flowers," Koh recalled Moreno saying as Moreno walked out of the meeting.

Moreno never sent the flowers, but she did plead out of the case. At a preparatory meeting on Sunday evening, the day before the hearing was to begin, the other eight students all voted to continue and face the Administrative Board. They would not consider any other proposals Fisher was still offering, something he would do until the last hour of the hearing. They would try to show that they had not intimidated any of Clark's secretaries and were not your typical radical activists, but moderates who were driven to sit in because of the school's unwillingness to tenure women of color and minorities. Their several weeks of planning this defense would finally be put to the test the next day at 4:15 P.M.

On National Public Radio's "Morning Edition," early on Monday, May 4, the day the Griswold Nine hearings were scheduled to start, host Bob Edwards brought the controversies at Harvard to the listening public's attention. And Tribe and Dershowitz continued their feud on the air. An exchange that occurred during this broadcast revealed how deeply their animosity toward each other now ran.

Professor Laurence Tribe: "It was dancing on the grave of a murder victim. . . . It was published on the first anniversary of her murder. It called her the 'rigor mortis' professor. It makes fun generally of violence against women. It seems to me that should be taken as a symptom of something gone badly wrong. My question is: What does it say about an institution like this?"

David Wright, reporting from Boston, explained how Tribe was among fifteen faculty members who called the parody a symptom of institutional sexism and misogyny. He moved to Dershowitz, and described how Dershowitz saw the incident as a question of free speech. Dershowitz launched into the same attack on the liberals that he had made in his op-ed piece. But this time his words had a sharper and more personal edge to them:

"Free speech is wonderful as long it applies to other people, but as soon as it comes home—as soon as the free speech offends us, my God, all the rules are off it. All the brains at the Harvard Law School, the brilliant brains of the radical left, get together, and they figure out ways of constructing freedom of speech and the First Amendment just so as not to include this particular genre of offensive speech. How many times have we heard that? 'I'm offended, it must be wrong.'"

Tribe: "And when those of us who say we would like to engage in further inquiry about the environment are told, 'Oh, you mustn't do that. You are silencing debate.' . . . They are the ones who are silencing debate by bandying about the convenient label of political correctness."

Dershowitz: "There's no harassment here. This is a spoof. . . . You know, he sounds just like Joseph McCarthy when he says that. What's wrong with an inquiry? . . . What's wrong with having some hearings? . . . My God, doesn't he remember? Has he no historical sense of perspective? He knows better."

Wright correctly observed how the gloves were off. Then he mentioned how the administration had been unwilling to discipline the authors of the parody, but, later that day, was going to begin disciplinary hearings against nine students who had occupied the dean's office for two days to protest the lack of faculty diversity. Marilynn Sager, the 3L who had helped draft the statement by the women students upset by the parody, denounced that disparity. Wright reported how Law School officials denied the existence of any double standards and claimed that preventing someone from working is against the rules. Publishing something—even something offensive—is not.

Law Review president Emily Schulman offered an insightful assessment of what was at the heart of the problem. "It may very well be the case that law school education, at least at Harvard Law School, certainly doesn't promote and may very well school out of its students any real sense of human compassion and moral conviction."

Later that day, as school administrators and prosecutor Detlev Vagts stood poised to suspend the eight students who admitted to holding a nonviolent sit-in at the dean's office to highlight a problem at the school, Schulman's poignant words hung in the air. So did the raw aggression displayed by professors Dershowitz and Tribe. The great, mistaken tragedy of this tumultuous spring was about to be played out.

Once again, students, faculty members, employees, and their friends and relatives filled all 250 seats located around the perimeter of the Ames Courtroom. Another hundred people stood in the aisles and along the wall. It was 4:15 P.M., the precise time set for the hearing, and standing room only. According to the schedule set by the Administrative Board, the proceeding would run until 6:45 P.M., and, if necessary, would reconvene at 7:30 and last to 9:30. If more time was needed, it would resume the next day at 4:15 P.M. and run to 7:00 P.M.

With its fifty-foot vaulted ceilings, wood-paneled walls, and cavernous feeling, Ames was an exact replica of a courtroom, built for moot-court competitions. Auditorium-style seats ran along the perimeter of the room, and in front was a judge's bench and a witness stand. For this hearing, hardly a mock trial, eight six-foot, rectangular tables were put in the center of the room into a huge square with a large hole in the middle. At about twelve o'clock on the square was one lone chair with a microphone, where witnesses would sit. To the right of the witness were the eight defendants and their counsel, Cicchino and Fisher. To the left was the prosecutor-presenter, Vagts, and a woman assisting him. Directly in front of the witness, at the opposite side of the square, just below the judge's bench, sat the eight members of the Administrative Board. Professor David Shapiro chaired the proceeding.

To Cicchino: "It could not have been more theatrical. It was really 'Twin Peaks on the Charles.' " Another observer said, "For drama and intensity, it seemed like an episode of 'L.A. Law.' "

Shapiro began by giving a brief opening statement about the need for order and about the fact that in the course of the hearing the board planned to receive evidence that might be relevant to the question of violations, to the question of appropriate sanctions if a violation is found or to both. He then explained the roles of Professors Vagts and Fisher and Cicchino, and of Vagts's assistant, Janet Katz.

Substantively, the case was rather simple. The administration wanted to show that the students had obstructed access to the offices located off the corridor, interfered with the "normal" duties of various employees, and refused to leave after being asked. The students hoped to show that their sit-in was entirely nonviolent and minimally disruptive, merely an expressive act of dissent motivated by a legitimate concern for the Law School's treatment of women and minorities. Vagts would present the school's case first, then Fisher and Cicchino would attempt to make the students' defense, and then members of the Administrative Board would ask questions. The proceeding took eleven hours over two days, and involved the questioning and cross-examining of nearly twenty witnesses.

Vagts, a thin, white-haired man, who appeared grim, spent hours eliciting testimony from Harvard's security officers and from Vice-Dean Smith and Dean Clark's secretaries, to show that the students caused a major interference. And although Clark himself was not at the hearing, he was relying on his witnesses to explain that from what they saw happening, if

Clark had tried hard to enter his office, the tension level of the sit-in would have risen.

Vagts was more successful with some witnesses than others, for instance, he asked Sergeant John Francis how the students acted toward him. He said their behavior was mixed. Some had tried to be friendly with him and talked to him about the origin of his name. Officer Rocco Forgione said the students had made him angry and he hadn't spoken to any of them. In the past, he had been helpful to students during other sit-ins, trying to accommodate them while seeing that events proceeded in an orderly fashion. A veteran employee of the university, he said this time he had had to offer more help to the secretaries because the students had intimidated them.

Vice-Dean Smith proved to be a strong witness for the administration. He testified that he had passed through the area several times, usually after stepping over and around the students sitting on the floor. At one time he had decided not to go into the corridor because, he said, he had been afraid there might be a physical altercation. Later, when the students testified, they said that they hadn't deliberately tried to block Smith or Clark from entering the corridor, though they might have made it more difficult for them to maneuver or pass through it.

Four secretaries testified about whether their freedom of movement had been restricted. Smith's secretary, named Sissy Amato, said she had been allowed to move freely, except one time when a male student's arm blocked her as she was entering the office. "I didn't think it was a big deal," she had told the *Crimson*. She had had the most direct contact with the protesters; there had been a moment when she seemed to lose her balance while trying to step over the students to get into the dean's office, and someone had had to hold her arm to keep her from falling. Yet her testimony was not nearly as damaging as the administration might have hoped. "She was the friendliest towards us," one of the defendants later commented. A few other secretaries, however, testified that the protesters had been rude and unpleasant toward them.

Finally, Vagts put forward witnesses to attest to the financial injury the students had cost the school. The money spent for increased security during protests, and administrative time to investigate the sit-ins and to consider whether to bring charges, ran close to $200,000, Vice-Dean Sandra Coleman testified. With that the administration rested.

Fisher called each of the remaining eight students facing charges to testify. In addition to describing the events as they saw them, the defendants, six women and two men, also made brief statements about why they had chosen to hold a sit-in. When they described their backgrounds, it was clear that these students weren't terrorists or far-left radicals. For the most part, these students were mainstream and moderate. They had been the pride and joy of their colleges and universities. They were school leaders, had enjoyed good relationships with their school administrators, and were involved in charitable organizations. Few had engaged in this level of political action or risked being suspended before. These were good citizens. Fisher hoped the Administrative Board would see that they had been motivated by the seriousness of the lack of faculty diversity.

Jodi Grant, a 2L and a Yale graduate, was active in the Law School's Student Funded Fellowships and the Big Brother/Big Sister Program. At Yale, she had been president of her class.

Jill Newman, a 2L, had graduated Phi Beta Kappa from Cornell University. At Harvard, she was involved in the Women's Law Association.

Marie-Louise Ramsdale was outgoing co-chair of the Women's Law Association. As a 2L, she was running for president of the Law School Council. As an undergraduate at the University of South Carolina, she had been student body president, president of the Student Alumni Association, and a representative to the University Board of Trustees.

Lucy Koh was a 2L who had graduated from Harvard-Radcliffe. In college, she had been a member of the undergrad council, had taught at a high school in Dorchester, Boston, and had volunteered with Big Sister. At Harvard, she had won the honor of writing the best brief in the semifinal round of the Ames Moot Court Competition, and participated in the Tenant Advocacy Project, the Battered Women's Advocacy Project, and the Asian American Law Students Association. She had also lived and worked in Mexico, Nigeria, and Thailand.

Julie Su, the only 1L, was a Phi Beta Kappa graduate from Stanford University. She had worked for Senator Cecil Green, for the Organization of Chinese Americans, and as a Peace Corps volunteer in Belize. She was the incoming co-chair of the Asian American Law Students Association.

Derek Honore, from South Central Los Angeles, was a graduate of UCLA. A 2L, he was chairman of the Black Law Students Association's Academic Affairs Committee. He also worked as a tutor and mentor in Roxbury, Boston.

William Anspach, a 2L, had graduated from Haverford College in 1986. Of all the protesters, he had the most experience in participating in acts of civil disobedience. He was in the process of establishing an Unemployment Compensation Advocacy Project through a temporary affiliation with Greater Boston Legal Services.

Charisse Carney, the only 3L, was the outgoing president of the Black Law Students Association. A graduate of Lincoln University, Justice Thurgood Marshall's alma mater, she was studying for a joint master's degree at the Kennedy School of Government. At Harvard, she had worked with the administration to establish the Charles Hamilton Houston Fellowship for minorities and women interested in law teaching. After graduation, she would begin clerking for a New Jersey Superior Court judge, and she would direct a children's play she had written about African-American culture.

These students, who began their testimony on Monday night, described the stuffy atmosphere, the use of a makeshift toilet during the sit-in, and other physical conditions that were imposed upon them. But this was not the hostile environment the administration was trying to portray. They described why they had worn masks, and explained that they weren't intended to be threatening. Their desire was always to be nonviolent and nondisruptive. They explained how they had cleaned up afterwards, so as not to appear disrespectful.

Nor were they as thoughtless and unkind to the secretaries as the administration was presenting the situation. There had been a few confusing moments, at first, because neither Clark nor Smith was there, and the secretaries didn't know what to do until they arrived later in the afternoon. The students said they had sent a letter to the clerical workers' union, notifying them of the sit-in. Vagts suggested the students should have known that the dean's secretaries were not members of the union.

Julia Gordon, who had participated in prior sit-ins, noted that the administration had never before issued charges, and said it was using this instance as a special case. Charisse Carney, who had spent her own money to take trips to recruit minorities to Harvard, and had been instrumental in creating a fellowship for prospective minority scholars, described how angry and disappointed she had felt after talking with Clark about his comments in *The Wall Street Journal.* It was compelling testimony.

Professors Frank Michelman, Chris Edley, Duncan Kennedy, and David Charny described the conversations they had had with the students on Tuesday morning, before they called off their protest. While Fisher was examining Charny, Vagts objected that Charny was using notes to refresh his memory about that morning's events and the advice he gave the students. Incensed at Vagts's objection, Charny suddenly threw his yellow notepad at Vagts and then reached into his pocket for his paperback copy of *The Brothers Karamazov,* and pitched that at Vagts too. The pad hit Vagts in the face and dropped on his arm. Vagts stood frozen, letting the pad sit on his arm until his assistant removed it.

Vagts was shaken. He said to everyone in the room, "Do you know how hard this has been for me? I'm doing this because Dean Clark asked me to." Charny, also flustered, apologized. He said that Vice-Dean Smith had been able to refresh his recollection by reading from a set of papers, and he thought he could use notes too. Everyone was shocked to see a professor throwing things at another professor. "It was so dramatic," said student defendant Koh.

In closing, Vagts apologized for having to prosecute the students, and said he had tried to make the hearing as easy as possible on everyone. Fisher closed by saying the *Law Review* parody had done more harm than the sit-ins, and asked that the students receive light punishment. On Friday, May 8, the Administrative Board issued an eight-page report saying that by a five-to-three vote, each student was receiving a warning, which would remain in his or her file until graduation. If they engaged in any more disruptive acts, the matter would be reported to state bar authorities. The board said the sanction was not stiff because this was the first time in many years that charges of that nature had been brought, and there had been other sit-ins that could also have been called "disruptive." Moreover, the "confrontational nature" of some students' actions were not premeditated, and students had apologized for any distress they may have caused.

The students felt relieved and vindicated. Because Moreno, who had settled early, had gotten a warning, they thought whatever they received would be worse. "It was a total surprise," recalled Koh. "Elizabeth had set the [minimum], so we were told we weren't to get a warning."

Vagts said later, "There was precious little chance there wouldn't be a warning. The dean wanted it, and other people thought there would be more [demonstrations, sit-ins, etc.] coming if we didn't stop it now." Vagts says he hadn't sought their expulsion. "I had no interest in trying to jack up the penalties. Why should I try to pull at the maximum penalty for them?" Overall, he said, "it was a little daunting, representing the State."

Cicchino found the entire process a disgrace. "It's totally a kangaroo court," he said. "It's totally ad hoc, a complete abuse of any due process. It purports to be a non-adversarial body, yet has all of the disadvantages of an adversarial process."

On Monday, May 11, a week after the hearings began, Clark sent a letter to "The Law School Community," announcing the Administrative Board's decision to the school. Defending the result, he said, "I believe it is important that we now move beyond the sit-in and hearing toward more constructive forms of dialogue. . . . As Dean, I wish very much to ensure that our students get the best legal education possible and that we provide a setting in which students can become skilled and ethical

lawyers who will serve as leaders in all parts of the profession."
He said he would welcome suggestions from everyone, and expected to announce some steps to advance his goal. Despite this open, acknowledging letter, the students, who believed the school had a long way to go before it would be a happy, diverse place, knew the administration would treat sit-ins more harshly in the future. The Administrative Board was just warming up.

But when it came to the editors of the *Harvard Law Review* who had authored the vicious parody of slain Professor Mary Joe Frug, the Administrative Board announced on May 20 that it would not punish them. In a letter to Professor David Kennedy, who had called for disciplinary action, the board said it would not take action because there were no rules limiting the content of the publication. Nor would it launch an investigation into charges of sexual harassment at the *Review*, though it would investigate individual complaints if they were filed.

Of course, the board could have found a basis by which to proceed against the editors. It could have charged those students with "interfering with members of the university in performance of their normal duties and activities," just as easily as it had done with the demonstrators. The fallout from the parody was taking up time, interrupting students' and professors' preparation for exams and classes. The editors of the Frug parody had compromised what were expressed in the school's statement on Rights and Responsibilities—under which the students had been prosecuted—as the essential characteristics of Harvard Law School: "respect for the dignity of others" and "mutual respect and trust." Its publication was truly "inappropriate behavior," in violation of school rules.

But the message was clear. Free speech at Harvard Law School was "for me but not for you." Tribe and other progressive professors had tried to open a dialogue on hostility to women at Harvard Law School, understanding that democratic speech was educational and redemptive. But the conservatives cried "political correctness" and, as a result, proved that they wanted to staunch public debate and let the hate-speakers get in the last word and have the last laugh. It was a great injustice at a once-great institution. Harvard Law School had become a "vile circus," as Boston University political scientist Abigail Thernstrom wrote in *The Wall Street Journal.* Thernstrom, though, was critical of the left for using the parody to press the diversity agenda and critical of the right for not embracing consistent academic standards.

On Wednesday, June 3, the day before graduation, former dean Erwin Griswold, faculty members, students, and guests gathered under a red and white striped tent on the lawn of Jarvis Field, adjacent to the Harkness Commons, for a quiet luncheon. It was supposed to be a party celebrating the school's one hundred and seventy-fifth anniversary. But no one was gleeful. Even Christopher Columbus Langdell, the first dean of the Harvard Law School, would have been embarrassed by the spectacle just witnessed at his alma mater.

There was no closure to this watershed year at Harvard Law. Graduation day, the next morning, was perhaps the sunniest day since the end of winter. The temperature was about seventy-five degrees, geraniums were set outside each building, and banners with the school's "Veritas" symbol hung from the lampposts and oak trees at Holmes Field. Harvard does pomp so well. At 8:45 A.M., students and their parents were treated to a champagne breakfast where the anniversary luncheon had taken place the previous day. Student activists were beginning to assemble too. John Bonifaz was distributing posters and placards bearing slogans such as "Resign Dean Clark," "Diversity Now," and "Down with Discrimination, Down with the Dean." They would carry these into the part of Harvard Yard between Memorial Church and Widener Library, known as the Tercentenary Theater, where all undergraduate and graduate degrees would be conferred.

The Yard was a splendor. Three giant crimson "Veritas" banners, bearing the ancient shield, billowed from the front of Widener Library. In brilliant colors hung the banners of the thirteen undergraduate houses. The male marshals sported morning coats and felt top hats, with fresh carnations in their lapels. Women ushers wore white dresses with red banners draped across their shoulders, and straw hats with red ribbons. They looked like guests at a large English garden party. All of the chairs and the lawn space were filled. It was a regal ceremony, marked by a grand processional of four divisions of faculty members, university officials, and dignitaries, all in long robes and brilliantly colored hats reflecting their fields and ranks.

Peter Cicchino won the honor of being one of three students from throughout the university to make a speech at commencement. He was mellifluous, praising Harvard while also describing its flaws. "I'd like to talk about three vices which this community possesses: arrogance, contentiousness, and a sense of entitlement. And how we might use those vices at the service of others." Instead of replacing vice with virtue, education was about capitalizing on those vices to do good. About arrogance, he said, "Talking about arrogance at Harvard is like talking about Catholicism at the Vatican. So pervasive is the reality, one hesitates to comment upon it." But he urged all the graduates to use that arrogance to help people.

About contentiousness, he said, there is a saying in the Koran: "Disagreement in my community is a sign of God's generosity." He went on, "Surely we are God's chosen people!"

As for entitlement, "On some deep level, each of us believes that he or she is, in the words of Bruce Springsteen, 'born to run.' Run businesses, run academic institutions, run the whole country! . . . So . . . my last bit of advice is that we embrace the responsibility to use what we have learned—yes, even the vices—to the advantage of those whom I once heard described as without voice and without choice."

It was a speech that alluded to the controversies that beset Harvard Law School in the last year. Cicchino tried to explain the reasons for those controversies and offered a way to learn from them. It was an address Dean Clark should have made long before any suits against the school, parodies, sit-ins, or administrative hearings ever happened. When it came time for Clark to present the class of students designated to receive their law degrees, he received an embarrassingly loud chorus of boos and hisses from the Law School graduates. Apparently not all students lose their appetite for activism upon graduation, and many had lost confidence in Clark.

Immediately after the main commencement exercise, students

and their guests moved to Holmes Field, where the class of '92—comprising 539 J.D.'s, 131 LL.M.'s, three S.J.D.'s, and twenty-nine masters in international tax—would receive their diplomas. Clark gave a soft, almost inaudible speech. "We've been through a lot together," he said. "We've had our ups and downs. Your concerns about legal education and Harvard have had a tremendous impact on me. I respect the energy you have put into making this a better place. I don't care what *U.S. News* or *USA Today* says about Yale. You are number one."

After everything that had happened, that was hard to believe. No period in the history of the Harvard Law School had been more controversial. Never had professors *and* students been so ruthless in their pursuit of what they thought was right, or to avenge what they thought was wrong. Driven by the force of the battles over Critical Legal Studies and Traditional Scholarship in the 1980s, the events of the 1991–92 academic year were both paradigmatic and enigmatic. The parody was a symbol of a sick school and sick society.

Harvard Law School had been "mugged," one professor said to writer Peter Collier. Many of its precious traditions, except its three vices of arrogance, contentiousness, and elitism, as Cicchino described them, had been overturned. But would it recover? The tally at the end of the day: still only five women and three African-American males out of sixty tenured professors; no minority woman, Latino, Asian, Native American, openly gay or lesbian, or physically disabled person. And there was little to indicate that, fundamentally, Harvard Law School could move beyond the moral disintegration of the 1980s, exemplified by the *Revue*, and rebuild itself as a moral force.

EPILOGUE

The crisp crimson and white banners with the Harvard Law School shield and insignia were still flying in Holmes Field a week after Harvard Law School dean Robert Clark had been booed at graduation by students seeking a more diverse faculty and by others upset about his handling of the malicious parody written by editors of the *Law Review*. But the dean was back at work, wasting no time in finding out if Derrick Bell, on whose behalf many of the students were protesting, would be returning to the faculty when his authorized leave of absence expired on June 30, 1992.

In a letter to Bell at New York University on June 12, just eight days after graduation, Clark told Bell he still hoped he would return to Harvard. However, he needed to know in writing no later than June 30. If he did not have a response by then, Bell would be deemed to have resigned.

Clark told Bell he knew Professor Frank Michelman had already written to Harvard University president Neil Rudenstein for an extension to the rule, and that Rudenstein was considering that request. He was writing Bell so that if his request was denied, he would be able to reconsider his plans.

Five days later, Rudenstein wrote Professor Michelman, who was acting as Bell's lawyer in this matter, to tell him that after talking with the university's incoming provost, Jerry Green, and general counsel, Daniel Steiner, he was not going to permit Bell to extend his leave of absence. Steiner had met with Michelman on June 3, the day before graduation.

Named a university professor in 1992, Michelman held one of the highest positions at Harvard. He was greatly respected for his constitutional scholarship and his level-headedness. People often said he had much more influence on the faculty than Tribe or Dershowitz. In a letter to Rudenstein, written May 7, Michelman argued that Harvard Law School had never established an affirmative action grievance procedure for faculty members. Moreover, the school had failed to improve the faculty's diversity. Indeed, some members of the faculty were opposed to affirmative action altogether, and the school itself treated affirmative action as a matter of individual choice and not an obligation. Not surprising, he said, considering Harvard Law School was so inbred. Granting Bell an exception to the two-year policy was clearly an appropriate remedy, he argued.

Rudenstein did not know Bell personally because Bell had been on leave since Rudenstein was appointed president in 1991, though he said he respected the efforts Bell had made to attract more women and minorities. But, he said, he did not agree with Bell's view, as articulated by Michelman, that the Law School's hiring practices were inconsistent with university affirmative-action policies.

Moreover, simply extending the rule, without a predetermined end, would set a bad precedent. Bell could follow his conscience, but he had to understand the consequences.

Bell wrote Clark back on June 24, with copies to Rudenstein and Michelman, saying he did not believe "that a fair basis ha[d] yet been laid for a deliberate, formal, administrative action, coming as close as these warnings do to a direct removal of my professional tenure." He felt they were trying to force him to leave, not really to work in a "collegial spirit" at all, as Rudenstein had commended Bell for doing in the letter to Michelman. Rudenstein hadn't even talked directly to Bell or Michelman, preferring instead to rely on the opinions of other university officials. Bell told Clark that Rudenstein had relied on "general arguments . . . against leave-taking . . . and on certain "characterizations" of Bell's activities and motives, which he said he found "inaccurate."

He implied that he was going to appeal to Harvard's two governing bodies, the Harvard Corporation and the Harvard Board of Overseers. In the meantime, he was not resigning or allowing himself to be terminated. "Feeling as I do that some further hearing and appeal procedures must be in order, I do not consider that I will have resigned on July 1. It is certainly not my intention to resign."

President Rudenstein was going to be out of town until mid-July, but provost-designate Jerry Green wrote Bell two days later to say that arrangements had been made for the Harvard Corporation to consider his request formally. The corporation's Joint Committee on Appointments and perhaps other members of the Board of Overseers would be reviewing materials pertaining to his leave request and a written statement from Bell if he chose to submit one. A meeting, sometime between July 22 and August 3, would be scheduled with some or all of these members of the Overseers' board. Bell could attend with Michelman, a student, and a faculty member, if he desired, Green wrote.

Green acknowledged the "difficult circumstances," but stressed that the process agreed upon was fair. He hoped that satisfied Bell's request for an appeal to the Harvard Corporation.

Clark also answered Bell's June 24 letter two days later, on June 26. It was a strange time for Bell. That weekend he was about to be married to a woman he had met in New York. But he was also fighting to save his job without abandoning the principle behind his leave of protest. Clark reiterated that he was considering Bell to have resigned from the faculty, that he felt Bell's protest was "unfortunate." But this time Clark's missive was more heartfelt and less matter-of-fact than earlier letters to Bell. He told Bell that whatever his decision, he would remain in their thoughts. Clark even congratulated Bell on his marriage.

Unfortunately, despite all of this apparent accommodation,

provost Jerry Green issued a terse, two-paragraph statement on June 30, refusing to allow an extended leave of absence and saying that the university regretted that Bell would not be rejoining the Law School faculty in the upcoming year. Green indicated that Bell would be allowed, at his request, to attempt to persuade the Harvard Corporation to grant a third year of absence.

Clark would say only that he was "saddened to receive Professor Bell's recent letter stating that he did not intend to return to active teaching at Harvard Law School this year. I wish he had chosen otherwise." Indeed, Bell had not written that in his letter to Clark at all; he had said he was not intending to resign and wanted to appeal to the highest officers of Harvard University.

Along with those statements, to counter unfavorable news that Harvard Law School was about to lose its first tenured black professor, the Law School released information on its efforts to recruit women and minorities. It mentioned the hiring of two women and two African-American male assistant professors since September 1991, the faculty's February resolution mandating the appointments committee to present several candidates who are not white males, and the creation of the Houston Fellowship program to help encourage members of minorities to become law professors. Two of those appointments came after the "ideologically correct" package deal of professors and only in reaction to public outcry. The Charles Hamilton Houston Fellowship was a program Bell had been trying for years to establish. Indeed, most of these "recent events" resulted from Bell's or students' suggestions, though the school would never say it had caved in to them.

In the days before Bell's meeting with members of the Harvard Corporation and the Board of Overseers, the Supreme Judical Court issued its decision in the law students' appeal of their suit alleging that the Law School's hiring practices discriminated against minorities and women. On July 9, the court affirmed the lower court's dismissal of the case, agreeing that the students lacked standing to sue because they were not past, present, or prospective employees of the school. "They have not claimed that the Law School denied or discharged them from employment, or discriminated in compensation, terms, conditions, or privileges," Justice Neil Lynch wrote for the court. "Likewise, the injuries they complain of—denial of 'perspectives, life experiences and access to role models'—are not within the area of concern of the statute."

On July 29, Bell and Michelman met with an advisory panel of the Harvard Corporation and the Board of Overseers. Not surprisingly, the corporation adopted the panel's recommendation to affirm President Rudenstein's decision rejecting Bell's request for an extension. The purpose of his leave had not been public service activities requiring his presence somewhere else, nor had he assured Harvard that he would return at the end of a third year, even if his request could have been granted.

Bell could not in good conscience return. The progress had been too small, and the hostility there too great. He would not relent on the question of faculty diversity. "My experience, though, indicates that you will come to understand why I found it necessary to place my position at risk rather than have my presence serve as a cover for the continuance of policies whose real aims are revealed clearly in the statistics that all deplore but very few truly wish to change," he responded to Rudenstein on August 19. To Senior Fellow Charles Slichter he wrote that the decision "to deny my request for a further leave ... is a disappointment, but ... I am strengthened in my belief that the course I have taken is both appropriate and perhaps essential to the major effort that will be required to achieve a meaningful diversity of the faculties at Harvard University." Bell would remain at New York University, where he would continue writing and speaking against racism.

By the time classes at the Law School resumed in the fall, Bell was gone and the students' suit was over. But the place was wounded. "Things are in ruins. There is rubble," said Michelman mournfully, at the start of the 1992–93 school year. The harm caused by the *Law Review*'s grotesque parody of murdered professor Mary Joe Frug and her work, the tragedy of students being subjected to a two-day trial for their nonviolent protest to seek improvements in the school, and the public spectacle created by the boisterous, combative exchange between professors Dershowitz and Tribe had left the faculty and students sullen and withdrawn. There was a personal toll as well as an institutional one. Even Robert Clark recognized that.

Clark began the school year with a new look and a new outlook. He shaved his beard, cut his hair, and returned looking younger and fresh-faced. Only deeper lines around his eyes gave away how besieged he had been just a few months earlier. But he knew his leadership and the Law School had been beaten. He opened the year by calling for healing. In a letter distributed to the entire school, he acknowledged that "the events of last spring were disturbing and difficult for many members of this community. . . . Most agree that issues relating to race and gender will require discussion and debate that is more open and more respectful. It has become apparent that the ways in which we deal with each other ought to be improved."

To begin that process, Clark asked negotiator Roger Fisher to establish a Project on Community to help build a stronger sense of community at the Law School. Fisher, an emeritus professor, agreed to commit two years to the effort. Professors Charles Ogletree and Alan Stone would assist Fisher in a working group that would include support staff, students, and other faculty members. Increasing the size of the faculty so that more students could attend seminars and enjoy smaller classes would remain a priority, as would hiring more women and minorities. Clark indicated that the appointments committee would be meeting with representative groups of students selected by the Law School Council, and that he would also be talking more often with students himself. He said he was "sorry" that Professor Bell would not be returning to the school that fall, because "he has been a valued member of our faculty." The door was not closed to Bell's return, Clark added. "It is my hope that Professor Bell will seek reappointment to our faculty in the near future."

Clark reminded the school that the "overall situation of the School" must be kept in "perspective." That viewpoint included an admission that confrontation was part of the culture of Harvard Law School. "More civil behavior can and should be fostered at the School, but real differences of opinion and occasional controversies are an essential part of its life." It was a law school, after all, he said, "specially adapted to training people in the art of argument," and the school's differences "should be an asset, not a liability."

But the truth is they had already become a liability, and it was just a matter of time before controversy struck again. In November, Kathleen Sullivan, perhaps Harvard's brightest star and certainly a woman on whom the school was pinning its hopes for the future, announced she had accepted an offer from Stanford University. A premier constitutional law scholar and popular teacher, Sullivan was a protégé of Laurence Tribe's. The class of '92 had given her the Outstanding Teacher award. Rumor had it that she was being groomed to be a future dean. In fact, during the summer, President Neil Rudenstein had asked Sullivan to be associate dean of the Law School because, as a moderate, she could help mend faculty relations. But she had already made her decision to leave. Some say she wanted to get out from under Tribe's shadow; others believe she simply preferred the California weather. In fact, after twelve years, she was simply tired of working on such a divided, hurtful faculty. Stanford had proven itself much more adept at accommodating divergent views, and professors there had also fallen in love with her and she with them.

Christopher Edley, former issues director for presidential nominee Michael Dukakis and a great supporter of the faculty diversity effort, was spending as little time as possible at Harvard, and as much time as he could advising the Clinton campaign. Later he would join the new administration. William (Terry) Fisher gladly accepted an opportunity to spend the fall semester conducting research in California. Not only was Harvard losing great young talent, but other professors were declining offers to join the faculty. That would have been almost unheard of fifteen years earlier. Yale's Carol Rose, Henry Hansmann, one of the original "four white men," and Elizabeth Warren, a visiting professor from the University of Pennsylvania School of Law, all turned down Harvard's entreaties.

Money still seemed to be pouring in from wealthy alumni who did not want to abandon their alma mater in a time of trouble, or to see the value of their diplomas drop. Harvard Law School had raised $82 million, more than half of its $150-million goal, and the end of the campaign was two years away. African-American financier and philanthropist Reginald Lewis, class of '68, gave Harvard $3 million in July, 1992, about six months before Lewis would die of brain cancer. It was the largest individual gift in the school's history. To be paid over five years, the donation from the chairman of TLC Beatrice International Holdings, the country's largest black-owned business, would be used to fund research, lectures, and fellowships for foreign students. Harvard was renaming the building that houses its international program after Lewis. Other contributions were already financing a new office and classroom building on the Law School campus, a new legal services center named for the benefactor firm of Hale and Dorr in the nearby Boston town of Jamaica Plain, and additional public-interest grants and fellowships.

Laurence Tribe and some other professors gave Clark the benefit of the doubt. Tribe seemed pleased with Clark's willingness to face up to problems, and he conceded that he may have "overreacted" to the parody himself. Tribe said Clark's desire to see the school heal was "an acknowledgment of a genuine need for discussion of issues relating to race and gender, and an acknowledgment that those discussions need to take place in a more open way." He also liked Clark's expression of hope regarding Bell's possible return. "I take it as a welcoming invitation. Not a promise—but certainly not frosty or dismissive." Clark was clearly not a "charismatic leader," as another professor said, but it looked as if he might have been learning from his mistakes.

But then came another controversy. Problems from the previous spring at the *Harvard Law Review* spilled over into the fall. President Emily Schulman, who appeared to have handled the turmoil surrounding the parody so well, found herself under fire. At a meeting on September 30, a black woman editor charged Schulman with racism. This charge was followed by other allegations of racism, sexism, and abuse of power.

One woman editor claimed that Schulman automatically presumed this editor would want Derrick Bell to write the foreword to the Supreme Court issue because she was black. Another woman alleged that Schulman had assigned two white men to perform additional editing tasks on two case comments because the woman editor was black. Two other women claimed that Schulman had refused to allow a black woman, who had been assigned by the articles editor, to edit Professor Charles Ogletree's tenure piece because she was black and might be too biased or too easy on a black professor, possibly hurting Ogletree's chances of obtaining a permanent appointment. Finally, Schulman had allegedly assigned two white male editors to edit a student note, instead of a black woman who had expressed an interest.

Schulman vehemently denied that race or sex had played a role in any of her decisions. Several editors asserted that the editors making these charges were just seeking to get back at Schulman for not having kicked the authors of the parody off the *Review,* and for having been too soft on other 3L editors who knew or should have known about the contents of the parody and the *Revue.* On October 4, the *Review* took an unprecedented vote of no confidence in the president that ended in a tie. "I thank God, it was not a white male president. We would have had a riot here," remarked Professor Paul Weiler.

At least, this time, Clark was wise enough to seek an independent review of the situation at Gannett House. On October 28, the Board of Trustees of the Harvard Law Review Association appointed Ralph Gants, a Boston lawyer and former notes editor of the *Review,* to investigate the latest furor at the *Review.* Schulman and the four women editors who had charged her with discrimination all retained lawyers. On January 29, Gants released an exhaustive 109-page report to the trustees. He found that Schulman had made "significant errors of judgment" in some situations, and had uttered comments that could have led others to question whether she was treating certain individuals differently, and maybe less favorably, because of their race or gender. But, he concluded, she was not "motivated by racial bias." The *Review*, however, later censured her and prohibited her from speaking at the 1993 spring banquet.

The whole affair seemed misplaced, a muddled and belated attempt to right the wrongs of the previous spring. Surely an independent investigator, called in then, could have found "errors of judgment," and that it was reasonable for some editors to conclude that they had been treated differently on the *Review* and in the *Revue* parody because of their gender. The same First Amendment arguments that had been used to defend Kenneth Fenyo and Craig Coben, the authors of the Frug parody, could have been made in Emily Schulman's case too. But they weren't. It was reflective of who Harvard was willing to blame. And it was much easier to blame Emily Schulman, a woman, than Coben and Fenyo, whose golden careers the school didn't want to blemish. Of course, Harvard could have punished those two authors. It is not a government entity, and it can regulate speech as well as behavior; the entire free-speech defense was merely a red herring.

The 1992–93 academic year continued to be a bitter one. The appointments committee, in reviewing all the women professors who had ever been visiting professors, decided to consider offering Catharine MacKinnon, the feminist theorist at the University of Michigan School of Law, a lateral appointment. She had been a guest lecturer at Harvard and had delivered the prestigious Holmes Lecture in 1987. Alan Dershowitz became one of her most vocal opponents. Dershowitz, who among other things was a defender of porn stars and a columnist for *Penthouse*, was distressed by MacKinnon, who had led an effort to seek ordinances outlawing pornography. Even if her ideas were radical to some, she was a star in her field.

She got 60 percent of the vote, but missed getting the two-thirds necessary for appointment. She was gracious about it, though, saying she had received more votes than she ever thought she would have. Faculty members were relieved. Her being denied "could have made it easy for students to continue to protest. We were all holding our breath. It could have been worse," said Weiler.

Charles Ogletree eventually won tenure unanimously, but only after a campaign to smear him. Vengeful editors retaliating against the way other black editors treated Schulman began circulating rumors that the *Review* had written his tenure piece for him. They said all Ogletree had done was to submit a three-page outline describing his former career as a public defender, and the editors had done the rest. Those claims turned out to be false. He had written a 289-page article and had shown drafts to at least six faculty members. The editors cut the piece substantially. But that was hardly uncommon. Ogletree, who had already been embarrassed by a parody of him in the *Revue*, handled the situation gracefully too. He admitted he had been working under a crammed schedule and had missed deadlines. But the piece was his.

In both the spring and fall incidents regarding the *Harvard Law Review*, people tried to make the *Review* a symbol of affirmative action gone wrong or about political correctness gone too far. But the parody in the *Revue*, the allegations about Schulman, and the attempt to discredit Ogletree were about something else: a lack of human decency. The parody reflected deep-seated racial, sexual, and economic divisions in society. And those problems were perpetuated by the failure of an institution like Harvard to instill respect and decency in those who would become America's future leaders. The other episodes were also signs of legal education gone awry. They demonstrated how law school sweeps human considerations under the rug and creates advocates who are numb to the feelings of others. This should not be the cost of breaking old traditions and inventing new, more inclusive ones.

Perhaps not surprisingly, Harvard Law School was not the favorite child of the Clinton administration. With the Clintons in the White House, Yale, their alma mater, overshadowed Harvard Law. The close-knit Yale, with its public-service spirit, was where the politically ambitious were going and from where they were being drawn. It had become the "hot ticket" in

American education—and politics, according to the *Washington Post.*

Harvard Law School graduates and professors fared well in appointments: Janet Reno, class of '63, was named attorney general; Professor Philip Heymann became deputy attorney general; Professor Edley became associate director of the Office of Management and Budget; and former Arizona governor Bruce Babbitt, class of '65, was selected secretary of the interior. With the appointment of Ruth Bader Ginsburg, who spent her first two years at Harvard before transferring to Columbia, and former Harvard law professor and graduate Stephen Breyer, Harvard Law still had a stronghold at the Supreme Court. But there was not a wholesale stockpiling of Harvard Law talent such as had been seen in the Johnson and Kennedy presidencies. Rather, many key administration officials, such as Solicitor General Drew Days, Secretary of Labor Robert Reich, National Economic Council chief Robert Rubin, CIA director James Woolsey, and the first-selected Secretary of Defense Les Aspin all hailed from Yale Law School.

Harvard was still perceived as a great institution. Its graduates were still commanding top dollar at major corporate law firms. But they no longer had a lock on the market. Nevertheless, Professor Frank Michelman, who was disheartened by the result of Derrick Bell's request for an extension and the other horrifying incidents at the school, believed Harvard was already becoming stronger from the consciousness and self-awareness that comes with pain. "Harvard Law School in [the fall of] 1992 is much better intellectually, and the quality of scholarship and scholarly output is much much higher, than it was in 1962," he said, though he admitted the students, the faculty, and the institution have paid "a high price."

In a fitting postscript, on September 20, 1993, Clare Dalton, the former assistant Harvard Law professor whose tenure denial after a close vote became a *cause célèbre* and sparked the battle over diversity and the legitimacy of Critical Legal Studies, won a $260,000 settlement of her 1987 gender-discrimination suit against Harvard Law School. Dalton is married to Labor Secretary Robert Reich. The case was settled the day before the Massachusetts Commission Against Discrimination was to begin a hearing on it. The commission had already found there was "probable cause" to believe Harvard had discriminated against her when it denied her tenure. That year, six assistant professors were up for tenure. Five males received offers; only Dalton, the one woman, didn't. Most of the tenured women on the faculty were prepared to testify about their own experiences.

Under the settlement, Harvard agreed to contribute the money to a new joint Northeastern-Harvard domestic violence institute, which she will run at Northeastern University when she returns from Washington. Harvard admitted no wrongdoing, but it agreed to pay a portion of Dalton's legal fees. "For the 1990s, we need decision-makers who understand the connections . . . between the blatant fact of disparate treatment and the unconscious dynamics of discrimination, of which only traces appear on the surface of institutional life," Dalton wrote in the *Boston Globe* about her case. Harvard Law School will never recapture its glory unless it makes that connection.

Notes

Prologue

Page 1. . . . "*Kit's freshmen.*" *The Law at Harvard: A History of Ideas and Men 1817–1967* by Arthur E. Sutherland (Cambridge, Mass.: Belknap Press of Harvard University Press, 1967), page 180.

Page 2. . . . *Langdell himself*. . . Sutherland, pages 163 and 165. Also see *Law School, Legal Education in America from the 1850s to the 1980s* by Robert Stevens (Chapel Hill, N.C.: University of North Carolina Press, 1983), pages 35–72.

Page 2. . . . *Nicola Sacco and Bartolomeo Vanzetti* . . . Sutherland, pages 259–262.

Page 2. . . . *feud between Frankfurter and* . . . *Legal Realism at Yale 1927–1960* by Laura Kalman (Chapel Hill, N.C.: University of North Carolina Press, 1986), page 58.

Page 3. . . . *resented Pound's timidity* . . . Kalman, pages 59–61.

Page 3. . . . *Pound's support for Hitler* . . . Kalman, page 60.

Page 3. *The School divided* . . . Kalman, page 60.

Page 3. . . . *clashed over the appointment* . . . Kalman, pages 59–62.

Page 3. . . . *"intelligence made theory irrelevant."* Kalman, page 58.

Page 3. . . . *they "prided themselves . . ."* Kalman, page 58.

Page 3. . . . *Zechariah Chafee advised* . . . *No Ivory Tower, McCarthyism and the Universities* by Ellen Schrecker (New York: Oxford University Press, 1986), pages 183–4.

Page 4. *". . . symbol of the Eastern Establishment."* Schrecker, page 183.

Page 4. . . . *called two twin brothers* . . . Schrecker, page 200; *The High Citadel, The Influence of Harvard Law School* by Joel Seligman with Lynne Bernabei (Boston: Houghton Mifflin, 1978), pages 85–87.

Page 4. ... *In the end, however, Griswold publicly opposed McCarthy.* Schrecker, page 199; Seligman, page 84, and interview with Erwin Griswold.

CHAPTER 1: A MATTER OF TRADITION

Pages 10–11. Election of David Ellen as *Law Review* president. Interview with David Ellen.

Page 11. ... *cites Harvard articles....* "The *Law Review* at 92" by David Margolick, *The Boston Sunday Globe,* May 13, 1979.

Page 11. ... *served as editors...* Margolick; "The *Harvard Law Review—* Glimpses of Its History, As Seen by an Aficionado" by Erwin Griswold, *Harvard Law Review Centennial Album,* 1987.

Page 12. ... *Joseph Califano, Jr., told the editors...* Margolick.

Page 13. ... *It is a curious place...* *The Harvard Mystique* by Enrique Hank Lopez (New York: Macmillan, 1979), page 31.

Page 13. "*... has had an incalculable influence...*" Lopez, page 31.

Pages 13–14. Harvard Law alumni on the Supreme Court and in Congress. Harvard Law School News Office.

Page 15. ... "*a second home for most of us*"... "*There were always lights on at night.*" Confidential interview.

Page 15. ... "*was crowded when I knew it*"... "*How the present administration operates...*" Griswold, page 17.

Page 16. A "*bookworm*" *and something of a* "*brilliant neurotic*"... Sutherland, page 165; "A Plea for Lawyer Schools" by Jerome Frank, *The Yale Law Journal,* September 1947.

Page 16. *The case method was built on...* Sutherland, pages 174–175.

Page 17. ... *that Harvard's journal might* "*show something of...*" Griswold, page 4.

Page 17. ... *the Review would contain* "*articles on subjects...*" Griswold, page 4.

Page 17. *Drafts were written...* "Report of the Internal Inquiry into Allegations of Race and Gender Discrimination at the *Harvard Law Review*" by Ralph Gants, January 27, 1993, pages 8–9. Hereafter known as "Gants Report."

Page 18. *At forty dollars per issue...* Griswold, page 5.

Page 18. *In 1984, Blue Book sales...* Harvard Law Review Association, Financial Report, 1984, Harvard Law Review Papers, Harvard Law School Library; ... *By 1993, Blue Book sales...* Confidential *Law Review* source.

Pages 19. *Adolf Augustus Berle, Jr.,... was blackballed...* Griswold, page 6, n. 24.

Page 19. *Thirty-five years later...* Griswold, page 7, n. 27.

Page 19. ... *three black members...* Griswold, page 8.

Page 20. "*... complete practices in democracy*"... *Felix Frankfurter Reminisces: An Intimate Portrait as Recorded in Talks with Dr. Harlan B. Phillips,* (Reynal, 1960), page 27.

Page 20. "... *the objectivity of the marking* ..." *Frankfurter Reminisces*, page 28.

Page 20. "*The fellow who gets an A* ..." *Frankfurter Reminisces*, page 28.

Page 20. ... *at the Boston law firm* ... Agenda for Ropes & Gray meeting, Harvard Law Review Papers, Harvard Law School Library.

Page 20. "*People know that the* Review *man* ..." Notes from Ropes & Gray meeting, April 27, 1949, Harvard Law Review Papers, Harvard Law School Library.

Page 20. ... "*certified brainpower*" ... Notes from Ropes & Gray meeting.

Page 21. ... "*reasonably accurate in measuring* ..." Griswold, page 7.

Page 21. ... *Review editors have a monopoly* ... Notes from Ropes & Gray meeting.

Page 21. ... "*just a bunch of lucky stiffs* ..." Minutes of meeting, March 24, 1949, between *Law Review* editors and Harvard Law School faculty members on the importance of the *Review* as an institution in the School. Harvard Law Review Papers, Harvard Law School Library.

Page 21. ... *in 1969, the ranks began to open.* Margolick.

Page 21. ... *criticized the change as* ... Margolick.

Page 22. ... *the writing competition yielded only* ... Harvard Law Review report to the Visiting Committee on the Adoption of Affirmative Action at the *Harvard Law Review*, April 1, 1981. Harvard Law Review Papers, Harvard Law School Library.

Page 22. ... *a plan emerged after a* ... Report to the Visiting Committee.

Page 22. ... *a radical departure from "absolute merit."* "Harvard Law Review's Ethnic Screening Criticized," *The New York Times*, February 24, 1981; "A Fairer Review," *Harvard Crimson*, February 24, 1981; "Drawing Distinctions at Harvard Law," *The New York Times*, March 3, 1981, Editorial; "Challenge to the White, Male Legal Establishment," letter to *The New York Times*, March 9, 1981; "Racial Unrest at Harvard" by Aric Press with Phyllis Malamud, *Newsweek*, March 9, 1981; "Eeeee! This Is Getting Serious!" *National Review*, March 20, 1981; "Right to Be White—and Male?" *The Economist*, March 28, 1981.

Page 22. ... *dean Albert Sacks formed a faculty committee* ... *and students* ... "Memorandum to the Faculty" by Harvard Law School dean Albert Sacks, March 5, 1981; "Memorandum to the Subcommittee of the Law School Visiting Committee," April 2, 1981, by Brent Abel, visiting committee chairman; "Report on the Method of Selection of the *Law Review*" by the Special Committee on *Law Review* Selection, April 25, 1981; "A Response to All Those Who Have Written Concerning *Harvard Law Review* Membership Selection" by Albert Sacks, June 29, 1981; compilation of student memos prepared for meeting on Alternative Selection Procedures, April 6, 1983. Harvard Law Review Papers, Harvard Law School Library.

Page 22. ... *at the height of the McCarthy era* ... Griswold, pages 15–16.

Page 23. ... *wanted the Lubells expelled* ... *But Griswold, reversing* ... Schrecker, page 200; Seligman, pages 85–87.

Page 23. ... *voted to reinstate* ... Griswold, page 15.

Page 23. . . . *they received certain perks* . . . Confidential interviews.

Page 24. . . . *needed to be less "hierarchical"* . . . Interview with Derek Bok.

Page 26. *At Harvard, for example* . . . Association of American Law Schools 1989 Directory of Law Teachers.

Page 26. . . . *"demeaning, distorting of values"* . . . *"arbitrary"* . . . *"Compared to medical schools* . . ." Seligman, page 177.

Page 26. *Some even arranged party weekends* . . . Interview with Jamin Raskin.

Page 27. *"It was her best work"* . . . Interview with David Ellen.

Page 28. . . . *"a struggle for the soul of this institution"* . . . "A Reporter at Large, Harvard Law" by Calvin Trillin, *The New Yorker,* March 26, 1984, page 54.

Page 28. *As it was* . . . Trillin, *The New Yorker,* March 26, 1984.

Page 29. *". . . a lot of political disrespect . . . The fault lines were . . ."* Interview with David Ellen.

CHAPTER 2: MURDER AMONG US

Page 31. *The peace of this enclave was shattered* . . . "Professor Is Slain on Street in Massachusetts," *The New York Times,* April 5, 1991; "Cambridge Police Have a Knife, No Motive in Professor's Murder" by Alexander Reid, *The Boston Globe,* April 6, 1991, page 1; "Murder Jolts Haven for Elite in Boston Area," *The New York Times,* April 9, 1991, page A-17.

Page 31. *Having finished dinner, she dialed* . . . "An Accomplished Life, a Brutal Death" by Matthew Brelis, *The Boston Globe,* April 14, 1991, page 1.

Page 32. . . . *at her memorial service* . . . "Hundreds Mourn Slain Professor" by David Arnold, *The Boston Globe,* April 9, 1991, page 17; "Memorial Service for Mary Joe Frug," *New England Law Review,* Spring 1992, pages 639–658; interview with John O'Brien, dean, New England School of Law.

Page 32. *"Her smile, her wit* . . . "Memorial Service," page 640.

Page 32. *". . . was indeed nature's therapist."* "Memorial Service," page 645.

Page 33. *"if she . . . had been his lawyer . . ."* "Memorial Service," page 645.

Page 33. *"ate the icing off the cake . . ."* "Memorial Service," page 656.

Page 33. *"I would think from the wounds. . . . It's a real nasty case."* Interview with Fidele Centrella, detective sergeant, Cambridge Police Department.

Page 33. *". . . was loaded up on hate . . ."* "Law Professor's Murder Still Unsolved" by Matthew Brelis, *The Boston Globe,* April 5, 1992.

Page 34. *The gossip began* . . . Brelis, *The Boston Globe,* April 14, 1991.

Page 34. *". . . was determined not to abandon . . ."* "Memorial Service," page 642.

Page 34. *"It was no coincidence . . ."* Interview with Marthalene Donaldson.

Page 35. . . . *Margaret Bean-Bayog* . . . "The Fatal Attraction of Psychiatrist and Patient" by Megan Rosenfeld, *The Washington Post,* April 17, 1992, page F1.

Page 35.... *"a Christian who happens to be gay."* "A Chaplain Comes Out Swinging" by Mary Jordan, *The Washington Post,* April 15, 1992, page F1.

Page 35.... *three-day conference in Madison, Wisconsin*... Initial outreach letter from the Organizing Committee of the Conference on Critical Legal Studies, January 17, 1977.

Page 35.... *two fundamental strains of CLS.* Letter from the Organizing Committee, January 17, 1977.

Page 35.... *"a wide and conflicting variety..."* *The Politics of Law: A Progressive Critique,* edited by David Kairys (New York: Pantheon Books, 1982), page 4.

Page 36. *The second strand of CLS...* Letter from the Organizing Committee, January 17, 1977.

Page 36. *"It was pretty memorable..."* Interview with Robert Gordon.

Page 37. *The downside was that CLS...* "CLS Approach Is 'Stiflingly Academic'" by William Pedersen, Jr., *Legal Times,* Commentary & Insight, May 12, 1986, page 22; "Duncan the Doughnut," *The New Republic,* March 17, 1986.

Page 38.... *CLS "was on the map..."* Interview with Gary Peller.

Page 38.... *"the smartest person in Brazil"...* Interview with David Trubek.

Page 38.... *"doctrinal deviation"...* *Knowledge and Politics* by Roberto Unger (New York: The Free Press, 1975); *The Critical Legal Studies Movement* by Roberto Unger (Cambridge, Mass.: Harvard University Press, 1983).

Page 39. *His massive history...* *The Transformation of American Law, 1780–1860* by Morton Horowitz (Cambridge, Mass.: Harvard University Press, 1977).

Page 39.... *an "inspired taunter."* Trillin, *The New Yorker,* March 26, 1984, page 76.

Page 39. *"a cross between Rasputin and Billy Graham"... at once "Machiavellian" and possessed a "gift for blarney"... could "work an audience ... with the seductiveness of a revivalist preacher."* "Notes toward an Intimate, Opinionated, and Affectionate History of the Conference on Critical Legal Studies" by John Henry Schlegel, *Stanford Law Review,* January 1984, page 392.

Page 40. *"... the critical techniques Kennedy employed..."* *Broken Contract* by Richard Kahlenberg (New York: Hill and Wang, 1992), page 166.

Page 40. *"... painted as a Crit with horns and a tail... really does get down and dirty..."* Interview with Keith Aoki.

Page 40.... *an "upper bohemian" family.* Interview with Duncan Kennedy.

Page 40.... *"didn't really have a lot of money"...* Duncan Kennedy interview.

Page 41. *" 'This is a pile of crap.' "... "I'm sitting there totally stunned"... "But he convinced me..."* Trubek interview.

Page 41. *"He knew everything..."* Trubek interview.

Page 42. *"He was remarkable..."* Interview with John Hart Ely.

Page 42.... *"wrote a very sensitive piece..."* Interview with Abraham Goldstein.

Pages 42.... *a polemic on "How the Law School Fails"...* and subsequent quotes. "How the Law School Fails: A Polemic" by Duncan Kennedy, *Yale Review of Law and Social Action,* Vol. 1, No. 1, 1970, pages 72–90.

Page 43. *"...ideological transmission belt for conservative legalism..."* "Laying Down the Law, The Empire Strikes Back" by Jamin Raskin, *How Harvard Rules,* edited by John Trumpbour, (Boston: South End Press, 1989), page 343.

Page 43. ... *"to study law [was] one way to know power."* Raskin, page 352.

Page 43.... *found such an "easy target for subversion"...* Raskin, page 352.

Page 43.... *his unique brand of "syndicalism"...* Duncan Kennedy interview.

Pages 43. *Another article by Kennedy...* and subsequent quotes. "Rebels from Principle: Changing the Corporate Law Firm from Within" by Duncan Kennedy, *Harvard Law School Bulletin,* Fall 1981, page 40.

Page 44. *He circulated...* "Notes of an Oppositionist in Academic Politics" by Duncan Kennedy (unpublished, 1982). Also see "First-Year Law Teaching as Political Action," speech by Duncan Kennedy, at the Second National Conference on Critical Legal Studies, Madison, Wisconsin, November 10, 1978.

Page 44.... *his "little red book"...* *Legal Education and the Reproduction of Hierarchy: A Polemic against the System* by Duncan Kennedy (Cambridge: FAR, 1983).

Page 44.... *to "reveal the hidden...," and were not necessarily...* Kahlenberg, page 164.

Page 44.... *testament to the nineteenth-century glory... The second-year curriculum... third-year was marked by...* Raskin, page 352–53.

Page 45.... *reminded Griswold... "the need of great teachers..."* Letter from Felix Frankfurter to Erwin Griswold, April 13, 1951, Library of Congress, Manuscript Division, Washington, D.C.

Pages 45.... *"to discover the potential Hamiltons, Jays... the rarest of all gifts..."* Letter from Felix Frankfurter to Erwin Griswold, January 17, 1955. Library of Congress, Manuscript Division, Washington, D.C.

Page 45.... *not merely follow those "who overvalue money..."* Letter from Felix Frankfurter to Erwin Griswold, January 17, 1955. Also see letter from Felix Frankfurter to Erwin Griswold, January 11, 1955, regarding gift made by the Ford Foundation to Harvard Law School. Library of Congress, Manuscript Division, Washington, D.C.

Page 46.... *good technicians and able craftsmen...* Interview with Derek Bok.

Page 46. *"People valued the institution.... wouldn't do anything to hurt it."* Interview with Archibald Cox.

Page 47. *"I found the law school..."* Bok interview.

Page 47.... *a president's report criticizing*... 1983–84 Annual President's Report to the Board of Overseers.

Page 47. *The tenured core of CLS survived*... Raskin, page 356.

Page 47.... *"committed to both academic freedom and..."* Raskin, page 356.

Page 47.... *never saw it as "Cubism versus Impressionism."* Interview with Christopher Edley.

Page 47. *"... the legal equivalent of auto mechanics."* Raskin, page 343.

Page 48. *"... all law is bullshit..."* "Harvard Defection a Coup for U. of C." by Mara Tapp, *Chicago Daily Law Bulletin*, September 6, 1985.

Page 48.... *disrupted the "Langdellian peace"... by showing how...*; also descriptions of courses. Raskin, page 353.

Page 48.... *made "a formal inroad"... with the "experimental sections"...* Raskin, page 354.

Page 48.... *because she was "not CLS."* Interview with Lea Brilmayer.

Page 49.... *"vilification, name-calling, back-stabbing, and character assassination"...* "The Split at Harvard Law Goes Down to Its Foundation" by David Margolick, *The New York Times*, October 6, 1985, Sec. 4, page 7.

Page 49. *He urged the CLS professors*... Trillin, *The New Yorker*, March 26, 1984, page 75.

Page 49.... *"the unhappiest place."* Trillin, page 53.

Page 49.... *"Missouri Compromise"*... Margolick.

Page 50. *Stanford's Robert Gordon explained*... "Harvard Tenure Battle Puts 'Critical Legal Studies' on Trial" by Jennifer Kingson, *The New York Times*, August 30, 1987, Sec. 4, page 5.

Page 50.... *Harvard University has never been patient*... Raskin, page 347.

Page 50.... *"a growing crisis in the American legal system"... "neo-Marxist" ... "radical in outlook"... "seeks by its manipulation..."* "Harvard Symposium to Examine Legal Education," *The Federalist Papers*, newsletter of the Federalist Society for Law and Public Policy Studies, Vol. 1, No. 1, February 1984. Also see "Of Law and the River" by Paul Carrington, *Journal of Legal Education*, Vol. 34 (1984), page 222.

Page 50. ... *"engaged in a ritual slaying of the elders"... "scholarship at the law school was deteriorating."* "Deep Philosophical Fractures Mar a Pillar of Legal Training" by David Margolick, *Los Angeles Daily Law Journal*, October 8, 1985. Also see "An Unconventional Traditionalist" by Daniel Golden, *The Boston Globe Magazine*, March 4, 1990, cover story.

Page 50. *"... didn't like seeing science dismissed..."* Interview with Robert Clark.

Page 51.... *didn't "meet the standards..."* "A Tenure Battle at Harvard Law" by Steve Curwood, *The Boston Globe*, July 19, 1987. Also see Raskin, pages 345–346.

Page 51.... *"an academic smear campaign..."* Raskin, page 344.

Page 51. *Lewis Sargentich told the Harvard Crimson*... "Law Profs Question Dalton Vote," *The Harvard Crimson*, May 13, 1987.

Page 51. *Stanford's Gordon circulated a letter*... Kingson, *The New York*

Times, Aug. 30, 1987; "Letter Calls for Harvard Probe; Academic Freedom in Peril" by David Kaplan, *The National Law Journal,* page 3; interview with Robert Gordon.

Page 52. *Derrick Bell... staged a four-day sit-in... to express his "disappointment and shame."...* Kingson, *The New York Times,* August 30, 1987.

Page 52. *... Harvard didn't want "women who..."* "Down and Out in Cambridge, Tenure Fights Raise Issues of Academic Freedom," by Geoffrey Cowley with Sue Hutchison, *Newsweek,* April 4, 1988, page 66.

Page 52. *"Divided?... They were armed camps already.... They were after Clare..."* Trubek interview.

Page 53. *He told the National Law Journal...* "Battle at Harvard Law over Tenure; So-called Crits v. Traditionalists" by David Kaplan, *The National Law Journal,* June 22, 1987, page 3.

Page 53. *"It was a backlash..."* Duncan Kennedy interview.

Page 53. *"It's difficult to go home..."* Margolick, *Los Angeles Daily Law Journal,* October 8, 1985.

Page 53. *... Arthur Miller said he was...* "Alumni Concerned, Students Aren't; Effect of Harvard Strife Uncertain" by Deborah Graham, *Legal Times,* January 6, 1986, page 1.

Page 53. *Nesson told his Evidence class...* Kahlenberg, page 81.

Page 54. *... "a terrible choice for the school."* "Conservative to Head Harvard Law" by Linda Matchen, *The Boston Globe,* February 18, 1989, Metro page 1.

Page 54. *... a groundbreaking article...* "Rereading Contracts: A Feminist Analysis of a Contracts Casebook," *American University Law Review,* 1985.

CHAPTER 3: FIGHTING WORDS

Page 57. *In her first sentence...* "A Postmodern Feminist Legal Manifesto (An Unfinished Draft)" by Mary Joe Frug, *Harvard Law Review,* March 1992, pages 1045–1075.

Page 60. *"... doing some unconventional things."* Ellen interview.

Page 61. *"... it systematically examined..."* Interview with Edith Ramirez.

Page 61. *"We were impressed..."* Interview with Janis Kestenbaum.

Page 61. *"... weren't sure it was the best thing... It was not as scholarly..."* Ellen interview.

Page 61. *Minow thought...* "Incomplete Correspondence: An Unsent Letter to Mary Joe Frug" by Martha Minow, *Harvard Law Review,* March 1992, page 1096; interview with Martha Minow.

Page 62. *"We recognized it was unfinished..."* Kestenbaum interview.

Page 62. *"I saw there was the word..."* Ellen interview.

Page 62. *The words...* Frug, *Harvard Law Review,* March 1992, page 1072.

Page 63. *... as if "Mary Joe were foreshadowing..."* "The Example of

Lesbians: A Posthumous Reply to Professor Frug" by Ruth Colker, *Harvard Law Review*, March 1992, page 1084.

Page 63. *. . . typical of "male talk."* Frug, *Harvard Law Review*, March 1992, page 1073.

Page 63. *". . . there's some stuff in here . . ."* Ellen interview.

Page 64. *. . . they said in the letter.* Interview with Carol Platt.

Page 64. *. . . "Those words had substantive content. . . ."* Kestenbaum interview.

Pages 65–66. *. . . had worked hard to air . . . "Conservatives liked that . . ."* Interview with Baruch Obama.

Page 66. *. . . "czars of the Blue Book" . . .* Ellen interview.

Page 66. *". . . more difficult than people realize" . . . "I felt that in some sense . . ."* Ellen interview.

Page 68. *"We realized no one was . . ."* Platt interview.

Page 68. *. . . simply trying to censor . . .* Ramirez, Kestenbaum, and Platt interviews.

Page 69. *"They didn't want compromise . . ."* Platt interview.

Page 69. *. . . "it was important to show them . . . compromise for the sake of compromise."* Ellen interview.

Page 70. *"We easily won."* Kestenbaum interview.

Page 70. *". . . an argument over power . . ."* Interview with Rebecca Eisenberg.

Page 70. *". . . most unceremoniously rejected . . . I felt personally betrayed . . ."* Platt interview.

Page 71. *". . . two inches from the finish line . . ."* Ellen interview.

Page 71. *"The weight of these disputes . . ."* Ellen interview.

CHAPTER 4: RINGING HARVARD'S BELL

Page 72. *. . . Clark finally reached . . .* Interview with Derrick Bell; letter from Derrick Bell to Robert Clark, February 26, 1992; memorandum written by Robert Clark.

Page 74. *. . . Bell mailed him a formal response . . .* Letter from Bell to Clark, February 26, 1992.

Page 76. *"This is a university . . ."* "Old Rights Campaigner Leads a Harvard Battle" by Fox Butterfield, *The New York Times*, May 21, 1990, page A18.

Page 77. *. . . "not something one should . . ."* Robert Clark interview.

Page 77. *"The university rule is a good one" . . . Moreover, "the faculty in general is not influenced . . ."* "Professor Steps Up Protest over Harvard Law School Hiring" by Fox Butterfield, *The New York Times*, February 28, 1992.

Page 77. *. . . blasted Bell in an editorial . . .* "Racial Ultimatum at Harvard Law," *New York Post*, May 2, 1990, page 24.

Page 77. *Columnist George Will . . .* "At Harvard Law, Intellectual Gerrymandering" by George Will, *Newsday*, May 17, 1990, page 80, and "Academic Set-Asides," by George Will, *The Washington Post*, May 17, 1990, page A27.

Page 77.... *"Bell's Solution Is No Solution."* "For Whom Bell Tolls," *The New Republic*, May 21, 1990, page 8. Also see "The Question of Merit at Harvard Law" by Richard Cohen, *The Washington Post*, May 15, 1990.

Page 78.... *the "permanence of racism"... Faces at the Bottom of the Well: The Permanence of Racism*, by Derrick Bell, (New York: Basic Books, 1992). Also see *And We Are Not Saved: The Elusive Quest for Racial Justice* by Derrick Bell (New York: Basic Books, 1987).

Page 78. *"... people who look black and think white." Derrick Bell*, statement to Harvard Law School, April 24, 1990.

Page 79. *"I lives to harass white folks."* Bell, *Faces*, page xii.

Page 79.... *never expected to topple his oppressors*. Bell, *Faces*, page xii.

Page 79.... *Bell told Muro*. "Derrick Bell-In Protest" by Mark Muro, *The Boston Globe*, March 25, 1992, page 69.

Page 80.... *Bell's father would caution*. Derrick Bell interview.

Page 80. *"... so my kids don't fall"... saw his mother win*... Butterfield, *The New York Times*, May 21, 1990. Also see "Bell at Harvard: A Unique Activism" by Anthony Flint, *The Boston Globe*, May 7, 1990, page B1; Bell interview.

Page 80. *"... I could see the difference..."* Derrick Bell interview.

Page 80. *"... treated me like I was Jesus... that I was fairly special."* Derrick Bell interview.

Page 81.... *didn't want his son*... Derrick Bell interview.

Page 81.... *the woman who ran it shouted*... Derrick Bell interview.

Page 82. *"Knows everything and... The Boston Globe*, page 72.

Page 83. *"... under the most extreme conditions."* Interview with Michael Meltsner.

Page 83. *"... had to be masters of themselves..."* Meltsner interview.

Page 86. *"... personally humiliating work."* Interview with Jean Fairfax.

Page 86. *"I hauled Derrick..."* Fairfax interview.

Page 86. *"... only time in my life I felt afraid..."* Fairfax interview.

Page 86. *"We were so hot and tired and dusty."* Interview with Winson Hudson.

Page 86.... *"He was with us all the way..."* Hudson interview.

Page 87. *"He was very personally involved..."* Fairfax interview.

Page 87. *"... woefully beyond reach today."* Bell, *Faces*, page 59.

Page 88. *"... the first of a long line..."* Interview with Judge Robert Bell.

Page 88.... *his "willful arc of guerrilla theater"*... Muro, *The Boston Globe*, March 25, 1992, page 69.

Page 89. *And Clark Byse*... Interview with Clark Byse.

Page 90.... *that he made them seem racist*. "For Whom Bell Tolls" by James Taub, *The New Republic*, March 1, 1993, page 17; confidential interview with University of Oregon Law School source.

Page 90. *...marked by his political framework*...Taub, *The New Republic,* March 1, 1993, page 19.

Page 90. *"I publicized the incident*...Derrick Bell interview.

Page 91. *...helped spawn a group of*..."Law Profs Fight the Power; Minority Legal Scholars" by Jon Wiener, *The Nation,* September 4, 1989, page 246.

Page 93. *"She was so accessible*..." Interview with Laura Hankins.

Page 94. *...why he felt he had to leave Harvard*...Derrick Bell, statement to Harvard Law School, April 24, 1990. Also see "Harvard Students Rally in Support of Bell's Vow" by John Kennedy, *The Boston Globe,* April 25, 1990, page B1.

Page 95. *"Her wanting me*..." "A Class Sends Message to Harvard Law School," special to *The New York Times,* November 21, 1990.

Page 95. *"I had been an 'A' student*..." Interview with Anita Allen.

Page 95. *She had never liked Harvard*....Derrick Bell interview.

CHAPTER 5: IF THE SUIT FITS, WEAR IT

Page 100. *That complaint prompted*...*Where They Are Now: The Story of the Women of Harvard Law 1974* by Jill Abramson and Barbara Franklin (New York: Doubleday, 1986), page 8.

Page 101. *...eliminated career counselor Ronald Fox*..."Clark Cuts Public Interest Position" by Patrick Miles, *Harvard Law Record,* September 8, 1989, page 1; "Harvard Dean Eliminates Office for Public Interest Counseling" by Terry Carter, *The National Law Journal,* September 11, 1989, page 4; "Clark Defends Move to Cut Counseling," *Harvard Crimson,* October 28, 1989, page 1.

Page 101. *...they held demonstrations and*..."Student Groups Meet with Clark, Rally Planned for Tuesday," *Harvard Law Record,* September 15, 1989, page 1; "Students Dump Protest Letters Outside Harvard Law Dean's Office," *The Boston Globe,* December 5, 1989, page 31; "The Abandonment of Public-Interest Law" by Jaron Bourke, *Legal Times,* October 30, 1989, page 21; interview with Jaron Bourke.

Page 101. *Clark was forced to backpedal*..."Harvard Law School Reinstates Public-Interest Career Counseling," *The Boston Globe,* September 30, 1990; "Harvard Law School Announces the Morris Wasserstein Public Interest Fellows Program to Counsel Students," *Harvard Law School News Release,* March 7, 1990.

Page 103. *...came through his house*...Interview with John Bonifaz.

Page 105. *"...afraid they might steal the show."* Interview with Keith Boykin.

Page 105. *...the coalition filed suit*..."Students Sue HLS over Faculty Hiring," *Harvard Law Record,* November 30, 1990, page 1; First Amended Complaint, *Harvard Law School Coalition for Civil Rights v. The President and Fellows of Harvard College,* Superior Court Department of the Trial Court of Middlesex County, Cambridge Division, November 20, 1990.

Page 106. *"We felt we had a significant victory... He didn't anticipate our fax."* Bonifaz interview.

Page 107. *... deep intrusion into the records...* Transcript of hearing for motion to dismiss, Febarury 15, 1991, Middlesex Superior Court.

Page 107. *"Courts have recognized repeatedly..."* Transcript of hearing.

Page 107. *Harvard has not met its burden..."* Transcript of hearing.

Page 108. *Their argument... "seems to be quite a stretch"...* Memorandum of Decision and Orders on Defendant's Motion to Dismiss and Other Pending Motions, Civil Action No. 90-7904-B, February 22, 1991.

Page 108. *... Steiner called a meeting...* Bonifaz interview.

Page 108. *... Steiner told the students...* Bonifaz interview.

Page 109. *"... It was an affirmation..."* Bonifaz interview.

Page 109. *"[Harvard] misread our conviction..."* Bonifaz interview.

Page 109. *... student advocate Wittcoff explained...* Transcript of oral argument, Supreme Judicial Court for the Commonwealth, Boston, Massachusetts, March 3, 1992.

Pages 111. *... submitted affidavits detailing...* First amended complaint, November 20, 1990.

Page 112. *"If there were no students at Harvard Law School..."* Oral argument, March 3, 1992.

Page 112. *Her classmate Laura Hankins...* Oral argument, March 3, 1992.

Page 115. *Richard Kahlenberg, a former student...* Kahlenberg, pages 237–238.

Page 115. *But Chief Justice Liacos...* Oral argument, March 3, 1992.

Pages 117–118. *... he wanted them to see their father at work.* Interview with Allan Ryan.

Page 118. *"You know," said Bonifaz...* Bonifaz interview.

Page 118. *"This case is not Brown v. Board of Education...* Oral argument, March 3, 1992.

Page 118. *"I wasn't just winging it..."* Ryan interview.

Page 118. *But Justice Wilkins stopped him....* Oral argument, March 3, 1992.

Page 120. *"... to keep those groups within the coalition..."* Boykin interview.

Page 120. *... since those groups were still in the complaint...* Oral argument, March 3, 1992.

CHAPTER 6: LET'S MAKE A DEAL

Page 124. *... "this was a breakthrough..."* Interview with Paul Weiler.

Page 125. *... log jam that had "constipated" appointments...* Interview with Daniel Meltzer.

Page 126. *He was unapologetic....* "The Law School in Brief, An Overview and an Introduction to Its Long-Range Plan and Comprehensive Campaign" by Robert Clark, December 4, 1991, description of career paths taken by the J.D. class of 1991, page 8. Also see "An Unconventional Traditionalist" by Daniel Golden, *The Boston Globe Magazine,* March

4, 1990, page 36, and "When Legal Titans Clash" by Ken Emerson, *The New York Times Magazine*, April 22, 1990.

Page 126. . . . *wasn't going to "heal" the differences* . . . "The Future of the Harvard Law School," a speech delivered by Dean-Designate Robert Clark to the Harvard Alumni Association of Washington, D.C., May 17, 1989. Also see "Flexibility, Determination, at Harvard Law" by Anthony Flint, *The Boston Globe*, October 30, 1990.

Page 127. . . . *learned about the vote* . . . "4 White Men offered Tenure," *Harvard Law Record*, March 6, 1992, page 1.

Page 128. . . . *"was a complete surprise."* Boykin interview.

Page 128. . . . *"the best deal he could make* . . ." Interview with Charles Nesson.

Page 128. . . . *Jackson arrived on campus* . . . "Jackson Exhorts HLS to Diversity" by Madeline Fain, *Harvard Law Record*, March 20, 1992, page 3. Also see "Jackson Says Eyes Are on Harvard" by Anthony Flint, *The Boston Globe*, May 9, 1990, page 41.

Page 129. . . . *they walked to Clark's house* . . . "Law Students Meet Dean, Debate Hiring Practices" by Perry Despeignes and Mark Ruberg, *The Harvard Crimson*, March 13, 1992, page 1; "Clark, Students Discuss Diversity on 'Zero day,'" *Harvard Law Record*, March 20, 1992, page 1.

Page 129. *"I was taking a shower* . . ." Ruberg, *The Harvard Crimson*, March 13, 1992, page 1.

Page 129. *Clark admitted it was a "muck-up"* . . . *Harvard Law Record*, March 20, 1992, page 1; Memorandum from Robert Clark to "Interested Members of the Law School Community," regarding "The Timing of Offers to Visiting Professors," March 5, 1992.

Page 130. . . . *chanting, "Diversity now, diversity now."* *Harvard Law Record*, March 20, 1992, page 7.

Page 131. *". . . must be taken seriously."* *Harvard Law Record*, March 20, 1992, page 7; "Law School Hiring Debate Continues, Students Demand 'More than Promises' from Clark" by Natasha Leland, *The Harvard Crimson*, March 13, 1992, page 3.

Page 131. *"There is a large enough group* . . ." *Harvard Law Record*, March 20, 1992, page 7.

Page 131. . . . *having to make political deals* . . . *Harvard Law Record*, March 20, 1992, page 7.

Page 131. *He would continue a dialogue* . . . *Harvard Law Record*, March 20, 1992, page 7; also see memorandum from Robert Clark, March 5, 1992.

Page 131. *". . . driven by my own compass."* Robert Clark interview.

Page 133. . . . *he told David Warsh.* "Rebuilding Beirut: A Liberal Vision for Harvard Law; Economic Principals," by David Warsh, *The Boston Globe*, February 11, 1990, page A1.

Page 133. . . . *"a neo-Langdellian" approach.* "Can New Harvard Dean Bring on a Calmer, Gentler Atmosphere?" by Lisa Green Markoff, *The Boston Globe*, March 20, 1989.

Page 133. *He was a "no-bullshit dean* . . ." "At Harvard Law, a New Era

Dawns" by Terry Carter, *The National Law Journal*, August 7, 1989, page 1.

Page 133. . . . *"out of step with . . ."* Matchen, *The Boston Globe*, February 18, 1989, Metro page 1.

Page 133. . . . *pledge to make Harvard* . . . Matchen, *The Boston Globe*, February 18, 1989.

Page 133. *Morton Horowitz . . . denounced Clark . . .* Matchen, *Boston Globe*, February 18, 1989.

Page 134. . . . *5,400 acres of cow pasture . . . "You didn't go there . . ."* Robert Clark interview.

Page 135. . . . *a serious, studious side to the family.* Interview with George Stephen Hotz.

Pages 135. . . . *Most of his friends weren't interested in* . . . Interview with Gus Cantrell.

Page 136. *". . . reading while everyone was sleeping."* Interview with Thomas Clark.

Page 136. *"I don't think Bob ever . . ."* Hotz interview.

Page 136. *". . . little patience for the mundane . . ."* Hotz interview.

Page 136. *". . . just wasn't into wasting time."* Hotz interview.

Page 136. . . . *during a Boy Scout outing* . . . Cantrell interview.

Page 137. *"If he's doing something he wants to do . . ."* Hotz interview.

Page 137. . . . *a broken piano on the street* . . . Golden, *The Boston Globe Magazine*, March 4, 1990, page 27.

Page 137. *"I just want to play desperately . . ."* Robert Clark interview.

Page 137. *"Does he have a piano?" . . .* Hotz interview.

Page 138. *"We took lessons . . ."* Hotz interview.

Page 138. *None of his friends were surprised* . . . Cantrell interview.

Page 138. *Clark called it* . . . Robert Clark interview.

Page 138. *Father Eugene Kennedy could tell . . .* Golden, *The Boston Globe Magazine*, March 4, 1990, page 27; interview with Eugene Kennedy.

Page 138. *". . . that he was singular . . ."* Eugene Kennedy interview.

Pages 138–139. *". . . he observed and sensed the world . . ."* Golden, *The Boston Globe Magazine*, March 4, 1990, page 27.

Page 139. . . . *to do his own "intellectual adventuring."* Golden, page 27.

Page 139. . . . *read from Alice in Wonderland.* Golden, page 28.

Page 139. . . . *Patrick Gunkel* . . . Golden, page 28; Robert Clark interview.

Page 140. *". . . couldn't do it, live a lie . . ."* Robert Clark interview.

Page 141. . . . *opposed the war, but took a detached view* . . . Golden, page 28; Robert Clark interview.

Page 141. *"The real motivating force was fear . . ."* Golden, page 28.

Pages 141–142. *"My whole interest in behaviorism . . ."* Robert Clark interview. Also see "Robert Clark, Dean, Corporate Law Expert, Philosopher, Musician," *Harvard Law Bulletin*, September 1989.

Page 142. *"Reading Skinner's early works was 'just like a revelation,' . . ."* Robert Clark interview.

Page 142. *He even mimicked Skinner* . . . Robert Clark interview; Golden, page 28.

Page 142.... *"Three more years?..."* Robert Clark interview.

Page 143.... *the air of an older, more mature student.* Interview with Barton Fisher.

Page 143. *His grades just missed*... Golden, page 29.

Page 143. *He wrote a paper*... Golden, page 29.

Page 143.... *Truman Casner interviewed Clark*... Interview with Truman Casner; Golden, page 29.

Page 144.... *tried to get Harvard to*... Casner interview.

Page 145.... *Clark had to choose sides*... Golden, page 30.

Page 145. *... became what he calls a moderate Republican.* "Freedom to Think at Harvard Law" by Eric Felten, *The Washington Times,* July 17, 1991, page E1.

Page 145. *His public attack... was a declaration of war.* Golden, page 30.

Page 145. *... the CLS faculty "had somewhat radical answers to give"... "infusing a political element..."* Bok interview.

Page 147. *Additionally, he set himself against the faculty*... Golden, page 36.

Chapter 7: The Ides of May

Page 149. ... *two-all night occupations*... "Protesters Camp Out at Law Dean's Office" by Linda Killian, *The Boston Globe,* March 4, 1990.

Page 149. ... *a tougher stance, and warned*... Memorandum to the Law School Community from Dean Robert Clark, March 31, 1992, saying that "interference with the rights of others at the School simply cannot be tolerated."

Page 149.... *the statement of "Rights and Responsibilities"*... Harvard Law School Catalog, 1991–1992, page 185.

Page 151. *In the winter of 1985, Charles Fried... says he shared... Order & Law: Arguing the Reagan Revolution—A Firsthand Account* by Charles Fried (New York: Simon & Schuster, 1991), pages 13–14.

Page 151.... *a distaste for the*... Fried, page 15.

Page 151.... *the "cynicism" and "self-hatred"*... Fried, page 15.

Page 151.... *a "less intrusive government"*... Fried, page 17.

Page 151.... *the "David Stockman of the legal agenda."*... Fried, page 17.

Page 152. ... *"taught more subjects and practiced less law"... The Tenth Justice: The Solicitor General and the Rule of Law* by Lincoln Caplan (New York: Vintage Books, 1988), page 178. Also see "A Champion of the Reagan Agenda; Solicitor General States Case with 'Vigor'" by David Lauter, *The National Law Journal,* January 27, 1987.

Page 152. *He called Roe... a "symptom of a mistaken approach to judging" that "confused and threatened..."* Fried, page 20.

Page 152. *"...judicial overreaching."* Fried, page 33.

Page 152.... *a "serious misuse of... example of twisted judging."* Fried, page 75.

Page 152. ... *the political engines of the left-liberal agenda*... Fried, page 57.

Page 152. *In the first brief*... Fried, page 75.

Page 153. . . . *the most strident ever* . . . Caplan, page 143.

Page 153. *". . . government taking over too many . . ."* Fried, page 20; . . . *"dangerously aggrandizes government."* Fried, page 90; . . . *somehow cheated on* . . . Fried, page 100; *degenerated "into stifling political entrepreneurship . . ."* Fried, page 130; *Hardliners* . . . Fried, page 106.

Page 154. . . . *minority set-asides for city contractors* . . . City of Richmond v. J.A. Crowson Co., 488 U.S. 469 (1989); *Another case held* . . . Wards Cove Packing Co. v. Atonio, 490 U.S. 642 (1989).

Page 154. . . . *could legally pass a law prohibiting* . . . Employment Div., Dept. of Human Resources v. Smith, 110 S. Ct. 1595, 1599–1602 (1990); . . . *the police could destroy potentially exculpatory evidence* . . . Arizona v. Youngblood, 488 U.S. 51, 57–58 (1988); . . . *police misconduct was not actionable* . . . Anderson v. Creighton, 483 U.S. 635, 642–46 (1987).

Page 155. . . . *the root of his philosophy of law* . . . Caplan, page 137.

Page 155. *". . . our liberty is more secure . . ."* Fried, page 59.

Page 155. *". . . something that any right-minded lawyer can see."* Philip Heymann quoted in Caplan, page 139.

Page 155. . . . *nothing immoral about doing a corporation's bidding.* "Lawyer as Friend," as cited in Caplan, page 136; . . . *the Massachusetts Institute of Technology* . . . Caplan, page 137. Also see Lauter, *The National Law Journal*, January 27, 1987.

Page 156. *"It is not our job . . ."* Interview with Charles Fried.

Page 156. *He regarded CLS as* . . . Fried interview.

Page 156. . . . *ironically proved the wisdom of CLS* . . . Caplan, page 272.

Page 156. . . . *"they tried to colonize the law school. . . ."* Fried interview.

Page 157. . . . *as events became more "disagreeable"* . . . Fried, page 30.

Page 157. *Tribe attacked Fried* . . . Caplan, page 143.

Page 157. *Fried, Tribe told reporters* . . . Caplan, page 206.

Page 158. . . . *to deny Fried's reappointment* . . . Derrick Bell interview.

Page 158. *And Fried regarded Bell's protest.* . . . Fried interview.

Page 158. . . . *just another way of playing to the crowd* . . . *"His tactics were not admirable . . ."* Fried interview.

Page 159. . . . *Fried reintroduced Roman Law* . . . Sutherland, page 336.

Pages 159–160. . . . *sat down to begin a silent vigil* . . . Interviews with John Bonifaz, Sarah Wald, and Charles Fried.

Page 160. *"I can't guarantee you anything"* . . . Wald interview.

Page 161. *"It was intended to be offensive . . ."* Fried interview.

Page 161. *Kraakman* . . . *dealt with student protesters* . . . Bonifaz interview.

Page 163. *For the second year in a row, Yale Law School ranked* . . . "Yale #1 Again!!" by Jason Levine, *Harvard Law Record*, March 20, 1992, page 1.

Page 165. . . . *Crovitz hailed Clark* . . . "Harvard Law School Finds Its Counterrevolutionary" by L. Gordon Crovitz, *The Wall Street Journal*, March 25, 1992, page A13.

Page 165. . . . *the plaintiff only imagined* . . . "CCR Asks for a Public Apology from Dean Clark," letter to the *Harvard Law Record*, by Camille Holmes and Jeffrey Lubell, April 7, 1992.

Page 166. *"People were furious..."* Hankins interview.
Page 166. *... expressing his "dismay" at the protests...* Memorandum to the Law School Community from Dean Robert Clark, March 31, 1992.
Page 167. *"If anyone was unruly, it was Fried"...* Bonifaz interview.

CHAPTER 8: CRUEL AND UNUSUAL *LAW REVIEW* HUMOR

Page 171. *"... making fun of them as much as anything else."* Interview with Luke Cole.
Page 171. *"... we had a clear political mission..."* Aoki interview.
Page 174. *... a pinprick at the bloated...* "The Parody That Missed the Mark" by David Von Drehle, *The Washington Post*, May 7, 1992.
Page 174. *Other 3L editors weren't surprised...* Kestenbaum interview.
Page 175. *... remembered that planning session...* Platt interview.
Page 175. *"... difference between pinpricks and a sledgehammer...."* Platt interview.
Page 177. *"... dismissing my point of view constantly..."* Eisenberg interview.
Page 177. *... deprecating comments about women.* Eisenberg interview.
Page 178. *... she too experienced a backlash.* Eisenberg interview.
Page 179. *"I personally didn't want to believe it..."* Eisenberg interview.
Page 180. *"He's a bull in a china shop"...* Confidential interview with an editor at the *Harvard Law Review.*
Page 180. *One night, Eisenberg confronted Coben...* Eisenberg interview.
Page 181. *Carol Platt planned to tell the males...* Platt interview.
Page 181. *... also had qualms about...* Ellen interview.
Page 183. *... invited Vice President Richard Nixon...* Letter from Richard Goodwin to Vice President Richard Nixon, Jan. 16, 1958, Harvard Law Review Papers, Harvard Law School Library.
Page 183. *... Humphrey gladly accepted...* Letter from Richard Goodwin to Senator Hubert Humphrey, March 14, 1958. Harvard Law Review Papers, Harvard Law School Library.
Page 183. *... Earl Warren had attended the year before...* List of attendees, Harvard Law Review Papers, Harvard Law School Library.
Page 183. *... important figures of their time.* History of banquet events and speakers, confidential *Harvard Law Review* business office source.
Page 184. *... the one hundredth Anniversary...* "Harvard Law Review Celebrates 100th Anniversary in April," *Harvard Law Review* news release.
Page 184. *Justice William Brennan...* "Review Marks Anniversary, Justice Brennan Ill, Unable to Deliver Address" by Emily Bernstein, *Harvard Law Record*, April 15, 1987, Harvard Law Review Papers, Harvard Law School Libary.
Page 184. *... the panel dealt with a serious topic too.* Bernstein, *Harvard Law Record*, April 15, 1987.
Page 186. *... distributed the armbands...* "Fried Riles *Review* at Annual Banquet" by Steve Yarian, *Harvard Law Record*, April 10, 1992, page 1.

Page 186.... *"needed protection from diversity protesters."*... Yarian, *Harvard Law Record*, April 10, 1992.

Page 187. *Fried then turned his sarcasm on*... Yarian, *Harvard Law Record*, April 10, 1992; account contained in "We Will Not Laugh. We Will Not Be Silent: A Response to the *Harvard Law Revue*'s Attack on Professor Mary Joe Frug," April 10, 1992.

Page 187. *"I found his reference to the Paschal lamb offensive*..." Yarian, *Harvard Law Record*, April 10, 1992.

Page 188.... *the souvenir they carried*... *Harvard Law Revue*, Volume 105, April 1992.

Page 198.... *no one expected that more than a limited audience would see it.* Interview with a *Harvard Law Review* editor.

CHAPTER 9: CAUSE AND EFFECT

Page 200. *A lot of the footnotes bothered her*... Eisenberg interview.

Page 201.... *"dime-store moralism of yesteryear"*... *Backlash: The Undeclared War Against American Women* by Susan Faludi, (New York: Doubleday, 1991), page xviii.

Page 201. *"... creates countercurrents and treacherous undertows." Backlash*, page xxi.

Page 201.... *Eisenberg posted a memo.* Eisenberg interview.

Page 202. *"... they just ignored it."* Eisenberg interview.

Page 202.... *what was to become a twenty-four hour sit-in*... "Griswold 9 Take Over Dean's Office" by Ashley Barr, *Harvard Law Record*, April 10, 1992, page 1; interview with Lucy Koh and John Bonifaz (not one of the Griswold 9).

Page 205. *"... even more angry after he came in"*... Koh interview.

Page 210.... *for the Administrative Board to reach a preliminary decision*... Barr, *Harvard Law Record*, April 10, 1992.

Page 210. *"We have reached our goal today*..." Barr, *Harvard Law Record*, April 10, 1992.

Page 211. *"... no way they could not have known*... *acting in willful blindness."* Eisenberg interview.

Page 212. *"... Everything has an effect on everything else,"*... Eisenberg interview.

Page 212. "We Will Not Laugh. We Will Not Be Silent: A Response to the *Harvard Law Revue*'s Attack on Professor Mary Joe Frug," April 10, 1992.

Page 214. *They were informed*... "Ad Board Moves against Students" by John Regis, *Harvard Law Record*, April 17, 1992, page 1.

Page 214.... *an editorial praising the Griswold Nine*... "No Limits to Appropriate Behavior" by Robert Arnold, *Harvard Law Record*, April 10, 1992, page 6.

Page 214.... *cartoon on the editorial page*... *Harvard Law Record*, April 10, 1992, page 6.

Page 215. . . . *letter to the editor* . . . *Harvard Law Record,* April 10, 1992, page 6.

Page 216. . . . *"Liabilities"* . . . *Harvard Law Record,* April 10, 1992, page 8.

Page 216. . . . *what students like Andrea Brenneke hoped* . . . Interview with Andrea Brenneke.

Page 218. *Eisenberg was infuriated.* Eisenberg interview.

Page 218. . . . *Mary Joe Frug had recognized* . . . Frug, *Harvard Law Review,* March 1992, page 1047.

Page 219. . . . *female suffering is buried* . . . Andrea Dworkin, *Right-Wing Women* (1983), quoted in Frug, *Harvard Law Review,* March 1992, page 1047.

Page 219. *". . . so it wasn't hurtful."* Eisenberg interview.

Page 219. . . . *a weekend long "Crit Networks Conference"* . . . A Crit Networks Conference, April 10–12, 1992, Final Conference Program.

Page 220. . . . *and stormed in.* "Revue Sparks Outrage, Campus Roiled in Pain and Anger" by Glennis Gill, *Harvard Law Record,* April 17, 1992, page 1; interview with Marilynn Sager.

Page 221. . . . *voted to let Schulman* . . . "Revue Sparks Outrage, Parody 'Vicious and Indefensible' " by Steve Yarian, *Harvard Law Record,* April 17, 1992, page 1; "Parody of Frug Article Draws Angry Response" by Caralee Caplan and Daniel Steinman, *Harvard Crimson,* April 11, 1992, page 1.

Page 221. *On Saturday* . . . Interviews with *Law Review* editors who requested not to be identified.

Page 222. *". . . this grand scheme of evil."* Platt interview.

Page 222. *". . . It's disembodied. . . . "* Platt interview.

Page 223. *". . . so much hysteria"* . . . Platt interview.

Page 223. *". . . this got out of hand."* Platt interview.

Page 224. *". . . an issue for the 2L's . . ."* Eisenberg interview.

Page 224. . . . *read her statement aloud.* Letter to Harvard Law Students by Emily Schulman, President, *Harvard Law Review,* April 11, 1992; "*Law Review* Apologizes for Parody of Frug Piece" by Marion Gammill, *The Harvard Crimson,* April 13, 1992.

Page 225. *". . . he was getting dragged . . ."* Ellen interview. Also see "Harvard in Uproar over Spoof of Dead Professor," *The Boston Sunday Herald,* April 12, 1992, page 1.

Page 226. . . . *penned one of the most* . . . Letter to Fellow Editors by David Ellen, outgoing President, *Harvard Law Review,* April 12, 1994.

CHAPTER 10: TRIBAL WARFARE

Page 228. . . . *speaking at a bagel brunch* . . . "Tribe Denounces Spoof as Hateful" by Caralee Caplan, *The Harvard Crimson,* April 13, 1992, page 1; "Revue Sparks Outrage, Campus Roiled in Pain and Anger" by Glennis Gill, *Harvard Law Record,* April 17, 1992, page 1; "*Harvard Law Review* Scraps Parody After Uproar" by Andrea Estes, *The Boston Herald,* April 13, 1992, page 7.

Page 229.... *affected him at a deeper level* ... Interview with Laurence Tribe.

Page 229. *"What is the point of teaching?* ... " Caplan, *The Harvard Crimson*, April 13, 1992.

Page 229.... *opened the floor for questions* ... Caplan, *The Harvard Crimson*, April 13, 1992; Gill, *Harvard Law Record*, April 17, 1992, page 3.

Page 233. *"... I can hardly be suspected. ...* " "At Harvard Law, Turmoil Is an Outward Sign of Progress" by Laurence Tribe, To the Editor, *The New York Times*, October 21, 1985.

Page 233. *"If a young, relatively conservative male. ...* " "Law Profs Question Dalton Vote" by Emily Bernstein, *The Harvard Crimson*, May 13, 1987.

Page 233. *"Anyone who believes [those decisions] ...* " "Battle at Harvard Law Over Tenure; So-called Crits v. Traditionalists" by David Kaplan, *The National Law Journal*, June 22, 1987, page 3.

Page 233.... *dubious of Bok's choice of Clark* ... "Harvard's New Leader" by Lisa Green Markoff, *The National Law Journal*, March 6, 1989, page 4.

Page 235. *"... my sympathy for people ...* " "Laurence Tribe" by Andrea Sachs, *Constitution*, Spring–Summer 1991, page 27.

Page 235.... *"fat little kid"* ... "Labors of the Legal Mind; Laurence Tribe, Teaching, Arguing, and Keeping a Scholarly Eye on the High Court" by Steve Coll, *The Washington Post*, November 26, 1985, page B1.

Page 236. ... *"communing with a blackboard ...* " Coll, *The Washington Post*, November 26, 1985; Sachs, page 27.

Page 236.... *didn't want to be overshadowed* ... Coll, *The Washington Post*, November 26, 1985.

Page 237.... *before "he felt comfortable ...* " Sachs, page 28.

Page 237.... *left his mark on several opinions* ... Sachs, page 28; Laurence Tribe résumé.

Page 237.... *cited more than 1,365 times* ... Sachs, page 28.

Page 237. *"It may well be ...* " *Battle for Justice: How the Bork Nomination Shook America* by Ethan Bronner (New York: Anchor Books 1989), page 135, quoting *The Wall Street Journal*, Dec. 18, 1987, page 25.

Page 238.... *ten days after his father died* ... Bronner, page 132.

Page 238. *He successfully defended* ... *Fisher v. City of Berkeley* (1986); *Pacific Gas & Electric Co. v. California Energy Resources Conservation and Development Commission* (1983); *Northeast Bancorp v. Federal Reserve System* (1985); *Adams Fruit Co. v. Barrett* (1990); and *White v. Mass. Council of Construction Employers* (1983).

Page 239. *"The issue is not what Michael Hardwick ...* " Sachs, page 29.

Page 239. *Of Tribe that day, Hardwick said* ... *The Courage of Their Convictions* by Peter Irons (New York: Penguin, 1990), page 399.

Page 239. *"... one of my biggest disappointments"* ... Tribe interview.

Page 239.... *felt further vindicated when* ... "Powell Regrets Backing Sodomy Law" by Ruth Marcus, *The Washington Post*, November 8, 1990, page A3.

Page 239. *"... not my favorite industry."* Sachs, page 29.

Page 239. *Before Tribe agreed to defend...* Tribe interview.

Page 240. *He pulls in...* "The Croesus of Cambridge" by Stewart Yerton, *The American Lawyer*, April 1994, page 63.

Page 240. *Embarrassing details about his fees...* Coll, *The Washington Post*, November 26, 1985.

Page 241. *But he has criticized...* Bronner, page 128.

Page 241. *"...deliberate models of ambiguity,"... God Save This Honorable Court: How the Choice of Supreme Court Justices Shapes Constitutional Choices* by Laurence Tribe (New York: Random House, 1985), page 42.

Page 241. *which "compel the Supreme Court..."* Tribe, pages 42–43.

Page 241. *Concepts of original intent... are "inconclusive"....* Tribe, page 46; *and abdicate responsibility...* Tribe, page 47.

Page 241. *... the Senate has rejected...* Tribe, page 78.

Page 242. *... "he who lives by the crystal ball..."* Tribe, page 50.

Page 242. *... also "oddly naïve..."* Bronner, page 128.

Page 242. *... an entire issue to tarring Tribe...* "A Preemptive Strike against Laurence Tribe, by Those Who Do Not Care to Call Him 'Mr. Justice'" by David Margolick, *The New York Times*, October 12, 1990.

Page 242. *... tried to brush off the attack.* Sachs, page 24.

Page 244. *... several Law Review editors still felt...* "An Open Letter to the Editors of the Harvard Law Review" by Rebecca Eisenberg, Renee Jones, Marie Milnes-Vasquez, Kunal Parker, and Annelise Riles, April 12, 1992.

Page 244. *It was the fault of Harvard Law...* Open Letter from the Battered Women's Advocacy Project to All Members of the Harvard Law School Community, April 13, 1992.

Page 244. *... the "community must get tough on hate..."* Open Letter from the *Harvard Civil Rights/Civil Liberties Law Review* to All Members of the Harvard Law School Community, April 13, 1992.

Page 245. *... "reflects and reinforces a campus climate..."* Open Letter from the Harvard Women's Law Association to the Harvard Law School Community, April 13, 1992.

Page 245. *"... offends all standards of decency..."* Letter from Dean Robert Clark to the Law School Community, April 13, 1992.

Page 245. *... admitted that what they had written...* Letter from Craig Coben and Ken Fenyo to the Harvard Law School Community, distributed April 14, 1992.

Page 246. *Eight other editors...* Letter from eight *Law Review* editors to the Members of the Law School Community, April 14, 1992.

Page 246. *... let the Frug parody slip through...* Letter from Janis Kestenbaum and Edith Ramirez to the Law School Community, April 13, 1992.

Page 246. *The professors...* Letter from a group of five faculty members to the *Harvard Law Review*, April 14, 1992; Letter from forty-seven faculty members to the Editors, April 14, 1992.

Page 247. *Hoping to correct the misimpression...* An Open Letter to the Harvard Law School Community from three *Law Review* editors, distributed April 14, 1992.

Page 247. . . . *recalling how he had once signed* . . . "Cambridge March Protests School's Relocation" by Jordana Hart, *The Boston Globe,* October 5, 1989, Metro/Region, page 1. Also see "Embattled Day School to Close; Cambridge Seen as 'Beginning of End' " by Patricia Nealon, *The Boston Globe,* August 14, 1993, Metro/Region, page 1.

Page 248. . . . *"wanted" posters* . . . "Posters Target Law Students; Apparent Retaliation for *Law Review* spoof Draws Fire" by Andre Estes, *The Boston Herald,* April 16, 1992.

Page 248. . . . *to withdraw letters of recommendation for clerkships* . . . "Harvard Law Students' Parody of Slain Professor's Text Decried" by Linda Matchen, *The Boston Globe,* April 13, 1992; "Spoof Authors' Apology Slammed" by Andrea Estes and Samson Mulugeta, *The Boston Herald,* April 15, 1992.

Page 249. *". . . The apple is rotten."* "Feminism Terrifies Men and Law at Harvard" by Margery Eagan, *The Boston Herald,* April 14, 1992.

Page 249. . . . *in the context of sexual harassment.* "Harvard Law Sorely Split in the Parody's Wake" by Anthony Flint, *The Boston Globe,* April 16, 1992; Letter to the Editor from Laurence Tribe, *The Boston Globe,* April 17, 1992.

Page 250. *". . . rock-bottom on the scale of morality"* . . . "Under *Revue,* Parody Renews Concerns over Diversity at HLS" by Amy Finkelstein, *The Harvard Independent,* April 16, 1992; Bonifaz interview.

Page 250. *". . . can only come out in an atmosphere . . ."* Finkelstein, *Harvard Independent,* April 16, 1992.

Page 250. . . . *called for Clark's resignation.* "Student Groups Call for Dean Clark's Resignation," *Harvard Law Record,* April 17, 1992, page 15; "Student Coalition Wants Harvard Law Dean to Quit" by Rebecca Walkowitz, *The Boston Globe,* April 17, 1992; "Law Students Want Dean Out, 'Animosity' to Minorities and Women Cited" by Andrea Estes, *The Boston Herald,* April 17, 1994; "In Attacking the Work of a Murdered Professor, Harvard's Elite Themselves Become a Target" by David Margolick, *The New York Times,* April 17, 1992.

Page 250. *"Look what happened after . . ."* Walkowitz, *The Boston Globe,* April 17, 1992.

Page 250. . . . *Boykin drew on his experience* . . . Boykin interview.

Page 251. . . . *explaining why Clark had to resign* . . . "A Realization for the Good of Harvard Law School, An Open Letter to Dean Robert Clark" by Peter Cicchino, *Harvard Law Record,* April 17, 1992, page 9.

Page 251. *The same day* . . . "Ad Board Moves Against Students" by John Regis, *Harvard Law Record,* April 17, 1992, page 1.

Page 252. *Tribe told Edley* . . . Edley and Tribe interviews.

CHAPTER 11: DEFENDING THEIR RIGHT, STARRING ALAN DERSHOWITZ

Page 253. . . . *letter condemning the climate* . . . An Open Letter to the Harvard Law School Community from fifteen professors, April 20, 1992.

Also see, "Faculty Letter Condemns Hiring, Climate at Harvard Law" by Rebecca Walkowitz, *The Boston Globe*, April 21, 1992, page 1; "Profs Demand Inquiry into Sexism at Harvard Law," *The Boston Herald*, April 21, 1992, page 1, and "Meanness on All Sides," editorial, *The Boston Herald*, April 21, 1992, page 24.

Page 254. "*. . . a leadership vacuum."*. . . Tribe interview.

Page 254. *Five professors*. . . Memorandum to Recipients of the Open Letter to the Harvard Law School Community from five professors, April 20, 1992.

Page 255. "*. . . collectively criticized the institution . . ."* "Parody Puts Harvard Law Faculty in Sexism Battle" by Fox Butterfield, *The New York Times*, April 27, 1992, page A10.

Page 255. It was *a "public admission"*. . . "Law Profs Urge New Faculty Hiring Process, Ask Dean to Dissolve Present Committee" by Natasha Leland, *The Harvard Crimson*, April 21, 1993; interview with Caroline Wittcoff.

Pages 256–257. *. . . put Robert Clark on the defensive.* Letter from Dean Robert Clark to the Law School Community, April 20, 1992.

Page 257. *In a "letter of one"*. . . Memorandum to the Faculty from Charles Fried, Re: The open letter of fifteen of my colleagues, April 20, 1992.

Page 258. "*I am afraid this deplorable incident . . ."* As quoted in "Harvard Law Sorely Split in Parody's Wake" by Anthony Flint, *The Boston Globe*, April 16, 1992, page 1.

Page 258. *. . . chapter of the Federalist Society*. . . Letter to the HLS Community from Neil Glazer, President, Federalist Society, and Adrian Vermeule, Vice-President, April 20, 1990.

Page 259. *. . . happens in the "marketplace of ideas."* *The Boston Globe*, April 16, 1992.

Page 259. *. . . angriest at Tribe.* Interview with Alan Dershowitz.

Page 259. "*. . . kicking these students in the balls . . ."* As quoted in "Blood on the Charles" by Peter Collier, *Vanity Fair*, October 1992, page 144.

Page 259. *. . . on Dershowitz's nationally syndicated column . . .* "Harvard Witch Hunt Burns the Incorrect at the Stake" by Alan Dershowitz, *Los Angeles Times*, April 22, 1992. Also see "Harvard Law Profs Defend Frug Parody as Free Speech" by Andrea Estes, *The Boston Herald*, April 23, 1992, page 12.

Page 260. *. . . doesn't find Law School politics gratifying.* Dershowitz interview.

Page 261. *. . . to fight the "cheat elite"*. . . *The Best Defense* by Alan Dershowitz (New York: Vintage Books, 1983), page xxi.

Page 264. "*Not only is Alan a friend . . ."* "Harvard Law School," Letter to the Editor from Laurence Tribe, *The New York Times*, May 20, 1990.

Page 265. *. . . his Jewishness is always with him . . . Chutzpah* by Alan Dershowitz (Boston: Little Brown, 1991), page 10.

Page 265. *. . . would never work on the Sabbath.* Dershowitz, *Chutzpah*, page 26.

Pages 265–270. Biographical information, *Chutzpah*, pages 21–31, and *The Best Defense*, pages 3–9.

Page 267. *"He was good."*... Interview with Claire Dershowitz.

Page 267. *"You got a good mouth on you...."* *Chutzpah*, page 42.... *But his father*... Dershowitz, *Chutzpah*, page 43.

Page 267.... *"he was one of these, you know...."* Interview with Nathan Dershowitz.

Page 268. *"... case that changed my life."* *Best Defense*, page 17.

Page 268. *Sheldon Seigel....* *Best Defense*, pages 13–84.

Page 269. *"Rules of the Justice Game"*... *Best Defense*, pages xxi–xxii.

Page 269. *Tactics and ethics, he tells students....* "Courting Fame, Fanning Flames, Lawyer Alan Dershowitz, From Rogues to Riches" by Marjorie Williams and Ruth Marcus, *The Washington Post*, February 10, 1991, page F1.

Page 270. *"Qualms is good."*... *Broken Contract*, page 204.... *"lying works ... I wish it weren't so..."* *Broken Contract*, page 206.

Page 271.... *from his guiding principles. Contrary to Popular Opinion* by Alan Dershowitz (Pharos Books, 1992).

Page 271.... *"the voracious appetite..."* *Contrary to Popular Opinion*, page 78.... *"Free Speech For Me"*... *Contrary to Popular Opinion*, page 60.

Page 272.... *disapproved of the student left*... "Derrick Bell and Diversity at Harvard," May 1990, reprinted in *Contrary to Popular Opinion*, pages 98–100.

Page 272. *"I don't think anybody genuinely wants diversity...."* Dershowitz interview.

Page 272. *"... cannot kowtow to their every wish."* Dershowitz interview.

Page 272. *Tribe's problem was...* Vanity Fair, October 1992, page 164.

Page 272.... *Tribe wasn't pulling any punches*... Memorandum to the Faculty from Larry Tribe, April 23, 1992, Re: Alan Dershowitz' OpEd.

Page 273. *Of course, Dershowitz*... Vanity Fair, October 1992, page 164.

Page 273.... *riding the momentum*... An Open Letter to the Harvard Law School Community by twenty-one professors, April 23, 1992. Also see "The Not-So-Civil War at Harvard Law School" by Thomas Palmer, Jr., *The Boston Sunday Globe*, April 26, 1992, and "Out-of-Bounds," *Newsweek*, Periscope, page 4.

Page 274. *"... belittling and trivializing the incident..."* Memorandum to the Faculty from Betsy Bartholet, Re: Issues relating to the Special Committee or Ad. Board Inquiry and to "Collegiality" (see recent Dershowitz and Kaufman statements), April 23, 1992.

CHAPTER 12: TRIAL AND GRAVE ERROR

Page 276.... *the Administrative Board announced*... Statement of the Administrative Board, April 20, 1992; "Fried 4 Absolved, Griswold 9 Hearing Set for Monday" by Andy Ward, *Harvard Law Record*, May 1, 1992, page 1.

Page 276. . . . *understood that their activities* . . . Letter to the Administrative Board from Raul Perez, Julia Gordon, and John Bonifaz, April 9, 1992.

Page 277. . . . *"public" was being defined as* . . . Letter to Professor William Fisher III from David Shapiro, Harvard Law School Administrative Board, April 30, 1992.

Pages 278-280. *In the late afternoon* . . . " 'Community' Forum Underwhelming" by Troy Chandler, *Harvard Law Record,* May 1, 1992, page 1. Also see "Harvard Law Unrest Confronted at Forum" by Gary Chafetz, *The Boston Globe,* April 30, 1992, and "Law School Forum Draws 300, Clark Says He Is 'Here to Listen'; Atmosphere Tense" by Natasha Leland, *The Harvard Crimson,* May 1, 1992.

Page 281. *". . . the events in L.A. . . ."* Koh interview.

Page 282. *"This was not about FTD . . ."* Koh interview.

Page 282. *On National Public Radio's* . . . Transcript of "Harvard Law Review Article Sparks Debate," National Public Radio, Morning Edition, May 4, 1992.

Page 285. *". . . could not have been more theatrical. . . . "* Interview with Peter Cicchino. . . . *like an episode of 'L.A. Law.' "* "Beirut on the Charles" by John Sedgwick, *GQ,* February 1993, page 152.

Page 286. . . . *more successful with some witnesses* . . . "Law School Protesters Deny Charges at Hearing" by Natasha Leland, *The Harvard Crimson,* May 6, 1992, page 1.

Page 287. . . . *described their backgrounds* . . . " 'Griswold 9' Voluntarily Come Forward," *Harvard Law Record,* April 17, 1992, page 6.

Page 289. . . . *hit Vagts in the face* . . . Sedgwick, *GQ,* February 1993, page 156.

Page 289. *"It was so dramatic." . . .* Koh interview.

Page 290. . . . *each student was receiving* . . . Statement of the Administrative Board, May 8, 1992. Also see "Harvard Panel Won't Discipline Parody Authors" by Rebecca Walkowitz, *The Boston Globe,* May 22, 1992, and "Harvard Won't Punish Authors in Parody of Slain Professor's Work," *The New York Times,* May 23, 1992.

Page 290. *The students felt relieved* . . . Koh interview.

Page 290. *". . . little chance there wouldn't be a warning. . . . "* Interview with Detlev Vagts.

Page 290. . . . *the entire process a disgrace.* Cicchino interview.

Page 290. *Defending the result* . . . Letter to the Law School Community from Dean Robert Clark, May 11, 1992.

Page 291. *Nor would it launch* . . . Memorandum to David Kennedy from the Administrative Board, May 20, 1992, Re: Your memorandum of April 19, 1992.

Page 291. . . . *wanted to staunch public debate* . . . "A Murder, a Mockery and a Political-Correctness Cover-up" by Jamin Raskin, *In These Times,* June 24–July 7, 1992, page 18.

Page 292. . . . *a "vile circus"* . . . "The Vile Circus at Harvard Law" by Abigail Thernstrom, *The Wall Street Journal,* May 1, 1992.

Page 294. ... *had been "mugged," ...* "Blood on the Charles" by Collier, *Vanity Fair*, October 1992, page 164.

EPILOGUE

Page 295. *In a letter to Bell ...* Letter from Robert Clark to Derrick Bell, June 12, 1992.

Page 296. ... *not going to permit Bell ...* Letter from Neil Rudenstein to Professor Frank Michelman, June 17, 1992.

Page 297. *"... not my intention to resign."* Letter from Derrick Bell to Robert Clark, June 24, 1992.

Page 297. ... *to consider his request formally.* Letter from Harvard University Provost Jerry Green to Derrick Bell, June 26, 1992.

Page 297. *Clark also answered ...* Letter from Robert Clark to Derrick Bell, June 26, 1992.

Page 298. ... *a terse, two-paragraph statement ...* "Harvard Provost Issues Statement on Derrick Bell," Harvard University news release, June 30, 1992.

Page 298. *Clark would say only ...* "Statement from Dean Robert C. Clark," Harvard Law School news release, July 1, 1992.

Page 298. ... *students lacked standing ...* "CCR Suit Dismissed," *Harvard Law Record*, September 18, 1992, page 1.

Page 299. *"... you will come to understand ..."* Letter from Derrick Bell to Neil Rudenstein, August 19, 1992. *"... strengthened in my belief ..."* Letter from Derrick Bell to Charles Slichter, Senior Fellow of Harvard College, August 19, 1992.

Page 299. *"Things are in ruins ..."* Interview with Frank Michelman.

Page 300. ... *calling for healing ...* An Open Letter from Dean Robert Clark, September 9, 1992.

Page 302. *"... not frosty or dismissive."* "A Call for Healing, Harvard Law Dean Tackles Divisive Issues" by Charles Radin, *The Boston Globe*, September 10, 1992, page 1.

Page 302. *At a meeting on September 30 ...* "Review Working Through Problems" by Todd Hartman, *Harvard Law Review*, October 30, 1992. page 1.

Page 303. *"... would have had a riot here."* Interview with Paul Weiler.

Page 303. ... *an independent review ...* "HLS Alum Named to Probe *Review*, Former Editor Gants to Evaluate Accusations Against President" by Betsy McGrath, *Harvard Law Record*, November 13, 1992. Also see "Affirmative Action Backfires at Harvard Law Review" by Abigail Thernstrom, *The Wall Street Journal*, November 18, 1992, page A17.

Page 304. ... *distressed by MacKinnon.* "Vigil Supports MacKinnon" by Johanna Davis, *Harvard Law Record*, March 5, 1993, page 1. Also see "Patriarchy: 1, Feminists: 0" *Time*, April 12, 1993, page 15.

Page 305. *"... all holding our breath. ..."* Weiler interview.

Page 305. *Vengeful editors ...* "Hate Story, Racial Strife at Law School" by Ruth Shalit, *The New Republic*, June 7, 1993.

Page 305. *Yale . . . overshadowed Harvard Law . . .* "A Hot Ticket Enjoys Its Ivy Climb, As Yale Gains Prominence, View from Cambridge Can Be Crabby" by Mary Jordan, *The Washington Post,* January 19, 1993.

Page 306. *. . . have paid "a high price."* Michelman interview.

Page 306. *. . . a fitting postscript . . .* "Harvard Law Ends Bias Suit by Agreeing on Institute" by Alice Dembner, *The Boston Globe,* September 22, 1993, page 1; "Law Professor Settles Complaint vs. Harvard with 'Win-Win' Deal," *Cambridge Chronicle,* September 23, 1993, page 5.

Page 307. *". . . the unconscious dynamics of discrimination . . ."* "Discrimination at Its Most DANGEROUS" by Clare Dalton, *The Boston Sunday Globe,* October 3, 1993.

Index